A·N·N·U·A·L E·D·I·T·I·O·N

Psychology

02/03

Thirty-Second Edition

EDITOR

Karen G. Duffy

SUNY College, Geneseo

Karen G. Duffy holds a doctorate in psychology from Michigan State University and is currently a professor of psychology at SUNY at Geneseo. She sits on the executive board of the New York State Employees Assistance Program and is a certified community and family mediator. She is a member of the American Psychological Society and the Eastern Psychological Association.

McGraw-Hill/Dushkin

530 Old Whitfield Street, Guilford, Connecticut 06437

Visit us on the Internet
http://www.dushkin.com

Credits

1. **The Science of Psychology**
   Unit photo—Photo by Harvard University Press.
2. **Biological Bases of Behavior**
   Unit photo—WHO photo.
3. **Perceptual Processes**
   Unit photo—© 2002 by PhotoDisc, Inc.
4. **Learning and Remembering**
   Unit photo—Courtesy of Leslie Holmes Lawlor.
5. **Cognitive Processes**
   Unit photo—© 2002 by Cleo Freelance Photography.
6. **Emotion and Motivation**
   Unit photo—© 2002 by Cleo Freelance Photography.
7. **Development**
   Unit photo—© 2002 by Cleo Freelance Photography.
8. **Personality Processes**
   Unit photo—© 2002 by Cleo Freelance Photography.
9. **Social Processes**
   Unit photo—© 2002 by Cleo Freelance Photography.
10. **Psychological Disorders**
    Unit photo—© 2002 by Cleo Freelance Photography.
11. **Psychological Treatments**
    Unit photo—Courtesy of Cheryl Greenleaf.

Copyright

Cataloging in Publication Data
Main entry under title: Annual Editions: Psychology. 2002/2003.
1. Psychology—Periodicals. I. Duffy, Karen G., *comp.* II. Title: Psychology.
BF 149.A58   150'   79–180263   ISBN 0–07–250634–2   ISSN 0272–3794

Thirty-Second Edition

Cover image © 2002 PhotoDisc, Inc.
Printed in the United States of America   1234567890BAHBAH5432   Printed on Recycled Paper

Editors/Advisory Board

Members of the Advisory Board are instrumental in the final selection of articles for each edition of ANNUAL EDITIONS. Their review of articles for content, level, currentness, and appropriateness provides critical direction to the editor and staff. We think that you will find their careful consideration well reflected in this volume.

EDITOR

Karen G. Duffy
SUNY College, Geneseo

Staff

047995

To the Reader

In publishing ANNUAL EDITIONS we recognize the enormous role played by the magazines, newspapers, and journals of the public press in providing current, first-rate educational information in a broad spectrum of interest areas. Many of these articles are appropriate for students, researchers, and professionals seeking accurate, current material to help bridge the gap between principles and theories and the real world. These articles, however, become more useful for study when those of lasting value are carefully collected, organized, indexed, and reproduced in a low-cost format, which provides easy and permanent access when the material is needed. That is the role played by ANNUAL EDITIONS.

Ronnie's parents couldn't understand why he didn't want to be picked up and cuddled as did his older sister when she was a baby. As an infant, Ronnie did not respond to his parents' smiles, words, or attempts to amuse him. By the age of two, Ronnie's parents knew that he was not like other children. He spoke no English, was very temperamental, and often rocked himself for hours. Ronnie is autistic. His parents feel that some of Ronnie's behavior may be their fault; they both work long hours as young professionals and leave both children with an older woman during the weekdays. Ronnie's pediatrician assures his parents that their reasoning, while logical, probably holds no merit because the causes of autism are little understood and that are likely to be physiological rather than parental. What can we do about children like Ronnie? What is the source of autism? Can autism be treated or reversed? Can autism be prevented?

Psychologists attempt to answer these and other complex questions in a specific way, with scientific methods. Researchers, using carefully planned methods, try to discover the causes of complex human behavior, normal or not. The scientific results of most psychological research are published in professional journals, and therefore may be difficult for the lay person to understand.

Annual Editions: Psychology 02/03 is designed to meet the needs of lay people and introductory level students who are curious about psychology. This *Annual Edition* provides a vast selection of readable and informative articles primarily from popular magazines and newspapers. These articles are typically written by journalists, but a few are written by psychologists and retain the excitement of the discovery of scientific knowledge.

The particular articles in this volume were chosen to be representative of the most current work in psychology. They were selected because they are accurate in their reporting and provide examples of the types of psychological research discussed in most introductory psychology classes. As in any science, some of the findings discussed in this collection are startling, while others will confirm what we already know. Some articles will invite speculation about social and personal issues; others will demand careful thought concerning potential misuse of the applications of research findings. Readers are expected to make the investment of effort and critical reasoning necessary to answer such questions and concerns.

I believe that you will find *Annual Editions: Psychology 02/03* readable and useful. I suggest that you look at the organization of this book and compare it to the organization of your textbook and course syllabus. By examining the *topic guide* that follows the *table of contents,* you can identify those articles most appropriate for any particular unit of study in your course. Your instructor may provide some help in this effort or assign articles to supplement the text. As you read the articles, try to connect their contents with the principles you are learning from your text and classroom lectures. Some of the articles will help you better understand a specific area of research, while others are designed to help you connect and integrate information from various research areas. Both of these strategies are important in learning about psychology or any other science. It is only through intensive investigation and subsequent integration of the findings from many studies that we are able to discover and apply new knowledge.

Please take time to provide me with some feedback to guide the annual revision of this anthology by completing and returning the *article rating form* in the back of the book. With your help, this collection will be even better next year. Thank you.

Karen Grover Duffy

Karen Grover Duffy
Editor

Contents

UNIT 1
The Science of Psychology

Four articles examine psychology as the science of behavior.

UNIT 2
Biological Bases of Behavior

Three selections discuss the biological bases of behavior. Topics include brain functions and the brain's control over the body.

The concepts in bold italics are developed in the article. For further expansion, please refer to the Topic Guide and the Index.

UNIT 3
Perceptual Processes

Five articles discuss the impact of the senses on human perceptual processes.

UNIT 4
Learning and Remembering

Five selections examine how operant conditioning, positive reinforcement, and memory interact during the learning process.

The concepts in bold italics are developed in the article. For further expansion, please refer to the Topic Guide and the Index.

UNIT 5
Cognitive Processes

Four articles examine how social skills, common sense, and intelligence affect human cognitive processes.

The concepts in bold italics are developed in the article. For further expansion, please refer to the Topic Guide and the Index.

UNIT 6
Emotion and Motivation

Four articles discuss the influences of stress, mental states, and emotion on the mental and physical health of the individual.

UNIT 7
Development

Five articles consider the importance of experience, discipline, familial support, and psychological aging during the normal human development process.

The concepts in bold italics are developed in the article. For further expansion, please refer to the Topic Guide and the Index.

UNIT 8
Personality Processes

Three selections discuss a few of the processes by which personalities are developed. Topics include self-esteem, empathy, and the secrets of happiness.

Unit Overview **142**

UNIT 9
Social Processes

Five selections discuss how the individual's social development is affected by genes, stereotypes, prejudice, and relationships.

Unit Overview **154**

The concepts in bold italics are developed in the article. For further expansion, please refer to the Topic Guide and the Index.

UNIT 10
Psychological Disorders

Four articles examine several psychological disorders. Topics include unexpected behavior, the impact of depression on a person's well-being, and phobias.

Unit Overview

UNIT 11
Psychological Treatments

Four selections discuss a few psychological treatments, including psychotherapy to alleviate depression, self-care, and the use of drugs.

Unit Overview

The concepts in bold italics are developed in the article. For further expansion, please refer to the Topic Guide and the Index.

The concepts in bold italics are developed in the article. For further expansion, please refer to the Topic Guide and the Index.

Topic Guide

This topic guide suggests how the selections in this book relate to the subjects covered in your course. You may want to use the topics listed on these pages to search the Web more easily.

On the following pages a number of Web sites have been gathered specifically for this book. They are arranged to reflect the units of this *Annual Edition.* You can link to these sites by going to the DUSHKIN ONLINE support site at *http://www.dushkin.com/online/.*

ALL THE ARTICLES THAT RELATE TO EACH TOPIC ARE LISTED BELOW THE BOLD-FACED TERM.

Adolescents
28. A World of Their Own
34. Disarming the Rage

Aging
29. Live to 100? No Thanks
30. Start the Conversation

Brain
7. The Future of the Brain
8. The Senses

Central nervous system
7. The Future of the Brain

Children
14. Different Strokes for Different Folks?
18. Cognitive Development in Social and Cultural Context
26. Fetal Psychology
27. Parenting: The Lost Art
32. Nurturing Empathy
34. Disarming the Rage
36. Nobody Left to Hate

Cognition
18. Cognitive Development in Social and Cultural Context
20. Can Animals Think?

Culture
5. The Tangled Skeins of Nature and Nurture in Human Evolution
18. Cognitive Development in Social and Cultural Context
37. Merits and Perils of Teaching About Other Cultures

Deafness
10. Noise Busters

Death
30. Start the Conversation

Deception
4. Psychology's Tangled Web: Deceptive Methods May Backfire on Behavioral Researchers

Depression
38. Finding Real Love
41. Up From Depression
45. The Quest for a Cure

Development, human
14. Different Strokes for Different Folks?
28. A World of Their Own
29. Live to 100? No Thanks

Diet
23. The Weighting Game

Dreams
12. Dreamspeak

Drug treatment
45. The Quest for a Cure

Emotional intelligence
25. Emotional Intelligence: What the Research Says

Emotions
24. What's in a Face?
25. Emotional Intelligence: What the Research Says
30. Start the Conversation
33. Secrets of Happiness
38. Finding Real Love

Empathy
32. Nurturing Empathy

Fear
42. Fear Not!

Fetus
26. Fetal Psychology

Freud
16. Repression Tries for Experimental Comeback

Genetics
5. The Tangled Skeins of Nature and Nurture in Human Evolution
6. Decoding the Human Body

Happiness
33. Secrets of Happiness

History of psychology
1. A Dance to the Music of the Century: Changing Fashions in 20th-Century Psychiatry

Intelligence
19. Who Owns Intelligence?
21. His Goal: Making Intelligence Tests Smarter

Learning
13. Memory and Learning
14. Different Strokes for Different Folks?
15. Regarding Rewards: Should You Be a Gold-Sticker Sticker?

Love
38. Finding Real Love

Memory
13. Memory and Learning
16. Repression Tries for Experimental Comeback

World Wide Web Sites

The following World Wide Web sites have been carefully researched and selected to support the articles found in this reader. The easiest way to access these selected sites is to go to our DUSHKIN ONLINE support site at *http://www.dushkin.com/online/*.

AE: Psychology 02/03

The following sites were available at the time of publication. Visit our Web site—we update DUSHKIN ONLINE regularly to reflect any changes.

General Sources

APA Resources for the Public

http://www.apa.org/psychnet/

Use the site map or search engine to access *APA Monitor,* the American Psychological Association newspaper, APA books on a wide range of topics, PsychINFO, an electronic database of abstracts on scholarly journals, and the HelpCenter.

Mental Help Net

http://mentalhelp.net

This comprehensive guide to mental health online features more than 6,300 individual resources. Information on mental disorders and professional resources in psychology, psychiatry, and social work are presented.

The Psych.com: Internet Psychology Resource

http://www.thepsych.com

Thousands of psychology resources are currently indexed at this site. Psychology Disciplines, Conditions & Disorders, Psychiatry, Assistance, and Self-Development are among the most useful.

School Psychology Resources Online

http://www.schoolpsychology.net

Numerous sites on special conditions, disorders, and disabilities, as well as other data ranging from assessment/evaluation to research, are available on this resouce page for psychologists, parents, and educators.

UNIT 1: The Science of Psychology

Abraham A. Brill Library

http://plaza.interport.net/nypsan/service.html

Containing data on over 40,000 books, periodicals, and reprints in psychoanalysis and related fields, the Abraham A. Brill Library's holdings span the literature of psychoanalysis from its beginning to the present day.

American Psychological Society (APS)

http://www.psychologicalscience.org/links.html

The APS is dedicated to advancing the best of scientific psychology in research, application, and the improvement of human conditions. Links to teaching, research, and graduate studies resources are available.

Psychological Research on the Net

http://psych.hanover.edu/APS/exponnet.html

This Net site provides psychologically related experiments. Biological psychology/neuropsychology, clinical psychology, cognition, developmental psychology, emotions, health psychology, personality, sensation/perception, and social psychology are some of the areas covered.

UNIT 2: Biological Bases of Behavior

Adolescence: Changes and Continuity

http://www.personal.psu.edu/faculty/n/x/nxd10/adolesce.htm

A discussion of puberty, sexuality, biological changes, cross-cultural differences, and nutrition for adolescents, including obesity and its effects on adolescent development, is presented here.

Division of Hereditary Diseases and Family Studies, Indiana University School of Medicine

http://medgen.iupui.edu/divisions/hereditary/

The Department of Medical and Molecular Genetics is primarily concerned with determining the genetic basis of disease. It consists of a multifaceted program with a variety of interdisciplinary projects. The areas of twin studies and linkage analysis are also explored.

Institute for Behavioral Genetics

http://ibgwww.colorado.edu/index.html

Dedicated to conducting and facilitating research on the genetic and environmental bases of individual differences in behavior, this organized research unit at the University of Colorado leads to Genetic Sites, Statistical Sites, and the Biology Meta Index, as well as to search engines.

Serendip

http://serendip.brynmawr.edu/serendip/

Serendip, which is organized into five subject areas (brain and behavior, complex systems, genes and behavior, science and culture, and science education), contains interactive exhibits, articles, links to other resources, and a forum area.

UNIT 3: Perceptual Processes

Psychology Tutorials and Demonstrations

http://psych.hanover.edu/Krantz/tutor.html

Interactive tutorials and simulations, primarily in the area of sensation and perception, are available here.

A Sensory Adventure

http://illusionworks.com/html/jump_page.html

This multimedia site on illusions will inform (and perhaps delight) about how we think and perceive.

UNIT 4: Learning and Remembering

The Opportunity of Adolescence

http://www.winternet.com/~webpage/adolescencepaper.html

According to this paper, adolescence is the turning point, after which the future is redirected and confirmed. The opportunities and problems of this period are presented with quotations from Erik Erikson, Jean Piaget, and others.

Project Zero

http://pzweb.harvard.edu

The Harvard Project Zero has investigated the development of learning processes in children and adults for 30 years. Today, Project Zero's mission is to understand and enhance learning,

www.dushkin.com/online/

thinking, and creativity in the arts and other disciplines for individuals and institutions.

UNIT 5: Cognitive Processes

Chess: Kasparov v. Deep Blue: The Rematch
http://www.chess.ibm.com/home/html/b.html

Clips from the chess rematch between Garry Kasparov and IBM's supercomputer, Deep Blue, are presented here along with commentaries on chess, computers, artificial intelligence, and what it all means.

Cognitive Science Article Archive
http://www.helsinki.fi/hum/kognitiotiede/archive.html

This excellent Finnish source contains articles on various fields of cognitive science.

Introduction to Artificial Intelligence (AI)
http://www-formal.stanford.edu/jmc/aiintro/aiintro.html

A description of AI is presented here along with links to other AI sites.

UNIT 6: Emotion and Motivation

CYFERNET-Youth Development
http://www.cyfernet.mes.umn.edu/youthdev.html

CYFERNET presents many articles on youth development, including a statement on the concept of normal adolescence and impediments to healthy development.

Nature vs. Nature: Gergen Dialogue With Winifred Gallagher
http://www.pbs.org/newshour/gergen/gallagher_5-14.html

Experience modifies temperament, according to this TV interview. The author of *I.D.: How Heredity and Experience Make You Who You Are* explains a current theory about temperament.

UNIT 7: Development

American Association for Child and Adolescent Psychiatry
http://www.aacap.org

This site is designed to aid in the understanding and treatment of the developmental, behavioral, and mental disorders that could affect children and adolescents. There is a specific link just for families about common childhood problems that may or may not require professional intervention.

Behavioral Genetics
http://www.uams.edu/department_of_psychiatry/slides/html/genetics/index.htm

A slide show on Behavioral Genetics, which includes objectives, methods of genetic investigation, family and twin studies, personality, intelligence, mental disorders, and Alzheimer's Disease, is presented on this Web site.

UNIT 8: Personality Processes

The Personality Project
http://personality-project.org/personality.html

This Personality Project (by William Revelle) is meant to guide those interested in personality theory and research to the current personality research literature.

UNIT 9: Social Processes

National Clearinghouse for Alcohol and Drug Information
http://www.health.org

Information on drug and alcohol facts that might relate to adolescence and the issues of peer pressure and youth culture is

presented here. Resources, referrals, research and statistics, databases, and related Net links are available.

UNIT 10: Psychological Disorders

Anxiety Disorders
http://www.adaa.org/aboutanxietydisorders/

Anxiety disorders in children, adolescents, and adults are reviewed by the Anxiety Disorders Association of America (ADAA). A detailed glossary is also included.

Ask NOAH About: Mental Health
http://www.noah-health.org/english//illness/mentalhealth/mental.html

Information about child and adolescent family problems, mental conditions and disorders, suicide prevention, and much more is available here.

Mental Health Net Disorders and Treatments
http://www.mentalhelp.net/dxtx.htm

Presented on this site are hotlinks to psychological disorders pages, which include anxiety, panic, phobic disorders, schizophrenia, and violent/self-destructive behaviors.

Mental Health Net: Eating Disorder Resources
http://www.mentalhelp.net/guide/eating.htm

This mental health Net site provides a complete list of Web references on eating disorders, including anorexia, bulimia, and obesity.

National Women's Health Resource Center (NWHRC)
http://www.healthywomen.org

NWHRC's site contains links to resources related to women's substance abuse and mental illnesses.

SAVE: Suicide Awareness/Voices of Education
http://www.save.org

This SAVE suicide site presents data on suicide prevention. It includes symptoms/danger signs, misconceptions, facts, hospitalization, and other details on depression and suicide.

UNIT 11: Psychological Treatments

Knowledge Exchange Network (KEN)
http://www.mentalhealth.org

Information about mental health (prevention, treatment, and rehabilitation services), is available via toll-free telephone services, an electronic bulletin board, and publications.

Links to the World of Carl Jung
http://www.cisnet.com/teacher-ed/jung.html

Dedicated to the work of Carl Jung, this is a comprehensive resource for Jungian psychology with links to Jung's complete works the Dream Room, reference materials, and the Keirsey Temperament Sorter.

Sigmund Freud and the Freud Archives
http://plaza.interport.net/nypsan/freudarc.html

Internet resources related to Sigmund Freud, which include a collection of libraries, museums, and biographical materials, as well as the Brill Library archives, can be found here.

We highly recommend that you review our Web site for expanded information and our other product lines. We are continually updating and adding links to our Web site in order to offer you the most usable and useful information that will support and expand the value of your Annual Editions. You can reach us at: *http://www.dushkin.com/annualeditions/*.

UNIT 1

The Science of Psychology

Unit Selections

1. **A Dance to the Music of the Century: Changing Fashions in 20th-Century Psychiatry**, David Healy
2. **Science and Pseudoscience**, APS Observer
3. **Good and Evil and Psychological Science**, Ervin Staub
4. **Psychology's Tangled Web: Deceptive Methods May Backfire on Behavioral Researchers**, Bruce Bower

Key Points to Consider

- Which area of psychology do you think is the most valuable and why? Many people are most aware of clinical psychology by virtue of having watched films and television. Is this the most valuable area of the discipline? About which other areas of psychology do you think the public ought to be informed?

- How do you think psychology is related to other scientific disciplines, such as sociology, biology, and human medicine? Are there nonscience disciplines to which psychology might be related, for example, philosophy and mathematics? How so?

- Is there one psychological theory to which you are especially attracted? Why? Which theories do you think will continue to be important to the field of psychology? Do you think psychologists will ever be able to piece together a single grand theory of human psychology? Do you have your own theory of human behavior? If yes, on what do you base your theory—your own observations? In developing a theory of human behavior, should psychologists rely extensively on research?

- Why is research important to psychology? What kinds of information can be gleaned from psychological research? Do you think it is ethical to deceive research participants? Under what circumstances do you think participants should be deceived; when should they not be deceived? How frequently do you think deception is used in psychological research? What kinds of research do you think are most likely to utilize deception? Would you ever deceive research participants if you were conducting research?

 **Links: www.dushkin.com/online/**
These sites are annotated in the World Wide Web pages.

Abraham A. Brill Library
http://plaza.interport.net/nypsan/service.html

American Psychological Society (APS)
http://www.psychologicalscience.org/links.html

Psychological Research on the Net
http://psych.hanover.edu/APS/exponnet.html

Little did Wilhelm Wundt realize his monumental contribution to science when, in 1879 in Germany, he opened the first psychological laboratory to examine consciousness. Wundt would barely recognize today's science of psychology as he practiced it.

Contemporary psychology is defined as *the science or study of individual mental activity and behavior.* This definition reflects the two parent disciplines from which psychology emerged: philosophy and biology. Compared to its parents, psychology is very much a new discipline. Some aspects of modern psychology are particularly biological, such as neuroscience, perception, psychophysics, and behavioral genetics. Other aspects are more philosophical, such as the study of personality, while others approximate sociology, as does social psychology.

Today's psychologists work in a variety of settings. Many psychologists are academics, teaching and researching psychology on university campuses. Others work in applied settings such as hospitals, mental health clinics, industry, and schools. Most psychologists also specialize in psychology after some graduate training. Industrial psychologists specialize in human performance in organizational settings, while clinical psychologists are concerned about the assessment, diagnosis, and treatment of individuals with a variety of mental disorders.

There are some psychologists who think that psychology is still in its adolescence and that the field seems to be experiencing some growing pains. Since its establishment, the field has expanded to many different areas. As mentioned above, some areas are very applied; other areas appear to emphasize theory and research. The growing pains resulted in some conflict over what the agenda of the first national psychological association, the American Psychological Association, should be. Because academics perceived this association as mainly serving practitioners, academics and researchers established their own competing association, the American Psychological Society. But despite its varied nature and growing pains, psychology remains a viable and exciting field. The first unit of the book is designed to introduce you to the nature and history of psychology.

In the opening article, "A Dance to the Music of the Century: Changing Fashions in 20th Century Psychiatry," David Healy reviews the history and theories of psychology and psychiatry. He also anticipates where these disciplines are headed and which theories will continue to play a role in shaping psychological thought.

In the second article, "Science and Pseudoscience," experts in psychology debate what science really is. They conclude that science has different meanings, depending upon the constitu-

ency. Lay people for example, often embrace as science simple anecdotal observations. Examples of science and anecdote are given.

The next article also pertains to psychological science. The authors ask a cogent question: Can psychology be used for both good and evil? The answer is yes. Author Ervin Staub, using his own research on several different topics, demonstrates the good uses and misuses of findings from psychological research.

The third introductory article on psychology is also about psychological research. In some research, psychologists utilize deception. For example, the instructions tell participants that the study is about creativity and that they will write a story after viewing a stimulus. The true nature of the study may really pertain to participants' reactions to sexual stimuli. In other words, the study is not examining creativity at all. The author of the article contends that when psychologists deceive and debrief research participants about the deception, they delve into muddy ethical water.

A dance to the music of the century:

Changing fashions in 20th-century psychiatry

David Healy, Director

North Wales Department of Psychological Medicine,
Hergest Unit, Bangor LL57 2PW

Modern psychiatry began in the early 19th century from a social psychiatric seed. The early alienists, Pinel and Tuke, Esquirol and Connolly believed that managing the social milieu of the patient could contribute significantly to their chances of recovery. These physicians produced the first classificatory systems in the discipline. At the turn of the century, university psychiatry, which was biologically oriented, began to impact on psychiatry, especially in Germany. This is seen most clearly in the work and classificatory system of Emil Kraepelin (Healy, 1997). At the same time, a new psychodynamic approach to the management of nervous problems in the community was pioneered most notably by Sigmund Freud. This led to yet another classification of nervous problems.

In the first half of the century, unlike German and French psychiatry, British psychiatry remained largely aloof from the influences of both university and psychodynamic approaches. It became famously pragmatic and eclectic. Edward Mapother, the first director of the Maudsley Hospital, typified the approach. Aubrey Lewis, who succeeded him, as well as David Henderson in Edinburgh, both of whom trained with Adolf Meyer in the USA, were committed to Meyer's biopsychosocial approach (Gelder, 1991). The social psychiatry that stemmed from this was to gain a decisive say in European and world psychiatry in the decades immediately following the Second World War.

Things at first unfolded no differently in that other bastion of English-speaking psychiatry—America. In the first decade of the 20th century, Meyer introduced Kraepelin's work to North America, where it had a modest impact, failing to supplant Meyer's own biopsychosocial formulations. In 1909, Freud visited the USA. He appears to have regarded it as an outpost of the civilised world, one particularly prone to enthusiasms. At this point, Freudian analysis restricted itself to handling personalities and their discontents. It initially made little headway in the USA.

There was another development in the USA that was to have a decisive impact on British and world psychiatry in due course. In 1912, the USA legislature passed the Harrison's Narcotics Act, the world's first piece of legislation which made drugs available on prescription only, in this case, opiates and cocaine. While substance misuse was not at the time a part of psychiatry, which confined itself worldwide almost exclusively to the management of the psychoses, this move to prescription-only status by involving medical practitioners in managing the problem almost by necessity meant that the issue of personalities and their disorders would at some point become part of psychiatry.

The years before the Second World War led to two sets of developments. First, there was a migration of psychoanalysts from Europe to North America, so that by the 1940s a majority of the world's analysts lived there. In America, what had been a pessimistic worldview was recast with an optimistic turn, in part perhaps because the War demonstrated that nervous disorders could be environmentally induced and at the same time genetic research was temporarily eclipsed. This new remodelled psychoanalysis abandoned Freud's reserve about treating psychosis. It triumphed and drove American psychiatry to a view that everyone was at least latently ill, that everyone was in need of treatment and that the way to put the world's wrongs right was not just to treat mental illness, but to resculpt personalities and promote mental health (Menninger, 1959).

Second, sulphonamides were discovered and the War stimulated research, which made penicillin commercially available. The success that stemmed from these led to explosive growth in the pharmaceutical sector. The search for other antibiotics led to the discovery in France of antihistamines, one of which turned out to be chlorpromazine. The Food and Drug Administration in the USA responded to these new drugs by making all new drugs available on prescription only. European countries followed suit. This was to bring not only problems of personality but also the vast pool of community nervousness within the remit of non-analytic psychiatry.

The psychoanalysts gained control of American psychiatry in the decade before the introduction of the psychotropic drugs. By 1962, 59 of 82 psychiatric departments were headed by analysts, all graduate programmes were based on analytical principles and 13 of the 17 most recommended texts were psychoanalytical (Shorter, 1996). As a director of the National Institute of Mental Health put it:

> "From 1945 to 1955, it was nearly impossible for a non-psychoanalyst to become a chairman of a department or professor of psychiatry" (Brown, 1976).

As early as 1948, three-quarters of all committee posts in the American Psychiatric Association (APA) were held by analysts (Shorter, 1996).

One of the features of these developments was that a rootless patois of dynamic terms seeped out into the popular culture to create a psychobabble, with untold consequences for how we view ourselves. Another feature that is regularly cited was the way the analytical totalitarianism that resulted handled failures of patients to get well or of critics to come on side. These were turned around and viewed as further indicators of the psychopathology afflicting patients and critics respectively (Dolnick, 1998).

Walter Reich (1982) argued that this style was a defence against pessimism that stemmed at least in part from America's peculiar needs for solutions to complexity. He was writing at a time of change, just after the publication of DSM-III (American Psychiatric Association, 1980). DSM-III, which is commonly cited as marking the triumph of a neo-Kraepelinian revolution in American psychiatry, was widely seen as changing the rules to favour a newly emerging biological psychiatry. Its message, that psychiatry's business was to treat diseases, was a counter to perceptions that the analytical agenda had become a crusade that had taken "psychiatrists on a mission to change the world which had brought the profession to the verge of extinction" (Bayer & Spitzer, 1985).

Part of the stimulus to DSM-III had come from participation in the International Pilot Study of Schizophrenia, where American psychiatrists had felt keenly the disdain with which their diagnostic views were regarded by their European counterparts, who were British or who, like Norman Sartorius, Assen Jablensky and others, had close links with the Maudsley (Spitzer, 2000). The DSM-III was fiercely resisted in the UK, whose leading authorities had been the key figures behind the international system of classification (ICD) for several decades. The new system was dismissed—"serious students of nosology will continue to use the ICD" (Shepherd, 1981). But an empire was slipping from British hands (Spitzer, 2000). The World Psychiatric Association took as its banner for its 1996 meeting the slogan "One World, One Language". Few people, attending the meeting at least, thought this language was anything other than biological or neo-Kraepelinian.

Reich (1982) commented on the change in American psychiatry from analysis to a more biologically-based discipline but this change, he suggested, was likely to be governed by similar dynamics to those that drove the earlier turn to psychoanalysis. By the 1990s, the rise of psychopharmacology and biological psychiatry was complete. The chances of a non-neuroscientist becoming a head of a psychiatric department in the USA was highly unlikely and not much more likely in the UK. The standard textbooks were heavily neuroscientific in their emphasis. Where once the APA was controlled by analysts, annual meetings now generated millions of dollars—largely from pharmaceutical company sponsored satellite symposia, of which there were 40 in 1999, at approximately $250 000 per symposium in addition to fees for exhibition space and registration fees for several thousand delegates brought to the meeting by pharmaceutical companies, as well as several million dollars per annum from sales of successive versions of the DSM.

The UK, which had once stood dismissive of American trends and diagnoses, increasingly followed American leads. Fashions in recovered memory therapies or fluoxetine-taking rapidly crossed the Atlantic, influenced in part perhaps by the ever-increasing attendance of British psychiatrists at APA meetings. By 1999, it was possible that greater numbers of British psychiatrists, sponsored largely by pharmaceutical companies, attended the APA meeting than the annual meeting of the Royal College of Psychiatrists, a development that would have been incredible a decade before.

Biological psychiatry, meanwhile, had not restricted itself to the psychoses from whence it came. By the end of the century, the complete transformation of personality rather than simply the treatment of disease was becoming the goal. This was most clearly articulated in Peter Kramer's *Listening to Prozac* (Kramer, 1993). Where once the psychiatric concern had been for symptoms as these reflected diseases, the emphasis was increasingly on the management of problems by biological means. The extent to which community nervousness stems from social arrangements rather than diseases is clearly uncertain, but where the best estimates of annual prevalence rates of depressive disease stood at between 50 and 100 per million in 1950, by the mid-1990s they had risen to 100,000 per million for depressive disorders as defined by the DSM, with even higher rates for depressive symptoms (Healy, 1997).

Despite the neo-Kraepelinian revolution, some American opinion leaders were beginning to argue that the profession faced disaster if it did not stop offering to solve social ills and if it did not pull back to a medical focus (Detre & McDonald, 1997). Where once blame had been put on families, or mothers in particular, the 1990s became the decade of blaming the brain (Valenstein, 1998). By the end of the decade, the psychobabble of yesteryear was fast being replaced by a newly minted biobabble. *The Guardian* newspaper ran a feature on "Oh no! We're not really getting more depressed are we?" in which a psychologist, Oliver James, pondered whether the British have become a low-serotonin people (James, 1997). Finally, an ever increasing emphasis on long-term treatment with psychotropic agents, along with difficulties with withdrawal from them (a perennial British concern), inevitably recalls Karl Kraus' quip about analysis becoming the illness it purported to cure.

The mass treatment of problems with psychotropic drugs could not but in itself run into problems. Reports of suicides, homicides and other events while taking fluoxetine (Healy *et al*, 1999) led Eli Lilly to devise a strategy to manage criticism which involved blaming the disease, not the drug (Cornwell, 1996). On 20 April 1999, two students took firearms into a high school in Littleton, Colorado, killing 12 students, one staff member and then themselves. Within days of suggestions that one of the teenagers had an antidepressant in their blood stream, the APA Website carried a statement from the Association's president:

> "Despite a decade of research, there is little valid evidence to prove a causal relationship between the use of antidepressant medications and destructive behavior. On the other hand, their [sic] is ample evidence that undiagnosed and untreated mental illness exacts a heavy toll on those who suffer from these disorders as well as those around them" (American Psychiatric Association, 1999).

Many of those who take up psychiatry as a career might be thought to do so for fairytale or romantic reasons. At some point they will have nourished fantasies of helping patients with neuroses or psychoses to recover to the point of being invited to participate in the ball of life once more. In the course of a century, psychiatrists attending the ball have elegantly changed partners on a number of occasions. It is less clear that those who are not invited to the ball have seen much difference as a consequence of changes on the dance floor. When the clock strikes for the new millennium, are any of the dancers likely to be bothered by a stray glass slipper or does that just happen in fairytales?

References

AMERICAN PSYCHIATRIC ASSOCIATION (1980) *Diagnostic and Statistical Manual of Mental Disorders* (3rd edn.) (DSM-III). Washington, DC: American Psychiatric Association.

AMERICAN PSYCHIATRIC ASSOCIATION (1999) *Online News Stand*, release no. 99–19. www.psych.org/news.stand/nr.990428.html.

BAYER R. & SPITZER, R. L. (1985) Neurosis, psychodynamics and DSM-III. *Archives of General Psychiatry*, **25**, 123–130.

BROWN, B. S. (1976) The life of psychiatry. *American Journal of Psychiatry*, **133**, 489–495.

CORNWELL, J. (1996) *The Power to Harm. Mind, Medicine and Money on Trial*. London: Viking Press.

DETRE, T. & McDONALD, M. C. (1997) Managed care and the future of psychiatry. *Archives of General Psychiatry*, **54**, 201–204.

DOLNICK, E. (1998) *Madness on the Couch. Blaming the Victim in the Heyday of Psychoanalysis*. New York: Simon & Schuster.

GELDER, M. (1991) Adolf Meyer and his influence in British psychiatry. In *150 Years of British Psychiatry 1841–1991* (eds. G. E. Berrios & H. Freeman), pp. 419–435. London: Gaskell.

JAMES, O. (1997) Oh no! We're not really getting more depressed are we? *The Guardian*, G2, pp. 1–3. Monday 15 September.

HEALY, D. (1997) *The Antidepressant Era*. Cambridge, MA: Harvard University Press.

HEALY, D., LANGMAACK, C. & SAVAGE, M. (1999) Suicide in the course of the treatment of depression. *Journal of Psychopharmacology*, **13**, 94–99.

KRAMER, P. (1993) *Listening to Prozac*. New York: Viking Press.

MENINGER, K. (1959) Hope. *American Journal of Psychiatry*, **116**, 481–491.

REICH, W. (1982) American psychoideology. *Psychiatric Bulletin*, **6**, 43.

SHEPHERD, M. (1981) Diagnostic and Statistical Manual, 3rd Edition. American Psychiatric Association Press. *Psychological Medicine*, **11**, 215.

SHORTER, F. (1996) *A History of Psychiatry. From the Age of the Asylum to the Era of Prozac*. New York: John Wiley & Sons.

SPITZER, R. (2000) A manual for diagnosis and statistics. In *The Psychopharmacologists*, volume 3 (ed. D. Healy). London: Arnold.

VALENSTEIN, E. S. (1998) *Blaming the Brain*. New York: Free Press.

Science and Pseudoscience

W hat makes something science? How do we identify what isn't science?

And how do we prevent that pseudoscience from being accepted and promoted as science?

These and other equally loaded questions were taken on at the APS Convention's Presidential Symposium, coordinated this year by then-APS President and current APS Past President Elizabeth Loftus, of the University of Washington.

"We live in a land transformed by science, and yet pseudoscientific ideas are rampant," said Loftus. "Many of these beliefs concern topics that have benefitted from widespread study by psychological scientists. Science and rationality are continually under attack and threatened by a rise of pseudoscience, so I organized this year's Presidential Symposium to illuminate these problems in hopes of fostering critical thinking, educating the public, and ourselves."

Loftus invited several well-known researchers and scholars in the field to help her in her quest, including:

1. Yale University's Robert Sternberg, who spoke on "How more and more research can tell you less and less until finally you know much less than when you started";
2. Carol Tavris, who gave her perspective on "Power, politics,

money, and fame: Sources of pseudoscience in research and therapy"; and

3. Ray Hyman, of the University of Oregon, who served as the discussant for these intriguing concepts.

In the Beginning...

Loftus kicked off the symposium discussing the tendency of humans, throughout their existence, to find some kind of explanation for the mysteries of the universe, natural events, and life itself. Loftus favorably mentioned and then paraphrased from a book—*Mind Myths: Exploring popular assumptions about the mind and brain*, edited by Sergio Della Sala—that, she said, captured the paradox:

"The changing seasons, growth and decay, storms, floods, droughts, and good and bad fortune, for example, were all attributed to supernatural beings, to famous ancestors, or ancient heroes," she said. "We now have a better understanding of, for instance, thunder and lightning and they don't terrify us as much, but in the absence of this kind of understanding of the mechanisms of the mind, the brain, and the effects of diseases on the mind and brain, we tackle mysteries still by focusing on divine intervention or we take shelter in simplistic superstition."

Loftus then gave a number of examples of how, even today, pseudoscience and misinformation abounds.

"Educated people have been known to recently express beliefs in alien abduction, fire walking, possession, creationism, and even that 90 percent of handicapped people have parents who were not virgins when they married," said Loftus, who then referred to a survey she conducted with her colleagues of non-psychology graduate students that indicated a good percentage of them believed that therapeutic techniques could be used to remember prenatal accounts.

"One problem here is that the books written by believers—full of enchanting anecdotes that are mistaken for science—sell like hot cakes, while books by skeptics trying to debunk these beliefs don't sell as well or at all," she said.

Loftus cited another example of a self-described "personologist" who has written a book on using a person's facial features to determine their personality and nature.

"Why do people persist in believing in impossible or improbable things?" asked Loftus, who turned the podium over the Sternberg, who explored the phenomenon of quasi science and challenged the assumption that the more data collected about a phenomenon indicates the more we know about that phenomenon.

This assumption is flat out wrong, says Sternberg, who argues that scientists tend to build in certain limited assumptions in collecting data. The result, he says, is that scientists keep getting the same wrong or limited result and then gain confidence in that result so that they eventually become more confident of something that is not true.

"If you misplace your confidence in your quasi-scientific results, you can end up doing more and more research on a topic and know less and less," he said. "In collecting data, we always build in certain limited assumptions. For example, we may limit the participants we test. Or we may limit the kinds of test materials we use. Or we may limit the situations in which we test people."

The result, said Sternberg, is that we keep getting the same wrong, or at least limited, result and gain confidence in it.

"We are thus becoming more and more confident of something that is not true," he said and gave as a case study the example of intelligence. "Hundreds of studies reviewed by Carroll, Jensen, Brand, and others appear to show that there is a general factor. They are right—but only under the assumptions of these studies."

Sternberg presented data that showed that when one expands the range of participants (e.g., to participants in various African and Asian countries, or even culturally diverse populations in the United States), the range of materials used to test intelligence (not just academic-analytical kinds of problems, but creative and practical ones as well), and the kinds of situations in which testing is done (e.g., getting outside classrooms or psychologists' testing rooms), the "G" factor disappears. Nor do such tests provide very good prediction of real-world performance, he said.

"The punch line is that continued heavy reliance on IQ-based measures, including the SAT, GRE, LSAT, GMAT, and so forth, depends on reliance on a narrow base of assumptions in research," he said. "Because people do not realize they are making these assumptions and because the assumptions often benefit them, they are blind to the assumptions. But these assumptions are there nevertheless, distorting the conclusions that are drawn. We need

a broader conception of intelligence and, more generally, we have to be careful… collecting more data does not tell us less rather than more."

You Know It When You See It

Tavris then presented her perspective on "Power, Politics, Money, and Fame: Sources of pseudoscience in research and therapy" in which she assessed what qualifies as science, what qualifies as pseudoscience, how to tell the difference, and why it matters.

Pseudoscience, said Tavris, is like pornography: we can't define it, but we know it when we see it.

"But what we are arguing about here and what remains a source of confusion for the public is: what is science?" she said. "Philosophers of science have been arguing this for a long time. Some define science by its goal; it is the search for permanent universal laws of behavior. Others define science by its tools; a PET scan is science, an interview is not. Others define it by its subject; a brain is a tangible thing you can study scientifically, whereas love and wisdom and other intangible psychological states are not science. Science for me is one thing: it is an attitude of questioning received wisdom combined with the deepest and most entrenched human cognitive bias—the conformational bias."

Tavris went on to define pseudoscience as the determined pursuit of confirmation of one's beliefs.

"Pseudoscience wears the veneer of science but lacks its central infusing spirit of inquiry and the willingness to come up wrong," she said. "More than ever, I think psychological science has a role to play in counteracting its influence in our culture. Of course, pseudoscience flourishes everywhere in the world and always has. It is a human predilection and not uniquely an American one, however, there are two aspects of the American culture that I think foster its particular incarnation in America."

The first aspect, said Tavris, is the American culture's need for certainty. Pseudoscience is popular because it confirms what we believe, she said. The second aspect of our

culture that fosters pseudoscience, added Tavris, is the capitalistic quick fix.

"We love instant cures and tonics for what ails us," she said. "From chubbiness to the blues, from serious problems to tragedies. 'We can fix you' is the American credo, and we can fix you especially fast if you take this magic pill or use this magic technology."

These forces, she argues, foster the pseudoscientific effect in research.

"The harmony now between drug researchers and the pharmaceutical industry is stronger and more worrisome than people tend to recognize. Drug companies set up their own research institutes. They sponsor seminars and conferences," she said. "I went to one on new advances in the treatment of depression. All of the advancements were—guess what—antidepressants. So increasingly, biomedical research, even if it is well done, is only giving us part of the story. The public rarely hears the rest—the rest being done by psychological scientists. For example, in the case with the antidepressants, the public rarely hears that upwards of 75 percent of the effectiveness of antidepressants is due to the placebo effect."

Critics of science, said Tavris, are right to remind scientists that they must now assume they have the truth.

"We won't ever have the truth, but, unlike pseudoscience, science give us the ability to be critically demanding," she said. "Demand evidence. Resist the confirmation bias. There are tools that can help us get closer to the answers. Maybe, sometimes, even close enough."

Science in Another Dimension

Discussant Hyman examined how learned scientists can sometime engage in, and fall victim to, pseudoscience.

"I have always been fascinated by the scientist who recognizes good science in one area while at the same time is considered to be doing pseudoscience in another area," he said. "This raises a variety of interesting issues."

Hyman has had extensive experience in debunking pseudoscientific issues. For example, earlier in the decade, he was appointed to a blue ribbon panel to evaluate previously secret programs of psychic spying conducted by the CIA over the past 20 years. In addition, he appears frequently on television shows presenting the skeptical views of various paranormal claims. He is also a founding member of the Committee of Scientific Investigation for the Claims of the Paranormal and serves on the editorial board of the journal the *Skeptic Inquirer*. He conducts an annual workshop titled "The Skeptics Toolbox," that is intended to provide participants with the knowledge and tools to properly evaluate paranormal claims.

Hyman used as an example the case of a recognized astrophysicist who published a book in which he claimed to have proven the existence of the fourth dimension from his investigations of a spiritualistic medium.

"Here we have a person who has earned his credentials and reputation in a recognized field of science," said Hyman. "He then develops and supports a theory that his colleagues categorize as pseudoscience. If this is true, then the same person can practice both science and pseudoscience."

Good and Evil and Psychological Science

ERVIN STAUB
Guest Columnist

To me, evil means great human destructiveness. Evil can come in an obvious form, such as a genocide. Or it can come in smaller acts of persistent harm doing, the effects of which accumulate, like parents being hostile and punitive, or a child being picked on by peers day after day for a long time. Goodness means bringing about great benefit to individuals or whole groups. It too can come in an obvious form, like a heroic effort to save someone's life, or great effort in pursuit of significant social change, or in smaller, persistent acts.

Nations often act in selfish and destructive ways. But goodness by groups, small and large, does exist. In the case of nations, goodness often comes from mixed motives, as in the case of the Marshall Plan that rebuilt Europe, but also was aimed at preventing the spread of Communism. At other times, as in Somalia—where intervention to help reduce starvation ended in violence and confusion—seemingly altruistic motives come to bad ends. The work of the Quakers in the abolition of slavery, and the village of LaChambon in France saving thousands of Jews during the Holocaust, illustrate goodness born of humane values and altruism.

What is the role of psychology in relation to goodness and evil? One obvious role is to study the influences that lead to great or persistent acts of harm or benefit. We can study the psychological processes, such as anger, hostility, the devaluation of groups of people, empathy or its absence, and a feeling of responsibility for others' welfare, that make a person act in destructive or caring ways. We can study the characteristics of persons, cultures, social/political systems and existing conditions that make either destructive or benevolent behavior likely. What are these processes and characteristics and how do they evolve?

Cultures and social systems influence not only group behavior but also shape individual psychology. Until not long ago, children were seen in many Western cultures as inherently willful. It was thought that to become good people, their will must be broken early, using severe punishment to do so. Such practices enhance the potential for both individual and group violence.

I will briefly discuss role of psychological science in a few specific domains of "good and evil": child rearing; the origins of genocide; and healing and reconciliation.

RAISING CARING, NOT VIOLENT, CHILDREN

On the basis of my own research on child rearing and the research of many others, and my own experiences with the application of research, I believe that we know a great deal about raising caring and nonaggressive children. Affection and nurturance that help fulfill a child's important needs; guidance that is both firm and responsive to the child, democratic and nonpunitive, based on values that are explained to children; and leading children to actually engage in behavior that benefits others are among the important elements.

So are positive peer relations. In our recent work in evaluating children's perception of their lives in school, from second grade to high school, we found, as have others, that even in good schools some children are the object of negative behavior, of bullying by others. Other children are excluded. Both groups report that they experience fewer positive emotions and more negative emotions in school. Bystanders, peers and teachers mostly remain passive. When they act, children who receive some protection feel better. So do the active bystanders themselves.

Psychologists ought to move, at this point, from piecemeal studies to holistic interventions, carefully evaluated, that aim to foster the development of caring, helpful and nonaggressive children. Doing so requires working not only with children but also with adults, since it is adults who have to provide affection, nurturance and guidance.

Intervention can center on creating caring schools, with communities that include every child and promote positive peer relations and constructive bystandership. Such intervention would help children who are badly treated and disconnected from people at home, and protect children in school. It may even stop such horrors as school shootings. Schools can also call on parents as allies, provide training, and help parents create a supportive community that fosters positive socialization.

An important point for me is that "intervention" is an essential aspect of the work of psychological science. Intervention aims to create a better world. But it is also a means of essential new learning. Only by combining the influences explored, usually individually, in controlled research, can we learn whether the whole is what we expect from a combination of the parts, whether the combination of influences usually required to create real change in the world actually does so. Our observation and experience in the course of such interventions—and careful evaluation with controls—can confirm old knowledge, but is almost certain to also give rise to new knowledge.

ORIGINS OF GENOCIDE AND OTHER GROUP VIOLENCE

I have studied the origins of genocide and other group violence for a long time. Psychologists, who with some exceptions have just begun paying attention to this realm, have a great deal to do. Their research has to extend beyond the laboratory. The data we need include economic and political conditions in a society; a history of relationships between groups such as conflict and enmity; characteristics of cultures—such as devaluation of another group, strong respect for authority, past woundedness and the absence of pluralism; the actions of leaders; the evolution of increasing harmdoing; and the behavior (passivity versus action) of bystanders. All of these have important roles (Staub, 1989; 1999).

It is essential to understand the characteristics and psychological processes of individuals and groups: Turning to a group for identity; scapegoating; ideologies or visions of life that iden-

tify enemies; changes in individuals and in group processes in the course of the evolution of increasing harmdoing; the psychology of leaders; and reasons for the passivity of internal and external bystanders. These are the proximal influences leading to violence.

Just as important is the issue of prevention. Understanding origins points to avenues for prevention. Some of these origins are not traditionally in the realm of psychology, but ought to be. For example, the passivity of nations encourages perpetrators. But such passivity has psychological elements, for example, the way leaders combine values and "interests" in decision making. Or the way leaders of genocidal groups make decisions. It is often assumed, by political scientists and sociologists, that such leaders act to enhance their own power and influence. But I strongly believe that they are impacted by social conditions and culture, as are other members of their group. Their actions are the results of complex psychological processes that arise under violence-generating conditions. We must understand these to ultimately deal with them in preventive ways.

HEALING AND RECONCILIATION

My work in Rwanda, in collaboration with Laurie Anne Pearlman, Alexandra Gubin and Athanase Hagengimana, has focused on helping people heal and reconcile in the aftermath of genocide, as a way of preventing renewed violence there (for early partial reports, see Staub 2000; Staub and Pearlman, in press).

Without healing, people so victimized will feel extremely vulnerable and see the world as dangerous. They may engage in violence, believing that they need to defend themselves, but in the process become perpetrators (Staub, 1998). Healing by them is essential. So is healing by perpetrators. Past victimization and other traumatic events are among the influences that contribute to perperation. In addition, perpetrators of mass violence are wounded by their own horrible actions. Perpetrator and victims groups, or two groups that have inflicted violence on each other, both need to heal if they are to overcome hostility, reconcile, and stop a continuing cycle of violence.

In Rwanda we trained people who worked for organizations that work with groups in the community. We talked to them and with them about the origins of genocide, about basic human needs—the frustration of which contributes to genocide and which are deeply frustrated in survivors of a genocide, about the traumatic effects of genocide on people, and about avenues to healing. We had them talk to each other in small groups about their painful experiences during the genocide.

Afterwards, some of the people we trained worked with groups in the community. In both training and application, Hutus and Tutsis participated together. The people in these community groups reported fewer trauma symptoms after this intervention and a more positive orientation to people in the other ethnic group. These changes occurred both over time and in comparison to changes in people who participated in groups led by facilitators we did not train, or were in control groups that received no treatment.

Doing such work is difficult and demanding, but highly rewarding. Working on the prevention of group violence is a field with newly emerging theories, limited experience, and little research. Psychological scientists are much needed to contribute to our knowledge, as well as to actually reduce evil and promote goodness.

REFERENCES

Staub, E. (1989). The roots of evil: The origins of genocide and other group violence. New York: Cambridge University Press.

Staub, E. (1998). Breaking the cycle of genocidal violence: Healing and reconciliation. In J. Harvey (ed.). Perspectives on loss: A sourcebook. Philadelphia: Taylor and Francis.

Staub, E. (1999). The origins and prevention of genocide, mass killing, and other collective violence. Peace and Conflict: Journal of Peace Psychology, 5(4), 303–336.

Staub, E. (2000). Genocide and mass killing: Origins, prevention, healing, and reconciliation. Political Psychology, 21(2), 367–382.

Staub, E., & Pearlman, L.A. (In press). Healing, reconciliation and forgiving after genocide and other collective violence. Forgiveness and Reconciliation, Radnor, PA. Templeton Foundation Press.

ERVIN STAUB is Professor of Psychology at the University of Massachusetts. He is President of the International Society for Political Psychology. His books include Positive Social Behavior and Morality *Vol 1, 1978; Vol 2, 1979, Academic Press, and* The Roots of Evil. *He is currently working on* A Brighter Future: Raising Caring and Nonviolent Children.

Psychology's Tangled Web

Deceptive methods may backfire on behavioral researchers

By BRUCE BOWER

In *Marmion*, Sir Walter Scott describes with memorable succinctness the unanticipated pitfalls of trying to manipulate others: "O, what a tangled web we weave, when first we practice to deceive."

The poet's tangled web aptly symbolizes the situation that some psychological researchers now find themselves struggling with.

Consider a study conducted recently by Kevin M. Taylor and James A. Shepperd, both of the University of Florida in Gainesville. Seven introductory psychology students took part in their pilot investigation, which measured the extent to which performance on a cognitive task was affected by experimenter-provided feedback after each of several attempts. Because of a last-minute cancellation by an eighth study recruit, the researchers asked a graduate student to pose as the final participant.

Only the graduate student knew beforehand that feedback was designed to mislead participants in systematic ways about their successes and failures on the task.

At the conclusion of the trials, an experimenter who had monitored the proceedings briefly left the room. Although they had been warned not to talk to one another, the seven "real" participants began to discuss the experiment and their suspicions about having been given bogus feedback. A brief comparison of the feedback they had received quickly uncovered the researchers' deceptive scheme.

When the experimenter returned, participants acted as though nothing had happened. The experimenter announced that the trials had included deception and asked

students on three separate occasions if they had become suspicious of anything that happened during the laboratory experience. All of them denied having had any misgivings, in interviews as well as on questionnaires, and divulged nothing about their collective revelation.

At that point, the experimenter dismissed the students and expressed confidence that they had provided useful data. The graduate stand-in, who purely by chance had witnessed the participants' secret deliberations, unburdened him of that illusion.

In a letter published in the August 1996 AMERICAN PSYCHOLOGIST, Taylor and Shepperd bravely fessed up to having had the tables turned on them by their own students. In the process, they rekindled a long-running debate about whether psychologists should try to fool research subjects in the name of science.

"Our seven participants do not represent all experimental participants," the Florida investigators concluded. "Nevertheless, their behavior suggests that, even when pressed, participants cannot be counted on to reveal knowledge they may acquire or suspicions they may develop about the deception or experimental hypotheses."

Deceptive techniques have gained prominence in psychological research, and particularly in social psychology, since the 1960s. Moreover, studies that place participants in fabricated situations featuring

role-playing confederates of the investigator have attracted widespread attention.

Consider a 1963 investigation conducted by the late Stanley Milgram, which still pervades public consciousness. Although ostensibly recruited for a study of learning and memory, volunteers unwittingly took part in Milgram's exploration of the extent to which people will obey authority figures.

Many volunteers accepted the exhortations of a stern experimenter to deliver increasingly stronger electric shocks to an unseen person in an adjoining room every time that person erred in recalling a list of words. Nearly two-thirds of the participants agreed to deliver powerful shocks to the forgetful individual—a confederate of Milgram's who received no actual shocks but could be heard screaming, pounding the wall, and begging to leave the room.

Milgram's study inspired much debate over the ethics of deceiving experimental subjects and whether data collected in this way offer clear insights into the nature of obedience or anything else. It also heralded a growing acceptance of deceptive practices by social psychologists.

Researchers have tracked this trend by monitoring articles appearing in the JOURNAL OF PERSONALITY AND SOCIAL PSYCHOLOGY, regarded by most as a premier publication. Only 16 percent of empirical studies published there in 1961 used deception. That proportion rose to nearly 47 percent in 1978, dipped to 32 percent in 1986, and returned to 47 percent in 1992. The investigators generally agree that an even larger portion of studies published in other social psychology journals have included deceptive techniques.

Deception still occurs relatively frequently in social psychology studies, although less often than in 1992, holds psychologist James H. Korn of Saint Louis University, who has investigated the prevalence of these practices and written a book titled *Illusions of Reality: A History of Deception in Social Psychology* (1997, State University of New York Press). Dramatic cases of experimental manipulation like Milgram's obedience study rarely appear anymore, he adds.

Instead, deception now usually involves concealing or camouflaging an experiment's true purpose in order to elicit unguarded responses from volunteers. For instance, researchers running a study of the effects of misleading information on memories of a traffic accident presented in a series of slides may simply tell participants that they're conducting an analysis of attention. After completing the study, volunteers get a full explanation of its methods and goals from experimenters in a debriefing session.

In Korn's view, this mellowing of deceptive tactics partly reflects an injunction in the current ethical guidelines of the American Psychological Association that "psychologists never deceive research participants about significant aspects that would affect their willingness to participate, such as physical risks, discomfort, or unpleasant emotional experiences."

Yet, as Taylor and Shepperd's humbling experience demonstrates, even the softer side of deception can have rough edges. In fact, the clandestine knowledge of the Florida recruits underscores the need to do away entirely with deception in psychological research, argue economist Andreas Ortmann of Bowdoin College in Brunswick, Maine, and psychologist Ralph Hertwig of the Max Planck Institute for Human Development in Munich, Germany. Suspicions of being misled may affect subjects' responses and complicate interpretation of the results.

A number of like-minded critics have challenged the ethics of using deceptive techniques, whether or not they generate compelling findings. Ortmann and Hertwig take a more practical stand. They regard deceptive procedures—even in mild forms promulgated by a significant minority—as the equivalent of methodological termites eating away at both the

reputation of all psychological researchers and the validity of their findings.

People in general, and the favorite experimental guinea pigs—college undergraduates—in particular, have come to expect that they will be misled in psychology experiments, Ortmann and Hertwig argue. Each new experiment in which participants are deceived and debriefed sets off another round of extracurricular discussions about psychologists' sneaky ruses, they say.

This process transforms interactions between a researcher and a participant into a real-life episode of a repeated prisoner's dilemma game, the researchers contended in the July 1997 AMERICAN PSYCHOLOGIST. In these games, two or more people choose either to cooperate or to pursue self-interest in some task over many trials.

A selfish choice by one person yields a big payoff to that player and virtually nothing for everyone else; cooperation by all players moderately benefits everyone; and multiple selfish moves leave everyone with little or nothing. Cooperation in these games quickly unravels when an identifiable player consistently opts for self-interest (SN: 3/28/98, p. 205). Likewise, participants who have reason to believe that they will somehow be deceived by psychologists are likely to turn uncooperative in the laboratory—and in ways that a researcher may not notice, according to Ortmann and Hertwig.

"Psychologists have good intentions and follow their ethical manual, but they still foster mistrust in their subjects when they use deception," Ortmann says. "This is a question of clean research design, not just ethics."

Most experimental economists avoid using deceptive methods because of concerns about their corrosive effects on the discipline's reputation among potential research participants, the Bowdoin researcher holds. Economics studies depend on highly structured games, such as the prisoner's dilemma, which require volunteers to enact an explicit scenario; investigators monitor changes in behavior over a series of trials. Each participant receives a monetary payment based on his or her overall performance in the experiment.

In contrast, Ortmann and Hertwig assert, psychologists usually do not ask volunteers to assume a specific role or perspective in performing mental tasks, do not conduct multiple trials, and pay participants a flat fee or nothing. Recruits get a poor feel for the purpose of these experiments and are likely to second-guess the

scientist's intentions, especially if they suspect that a study includes deception.

Such suspicions flare up all too easily in studies of ongoing social interactions in which one participant secretly plays a fixed role at the researcher's behest, notes psychologist William Ickes of the University of Texas at Arlington. Volunteers who try to talk spontaneously with such a confederate often note an unnatural or bizarre quality to the conversation and become wary of the entire experiment, Ickes says.

The Texas scientist, who studies empathic accuracy (SN: 3/23/96, p. 190), focuses on undirected and unrehearsed encounters between volunteers.

Deception-free methods do not sift out all experimental impurities. Economics research, for instance, places individuals in abstract, potentially confusing situations that may have limited applicability to real-life exchanges of money and goods, Ortmann says. Still, the use of deceptive techniques would stir up mistrust among research subjects and throw the whole enterprise off course, he argues.

Critics of Ortmann and Hertwig's call to outlaw all forms of experimental deception defend its use in judicious moderation. Three psychologists elaborate on this view in the July AMERICAN PSYCHOLOGIST.

"The preponderance of evidence suggests that deceived participants do not become resentful about having been fooled by researchers and that deception does not negatively influence their perceptions about psychology or their attitudes about science in general," states Allan J. Kimmel of the Ecole Supérieure de Commerce de Paris, France.

Several surveys of people who have participated in psychological studies that included deceptive tactics find that, compared to their counterparts in nondeceptive experiments, they report having enjoyed the experience more and having learned more from it, Kimmel says.

Deceptive studies that include careful debriefing sessions preserve psychology's reputation, adds Arndt Bröder of the University of Bonn in Germany. In his own department, Bröder notes, during the debriefing the researchers explain the nature and necessity of experimental deceptions to all participants, most of whom agree to take part in further studies.

Sometimes researchers have no alternative but to hide their intentions from participants, contends Korn. A total ban on deception would obstruct certain types of work, he says, such as explorations of how people form and use ethnic and religious stereotypes.

Positive attitudes expressed on surveys and continued willingness to show up for experiments do not reassure Ortmann and Hertwig that participants accept experimental situations and researchers' directions at face value.

It is not necessarily deception when a researcher fails to tell participants the purpose of an experiment, they say, but it is always deception if a researcher tells falsehoods to participants in the course of an experiment.

At that point, a tangled web of social interactions may begin to trip up scientific progress. Participants who unravel a scientific fib may feel that they should not know more about an experiment than the re-searcher tells them and that such knowledge may invalidate their responses, maintain Taylor and Shepperd. As a result, perceptive volunteers zip their lips and make nice for the investigator.

All sorts of unspoken inferences by participants can intrude on the best-laid research plans, even if they exclude deception, argues Denis J. Hilton of the Ecole Supérieure des Sciences Economiques et Commerciales in Cergy-Pontoise, France.

In the September 1995 PSYCHOLOGI-CAL BULLETIN, Hilton analyzed how volunteers' assumptions about the meaning of experimental communications in several areas of psychological research can affect their responses.

For example, participants often read more into response scales than experimenters had intended. In a study noted by Hilton that asked volunteers how often they had felt irritated recently, those given a scale ranging from "several times daily" to "less than once a week" reported relatively minor irritations, such as enduring slow service at a restaurant. Those given a scale ranging from "several times a year" to "less than once every 3 months" cited more extreme incidents, such as a marital fight. The time frame provided by the scales shaped the way in which irritating episodes were defined and tallied.

Further complications in interpreting responses ensue when participants mistrust a researcher's objectives, Ortmann asserts.

"The question of whether deception matters deserves further inquiry," he remarks. "Too often, we as scientists don't think carefully about methodological issues and take for granted our experimental conditions."

UNIT 2
Biological Bases of Behavior

Unit Selections

5. **The Tangled Skeins of Nature and Nurture in Human Evolution**, Paul R. Ehrlich
6. **Decoding the Human Body**, Sharon Begley
7. **The Future of the Brain**, Norbert R. Myslinski

Key Points to Consider

- What do you think contributes most to our psychological make-up and behaviors: the influence of the environment, the expression of genes, or the functioning of the nervous system? Do you believe that perhaps some combination of these factors accounts for psychological characteristics and behaviors? How are these various contributors to behavior studied?

- What is genetic research? How is it conducted? How much of human behavior is influenced by genes? Can you give some examples of the influence of genes on human behavior? How could such research help experts in psychology and medicine predict and treat various disorders? What environmental factors affect genetic expression?

- What is the human genome project? Do you have ethical concerns about the human genome project? Or do you believe that the advantages of the project outweigh any concerns?

- How does the brain influence human behavior and psychological characteristics? What functions does the brain control? How do we study the brain? What new techniques do we have at our disposal to study the brain? What are the advantages of these techniques? How might these techniques influence how physicians and surgeons now deal with brain disorders or do surgery on the brain? What are some of the types of brain disorders and their symptoms?

 **Links: www.dushkin.com/online/**
These sites are annotated in the World Wide Web pages.

Adolescence: Changes and Continuity
http://www.personal.psu.edu/faculty/n/x/nxd10/adolesce.htm

Division of Hereditary Diseases and Family Studies, Indiana University School of Medicine
http://medgen.iupui.edu/divisions/hereditary/

Institute for Behavioral Genetics
http://ibgwww.colorado.edu/index.html

Serendip
http://serendip.brynmawr.edu/serendip/

As a child, Nancy vowed she did not want to turn out like either of her parents. Nancy's mother was very passive and acquiescent about her father's drinking. When Dad was drunk, Mom always called his boss to report that Dad was "sick" and then acted as if there was nothing wrong at home. Nancy's childhood was a nightmare. Her father's behavior was erratic and unpredictable. If he drank just a little bit, most often he was happy. If he drank a lot, which was usually the case, he often became belligerent.

Despite vowing not to become her father, as an adult Nancy found herself in the alcohol rehabilitation unit of a large hospital. Nancy's employer could no longer tolerate her on-the-job mistakes or her unexplained absences from work, and he referred her to the clinic for help. As Nancy pondered her fate, she wondered whether her genes pre-ordained her to follow in her father's inebriated footsteps or whether the stress of her childhood had brought her to this point in her life. After all, being the child of an alcoholic is not easy.

Just as Nancy was, psychologists also are concerned with discovering the causes of human behavior. Once the cause is known, treatments for problematic behaviors can be developed. In fact, certain behaviors might even be prevented when the cause is known. But for Nancy, prevention was too late.

One of the paths to understanding humans is to understand the biological underpinnings of their behavior. Genes and chromosomes, the body's chemistry (as found in hormones, neurotransmitters, and enzymes), and the central nervous system (comprised of the brain, spinal cord, and nerve cells) are all implicated in human behavior. All represent the biological aspects of behavior and ought, therefore, to be worthy of study by psychologists.

Physiological psychologists and psychobiologists are often the ones who examine the role of biology in behavior. The neuroscientist is especially interested in brain functioning; the psychopharmacologist is interested in the effects of various psychopharmacological agents or psychoactive drugs on behavior.

These psychologists often utilize one of three techniques to understand the biology-behavior connection. Animal studies involving manipulation, stimulation, or destruction of certain parts of the brain offer one method of study. For psychologists there is also a second available technique that includes the examination of unfortunate individuals whose brains are defective at birth or damaged later by accidents or disease.

We can also use animal models to understand genetics; with animal models we can control reproduction and develop various strains of animals if necessary. Such tactics with humans would be considered extremely unethical. However, a third technique, studying an individual's behavior in comparison to both natural and adoptive parents or by studying identical twins reared together or apart, allows psychologists to begin to understand the role of genetics versus environment in human behavior.

The articles in this unit are designed to familiarize you with the knowledge psychologists have gleaned by using these and other techniques to study physiological processes and other un-

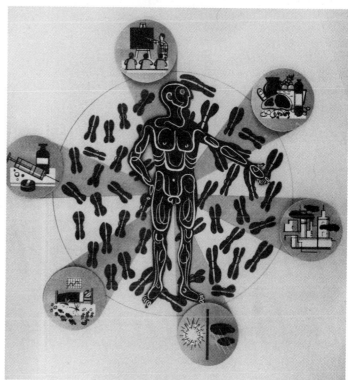

derlying mechanisms in human behavior. Each article should interest you and make you more curious about the role of biology in human endeavors.

The first article in this unit reviews almost all aspects of the biological bases of behavior. In "The Tangled Skeins of Nature and Nurture in Human Evolution," the author discusses the nature versus nurture debate, which questions whether genetics or the environment (in the form of culture) contribute to our psychological make-up. The author suggests that both nature and nurture are intricately intertwined to produce the characteristics of each individual.

The next selection for this unit examines the role of genes in human behavior. In "Decoding the Human Body," Sharon Begley reviews the human genome project. In this research, scientists are mapping the genetic code for humans. This project is exciting in that it will help us predict who is at risk for various illnesses and other genetically carried factors. The project, however, has caused some controversy in that such information could be misused in the hands of the wrong people.

Genes aren't the only biological underpinnings of human psychology. The next article covers information about the central nervous system, another important biological aspect of human behavior. In "The Future of the Brain," Norbert Myslinski describes new brain imaging techniques. These techniques are helping scientists understand what functions each part of the brain serves. These imaging techniques might also allow physicians to conduct brain surgery in less invasive and therefore in less detrimental ways.

The Tangled Skeins of Nature and Nurture in Human Evolution

By Paul R. Ehrlich

Wʜᴇɴ we think about our behavior as individuals, "Why?" is a question almost always on the tips of our tongues. Sometimes that question is about perceived similarities: why is almost everyone religious; why do we all seem to crave love; why do most of us like to eat meat? But our differences often seem equally or more fascinating: why did Sally get married although her sister Sue did not, why did they win and we lose, why is their nation poor and ours rich? What were the fates of our childhood friends? What kinds of careers did they have; did they marry; how many children did they have? Our everyday lives are filled with why's about differences and similarities in behavior, often unspoken, but always there. Why did one of my closest colleagues drink himself to death, whereas I, who love wine much more than he did, am managing to keep my liver in pretty good shape? Why, of two very bright applicants admitted to our department at Stanford University for graduate work, does one turn out pedestrian science and another have a spectacular career doing innovative research? Why are our natures often so different, and why are they so frequently the same?

The background needed to begin to answer all these *whys* lies within the domain of human biological and cultural evolution, in the gradual alterations in genetic and cultural information possessed by humanity. It's easy to think that evolution is just a process that sometime in the distant past produced the physical characteristics of our species but is now pretty much a matter of purely academic, and local school board, interest. Yet evolution is a powerful, ongoing force that not only has shaped the attributes and behaviors shared by all human beings but also has given every single individual a different nature.

A study of evolution does much more than show how we are connected to our roots or explain why people rule Earth—it explains why it would be wise to limit our intake of beef Wellington, stop judging people by their skin color, concern ourselves about global warming, and reconsider giving our children antibiotics at the first sign of a sore throat. Evolution also provides a framework for answering some of the most interesting questions about ourselves and our behavior.

When someone mentions evolution and behavior in the same breath, most people think immediately of the power of genes, parts of spiral-shaped molecules of a chemical called DNA. Small wonder, considering the marvelous advances in molecular genetics in recent decades. New subdisciplines such as evolutionary medicine and evolutionary psychology have arisen as scientists have come to recognize the importance of evolution in explaining contemporary human beings, the network of life that supports us, and our possible fates. And the mass media have been loaded with stories about real or imagined links between every conceivable sort of behavior and our genes.

Biological evolution—evolution that causes changes in our genetic endowment—has unquestionably helped shape human natures, including human behaviors, in many ways. But numerous commentators expect our genetic endowment to accomplish feats of which it is incapable. People don't have enough genes to program all the behaviors some evolutionary psychologists, for example, believe that genes control. Human beings have something on the order of 100,000 genes, and human brains have more than one *trillion* nerve cells, with about 100–1,000 trillion connections (synapses) between them. That's at least one *billion* synapses per gene, even if each and every gene did nothing but control the production of synapses (and it doesn't). Given that ratio, it would be quite a trick for genes typically to control more than the most general aspects of human behavior. Statements such as "Understanding the genetic roots of personality will help you 'find yourself' and relate better to others" are, at today's level of knowledge, frankly nonsensical.

The notion that we are slaves to our genes is often combined with reliance on the idea that all problems can be solved by dissecting them into ever smaller components—the sort of reductionist approach that has been successful in much of science but is sometimes totally unscientific. It's like the idea that knowing the color of every microscopic dot that makes up a picture of your mother can explain why you love her. Scientific problems have to be approached at the appropriate level of organization if there is to be a hope of solving them.

There are important "coevolutionary" interactions between culture and genetics. For example, our farming practices change our physical environment in ways that alter the evolution of our blood cells.

That combination of assumptions—that genes are destiny at a micro level and that reductionism leads to full understanding—is now yielding distorted views of human behavior. People think that coded into our DNA are "instructions" that control the details of individual and group behavior: that genetics dominates, heredity makes us what we are, and what we are is changeable only over many generations as the genetic endowment of human populations evolves. Such assertions presume, as I've just suggested, that evolution has produced a level

of genetic control of human behavior that is against virtually all available evidence. For instance, ground squirrels have evolved a form of "altruistic" behavior—they often give an alarm call to warn a relative of approaching danger. Evidence does indicate that this behavior is rooted in their genes; indeed, it probably evolved because relatives have more identical genes than do unrelated individuals. But some would trace the "altruistic" behavior of a business executive sending a check to an agency helping famine victims in Africa, or of a devout German Lutheran aiding Jews during the Holocaust, to a genetic tendency as well. In this view, we act either to help relatives or in the expectation of reciprocity—in either case promoting the replication of "our" genes. But experimental evidence indicates that not all human altruistic behavior is self-seeking—that human beings, unlike squirrels, are not hereditarily programmed only to be selfish.

ANOTHER FALSE ASSUMPTION of hereditary programming lies behind the belief that evolution has resulted in human groups of different quality. Many people still claim (or secretly believe), for example, that blacks are less intelligent than whites and women less "logical" than men, even though those claims are groundless. Belief in genetic determinism has even led some observers to suggest a return to the bad old days of eugenics, of manipulating evolution to produce ostensibly more skilled people. Advocating programs for the biological "improvement of humanity"—which in the past has meant encouraging the breeding of supposedly naturally superior individuals—takes us back at least to the days of Plato, more than two millennia ago, and it involves a grasp of genetics little more sophisticated than his.

Uniquely in our species, changes in culture have been fully as important in producing our natures as have changes in the hereditary information passed on by our ancestors. Culture is the nongenetic information (socially transmitted behaviors, beliefs, institutions, arts, and so on) shared and exchanged among us. Indeed, our evolution since the invention of agriculture, about 10,000 years ago, has been overwhelmingly cultural because, as we shall see, cultural evolution can be much more rapid than genetic evolution. There is an unhappy predilection, especially in the United States, not only to overrate the effect of genetic evolution on our current behavior but also to underrate that of cultural evolution. The power of culture to shape human activities can be seen immediately in the diversity of languages around the world. Although, clearly, the ability to speak languages is a result of a great deal of genetic evolution, the specific languages we speak are just as clearly products of cultural evolution. Furthermore, genetic evolution and cultural evolution are not independent. There are important "coevolutionary" interactions between them. To take just one example, our farming practices (an aspect of our culture) change our physical environment in ways that alter the evolution of our blood cells.

Not only is the evolution of our collective nongenetic information critical to creating our natures, but also the rate of that evolution varies greatly among different aspects of human culture. That, in turn, has profound consequences for our behavior and our environments. A major contemporary human problem, for instance, is that the rate of cultural evolution in science and technology has been extraordinarily high in contrast with the snail's pace of change in the social attitudes and political institutions that might channel the uses of technology in more beneficial directions. No one knows exactly what sorts of societal effort might be required to substantially redress that imbalance in evolutionary rates, but it is clear to me that such an effort, if successful, could greatly brighten the human prospect.

Science has already given us pretty good clues about the reasons for the evolution of some aspects of our natures; many other aspects remain mysterious despite a small army of very bright people seeking reasons. Still others (such as why I ordered duck in the restaurant last night rather than lamb) may remain unanswerable—for human beings have a form of free will. But even to *think* reasonably about our natures and our prospects, some background in basic evolutionary theory is essential. If Grace is smarter than Pedro because of her genes, why did evolution provide her with "better" genes? If Pedro is actually smarter than Grace but has been incorrectly evaluated by an intelligence test designed for people of another culture, how did those cultural differences evolve? If I was able to choose the duck for dinner because I have free will, what exactly does that mean? How did I and other human beings evolve that capacity to make choices without being complete captives of our histories? Could I have exercised my free will to eat a cockroach curry had we been in a restaurant that served it (as some in Southeast Asia do)? Almost certainly not—the very idea nauseates me, probably because of an interaction between biological and cultural evolution.

Trying to separate nature and nurture is like trying to separate the contributions of length and width to the area of a rectangle, which at first seems easy. When you think about it, though, it proves impossible.

Every attribute of *every* organism is, of course, the product of an interaction between its genetic code and its environment. Yes, the number of heads an individual human being possesses is specified in the genes and is the same in a vast diversity of environments. And the language or languages a child speaks (but not her capacity to acquire language) is determined by her environment. But without the appropriate internal environment in the mother's body for fetal development, there would be no head (or infant) at all; and without genetically programmed physical structures in the larynx and in the developing brain, there would be no capacity to acquire and speak language. Beyond enabling us to make such statements in certain cases, however, the relative contributions of heredity and environment to various human attributes are difficult to specify. They clearly vary from attribute to attribute. So although it is informative to state that human nature is the product of genes interacting with environments (both internal and external), we usually can say little with precision about the processes that lead to interesting behaviors in adult human beings. We can't partition the responsibility for aggression, altruism, or charisma between DNA and upbringing. In many such cases, trying to separate the contributions of nature and nurture to an attribute is rather like trying to separate the contributions of length and width to the area of a rectangle, which at first glance also seems easy. When you think about it carefully, though, it proves impossible.

Diverse notions of inherited superiority or inferiority and of characteristic innate group behaviors have long pervaded human societies: beliefs about the divine right of kings; "natural" attributes that made some people good material for slaves or slave masters; innate superiority of light-skinned people over dark-skinned people; genetic tendencies of Jews to be moneylenders, of Christians to be sexually inhibited, and of Asians to be more hardworking than Hispanics; and so on. Consider the following quote from a recent book titled *Living With Our Genes*, which indicates the tone even among many scientists: "The emerging science of molecular biology has made startling discoveries that show beyond a doubt that genes are the single most important factor that distinguishes one person from another. We come in large part ready-made from the factory. We accept that we *look* like our parents and other blood relatives; we have a harder time with the idea we *act* like them."

In fact, the failure of many people to recognize the fundamental error in such statements (and those in other articles and books based on genetic determinism, such as Richard J. Herrnstein and Charles Murray's famous *The Bell Curve*) is itself an environmental phenomenon—a product of the cultural milieu in which many of us have grown up. Genes do not shout commands to us about our behavior. At the very most, they whisper suggestions, and the nature of those whispers is shaped by our internal environments (those within and between our cells) during early development and later, and usually also by the external environments in which we mature and find ourselves as adults.

How do scientists know that we are not simply genetically programmed automata? First, biological evolution has produced what is arguably the most astonishingly adaptable device that has ever existed—the human nervous system. It's a system that can use one organ, the brain, to plan a marriage or a murder, command muscles to control the flight of a thrown rock or a space shuttle, detect the difference between a 1945 Mouton and a 1961 Latour, learn Swahili or Spanish, and interpret a pattern of colored light on a flat television screen as a three-dimensional world containing real people. It tries to do whatever task the environment seems to demand, and it usually succeeds—and because many of those demands are novel, there is no way that the brain could be preprogrammed to deal with them, even if there were genes enough to do the programming. It would be incomprehensible for evolution to program such a system with a vast number of inherited rules that would reduce its flexibility, constraining it so that it could not deal with novel environments. It would seem equally inexplicable if evolution made some subgroups of humanity less able than others to react appropriately to changing circumstances. Men and people with white skin have just as much need of being smart and flexible as do women and people with brown skin, and there is every reason to believe that evolution has made white-skinned males fully as capable as brown-skinned women.

A SECOND TYPE OF EVIDENCE that we're not controlled by innate programs is that normal infants taken from one society and reared in another inevitably acquire the behaviors (including language) and competences of the society in which they are reared. If different behaviors in different societies were largely genetically programmed, that could not happen. That culture dominates in creating intergroup differences is also indicated by the distribution of genetic differences among human beings. The vast majority (an estimated 85 percent) is not between "races" or ethnic groups but *between individuals within groups*. Human natures, again, are products of similar (but not identical) inherited endowments interacting with different physical and cultural environments.

Thus, the genetic "make-brain" program that interacts with the internal and external environments of a developing person doesn't produce a brain that can call forth only one type of, say, mating behavior—it produces a brain that can engage in any of a bewildering variety of behaviors, depending on circumstances. We see the same principle elsewhere in our development; for instance, human legs are not genetically programmed to move only at a certain speed. The inherited "make-legs" program normally produces legs that, fortunately, can operate at a wide range of speeds, depending on circumstances. Variation among individuals in the genes they received from their parents produces some differences in that range (in any normal terrestrial environment, I never could have been a four-minute miler—on the moon, maybe). Environmental variation produces some differences, too (walking a lot every day and years of acclimatization enable me to climb relatively high mountains that are beyond the range of some younger people who are less acclimatized). But no amount of training will permit any human being to leap tall buildings in a single bound, or even in two.

Similarly, inherited differences among individuals can influence the range of mental abilities we possess. Struggle as I might, my math skills will never approach those of many professional mathematicians, and I suspect that part of my incapacity can be traced to my genes. But environmental variation can shape those abilities as well. I'm also lousy at learning languages (that may be related to my math incompetence). Yet when I found myself in a professional environment in which it would have been helpful to converse in Spanish, persistent study allowed me to speak and comprehend a fair amount of the language. But there are no genetic instructions or environmental circumstances that will allow the development of a human brain that can do a million mathematical calculations in a second. That is a talent reserved for computers, which were, of course, designed by human minds.

Are there any behavioral instructions we can be sure are engraved in human DNA? If there are, at least one should be the urge to have as many children as possible. We should have a powerful hereditary tendency to maximize our genetic contributions to future generations, for that's the tendency that makes evolution work. Yet almost no human beings strictly obey this genetic "imperative"; environmental factors, especially cultural factors, have largely overridden it. Most people choose to make smaller genetic contributions to the future—that is, have fewer children—than they could, thus figuratively thwarting the supposed maximum reproduction "ambitions" of their genes.

If genes run us as machines for reproducing themselves, how come they let us practice contraception? We are the only animals that deliberately and with planning enjoy sex while avoiding reproduction. We can and do "outwit" our genes—which are, of course, witless. In this respect, our hereditary endowment made a big mistake by "choosing" to encourage human reproduction not through a desire for lots of children but through a desire for lots of sexual pleasure.

There are environments (sociocultural environments in this case) in which near-maximal human reproduction has apparently occurred. For example, the Hutterites, members of a Mennonite sect living on the plains of western North America, are famous for their high rate of population growth. Around 1950, Hutterite women over the age of 45 had borne an average of 10 children, and Hutterite population growth rates exceeded 4 percent per year. Interestingly, however, when social conditions changed, the growth rate dropped from an estimated 4.12 percent per year to 2.91 percent. Cultural evolution won out against those selfish little genes.

Against this background of how human beings can overwhelm genetic evolution with cultural evolution, it becomes evident that great care must be taken in extrapolating the behavior of other animals to that of human beings. One cannot assume, for example, that because marauding chimpanzees of one group sometimes kill members of another group, selection has programmed warfare into the genes of human beings (or, for that matter, of chimps). And although both chimp and human genetic endowments clearly can interact with certain environments to produce individuals capable of mayhem, they just as clearly can interact with other environments to produce individuals who are not aggressive. Observing the behavior of nonhuman mammals—their mating habits, modes of communication, intergroup conflicts, and so on—can reveal patterns we display in common with them, but those patterns certainly will not tell us which complex behaviors are "programmed" inalterably into our genes. Genetic instructions are of great importance to our natures, but they are not destiny.

THERE are obviously limits to how much the environment ordinarily can affect individual characteristics. No known environment, for example, could have allowed me to mature with normal color vision: like about 8 percent of males, I'm color-blind—the result of a gene inherited from my mother. But the influence on many human attributes of even small environmental differences should not be underestimated. Consider the classic story of the "Siamese twins" Chang and Eng. Born in Siam (now Thailand) on May 11, 1811, these identical twins were joined at the base of their chests by an arm-like tube that in adulthood was five or six inches long and about eight inches in circumference. They eventually ended up in the United States, became prosperous as sideshow attractions, and married sisters. Chang and Eng farmed for a time, owned slaves before the Civil War, and produced both many children and vast speculation about the circumstances of their copulations. They were examined many times by surgeons who, working before the age of X-rays, concluded that it would be dangerous to try to separate them.

From our perspective, the most interesting thing about the twins is their different natures. Chang was slightly shorter than Eng, but he dominated his brother and was quick-tempered. Eng, in contrast, was agreeable and usually submissive. Although the two were very similar in many respects, in childhood their differences once flared into a fistfight, and as adults on one occasion they disagreed enough politically to vote for opposing candidates. More seriously, Chang drank to excess and Eng did not. Partly as a result of Chang's drinking, they developed considerable ill will that made it difficult for them to live together—they were constantly quarreling. In old age, Chang became hard of hearing in both ears, but Eng became deaf only in the ear closer to Chang. In the summer of 1870, Chang suffered a stroke, which left Eng unaffected directly but bound him physically to an invalid. On January 17, 1874, Chang died in the night. When Eng discovered his twin's death, he (although perfectly healthy) became terrified, lapsed into a stupor, and died two hours later, before a scheduled surgical attempt was to have been made to separate the two. An autopsy showed that the surgeons had been correct—the twins probably would not have survived an attempt to separate them.

Chang and Eng demonstrated conclusively that genetic identity does not necessarily produce identical natures, even when combined with substantially identical environments—in this case only inches apart, with no sign that their mother or others treated them differently as they grew up. Quite subtle environmental differences, perhaps initiated by different positions in the womb, can sometimes produce substantially different behavioral outcomes in twins. In this case, in which the dominant feature of each twin's environment clearly was the other twin, the slightest original difference could have led to an escalating reinforcement of differences.

The nature-nurture dichotomy, which has dominated discussions of behavior for decades, is largely a false one—all characteristics of all organisms are truly a result of the simultaneous influences of both. Genes do not dictate destiny in most cases (exceptions include those serious genetic defects that at present cannot be remedied), but they often define a range of possibilities in a given environment. The genetic endowment of a chimpanzee, even if raised as the child of a Harvard professor, would prevent it from learning to discuss philosophy or solve differential equations. Similarly, environments define a range of developmental possibilities for a given set of genes. There is no genetic endowment that a child could get from Mom and Pop that would permit the youngster to grow into an Einstein (or a Mozart or a García Marquez—or even a Hitler) as a member of an isolated rain-forest tribe without a written language.

Attempts to dichotomize nature and nurture almost always end in failure. Although I've written about how the expression of genes depends on the environment in which the genes are expressed, another way of looking at the development of a person's nature would have been to examine the contributions of three factors: genes, environment, *and* gene-environment interactions. It is very difficult to tease out these contributions, however. Even under experimental conditions, where it is possible to say something mathematically about the comparative contributions of heredity and environment, it can't be done completely because there is an "interaction term." That term cannot be decomposed into nature or nurture because the effect of each depends on the contribution of the other.

To construct an artificial example, suppose there were a gene combination that controlled the level of a hormone that tended to make boys aggressive. Further, suppose that watching television also tended to make boys aggressive. Changing an individual's complement of genes so that the hormone level was doubled and also doubling the television-watching time might, then, quadruple some measure of aggressiveness. Or, instead, the two factors might interact synergistically and cause the aggression level to increase fivefold (perhaps television is an especially potent factor when the viewer has a high hormone level). Or the interaction might go the other way—television time might increase aggression only in those with a relatively low hormone level, and doubling both the hormone level and the television time might result in only a doubling of aggression. Or perhaps changing the average *content* of television programming might actually reduce the level of aggressiveness so that even with hormone level and television time doubled, aggressiveness would decline. Finally, suppose that, in addition, these relationships depended in part on whether or not a boy had attentive and loving parents who provided alternative interpretations of what was seen on television. In such situations, there is no way to make a precise statement about the contributions of "the environment" (television, in this case) to aggressiveness. This example reflects the complexity of relationships that has been demonstrated in detailed studies of the ways in which hormones such as testosterone interact with environmental factors to produce aggressive behavior.

The best one can ordinarily do in measuring what genes contribute to attributes (such as aggressiveness, height, or I.Q. test score) is calculate a statistical measure known as heritability. That statistic tells how much, on average, offspring resemble their parents in a particular attribute *in a particular set of environments*. Heritability, however, is a measure that is difficult to make and difficult to interpret. That is especially true in determining heritability of human traits, where it would be unethical or impossible to create the conditions required to estimate it, such as random mating within a population.

Despite these difficulties, geneticists are gradually sorting out some of the ways genes and environments can interact in experimental environments and how different parts of the hereditary endowment interact in making their contribution to the development of the individual. One of the key things they are learning is that it is often very difficult for genetic evolution to change just one characteristic. That's worth thinking about the next time someone tells you that human beings have been programmed by natural selection to be violent, greedy, altruistic, or promiscuous, to prefer certain facial features, or to show male (or white) dominance. At best, such programming is difficult; often it is impossible.

TODAY'S DEBATES about human nature—about such things as the origins of ethics; the meanings of consciousness, self, and reality; whether we're driven by emotion or reason; the relationship between thought and language; whether men are naturally aggressive and women peaceful; and the role of sex in society—trace far back in Western thought. They have engaged thinkers from the pre-Socratic philosophers, Plato, and Aristotle to René Descartes, John Locke, Georg Wilhelm Friedrich Hegel, Charles Sanders Peirce, and Ludwig Wittgenstein, just to mention a tiny handful of those in the Western tradition alone.

What exactly *is* this human nature we hear so much about? The prevailing notion is that it is a single, fixed, inherited attribute—a common property of all members of our species. That notion is implicit in the universal use of the term in singular form. And I think that singular usage leads us astray. To give a rough analogy, *human nature* is to *human natures* as *canyon* is to *canyons*. We would never discuss the "characteristics of canyon." Although all canyons share certain attributes, we always use the plural form of the word when talking about them in general. That's because even though all canyons have more characteristics in common with one another than any canyon has with a painting or a snowflake, we automatically recognize the vast diversity subsumed within the category *canyons*. As with *canyon*, at times there is reason to speak of human nature in the singular, as I sometimes do when referring to what we all share—for example, the ability to communicate in language, the possession of a rich culture, and the capacity to develop complex ethical systems. After all, there are at least *near*-universal aspects of our natures and our genomes (genetic endowments), and the variation within them is small in relation to the differences between, say, human and chimpanzee natures or human and chimpanzee genomes.

I argue, contrary to the prevailing notion, that human nature is not the same from society to society or from individual to individual, nor is it a permanent attribute of *Homo sapiens*. Human natures are the behaviors, beliefs, and attitudes of *Homo sapiens* and the changing physical structures that govern, support, and participate in our unique mental functioning. There are many such natures, a diversity generated especially by the overwhelming power of cultural evolution—the super-rapid kind of evolution in which our species excels. The human nature of a Chinese man living in Beijing is somewhat different from the human nature of a Parisian woman; the nature of a great musician is not identical with that of a fine soccer player; the nature of an inner-city gang member is different from the nature of a child being raised in an affluent suburb; the nature of someone who habitually votes Republican is different from that of her identical twin who is a Democrat; and my human nature, despite many shared features, is different from yours.

The differences among individuals and groups of human beings are, as already noted, of a magnitude that dwarf the differences within any other nondomesticated animal species. Using the plural, *human natures*, puts a needed emphasis on that critical diversity, which, after all, is very often what we want to understand. We want to know why two genetically identical individuals would have different political views; why Jeff is so loud and Barbara is so quiet; why people in the same society have different sexual habits and different ethical standards; why some past civilizations flourished for many centuries and others perished; why Germany was a combatant in two horrendous 20th-century wars and Switzerland was not; why Julia is concerned about global warming and Juliette doesn't know what it is. There is no single human nature, any more than there is a single human genome, although there are features common to all human natures and all human genomes.

But if we are trying to understand anything about human society, past or present, or about individual actions, we must go to a finer level of analysis and consider human nature*s* as actually formed in the world. It is intellectually lazy and incorrect to "explain" the relatively poor school performance of blacks in the United States, or the persistence of warfare, or marital discord, by claiming that nonwhites are "naturally" inferior, that all people are "naturally" aggressive, or that men are "naturally" promiscuous. Intellectual performance, aggression, and promiscuity, aside from being difficult to define and measure, all vary from individual to individual and often from culture to culture. Ignoring that variance simply hides the causative factors—cultural, genetic, or both—that we would like to understand.

Permanence is often viewed as human nature's key feature; after all, remember, "you can't change human nature." But, of course, we *can*—and we do, all the time. The natures of Americans today are very different from their natures in 1940. Indeed, today's human natures everywhere are diverse products of change, of long genetic and, especially, cultural evolutionary processes. A million years ago, as paleoanthropologists, archaeologists, and other scientists have shown, human nature was a radically different, and presumably much more uniform, attribute. People then had less nimble brains, they didn't have a language with fully developed syntax, they had not developed formal strata in societies, and they hadn't yet learned to attach worked stones to wooden shafts to make hammers and arrows.

Human natures a million years in the future will also be unimaginably different from human natures today. The processes that changed those early people into modern human beings will continue as long as there are people. Indeed, with the rate of cultural evolution showing seemingly continuous acceleration, it would be amazing if the broadly shared aspects of human natures were not quite different even a million *hours* (about a hundred years) in the future. For example, think of how Internet commerce has changed in the past million or so minutes (roughly two years).

As evolving mental-physical packages, human natures have brought not only planetary dominance to our species but also great triumphs in areas such as art, music, literature, philosophy, science, and technology. Unhappily, though, those same packages—human behavioral patterns and their physical foundations—are also the source of our most serious current problems. War, genocide, commerce in drugs, racial and religious prejudice, extreme economic inequality, and destruction of society's life-support systems are all products of today's human natures, too. As Pogo so accurately said, "We have met the enemy, and they is us." But nowhere is it written that those problems have to be products of tomorrow's human natures. It is theoretically possible to make peace with ourselves and with our environment, overcome racial and religious prejudice, reduce large-scale cruelty, and increase economic equality. What's needed is a widespread understanding of the evolutionary processes that have produced our natures, open discourse on what is desirable about them, and conscious collective efforts to steer the cultural evolution of the more troublesome features of our natures in ways almost everyone would find desirable. A utopian notion? Maybe. But considering progress that already has been made in areas such as democratic governance and individual freedom, race relations, religious tolerance, women's and gay rights, and avoidance of global conflict, it's worth a try.

Paul R. Ehrlich is a professor of population studies and of biological sciences at Stanford University. This essay is adapted from his Human Natures: Genes, Cultures, and the Human Prospect, *published by Island Press in August 2000.*

DECODING THE
HUMAN BODY

The secrets of life: It is the most expensive, most ambitious biology mission ever. The Human Genome Project, at $250 million and counting, is biology's moon shot. In the eyes of boosters, it promises to provide no less than the operating instructions for a human body, and will revolutionize the detection, prevention and treatment of conditions from cancer to depression to old age itself. In the eyes of critics, it threatens to undermine privacy and bring on 'genetic discrimination' in insurance and employment. Near the finish line, one effect is indisputable: the genome has reignited the biotech industry. Explaining the genome—and what it means for you.

BY SHARON BEGLEY

EVERY FRIDAY morning at 11, the directors of the five labs leading the race to decipher the human genome confer by phone to assess their progress. In mid-March, it was clear they were closing in on the next big milestone: reading the 2 billionth chemical "letter" in human DNA. But since some of those letters were redundant, a count of 2 billion would not really tell how close they were to the finish line of 3.2 billion.

Greg Schuler, a molecular biologist turned computer jock at the National Institutes of Health, had just spent the weekend, sitting on the sofa with his laptop in front of his fireplace at home, writing a 674-line program to reanalyze the overlaps. When he sicced it on the redundant sequences, the answer popped out: the Human Genome Project had *already* passed the 2 billion mark, on March 9. It had taken four years to determine the first billion letters in the human genome, but only four months for what Schuler calls "that next odometer moment." The actual chemical letter was—drumroll, please—T.

All right, so it didn't really matter which of the four letters making up DNA claimed position number 2,000,000,000 in the largest, most expensive, most ambitious biology project ever undertaken. But after 13 years and $250 million, through the work of some 1,100 biologists, computer scientists and technicians at 16 (mostly university) labs in 6 countries, the announcement meant that the Human Genome Project was two thirds of the way toward its goal of determining the exact chemical sequence that constitutes the DNA in every cell of every human body. With competitors in the private sector goading them on, scientists in the public

project have tripled their pace, sequencing 12,000 letters every minute of every day, 24/7. By last weekend the project, financed by the U.S. government and Britain's Wellcome Trust, had sequenced 2,104,257,000 chemical letters. At this rate, it will complete its "working draft"— 90 percent of the genome, with an accuracy of 99.9 percent—in June. And Science will know the blueprint of human life, the code of codes, the holy grail, the source code of *Homo sapiens*. It will know, Harvard University biologist Walter Gilbert says, "what it is to be human."

That knowledge promises to revolutionize medicine and vault the biotech industry into the Wall Street stratosphere. But just as no one foresaw eBay or Amazon when Apple unveiled the first home computer in 1977, so there is no crystal ball clear enough to reveal how knowing

The Public Genome Team Races...

Going public: Collins has led the publicly financed genome project since 1993. This year he rebuffed an offer from the biotech firm Celera to join forces and thus speed up the work: he feared Celera would keep the results private, available only to those who pay, for too long. So the public project goes it alone, posting its discoveries every 24 hours (except weekends) at www.ncbi.nlm.nih.gov/genome/seq.

...The Upstart Master Of the Gene-iverse

To the swift: Venter's teams have sequenced the genomes of more organisms than anyone else. His policy of keeping data secret for six months ($5 million buys companies instant access for five years) riles some academics. But Venter's speed means that everyone gets data months sooner.

What We Know So Far

Fly boys: It took 195 scientists to decode *Drosophila's* genome. Why bother? Of 289 human-disease genes, 177 have analogs in the fly, including 68% of cancer genes.

Almost human? Half of the known human-disease genes have analogs in the genes of the worm C. elegans, raising hopes for the discovery of treatments

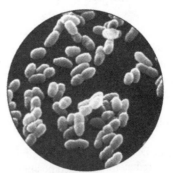

Tiny trailblazer: Haemophilus influenzae, a bacterium, was the first organism whose genome was fully sequenced

the entire human genome will change the way we live and even the way we think about who we are. It is a pretty good bet, though, that doctors will drip droplets of our genes onto a biochip to figure out if we have the kind of prostate cancer that will kill or not, or to figure out if ours is the kind of leukemia that responds to this drug rather than that one. They will analyze our children's genes to rank their chances of succumbing to heart disease or Alzheimer's. Scientists will learn which genes turn on when a wound heals, when a baby's fingers grow, when a scalp becomes bald or a brow wrinkled, when a song is learned or a memory formed, when hormones surge or stress overwhelms us— and they will learn how to manipulate those genes. Babies will be designed before conception. Employers will take your genetic profile before they offer you a job or withdraw an offer if they don't like the cut of your DNA. The human genome sequence "will be the foundation of biology for decades, centuries or millennia to come," says John Sulston, director of the Sanger Centre, the genome lab near Cambridge, England, where a spiral staircase in the lobby twists upward like the double helix itself.

And all of it will emerge from something like this: ATGCCGCGGCTC-CTCC... on and on, for about 3.2 billion

The Human Parts List

Scientists have identified more than 8,000 human genes, including those linked to breast and colon cancers and Alzheimer's disease. Figuring out how the genes work promises to lead to preventions and treatments. Some of the genes identified:

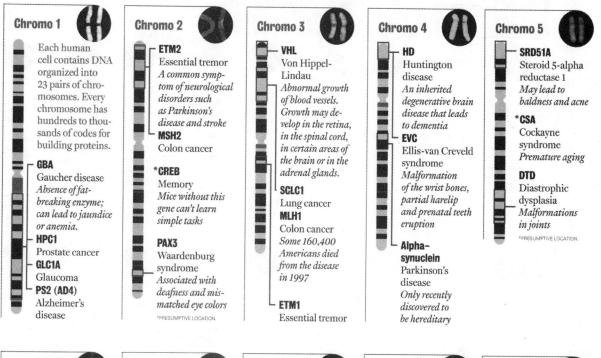

Chromo 1

Each human cell contains DNA organized into 23 pairs of chromosomes. Every chromosome has hundreds to thousands of codes for building proteins.

GBA
Gaucher disease
Absence of fat-breaking enzyme; can lead to jaundice or anemia.

HPC1
Prostate cancer

GLC1A
Glaucoma

PS2 (AD4)
Alzheimer's disease

Chromo 2

ETM2
Essential tremor
A common symptom of neurological disorders such as Parkinson's disease and stroke

MSH2
Colon cancer

*CREB
Memory
Mice without this gene can't learn simple tasks

PAX3
Waardenburg syndrome
Associated with deafness and mismatched eye colors

*PRESUMPTIVE LOCATION.

Chromo 3

VHL
Von Hippel-Lindau
Abnormal growth of blood vessels. Growth may develop in the retina, in the spinal cord, in certain areas of the brain or in the adrenal glands.

SCLC1
Lung cancer

MLH1
Colon cancer
Some 160,400 Americans died from the disease in 1997

ETM1
Essential tremor

Chromo 4

HD
Huntington disease
An inherited degenerative brain disease that leads to dementia

EVC
Ellis-van Creveld syndrome
Malformation of the wrist bones, partial harelip and prenatal teeth eruption

Alpha-synuclein
Parkinson's disease
Only recently discovered to be hereditary

Chromo 5

SRD51A
Steroid 5-alpha reductase 1
May lead to baldness and acne

*CSA
Cockayne syndrome
Premature aging

DTD
Diastrophic dysplasia
Malformations in joints

*PRESUMPTIVE LOCATION.

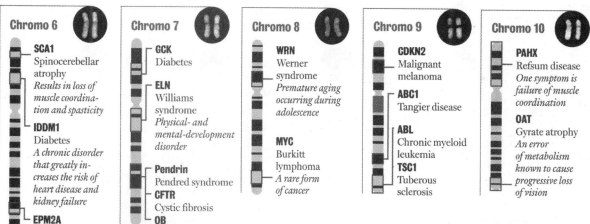

Chromo 6

SCA1
Spinocerebellar atrophy
Results in loss of muscle coordination and spasticity

IDDM1
Diabetes
A chronic disorder that greatly increases the risk of heart disease and kidney failure

EPM2A
Epilepsy

Chromo 7

GCK
Diabetes

ELN
Williams syndrome
Physical- and mental-development disorder

Pendrin
Pendred syndrome

CFTR
Cystic fibrosis

OB
Obesity

Chromo 8

WRN
Werner syndrome
Premature aging occurring during adolescence

MYC
Burkitt lymphoma
A rare form of cancer

Chromo 9

CDKN2
Malignant melanoma

ABC1
Tangier disease

ABL
Chronic myeloid leukemia

TSC1
Tuberous sclerosis

Chromo 10

PAHX
Refsum disease
One symptom is failure of muscle coordination

OAT
Gyrate atrophy
An error of metabolism known to cause progressive loss of vision

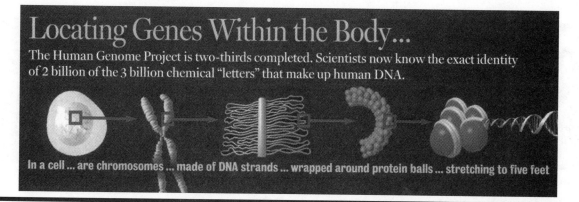

Locating Genes Within the Body...

The Human Genome Project is two-thirds completed. Scientists now know the exact identity of 2 billion of the 3 billion chemical "letters" that make up human DNA.

In a cell ... are chromosomes ... made of DNA strands ... wrapped around protein balls ... stretching to five feet

Photos by T. Ried–NHGRI–NIH

...Preparing for Study...

Shredding The DNA strand is cut into sections of 5,000 to 10,000 nucleotides

Freezing The DNA snippets are placed in vials and frozen for later analysis

Splicing The snippets are spliced into circular bacterial chromosomes

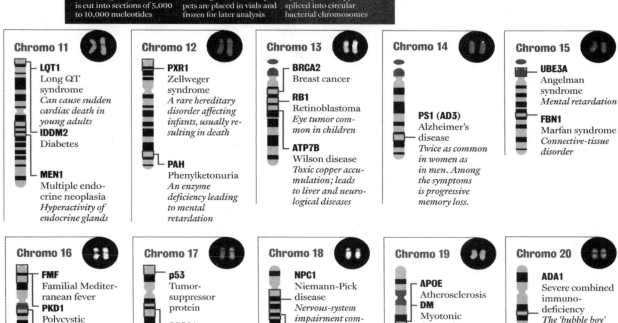

Chromo 11
LQT1 Long QT syndrome *Can cause sudden cardiac death in young adults*
IDDM2 Diabetes
MEN1 Multiple endocrine neoplasia *Hyperactivity of endocrine glands*

Chromo 12
PXR1 Zellweger syndrome *A rare hereditary disorder affecting infants, usually resulting in death*
PAH Phenylketonuria *An enzyme deficiency leading to mental retardation*

Chromo 13
BRCA2 Breast cancer
RB1 Retinoblastoma *Eye tumor common in children*
ATP7B Wilson disease *Toxic copper accumulation; leads to liver and neurological diseases*

Chromo 14
PS1 (AD3) Alzheimer's disease *Twice as common in women as in men. Among the symptoms is progressive memory loss.*

Chromo 15
UBE3A Angelman syndrome *Mental retardation*
FBN1 Marfan syndrome *Connective-tissue disorder*

Chromo 16
FMF Familial Mediterranean fever
PKD1 Polycystic kidney disease
Crohn's disease *Bowel disorder*

Chromo 17
p53 Tumor-suppressor protein
BRCA1 Breast cancer

Chromo 18
NPC1 Niemann-Pick disease *Nervous-system impairment common in children*
DPC4 (Smad4) Pancreatic cancer

Chromo 19
APOE Atherosclerosis
DM Myotonic dystrophy *Can cause mental deficiency, hair loss and cataracts*

Chromo 20
ADA1 Severe combined immuno-deficiency *The 'bubble boy' disease; leaves little or no immunity to viruses*

Chromo 21
SOD1 Amyotrophic lateral sclerosis
APS1 Autoimmune polyglandular syndrome

Chromo 22
BCR Chronic myeloid leukemia *Results when bone marrow is replaced by malignant leukemic cells*

Chromo Y
SRY (TDF) Testis-determining factor *One of the molecules that interacts with other genes in male sex determination*

Chromo X
DMD Duchenne muscular dystrophy
ATP7A Menkes syndrome *Severe cerebral degeneration*
FMR1 Fragile X syndrome *Mental retardation common in men*

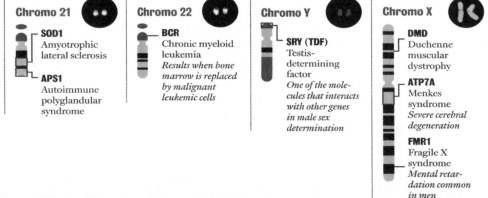

...And Sequencing the Strands for Analysis

Amplifying As the bacteria reproduce, they act like copy machines, multiplying DNA by the billions

Tagging The DNA strands are extracted and treated with special dyes visible under laser light

Sequencing The DNA fragments are then fed into 96 tubes inside a sequencing machine

Assembling Computers identify overlapping segments to re-create the original nucleotide order

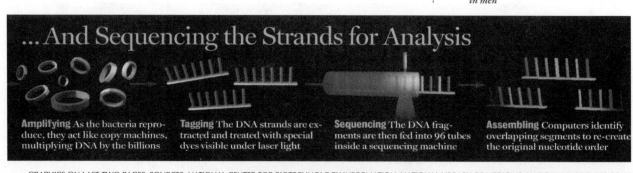

GRAPHICS ON LAST TWO PAGES: SOURCES: NATIONAL CENTER FOR BIOTECHNOLOGY INFORMATION, NATIONAL LIBRARY OF MEDICINE, NATIONAL INSTITUTES OF HEALTH

RESEARCH BY FE CONWAY AND STEPHEN TOTILO, DESIGN BY BONNIE SCRANTON, GENE-SEQUENCING ILLUSTRATIONS BY CHRISTOPH BLUMRICH--NEWSWEEK.

such letters. Each letter represents a molecule—adenine, cytosine, guanine, thymine. Every cell of every human body, from skin to muscle to liver and everything in between (except red blood cells), contains a copy of the same DNA. The totality of DNA present in the cells of a species is its genome. Although the genetic age has brought incessant reports about genes "for" homosexuality, risk-taking, shyness, anxiety, cancer, Alzheimer's and more, the only thing a gene is actually "for" is a protein. The A's, T's, C's and G's constitute a code. Each triplet of letters instructs special machinery inside a cell to grab onto a particular amino acid. TGG, for instance, snatches the amino acid tryptophan. If you string together enough amino acids, you have a protein—a stomach enzyme that digests food, insulin that metabolizes carbohydrates, a brain chemical that causes depression, a sex hormone that triggers puberty. A gene, then, is an instruction, like the directions in a bead-making kit but written in molecule-ese. Humans have perhaps 80,000 genes, and we are 99.9 percent identical. That is, at only one in 1,000 chemical letters does the genome of, say, Woody Allen differ from that of Stone Cold Steve Austin.

Even at its inception, the creators of the Human Genome Project suspected that it would transform biology, vaulting it past physics as the hot science. But at the moment of its creation, the project was an unwanted child. Charles DeLisi, newly arrived at the Department of Energy, was in charge of research into the biological effects of radiation. In October 1985, he was reading a government report on technologies for detecting heritable mutations, such as those in the survivors of Hiroshima. It hit him: given the slow pace at which biologists were deciphering genes, which you need to do in order to assess mutations, they would finish… oh, about when humans had evolved into a new species. "We just weren't going to get there," says DeLisi. So he dashed off memos, ordered up reports, begged scientists to serve on planning committees—and got responses like "I don't want to spin my wheels" on a project that had little chance of happening.

For biologists and the genome, it was far from love at first sight. Critics pointed out that some 97 percent of the human genome—3.1 billion of the 3.2 billion A's, T's, C's and G's—does not spell out a gene. Why bother sequencing this "junk" DNA, whose presence no one can explain, especially when there was no known way to tell what was junk and what was a gene?

But when a panel of leading scientists, including skeptics, unanimously endorsed the project in 1988, and it wrested funding from Congress, the Human Genome Project was out of the gate, headed toward a completion date of 2005 at a nice, sedate pace. It didn't last. In May 1998, gene-hunter extraordinaire J. Craig Venter and his newly formed Celera Genomics vowed to trounce the public project by finishing the human genome sequence in just three years. That made Francis Collins, director of the National Human Genome Research Institute, scramble. His labs had sequenced less than 3 percent of the genome at the original halfway point, so he ordered everyone to forget about the double-checking and the exploring of cool scientific puzzles and just churn out the *#@*ing A's, T's, C's and G's. It worked. In October 1998 Collins announced that his team would have a rough draft in 2001; in March 1999 he pushed it to this spring.

What will it mean to know the complete human genome? Eric Lander of MIT's Whitehead Institute compares it to the discovery of the periodic table of the elements in the late 1800s. "Genomics is now providing biology's periodic table," says Lander. "Scientists will know that every phenomenon must be explainable in terms of this measly list"—which will fit on a single CD-ROM. Already researchers are extracting DNA from patients, attaching fluorescent molecules and sprinkling the sample on a glass chip whose surface is speckled with 10,000 known genes. A laser reads the fluorescence, which indicates which of the known genes on the chip are in the mystery sample from the patient. In only the last few months such "gene-expression monitoring" has diagnosed a muscle tumor in a boy thought to have leukemia, and distinguished between two kinds of cancer that require very different chemotherapy. Soon, predicts Patrick Brown of Stanford University, expression analysis will distinguish prostate cancers that kill from prostate cancers that don't, neurons in a depressed brain from neurons in a normal brain—all on the basis of which genes are active.

Humankind's history is also written in its DNA. "Rare spelling differences in DNA can be used to trace human migrations," says Lander. "Scientists can recognize the descendants of chromosomes that ancient Phoenician traders left behind when they visited Italian seaports." Genetic data support the oral tradition that the Bantu-speaking Lemba of southern Africa are descendants of Jews who migrated from the Middle East 2,700 years ago. And they suggest that 98 percent of the Irish men of Connaught are descended from a single band of hunter-gatherers who reached the Emerald Isle more than 4,000 years ago.

But decoding the book of life poses daunting moral dilemmas. With knowledge of our genetic code will come the power to re-engineer the human species. Biologists will be able to use the genome as a parts list—much as customers scour a list of china to replace broken plates—and may well let prospective parents choose their unborn child's traits. Scientists have solid leads on genes for different temperaments, body builds, statures and cognitive abilities. And if anyone still believes that parents will recoil at playing God, and leave their baby's fate in the hands of nature, recall that couples have already created a frenzied market in eggs from Ivy League women.

Beyond the profound ethical issues are practical concerns. The easier it is to change ourselves and our children, the less society may tolerate those who do not, warns Lori Andrews of Kent College of Law. If genetic tests in utero predict mental dullness, obesity, short stature—or other undesirable traits of the moment—will society disparage children whose parents let them be born with those traits? Already, Andrew finds, some nurses and doctors blame parents for bringing into the world a child whose birth defect was diagnosable before delivery; how long will it be before the same condemnation applies to cosmetic imperfections? An even greater concern is that well-intentioned choices by millions of individual parents-to-be could add up to unforeseen consequences for all of humankind. It just so happens that some disease genes also confer resistance to disease: carrying a gene for sickle cell anemia, for instance, brings resistance to malaria. Are we smart enough, and wise enough, to know how knocking out "bad" genes will affect our evolution as a species?

From the inception of the genome project, ethicists warned that genetic knowledge would be used against people in insurance and employment. Sorting out whether this is happening is like judging whether HMOs provide quality care. Systematic surveys turn up few problems, but horror stories abound. One man underwent a genetic test and learned that he carried a marker for the blood disorder hemochromatosis. Although he was being successfully treated, his insurer dropped him on the ground that he might stop treatment and develop the disease. Another had a job offer withdrawn for "lying" during a pre-employment physical. He was healthy, but carried a gene for kidney disease. And last December Terri Seargent, 43, was fired from her job as an office manager after she tested positive for the genetic disease that killed her brother. She began receiving preventive treatments. When her self-insured employer got the first bill, she was fired.

So far 39 states prohibit, at least in part, discrimination in health insurance based on genetic tests; 15 have some ban on discrimination in employment. But many of the laws have loopholes. (One of the 15 is North Carolina, where Seargent lives.) Employers still, apparently, want genetic information about their workers. A 1999 survey by the American Management Association found that 30 percent of large and midsize firms obtain such information on employees. Seven percent use it in hiring and promotions. "It is still possible to have information about the genome used to take away your health insurance or your job," says Collins. "As yet, we have not seen effective federal legislation [to prevent this]. With genes getting discovered right and left, the opportunities for mischief are on an exponential curve."

Perhaps the greatest unknown is how the completion of the Human Genome Project—not just getting C's, G's, T's and A's, but learning the function of every gene—will shape our views of what we are. There is a great risk of succumbing to a naive biological determinism, ascribing to our genes such qualities as personality, intelligence, even faith. Studies of twins have already claimed (to great criticism, but claimed nonetheless) that genes even shape whether an individual will favor or oppose capital punishment. "We do ascribe some sort of quasi-religious significance to our DNA," says Collins. "We have a tendency to be more deterministic than we should." For now, the power, and the limits, of the genome can only be guessed at. The stage is set. The players are ready. After millions of dollars and millions of hours, the curtain is rising on what our children will surely, looking back in awe, see as the dawn of the century of the genome.

With THOMAS HAYDEN, WILLIAM UNDERHILL *in London and* GREGORY BEALS

The Future of the Brain

The pairing of innovative technologies with scientific discoveries about the brain opens new ways of handling information, treating diseases, and possibly creating robots with human characteristics.

Norbert R. Myslinski

For I dipp'd into the future,
far as human eye could see,
Saw the Vision of the world,
and all the wonder that would be.

—Alfred, Lord Tennyson

An understanding of the brain helps us understand our nature. Over the course of evolution, the brain has acquired greater functions and higher consciousness. The reptilian brain, for instance, exerts control over vegetative functions, such as eating, sleeping, and reproduction. Development of the mammalian brain added the ability to express emotions. The human brain has the additional powers of cognition—such as reasoning, judgment, problem solving, and creativity. The latter functions, which are controlled by an area of the brain called the prefrontal cortex (located behind the forehead), distinguish us from other forms of life and represent the flower of our humanity. They have allowed us to re-create ourselves and decide our destiny.

Besides these long-term changes, our brains undergo short-term modifications during our lifetime. Not only does the brain control behavior, but one's behavior leads to changes in the brain, in terms of both structure and function. Subjective experiences play a major role in brain functions and the manifestation of one's mind, consciousness, and personal values. Thus the brain adapts to each individual's changing world.

Modern society and technology have given us the time, protection, and freedom to focus on the higher powers of the brain. As individual freedoms and the free enterprise system are extended around the world, we will see a continuing rise of innovative ventures and scientific exploration. In addition, our success at eliminating brain diseases and expanding brain functions will depend on the uniquely human characteristics of the brain. Given the finances and technology, we will need vision and creativity.

But modern technology also raises a number of questions about our future. For instance, how will the continuing information explosion challenge the powers of our brains? What does the next century have in store for us regarding memory drugs, brain surgery, brain regeneration, and other treatments for brain disorders? How will the relationships between mind and body or brain and machine evolve? More important, are we prepared to handle such challenges, socially, psychologically, and ethically?

The Information Explosion

Information technologies have been increasingly successful in helping us acquire and communicate large new areas of knowledge. But the same success challenges the brain's capacity. How will the brain continue to cope with this information explosion? It will probably employ the same techniques it always has: filtering, organizing, and selective forgetting [see "Sherlock Holmes' Lesson," THE WORLD & I, June 2000, p. 316].

Our brains allow us to exert such uniquely human powers as reasoning, judgment, problem solving, and creativity—thereby guiding our own development and destiny.

Already, the brain filters out more than 99 percent of all sensory input before it reaches consciousness. In the future, it will be even more important to filter out the repetitive, boring, and unnecessary, and retain the novel, relevant, and necessary information. Actually, the brain is not good at remembering isolated facts but is great at organizing and associating thoughts and ideas. This ability will help it handle new information without suffering overload.

As the human genome is mapped, scientists hope to find cures for many genetically linked diseases, including those that affect the brain.

Just as important as the biology inside the brain is the technology outside. First with the introduction of books, and now computers, we have become increasingly reliant on artificial means of storing information. Thus the relative need for long-term (storage) memory in the brain and the time span for storage have decreased. As this trend continues, we will make greater use of our working memory and less use of our storage memory [see "Now Where Did I Put Those Keys?" THE WORLD & I, November 1998, p. 160].

Help for our memories may also come in the form of a pill. Research related to Alzheimer's disease has already produced a drug that can improve normal memory in small, healthy animals.

Furthermore, the rate at which we access and share information will most likely continue to accelerate. As a result, our brains will be challenged to think faster and make decisions more quickly. Anything less will be inefficient. Bureaucracy and red tape will be our enemies. We may be compelled to place greater emphasis on intuition and "gut feelings."

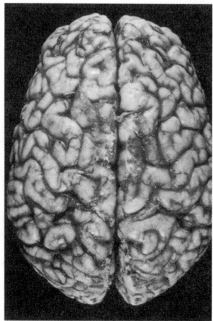

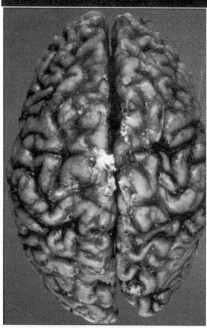

BOTH IMAGES COURTESY OF THE NATIONAL INSTITUTE OF NEUROLOGICAL DISORDERS AND STROKE/ NIH

Convolutions in the brain of an Alzheimer's patient show considerable shrinkage (bottom) compared with those in a normal brain (top). Cures for Alzheimer's and other brain diseases may be found through such approaches as genetic engineering or neural cell regeneration.

Treating hereditary brain disorders

In living organisms, another type of memory occurs in the form of ge-

netic material known as DNA (deoxyribonucleic acid). It is the blueprint for the body and the chemical memory for traits that are passed down from generation to generation. The DNA representing the human genome (complete set of genetic information) consists of over 3 billion subunits (base pairs) and contains the coding for anywhere between 40,000 and 100,000 genes.

Scientists are already tackling the ambitious goal of determining the sequence of base pairs and mapping the genes of the entire human genome. Two groups—a publicly funded, international consortium (whose work is known as the Human Genome Project) and the private company Celera Genomics Corporation (based in Rockville, Maryland)—have just recently submitted "working drafts," with the promise of more detailed, high-quality results in the near future.

The human genetic map will help locate biomarkers for the diagnosis and treatment of hereditary disorders, including those affecting the brain. One type of treatment, known as gene therapy, is directed toward replacing defective genes with undamaged ones [see "Doctoring Genes to Beat Disease," THE WORLD & I, December 1997, p. 178]. But the many gene therapy trials conducted over the past 10 years have met with a low success rate, indicating the need for further refinements to the technique. In the meantime, a promising new strategy called *chimeraplasty*, in which the cell is stimulated to repair its own defective genes, has emerged [see "The Promise of Genetic Cures," THE WORLD & I, May 2000, p. 147]. Either approach may also be used to fight noninherited disorders by increasing the body's production of substances (such as interleukin or interferon) that protect the body.

The genetic information will probably lead to tests performed *in utero* or early in life to detect markers that suggest predispositions to such conditions as obesity and alcoholism, or such diseases as schizophrenia and Alzheimer's. People would then have the opportunity to get genetic counseling and design a lifestyle that integrates medical surveillance to stay healthy. At the same time, however, we need to improve our system of laws to prevent discrimination against people—particularly in employment and insurance coverage—based on this information. In February this year, President Clinton prohibited federal employers from requiring or requesting genetic tests as a condition of being hired or receiving benefits.

Environment and behavior can alter our brains; free will can influence our behavior.

Moreover, knowledge of a person's genotype (gene structure and organization) will not necessarily enable us to predict his phenotype (body structure), which is the manifestation of not only the genetic information but environmental influences and life experiences as well. The phenotype for a brain disease, for example, could range anywhere from no symptoms to total disability. Even identical twins are not 100 percent concordant for most brain disorders. The health and character of the human brain (and the rest of the body) are neither predetermined nor inevitable. Environment and behavior can alter our brains; free will can influence our behavior.

It is also possible that a treatment that alters one gene may affect many traits, even those that we do not wish to change. The same gene linked to a brain disorder might also influence intelligence or creativity. The risk involved in altering a gene is especially great for disorders associated with multiple genes.

Vaccines, drugs, surgery, and brain regeneration

We have grown up in a world of miracle drugs, but most alleviate just the symptoms. The next century will focus on prevention and cures. Scien-

tists are already working on oral vaccines that would attack the pathological plagues and tangles of Alzheimer's disease, decrease brain damage after a stroke or seizure, and lower the number of seizures in epileptics. We will be able to administer specific substances (called trophic factors) that will stimulate brain cells to multiply and replace cells degenerating because of brain diseases such as Parkinson's and Huntington's.

The trial-and-error method of finding effective drugs is now being replaced by the use of computers to design molecules that will precisely fit into specific receptors for the purpose of treating diseases. In the future, we will also be able to manufacture and use larger quantities of disease-fighting chemicals—such as interleukins, interferon, and brain trophic factors—that occur naturally in the body.

One strategy for making large quantities of specific antibodies is called the monoclonal antibody technique. Antibodies of a particular type are produced in large quantities by fusing the specific antibody-producing cells with tumor cells that grow and proliferate indefinitely. We could even piggyback drugs onto antibodies that target specific parts of the brain, thereby reducing the drug dosage and minimizing side effects.

Another approach currently being pursued is genetically engineering plants to produce pharmaceuticals. Until recently, efforts have been directed at protecting crops and improving their taste and nutritional value. About two dozen companies are now working to enhance the availability and lower the cost of drugs by genetically engineering plants to produce them. Some of the drugs may be ingested by simply eating the plant food.

With the improvement of brain imaging and robotics, brain surgery will improve and become less invasive. The brain is ideally suited for robotic surgery. It is enclosed in a firm skull that's appropriate for mounting instruments and provid-

ing fixed reference points by which to navigate the brain. Robotics and microscopic brain imaging will be used for higher precision, fewer mistakes, and minimally invasive surgical techniques.

On Being Human

According to futurist Alvin Toffler, the new millennium will challenge our understanding of what it means to be human. The fusion of computer technology, genetic engineering, and research on the brain will allow us to control our own evolution. For instance, electronic microchips may be placed in our brains to repair lost functions or create new ones. Scientists can now make microchips that are part organic. What about computers that are part protoplasm? When do we stop calling them machines and start calling them life?

There is currently a debate about the ethics of producing human clones or designer babies with "better" abilities. Can we also modify the genes of animals to give them human intelligence? Or can we create robots that take on human characteristics, such as human behavior or even self-replication? If so, should they be considered part human?

Whatever the answers may turn out to be, our differing views of what it means to be human are likely to polarize society because of conflicting causes taken up by political, religious, and scientific groups. We may experience a moral divide that could exceed that seen with slavery or abortion.

—N.R.M.

While pharmacological and surgical treatments improve, another approach that's gaining in importance is the regeneration of neural tissue. This approach has become possible because of recent research on stem cells and trophic factors, along with the discovery that adult brain cells can divide and multiply. Neural regeneration is the hope for those who suffer from such disorders as paralysis, Lou Gehrig's disease (amyotrophic lateral sclerosis), Down syndrome, retina degeneration, and Parkinson's disease.

The mind-body relationship

Charles Schultz, the beloved creator of Charlie Brown and author of the comic strip *Peanuts* for 50 years, died this year on the very day that his farewell strip was published. It was as if he stayed alive just long enough to see it end. Was that just a coincidence?

Warm, loving relationships, as well as isolation, can influence longevity and the will to live. How often have we heard of a person dying soon after his spouse dies? The body is not a biological machine operating independently of the mind. Even Hippocrates proposed that health was a balance of mind and body in the proper environment.

Robotics and microscopic brain imaging will be used for higher precision, fewer mistakes, and minimally invasive surgical techniques.

The mind has a powerful effect on our physical health by influencing our immune, cardiovascular, and endocrine systems. It can change the levels of such body substances as cortisol, adrenaline, and natural killer cells. Happy people get sick less often. Angry people have more health problems. Stress, anger, depression, and loneliness suppress the immune system, overexert the heart, raise blood pressure, enhance blood clotting, increase bone loss, harden the arteries, and increase cholesterol and abdominal fat. These factors can increase the incidence and severity of cancer, heart disease, stroke, arthritis, and even the common cold.

Western medicine, however, has underappreciated this mind-body relationship. Now that brain imaging can be used to observe the effect of the mind on the body, we will see the medical establishment embrace this concept as the basis of a legitimate form of therapy. Support groups, meditation, and relaxation therapy will be prescribed to ward off disease and dampen its devastating effects.

Research has shown that people who derive strength and comfort from religion live healthier and longer lives [see "Is Religion Good for Your Health?" THE WORLD & I, February 1996, p. 291]. The benefits of religion go beyond social contact or the encouragement of healthier habits. It can be a mechanism to help cope with life and stressful situations. Faith in a Higher Being has been shown to be an important part of the successful Twelve Steps program of Alcoholics Anonymous—a program that has been extended to treat other addictions, such as gambling and overeating [see "Spirituality in Healing," THE WORLD & I, May 2000, p. 153]. Doctors will use it to increase the compliance of patients with the treatments prescribed for a wide range of acute and chronic medical problems.

People get better because they believe they will. This is called the placebo effect. A patient's belief that he is receiving effective medicine will alleviate his symptoms. The stronger his belief, the stronger the relief. This effect has been known and used by doctors for many years. It must be taken into account when testing new medicines and therapies.

The placebo effect is based on the brain's ability to anticipate the future and prepare for it. For example, the brain analyzes trajectories of objects in motion and predicts their future location, or it analyzes environmental temperatures and predicts the body's future temperature. Also, our senses are notorious for seeing what we hope to see and tasting what we expect to taste. The brain produces a placebo effect by stimulating cells

and releasing hormones that start the healing process in anticipation of getting better.

Brain Doctors

Technology will enable drugs to be more selective and surgeries to be more exact. But what about the doctors? How will they change? Their early training will involve greater use of virtual reality and less use of animals. They will emphasize prevention and cure rather than the treatment of symptoms. They will have to be genetic counselors and focus on the whole person rather than symptoms. They must put humanity back into medicine.

Today's neurologists tend to be technicians more than healers. They are trained primarily to diagnose and fix defective brains. Their success is determined by how effective they are at minimizing symptoms, restoring functions, and curing diseases. Although most patients are grateful, many find the doctor's help to be insufficient or lacking. Substituting a side effect for a symptom, or prolonging a life of pain and distress, may not be an improvement in the patient's quality of life.

In addition, the psychological and spiritual needs of the patient often go unattended. Patients need someone to appreciate their distress and relate to them on a human level. Recognizing these needs, medical education is now increasing its emphasis on treating the whole person. Doctors are realizing that the way to a healthy body is through the mind.

—N.R.M.

The brain-machine connection

Over the past century, we have aided our vision and hearing with lenses and amplifiers. During the next century, we will probably replace eyes and ears with light and sound detectors and computer chips that send signals to the brain.

Every year, the International NAISO Congress on Information Science Innovations holds a Robot Soccer Competition. Winners are those who create robots that can "see" with greater acuity, "think" more perceptively, and move faster and with greater agility. Software companies are already making advertising claims that their programs can "think." Will molecular electronics and nanotechnology, combined with genetic engineering, give us the power to create sentient robots?

We need to find ways to understand consciousness and how the brain is involved in the powers of reasoning, creativity, and love.

If so, a modern-day Pandora's box is being opened. Unlike scientific breakthroughs of the past, the robots and engineered organisms of the future could have the potential for self-replication. While the uncontrolled replication of mischievous programs on the Internet—as seen with the "Melissa" and "I Love You" viruses—can cause a lot of damage, the uncontrolled replication of sentient robots may pose a threat to our humanity. Will this evolution come suddenly, like the news about cloning the first mammal, or gradually, so that we will get used to it? Or will modern-day Luddites have the courage and foresight to say no and steer us in another direction?

We began the twentieth century looking at the brain's structure through a simple microscope and ended by examining its functions with such techniques as PET (positron emission tomography) and

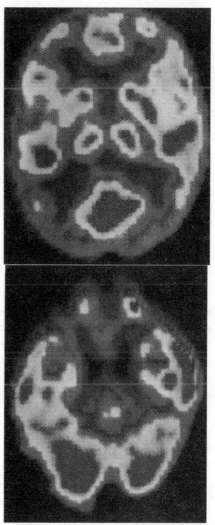

COURTESY OF THE NATIONAL INSTITUTE OF NEURO-
LOGICAL DISORDERS AND STROKE/NIH

Just as current PET scans (above) reveal general activity in the brain, future techniques may show microscopic details Top: The brain of a young man listening intently to a story uses a great deal of glucose in the auditory cortex (gray areas near the ears). Bottom: An image at a different level of the same brain shows activity in the hippocampus (gray spots at short distances in from the sides), where short-term learning is converted to long-term memory.

MRI (magnetic resonance imaging). We went through the stages of neuroanatomy, neurophysiology, and neurochemistry. We learned how the brain controls movement and processes sensory information. We scratched the surface in our attempts to clarify intelligence and emotions. Among the challenges of the new century will be to find ways to understand consciousness and how the brain is involved in the powers of reasoning, creativity, and love.

Speculating about the future, however, is daunting, even for experts. In a 1987 survey, medical scientists predicted that by the year 2000 we would probably have a cure for two-thirds of all cancers, AIDS would be eliminated, and coronary bypass surgery would be replaced by less invasive techniques.

Distinguishing between fact and fiction is difficult even today. On the first day of my neuroscience course in graduate school, our instructor told us that half of what he would teach us that semester would eventually prove to be wrong—the problem was, he could not tell which half was wrong. Since then, I have repeatedly witnessed the truth of that statement. Revisions of our knowledge will continue in the twenty-first century. We must keep testing our view of the world, and if it fails, replace it with a better one. We must remain flexible in our beliefs, just as our brains remain flexible in their structure and function.

Norbert R. Myslinski is associate professor of neuroscience at the University of Maryland and director of Maryland Brain Awareness Week.

This article appeared in the August 2000 issue of *The World & I*, pp. 152-159. *The World & I*, a publication of The Washington Times Corporation. © 2000.

UNIT 3
Perceptual Processes

Unit Selections

Key Points to Consider

- Why would psychologists be interested in studying sensations and perceptions? Can you differentiate the two? Isn't sensation the domain of biologists and physicians? Can you rank-order the senses, that is, place them in a hierarchy of importance? Can you justify your rankings?

- What role does the brain play in sensation and perception? Can you give specific information about the role of the brain in each sense? Are some senses "distant" senses and some "near" senses in terms of how we perceive a stimulus, whether the stimulus is physical or social? Can you think of other ways to categorize the various senses?

- Do you think visual experiences induce consciousness? If not, what is consciousness and what does induce it? From where do you think consciousness originates?

- What is deafness? What are some of the causes of deafness? Are Americans at risk for deafness? How much noise is too much noise? What can be done to reduce noise levels so that they are not detrimental to us?

- What is synesthesia? Can you provide some examples that would describe the experience of a synesthete? Would you want to experience synesthesia? Why or why not?

- What is an altered state of consciousness? Do you believe in extrasensory phenomena such as ESP? Do you believe in it even if there is scientific evidence against it? How do psychologists study parapsychological phenomena such as ESP or dreaming?

- What is REM sleep? What are some of the problems dream researchers encounter? What do dreams mean? Was Freud correct that dreams are repressed wishes that we want to forget? Or are dreams events we would rather remember? How do our night dreams affect our waking behaviors?

 **Links: www.dushkin.com/online/**
These sites are annotated in the World Wide Web pages.

Psychology Tutorials and Demonstrations
http://psych.hanover.edu/Krantz/tutor.html
A Sensory Adventure
http://illusionworks.com/html/jump_page.html

Susan and her roommate have been friends since freshmen year. Because they share so much in common, they decided to become roommates in their sophomore year. They both want to travel abroad one day. Both date men from the same fraternity, are education majors, and want to work with young children after graduation from college. Today they are at the local art museum. As they walk around the galleries, Susan is astonished at her roommate's taste in art. Whatever her roommate likes, Susan hates. The paintings and sculptures that Susan admires are the very ones to which her roommate turns up her nose. "How can our tastes in art be so different?" Susan wonders.

What Susan and her roommate are experiencing is a difference in perception or the interpretation of the sensory stimulation provided by the artwork. Perception and its sister area of psychology, sensation, are the foci of this unit.

For many years in psychology it was popular to consider sensation and perception as two distinct processes. Sensation was defined in passive terms as the simple event of some stimulus energy (i.e., a sound wave) impinging on the body or on a specific sense organ that then reflexively transmits appropriate information to the central nervous system. Both passivity and simple reflexes were stressed in this concept. Perception, on the other hand, was defined as an integrative and interpretive process that the higher centers of the brain accomplish based on sensory information and available memories for similar events.

The Gestalt psychologists, early German researchers, were convinced that perception was a higher order function compared to sensation. The Gestalt psychologists believed that the whole stimulus was more than the sum of its individual sensory parts; Gestalt psychologists believed this statement was made true by the process of perception.

For example, when you listen to a song, you hear the words, the loudness, and the harmony as well as the main melody. However, you do not really hear each of these units separately; what you hear is a whole song. If the song is pleasant to you, you may say that you like the song. If the song is raucous to you, you may say that you do not like it. However, even the songs you do not like on first hearing may become likable after repeated exposure. Hence perception, according to these early Gestalt psychologists, was a more advanced and complicated process than sensation.

This dichotomy of sensation and perception is no longer widely accepted. The revolution came in the mid-1960s when a psychologist published a then-radical treatise in which he reasoned that perceptual processes included all sensory events that he saw as directed by a searching central nervous system. Also, this view provided that certain perceptual patterns, such as recognition of a piece of artwork, may be species-specific. That is, all humans, independent of learning history, should share some of the same perceptual repertoires. This unit on perceptual processes is designed to further your understanding of these complex and interesting processes.

In the first article, "The Senses," one of the main topics of this unit is introduced to you. The author reviews many of the dominant senses in the human being and concludes that when we understand the senses, we also understand the brain.

The second article in this unit, "Vision: A Window on Consciousness," explores one of the most important senses in humans. The author, Nikos Logothetis, ties together our visual experiences and consciousness. Psychologists have long debated consciousness and tried to define it and find its source. Logothetis strongly suggests that we derive consciousness from our visual experiences. He demonstrates this by showcasing research on visual ambiguity, a situation in which a stimulus appears to be ambiguous to the eyes.

One of the other dominant senses in humans is audition or hearing. In the next article, "Noise Busters," *Smithsonian Magazine* discloses information about just how much noise Americans are exposed to and why certain noises can be detrimental. With enough exposure to certain sounds, individuals can become deaf. The article also reveals what can be done to save Americans' hearing.

The fourth article in this section, "For Some, Pain Is Orange," reveals information about a very unusual phenomenon—synesthesia. People who experience synesthesia combine sensations in unique ways such that pain may actually be perceived as a color, or a sound may conjure a vision. Susan Hornik explores the special world of synesthetes in this article.

The final selection of this unit, "Dream Speak," relates to an altered state of perception or altered state of consciousness (something outside of normal sensation and perception). This last article is about dreaming, something we all do and something that fascinates most individuals. By studying sleep, especially dream or REM sleep, researchers are beginning to understand why we dream and what dreams may mean. Freud's was the first theory to address these issues, but newer theories are making headway on the nature and causes of dreaming. Author Milton Kramer suggests that dreams are emotional dramas that affect our moods during the day.

THE SENSES

They delight, heal, define the boundaries of our world. And they are helping unlock the brain's secrets

To the 19th-century French poet Charles Baudelaire, there was no such thing as a bad smell. What a squeamish, oversensitive bunch he would have deemed the denizens of 20th-century America, where body odors are taboo, strong aromas are immediately suppressed with air freshener, and perfume—long celebrated for its seductive and healing powers—is banned in some places to protect those with multiple chemical sensitivities.

Indeed, in the years since Baudelaire set pen to paper, civilization has played havoc with the natural state of all the human senses, technology providing the ability not only to tame and to mute but also to tease and overstimulate. Artificial fragrances and flavors trick the nose and tongue. Advertisers dazzle the eyes with rapid-fire images. Wailing sirens vie with the beeping of pagers to challenge the ears' ability to cope.

Yet even as we fiddle with the texture and scope of our sensibilities, science is indicating it might behoove us to show them a bit more respect. Growing evidence documents the surprising consequences of depriving or overwhelming the senses. And failing to nurture our natural capabilities, researchers are discovering, can affect health, emotions, even intelligence. Hear-

ing, for example, is intimately connected to emotional circuits: When a nursing infant looks up from the breast, muscles in the middle ear reflexively tighten, readying the child for the pitch of a human voice. The touch of massage can relieve pain and improve concentration. And no matter how we spritz or scrub, every human body produces a natural odor as distinctive as the whorls on the fingertips—an aroma that research is showing to be a critical factor in choosing a sexual partner.

Beyond their capacity to heal and delight, the senses have also opened a window on the workings of the human brain. A flood of studies on smell, sight, hearing, touch and taste in the last two decades have upended most of the theories about how the brain functions. Scientists once believed, for example, that the brain was hard-wired at birth, the trillions of connections that made up its neural circuits genetically predetermined. But a huge proportion of neurons in a newborn infant's brain, it turns out, require input from the senses in order to hook up to one another properly.

Similarly, scientific theory until recently held that the sense organs did the lion's share of processing information about the world: The eye detected move-

ment; the nose recognized smells. But researchers now know that ears, eyes and fingers are only way stations, transmitting signals that are then processed centrally. "The nose doesn't smell—the brain does," says Richard Axel, a molecular biologist at Columbia University. Each of our senses shatters experience into fragments, parsing the world like so many nouns and verbs, then leaving the brain to put the pieces back together and make sense of it all.

In labs across the country, researchers are drafting a picture of the senses that promises not only to unravel the mysterious tangle of nerves in the brain but also to offer reasons to revel in sensuous experience. Cradling a baby not only feels marvelous, scientists are finding, but is absolutely vital to a newborn's emotional and cognitive development. And the results of this research are beginning to translate into practical help for people whose senses are impaired: Researchers in Boston last year unveiled a tiny electronic device called a retinal chip that one day may restore sight to people blinded after childhood. Gradually, this new science of the senses is redefining what it means to be a feeling and thinking human being. One day it may lead to an understanding of consciousness itself.

SIGHT

Seeing is believing, because vision is the body's top intelligence gatherer, at least by the brain's reckoning. A full quarter of the cerebral cortex, the brain's crinkled top layer, is devoted to sight, according to a new estimate by neuroscientist David Van Essen of Washington University in St. Louis—almost certainly more than is devoted to any other sense.

SIGHT
Cells in the retina of the eye are so sensitive they can respond to a single photon, or particle of light.

It seems fitting, then, that vision has offered scientists their most powerful insights on the brain's structure and operations. Research on sight "has been absolutely fundamental" for understanding the brain, says neurobiologist Semir Zeki of University College in London, in part because the visual system is easier to study than the other senses. The first clues to the workings of the visual system emerged in the 1950s, when Johns Hopkins neurobiologists David Hubel and Torsten Wiesel conducted a series of Nobel Prize–winning experiments. Using hair-thin electrodes implanted in a cat's brain, they recorded the firing of single neurons in the area where vision is processed. When the animal was looking at a diagonal bar of light, one neuron fired. When the bar was at a slightly different angle, a different nerve cell responded.

Hubel and Wiesel's discovery led to a revolutionary idea: While we are perceiving a unified scene, the brain is dissecting the view into many parts, each of which triggers a different set of neurons, called a visual map. One map responds to color and form, another only to motion. There are at least five such maps in the visual system alone, and recent work is showing that other senses are similarly encoded in the brain. In an auditory map, for example, the two sets of neurons that respond to two similar sounds, such as "go" and "ko," are located near each other, while those resonating with the sound "mo" lie at a distance.

Though we think of sensory abilities as independent, researchers are finding that each sense receives help from the others in apprehending the world. In 1995, psycholinguist Michael Tanenhaus of the University of Rochester videotaped people as they listened to sentences about nearby objects. As they listened, the subjects' eyes flicked to the objects. Those movements—so fast the subjects did not realize they'd shifted their gaze—helped them understand the grammar of the sentences, Tanenhaus found. Obviously, vision isn't required to comprehend grammar. But given the chance, the brain integrates visual cues while processing language.

The brain also does much of the heavy lifting for color vision, so much so that some people with brain damage see the world in shades of gray. But the ability to see colors begins with cells in the back of the eyeball called cones. For decades, scientists thought everyone with normal color vision had the same three types of cone cell—for red, green and blue light—and saw the same hues. New research shows, however, that everybody sees a different palette. Last year, Medical College of Wisconsin researchers Maureen Neitz and her husband, Jay, discovered that people have up to nine genes for cones, indicating there may be many kinds of cones. Already, two red cone subtypes have been found. People with one type see red differently from those with the second. Says Maureen Neitz: "That's why people argue about adjusting the color on the TV set."

HEARING

Hearing is the gateway to language, a uniquely human skill. In a normal child, the ears tune themselves to human sounds soon after birth, cementing the neural connections between language, emotions and intelligence. Even a tiny glitch in the way a child processes sound can unhinge development.

About 7 million American children who have normal hearing and intelligence develop intractable problems with language, reading and writing because they cannot decipher certain parcels of language. Research by Paula Tallal, a Rutgers University neurobiologist, has shown that children with language learning disabilities (LLD) fail to distinguish between the "plosive" consonants, such as b, t and p. To them, "bug" sounds like "tug" sounds like "pug." The problem, Tallal has long argued, is that for such kids the sounds come too fast. Vowels resonate for 100 millisec-onds or more, but plosive consonants last for a mere 40 milliseconds—not long enough for some children to process them. "These children hear the sound. It just isn't transmitted to the brain normally," she says.

Two years ago, Tallal teamed up with Michael Merzenich, a neurobiologist at the University of California–San Francisco, to create a set of computer games that have produced stunning gains in 29 children with LLD. With William Jenkins and Steve Miller, the neurobiologists wrote computer programs that elongated the plosive consonants, making them louder—"like making a yellow highlighter for the brain," says Tallal. After a month of daily three-hour sessions, children who were one to three years behind their peers in language and reading had leaped forward a full two years. The researchers have formed a company, Scientific Learning Corp., that could make their system available to teachers and professionals within a few years. (See their Web site: http://www.scilearn.com or call 415-296-1470.)

An inability to hear the sounds of human speech properly also may contribute to autism, a disorder that leaves children unable to relate emotionally to other people. According to University of Maryland psychophysiologist Stephen Porges, many autistic children are listening not to the sounds of human speech but instead to frightening noises. He blames the children's fear on a section of the nervous system that controls facial expressions, speech, visceral feelings and the muscles in the middle ear.

HEARING
At six months, a baby's brain tunes in to the sounds of its native tongue and tunes out other languages.

These muscles, the tiniest in the body, allow the ear to filter sounds, much the way muscles in the eye focus the eyeball on near or distant objects. In autistic children, the neural system that includes the middle ear is lazy. As a result, these children attend not to the pitch of the human voice but instead to sounds that are much lower: the rumble of traffic, the growl of a vacuum cleaner. In the deep evolutionary past, such noises signaled danger. Porges contends that autistic children feel too anxious to interact emotionally, and the neural system controlling many emotional responses fails to develop.

Porges says that exercising the neural system may help autistic kids gain language and emotional skills. He and his colleagues have begun an experimental treatment consisting of tones and songs altered by computer to filter out low sounds, forcing the middle ear to focus on the pitches of human speech. After five 90-minute sessions, most of the 16 children have made strides that surprised even Porges. Third grader Tomlin Clark, for example, who once spoke only rarely, recently delighted his parents by getting in trouble for talking out of turn in school. And for the first time, he shows a sense of humor. "Listening to sounds seems so simple, doesn't it?" says Porges. "But so does jogging."

TOUCH

The skin, writes pathologist Marc Lappé, "is both literally and metaphorically 'the body's edge'... a boundary against an inimical world." Yet the skin also is the organ that speaks the language of love most clearly—and not just in the erogenous zones. The caress of another person releases hormones that can ease pain and clear the mind. Deprive a child of touch, and his brain and body will stop growing.

This new view of the most intimate sense was sparked a decade ago, when child psychologist Tiffany Field showed that premature infants who were massaged for 15 minutes three times a day gained weight 47 percent faster than preemies given standard intensive care nursery treatment: as little touching as possible. The preemies who were massaged weren't eating more; they just processed food more efficiently, says Field, now director of the University of Miami's Touch Research Institute. Field found that massaged preemies were more alert and aware of their surroundings when awake, while their sleep was deeper and more restorative. Eight months later, the massaged infants scored better on mental and motor tests.

Being touched has healing powers throughout life. Massage, researchers have found, can ease the pain of severely burned children and boost the immune systems of AIDS patients. Field recently showed that office workers who received a 15-minute massage began emitting higher levels of brain waves associated with alertness. Af-

---

SIXTH SENSES

Wish you had that nose?

Folklore abounds with tales of animals possessing exceptional sensory powers, from pigs predicting earthquakes to pets telepathically anticipating their owners' arrival home. In some cases, myth and reality are not so far apart. Nature is full of creatures with superhuman senses: built-in compasses, highly accurate sonar, infrared vision. "Our worldview is limited by our senses," says Dartmouth College psychologist Howard Hughes, "so we are both reluctant to believe that animals can have capabilities beyond ours, and we attribute to them supernatural powers. The truth is somewhere between the two."

In the case of Watson, a Labrador retriever, reality is more impressive than any fiction. For over a year, Watson has reliably pawed his owner, Emily Ramsey, 45 minutes before her epileptic seizures begin, giving her time to move to a safe place. Placed by Canine Partners for Life, Watson has a 97 percent success rate, according to the Ramsey family. No one has formally studied how such dogs can predict seizure onset consistently. But they may smell the chemical changes known to precede epileptic attacks. "Whatever it is," says Harvard University neurologist Steven Schachter, "I think there's something to it."

Scientists have scrutinized other animals for decades, trying to decipher their sensory secrets. Birds, bees, moles and some 80 other creatures are known to sense magnetic fields. But new studies indicate birds have two magnetic detection systems: One seems to translate polarized light into visual patterns that act as a compass; the other is an internal magnet birds use to further orient themselves.

Dolphin sonar so intrigued government researchers that they launched the U.S. Navy Marine Mammal Program in 1960, hoping it would lead to more-sophisticated tracking equipment. But the animals still beat the machines, says spokesman Tom LaPuzza. In a murky sea, dolphins can pinpoint a softball two football fields away. A lobe in their forehead focuses their biosonar as a flashlight channels light, beaming 200-decibel clicks.

It took night-vision goggles for humans to replicate the infrared vision snakes come by naturally: A cameralike device in organs lining their lips lets them see heat patterns made by mammals. And humans can only envy the ability of sharks, skates and rays to feel electric fields through pores in their snouts—perhaps a primordial skill used by Earth's earliest creatures to scout out the new world.

BY ANNA MULRINE

---

ter their massage, the workers executed a math test in half their previous time with half the errors.

TOUCH
People with "synesthesia" feel colors, see sounds and taste shapes.

While such findings may sound touchy-feely, an increasing volume of physiological evidence backs them up. In a recent series of experiments, Swedish physiologist Kerstin Uvnas-Moberg found that gentle stroking can stimulate the body to release oxytocin, sometimes called the love hormone because it helps cement the bond between mothers and their young in many species. "There are deep, deep, physiological connections between touching and love," Uvnas-Moberg says. Oxytocin also blunts pain and dampens the hormones release when a person feels anxious or stressed.

For the babies of any species, touch signals that mother—the source of food, warmth and safety—is near. When she is gone, many young animals show physiological signs of stress and shut down their metabolism—an innate response designed to conserve energy until she returns. Without mother, rat pups do not grow, says Saul Schanberg, a Duke University pharmacologist, even when they are fed and kept warm. Stroking them with a brush in a manner that mimics their mother licking them restores the pups to robust health. "You need the right kind of touch in order to grow," says Schanberg, "even more than vitamins."

SMELL

Long ago in human evolution, smell played a prominent role, signaling who was ready to mate and who was ready to fight. But after a while, smell fell into disrepute. Aristotle disparaged it as the most animalistic of the senses, and Immanuel Kant dreamed of losing it. Recent research has restored the nose to some of its former glory. "Odor plays a far more important role in human behavior and physiology than we realize," says Gary Beauchamp, director of Philadelphia's Monell Chemical Senses Center.

SMELL

A woman's sense of smell is keener than a man's. And smell plays a larger role in sexual attraction for women.

A baby recognizes its mother by her odor soon after birth, and studies show that adults can identify clothing worn by their children or spouses by smell alone. In 1995, Beauchamp and colleagues at Monell reported that a woman's scent—genetically determined—changes in pregnancy to reflect a combination of her odor and that of her fetus.

The sense of smell's most celebrated capacity is its power to stir memory. "Hit a tripwire of smell, and memories explode all at once," writes poet Diane Ackerman. The reason, says Monell psychologist Rachel Herz, is that "smells carry an emotional quality." In her latest experiment, Herz showed people a series of evocative paintings. At the same time, the subjects were exposed to another sensory cue—an orange, for example—in different ways. Some saw an orange. Others were given an orange to touch, heard the word "orange" or smelled the fruit. Two days later, when subjects were given the same cue and were asked to recall the painting that matched it, those exposed to the smell of the orange recalled the painting and produced a flood of emotional responses to it.

Herz and others suspect that an aroma's capacity to spark such vivid remembrances arises out of anatomy. An odor's first way station in the brain is the olfactory bulb, two blueberry-sized lumps of cortex from which neurons extend through the skull into the nose. Smell molecules, those wafting off a cinnamon bun, for example, bind to these olfactory neurons, which fire off their signals first to the olfactory bulb and then to the limbic system—the seat of sexual drive, emotions and memory. Connections between the olfactory bulb and the neocortex, or thinking part of the brain, are secondary roads compared to the highways leading to emotional centers.

Scientists once thought all smells were made up of combinations of seven basic odors. But in an elegant series of experiments, research teams led by Columbia's Axel and Linda Buck of Harvard have shown the mechanics of smell to be much more complicated. In 1991, the scientists discovered a family of at least 1,000 genes corresponding to about 1,000 types of olfactory neurons in the nose. Each of these neuronal types responds to one—and only one—type of odor molecule.

ARE YOU A SUPERTASTER?

All tongues are not created equal. How intense flavors seem is determined by heredity. In this test, devised by Yale University taste experts Linda Bartoshuk and Laurie Lucchina, find out if you are a **nontaster**, an **average taster** or a **supertaster**. Answers on next page.

TASTE BUDS. Punch a hole with a standard hole punch in a square of wax paper. Paint the front of your tongue with a cotton swab dipped in blue food coloring. Put wax paper on the tip of your tongue, just to the right of center. With a flashlight and magnifying glass, count the number of pink, unstained circles. They contain taste buds.

SWEET. Rinse your mouth with water before tasting each sample. Put ½ cup of sugar in a measuring cup, and then add enough water to make 1 cup. Mix. Coat front half of your tongue, including the tip, with a cotton swab dipped in the solution. Wait a few moments. Rate the sweetness according to the scale shown below.

SALT. Put 2 teaspoons of salt in a measuring cup and add enough water to make 1 cup. Repeat the steps listed above, rating how salty the solution is.

SPICY. Add 1 teaspoon of Tabasco sauce to 1 cup of water. Apply with a cotton swab to first half inch of the tongue, including the tip. Keep your tongue out of your mouth until the burn reaches a peak, then rate the pain according to the scale.

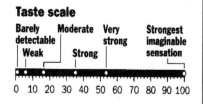

Taste scale

Barely detectable		Moderate		Very strong			Strongest imaginable
Weak			Strong				sensation

0 10 20 30 40 50 60 70 80 90 100

The average person, of course, can detect far more than 1,000 odors. That's because a single scent is made up of more than one type of molecule, perhaps even dozens. A rose might stimulate neurons A, B and C, while jasmine sets off neurons B, C and F. "Theoretically, we can detect an astronomical number of smells." says Axel—the equivalent of 10 to the 23rd power. The brain, however, doesn't have the space to keep track of all those possible combinations of molecules, and so it focuses on smells that were relevant in evolution, like the scent of ripe fruit or a sexually receptive mate—about 10,000 odors in all.

Axel and Buck have now discovered that the olfactory bulb contains a "map," similar to those the brain employs for vision and hearing. By implanting a gene into mice, the researchers dyed blue the nerves leading from the animals' olfactory bulbs to their noses. Tracing the path of these neurons, the researchers discovered that those responsible for detecting a single type of odor molecule all led back to a single point in the olfactory bulb. In other words, the jumble of neurons that exists in the nose is reduced to regimental order in the brain.

Smell maps may one day help anosmics, people who cannot smell. Susan Killorn of Richmond, Va., lost her sense of smell three years ago when she landed on her head while in-line skating and damaged the nerves leading from her nose to her brain. A gourmet cook, Killorn was devastated. "I can remember sitting at the dinner table and begging my husband to describe the meal I'd just cooked," she says. Killorn's ability to detect odors has gradually returned, but nothing smells quite right. One possibility, says Richard Costanzo, a neurophysiologist at Virginia Commonwealth University, is that some of the nerves from her nose have recovered or regenerated but now are hooked up to the wrong spot in her smell map.

Though imperfect, recoveries like Killorn's give researchers hope they may one day be able to stimulate other neurons to regenerate—after a spinal cord injury, for example. Costanzo and others are searching for chemicals made by the body that can act as traffic cops, telling neurons exactly where to grow. In the meantime, Killorn is grateful for every morsel of odor. "I dream at night about onions and garlic," she says, "and they smell like they are supposed to."

TASTE

Human beings will put almost anything into their mouths and consider it food, from stinging nettles to grubs. Fortunately, evolution armed the human tongue with a set of sensors to keep venturesome members of the species from dying of malnutrition or poison. The four simple flavors—sweet, salty, bitter and sour—tell human beings what's healthy and what's harmful. But as researchers are finding, the sense of taste does far more than keep us from killing ourselves. Each person tastes food differently, a genetically determined sensitivity that can affect diet, weight and health.

TASTE
Human beings are genetically hard-wired to crave sweetness; sugar on the lips of a newborn baby will bring a smile.

In a quest for novelty, people around the world have developed an affinity for foods that cause a modicum of pain. "Humans have the ability to say, 'Oh, that didn't really hurt me—let me try it again,'" says Barry Green, a psychologist at the John B. Pierce Laboratory in New Haven, Conn. Spicy food, Green has found, gives the impression of being painfully hot by stimulating the nerves in the mouth that sense temperature extremes. The bubbles in soda and champagne feel as if they are popping inside the mouth; in reality, carbon dioxide inside the bubbles irritates nerves that sense pain.

One person's spicy meatball, however, is another's bland and tasteless meal. Researchers have long known that certain people have an inherited inability to taste a mildly bitter substance with a tongue-twisting name: propylthiouracil, or PROP, for short. About a quarter of Caucasians are "nontasters," utterly insensitive to PROP, while the vast majority of Asians and Africans can taste it. Now, researchers

at Yale University led by psychologist Linda Bartoshuk have discovered a third group of people called "supertasters." So sensitive are supertasters' tongues that they gag on PROP and can detect the merest hint of other bitter compounds in a host of foods, from chocolate and saccharin to vegetables such as broccoli, "which could explain why George Bush hates it," Bartoshuk says. She has recently discovered that supertasters have twice as many taste buds as nontasters and more of the nerve endings that detect the feel of foods. As a consequence, sweets taste sweeter to supertasters, and cream feels creamier. A spicy dish can send a supertaster through the roof.

RESULTS OF TASTE TEST ON PREVIOUS PAGE		
	SUPER-TASTERS	NON-TASTERS
No. of taste buds	25 on average	10
Sweet rating	56 on average	32
Tabasco rating	64 on average	31

Average tasters lie in between.
Bartoshuk and Lucchina lack the data to rate salt.

In an ongoing study, Bartoshuk's group has found that older women who are nontasters tend to prefer sweets and fatty foods—dishes that some of the supertasters find cloying. Not surprisingly, supertasters also tend to be thinner and have lower cholesterol. In their study, the researchers ask subjects to taste cream mixed with oil, a combination Bartoshuk confesses she finds delicious. "I'm a nontaster, and I'm heavy," she says. "I gobble up the test." But tasting ability is not only a matter of cuisine preference and body weight. Monell's Marcia Pelchat and a graduate student recently completed a study indicat-

ing that nontasters also may be predisposed to alcoholism.

The human senses detect only a fraction of reality: We can't see the ultraviolet markers that guide a honeybee to nectar; we can't hear most of the noises emitted by a dolphin. In this way, the senses define the boundaries of mental awareness. But the brain also defines the limits of what we perceive. Human beings see, feel, taste, touch and smell not the world around them but a version of the world, one their brains have concocted. "People imagine that they're seeing what's really there, but they're not," says neuroscientist John Maunsell of Baylor College of Medicine in Houston. The eyes take in the light reflecting off objects around us, but the brain only pays attention to part of the scene. Looking for a pen on a messy desk, for example, you can scan the surface without noticing the papers scattered across it.

The word "sentience" derives from the Latin verb *sentire*, meaning "to feel." And research on the senses, especially the discovery of sensory mapping, has taken scientists one step further in understanding the state we call consciousness. Yet even this dramatic advance is only a beginning. "In a way, these sexy maps have seduced us," says Michael Shipley, director of neurosciences at the University of Maryland–Baltimore. "We still haven't answered the question of how do you go from visual maps to recognizing faces, or from an auditory map to recognizing a Mozart sonata played by two different pianists." The challenge for the 21st century will be figuring out how the brain, once it has broken the sensory landscape into pieces, puts them together again.

BY SHANNON BROWNLEE
WITH TRACI WATSON

Vision:
A Window on Consciousness

*In their search for the mind, scientists are focusing on visual perception—
how we interpret what we see*

by Nikos K. Logothetis

Whan you first look at the center image in the painting by Salvador Dalí, *Old Age, Adolescence, Infancy (The Three Ages)*, what do you see? Most people immediately perceive a man's face, eyes gazing skyward and lips pursed under a bushy mustache. But when you look again, the image rearranges itself into a more complex tableau. The man's nose and white mustache become the mob-cap and cape of a seated woman. The glimmers in the man's eyes reveal themselves as lights in the windows—or glints on the roofs—of two cottages nestled in darkened hillsides. Shadows on the man's cheek emerge as a child in short pants standing beside the seated woman—both of whom, it is now clear, are looking across a lake at the cottages from a hole in a brick wall, a hole we once saw as the outline of the man's face.

In 1940, when he rendered *Old Age, Adolescence, Infancy (The Three Ages)*—which contains three "faces"—Dalí was toying with the capacity of the viewer's mind to interpret two different images from the same set of brushstrokes. More than 50 years later researchers, including my colleagues and I, are using similarly ambiguous visual stimuli to try to identify the brain activity that underlies consciousness. Specifically, we want to know what happens in the brain at the instant when, for example, an observer comprehends that the three faces in Dalí's picture are not really faces at all.

Consciousness is a difficult concept to define, much less to study. Neuroscientists have in recent years made impressive progress toward understanding the complex patterns of activity that occur in nerve cells, or neurons, in the brain. Even so, most people, including many scientists, still find the notion that electrochemical discharges in neurons can explain the mind, and in particular consciousness, challenging.

Yet, as Nobel laureate Francis Crick of the Salk Institute for Biological Studies in San Diego and Christof Koch of the California Institute of Technology have recently argued, the problem of consciousness can be broken down into several separate questions, some of which can be subjected to scientific inquiry [see "The Problem of Consciousness," by Francis Crick and Christof Koch; SCIENTIFIC AMERICAN, September 1992]. For example, rather than worrying about what consciousness is, one can ask: What is the difference between the neural processes that correlated with particular conscious experience and those that do not?

Now You See It...

That is where ambiguous stimuli come in. Perceptual ambiguity is not a whimsical behavior specific to the organization of the visual system. Rather it tells us something about the organization of the entire brain and its way of making us aware of all sensory information. Take, for instance, the meaningless string of French words *pas de lieu Rhône que nous*, cited by the psychologist William James in 1890. You can read this over and over again without recognizing that it sounds just like the phrase "paddle your own canoe." What changes in neural activity occur when the meaningful sentence suddenly reaches consciousness?

In our work with ambiguous visual stimuli, we use images that not only give rise to two distinct perceptions but also instigate a continuous alternation between the two. A familiar example is the Necker cube [*see illustration*]. This figure is perceived as a three-dimensional cube, but the apparent perspective of the cube appears to shift every few seconds. Obviously, this alternation must correspond to something happening in the brain.

A skeptic might argue that we sometimes perceive a stimulus without being truly conscious of it, as when, for example, we "automatically" stop at a red light when driving. But the stimuli and the situations that I investigate are actually designed to reach consciousness.

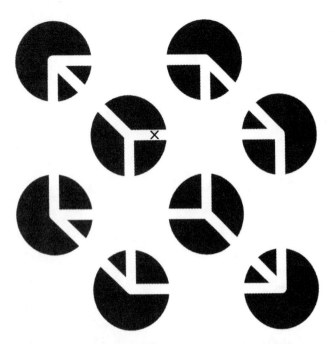

JOHNNY JOHNSON

NECKER CUBE can be viewed two different ways, depending on whether you see the "x" on the top front edge of the cube or on its rear face. Sometimes the cube appears superimposed on the circles; other times it seems the circles are holes and the cube floats behind the page.

We know that our stimuli reach awareness in human beings, because they can tell us about their experience. But it is not usually possible to study the activity of individual neurons in awake humans, so we perform our experiments with alert monkeys that have been trained to report what they are perceiving by pressing levers or by looking in a particular direction. Monkeys' brains are organized like those of humans, and they respond to such stimuli much as humans do. Consequently, we think the animals are conscious in somewhat the same way as humans are.

We investigate ambiguities that result when two different visual patterns are presented simultaneously to each eye, a phenomenon called binocular rivalry. When people are put in this situation, their brains become aware of first one perception and then the other, in a slowly alternating sequence.

In the laboratory, we use stereoscopes to create this effect. Trained monkeys exposed to such visual stimulation report that they, too, experience a perception that changes every few seconds. Our experiments have enabled us to trace neural activity that corresponds to these changing reports.

In the Mind's Eye

Studies of neural activity in animals conducted over several decades have established that visual information leaving the eyes ascends through successive stages of a neural data-processing system. Different modules ana-lyze various attributes of the visual field. In general, the type of processing becomes more specialized the farther the information moves along the visual pathway.

At the start of the pathway, images from the retina at the back of each eye are channeled first to a pair of small structures deep in the brain called the lateral geniculate nuclei (LGN). Individual neurons in the LGN can be activated by visual stimulation from either one eye or the other but not both. They respond to any change of brightness or color in a specific region within an area of view known as the receptive field, which varies among neurons.

From the LGN, visual information moves to the primary visual cortex, which is at the back of the head and conventionally abbreviated as V1. Neurons in V1 behave differently than those in the LGN do. They can usually be activated by either eye, but they are also sensitive to specific attributes, such as the direction of motion of a stimulus placed within their receptive field. Visual information is transmitted from V1 to more than two dozen other distinct cortical regions.

Some information from V1 can be traced as it moves through areas known as V2 and V4 before winding up in regions known as the inferior temporal cortex (ITC), which like all the other structures are bilateral. A large number of investigations, including neurological studies of people who have experienced brain damage, suggest that the ITC is important in perceiving form and recognizing objects. Neurons in V4 are known to respond selectively to aspects of visual stimuli critical to discerning shapes. In the ITC, some neurons behave like V4 cells, but others respond only when entire objects, such as faces, are placed within their very large receptive fields.

Other signals from V1 pass through regions V2, V3 and an area called MT/V5 before eventually reaching a part of the brain called the parietal lobe. Most neurons in MT/V5 respond strongly to items moving in a specific direction. Neurons in other areas of the parietal lobe respond when an animal pays attention to a stimulus or intends to move toward it.

One surprising observation made in early experiments is that many neurons in these visual pathways, both in V1 and in higher levels of the processing hierarchy, still respond with their characteristic selectivity to visual stimuli even in animals that have been completely anesthetized. Clearly, an animal (or a human) is not conscious of all neural activity.

The observation raises the question of whether awareness is the result of the activation of special brain regions or clusters of neurons. The study of binocular rivalry in alert, trained monkeys allows us to approach that question, at least to some extent. In such experiments, a researcher presents each animal with a variety of visual stimuli, usually patterns or figures projected onto a screen. Monkeys can easily be trained to report accurately what stimulus they perceive by means of rewards of fruit juice.

How to Experience Binocular Rivalry

To simulate binocular rivalry at home, use your right hand to hold the cardboard cylinder from a roll of paper towels (or a piece of paper rolled into a tube) against your right eye. Hold your left hand, palm facing you, roughly four inches in front of your left eye, with the edge of your hand touching the tube.

At first it will appear as though your hand has a hole in it, as your brain concentrates on the stimulus from your right eye. After a few seconds, though, the "hole" will fill in with a fuzzy perception of your whole palm from your left eye. If you keep viewing, the two images will alternate, as your brain selects first the visual stimulus viewed by one eye, then that viewed by the other. The alternation is, however, a bit biased; you will probably perceive the visual stimulus you see through the cylinder more frequently than you will see your palm.

The bias occurs for two reasons. First, your palm is out of focus because it is much closer to your face, and blurred visual stimuli tend to be weaker competitors in binocular rivalry than sharp patterns, such as the surroundings you are viewing through the tube. Second, your palm is a relatively smooth surface with less contrast and fewer contours than your comparatively rich environment has. In the laboratory, we select the patterns viewed by the subjects carefully to eliminate such bias.

—*N.K.L.*

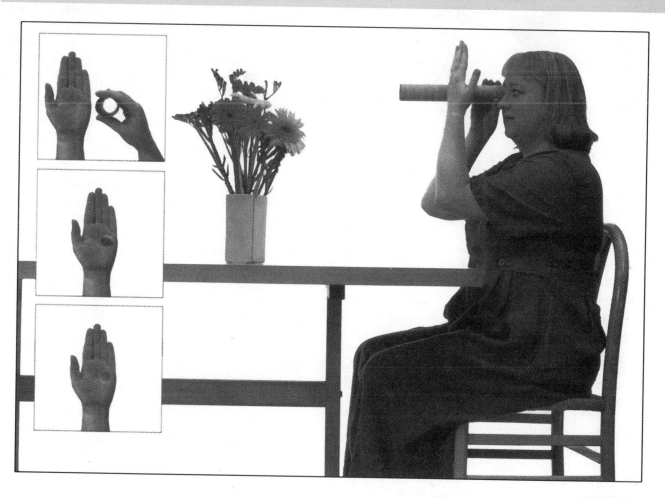

DAN WAGNER

During the experiment, the scientist uses electrodes to record the activity of neurons in the visual-processing pathway. Neurons vary markedly in their responsiveness when identical stimuli are presented to both eyes simultaneously. Stimulus pattern A might provoke activity in one neuron, for instance, whereas stimulus pattern B does not.

Once an experimenter has identified an effective and an ineffective stimulus for a given neuron (by presenting the same stimulus to both eyes at once), the two stimuli can be presented so that a different one is seen by each eye. We expect that, like a human in this situation, the monkey will become aware of the two stimuli in an alternating sequence. And, indeed, that is what the monkeys tell us by their responses when we present them with such rivalrous pairs of stimuli. By recording from neurons during successive presentations of rivalrous pairs, an experimenter can evaluate which neurons change their activity only when the stimuli change and which neurons alter their rate of firing when the animal reports a changed perception that is not accompanied by a change in the stimuli.

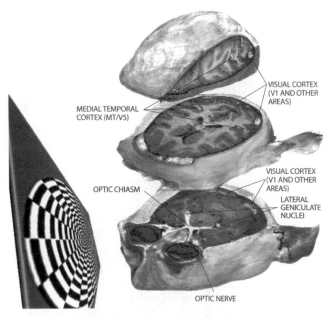

NIKOS K. LOGOTHETIS

IMAGES OF BRAIN ACTIVITY are from an anesthetized monkey that was presented with a rotating, high-contrast visual stimulus (lower left). These views, taken using functional magnetic resonance imaging, show that even though the monkey is unconscious, its vision-processing areas--including the lateral geniculate nuclei (LGN), primary visual cortex (V1) and medial temporal cortex (MT/V5)--are busy.

Jeffrey D. Schall, now at Vanderbilt University, and I carried out a version of this experiment in which one eye saw a grating that drifted slowly upward while the other eye saw a downward-moving grating. We recorded from visual area MT/V5, where cells tend to be responsive to motion. We found that about 43 percent of the cells in this area changed their level of activity when the monkey indicated that its perception had changed from up to down, or vice versa. Most of these cells were in the deepest layers of MT/V5.

The percentage we measured was actually a lower proportion than most scientists would have guessed, because almost all neurons in MT/V5 are sensitive to direction of movement. The majority of neurons in MT/V5 did behave somewhat like those in V1, remaining active when their preferred stimulus was in view of either eye, whether it was being perceived or not.

There were further surprises. Some 11 percent of the neurons examined were excited when the monkey reported perceiving the more effective stimulus of an upward/downward pair for the neuron in question. But a similar proportion of neurons, paradoxically, was most excited when the most effective stimulus was not perceived—even though it was in clear view of one eye. Other neurons could not be categorized as preferring one stimulus over another.

While we were both at Baylor College of Medicine, David A. Leopold and I studied neurons in parts of the brain known to be important in recognizing objects. (Leopold is now with me at the Max Planck Institute for Biological Cybernetics in Tübingen, Germany.) We recorded activity in V4, as well as in V1 and V2, while animals viewed stimuli consisting of lines sloping either to the left or to the right. In V4 the proportion of cells whose activity reflected perception was similar to that which Schall and I had found in MT/V5, around 40 percent. But again, a substantial proportion fired best when their preferred stimulus was not perceived. In V1 and V2, in contrast, fewer than one in 10 of the cells fired exclusively when their more effective stimulus was perceived, and none did so when it was not perceived.

The pattern of activity was entirely different in the ITC. David L. Sheinberg—who also moved with me from Baylor to the Max Planck Institute—and I recorded from this area after training monkeys to report their perceptions during rivalry between complex visual patterns, such as images of humans, animals and various man-made objects. We found that almost all neurons, about 90 percent, responded vigorously when their preferred pattern was perceived, but their activity was profoundly inhibited when this pattern was not being experienced.

So it seems that by the time visual signals reach the ITC, the great majority of neurons are responding in a way that is linked to perception. Frank Tong, Ken Nakayama and Nancy Kanwisher of Harvard University have used a technique called functional magnetic resonance imaging (fMRI)—which yields pictures of brain activity by measuring increases in blood flow in specific areas of the brain—to study people experiencing binocular rivalry. They found that the ITC was particularly active when the subjects reported they were seeing images of faces.

In short, most of the neurons in the earlier stages of the visual pathway responded mainly to whether their preferred visual stimulus was in view or not, although a few showed behavior that could be related to changes in the animal's perception. In the later stages of processing, on the other hand, the proportion whose activity reflected the animal's perception increased until it reached 90 percent.

A critic might object that the changing perceptions that monkeys report during binocular rivalry could be caused by the brain suppressing visual information at the start of the visual pathway, first from one eye, then from the other, so that the brain perceives a single image at any given time. If that were happening, changing neural activity and perceptions would simply represent the result of input switched from one eye to the other and would not be relevant to visual consciousness in other situations.

But experimental evidence shows decisively that input from both eyes is continuously processed in the visual system during rivalry.

Keeping Monkeys (and Experimenters) Honest

One possible objection to the experiments described in the main article is that the monkeys might have been inclined to cheat to earn their juice rewards. We are, after all, unable to know directly what a monkey (or a human) thinks or perceives at a given time. Because our monkeys were interested mainly in drinking juice rather than in understanding how consciousness arises from neuronal activity, it is possible that they could have developed a response strategy that appeared to reflect their true perceptions but really did not.

In the training session depicted below, for example, the monkey was being taught to pull the left lever only when it saw a sunburst and the right lever only when it saw a cowboy. We were able to ensure that the monkey continued to report truthfully by interjecting instances in which no rivalrous stimuli were shown (below). During these occasions, there was a "right" answer to what was perceived, and if the monkey did not respond correctly, the trial—and thus the opportunity to earn more juice rewards—was immediately ended. Similarly, if the monkey pulled any lever when presented with a jumbled image, in which the sunburst and the cowboy were superimposed (last panel), we knew the monkey was lying in an attempt to get more juice.

Our results indicate that monkeys report their experiences accurately. Even more convincing is our observation that monkeys and humans tested with the same apparatus perform at similar levels in different tasks. *N.K.L.*

Sees sunburst
Pulls left lever   **CORRECT=**   **JUICE REWARD**

We know this because it turns out that in humans, binocular rivalry produces its normal slow alternation of perceptions even if the competing stimuli are switched rapidly—several times per second—between the two eyes. If rivalry were merely a question of which eye the brain is paying attention to, the rivalry phenomenon would vanish when stimuli are switched quickly in this way. (The viewer would see, rather, a rapid alternation of the stimuli.) The observed persistence of slowly changing rivalrous perceptions when stimuli are switched strongly suggests that rivalry occurs because alternate stimulus representations compete in the visual pathway. Binocular rivalry thus affords an opportunity to study how the visual system decides what we see even when both eyes see (almost) the same thing.

A Perceptual Puzzle

What do these findings reveal about visual awareness? First, they show that we are unaware of a great deal of activity in our brains. We have long known that we are mostly unaware of the activity in the brain that maintains the body in a stable state—one of its evolutionarily most ancient tasks. Our experiments show that we are also unaware of much of the neural activity that generates—at least in part—our conscious experiences.

We can say this because many neurons in our brains respond to stimuli that we are not conscious of. Only a tiny fraction of neurons seem to be plausible candidates for what physiologists call the "neural correlate" of conscious perception—that is, they respond in a manner that reliably reflects perception.

We can say more. The small number of neurons whose behavior reflects perception are distributed over the entire visual pathway, rather than being part of a single area in the brain. Even though the ITC clearly has many more neurons that behave this way than those in other regions do, such neurons may be found elsewhere in future experiments. Moreover, other brain regions may be responsible for any decision resulting from whatever stimulus reaches consciousness. Erik D. Lumer and his colleagues at University College London have studied that possibility using fMRI. They showed that in humans the temporal lobe is activated during the conscious experience of a stimulus, as we found in monkeys. But other regions, such as the parietal and the prefrontal cortical areas, are activated precisely at the time at which a subject reports that the stimulus changes.

Learning more about the locations of, and connections between, neurons that correlate with conscious experience will tell us more about how the brain generates awareness. But the findings to date already strongly suggest that visual awareness cannot be thought of as the end product of such a hierarchical series of processing stages. Instead it involves the entire visual pathway as well as the frontal parietal areas, which are involved in higher cognitive processing. The activity of a significant minority of neurons reflects what is consciously seen even in the lowest levels we looked at, V1 and V2; it is only the proportion of active neurons that increases at higher levels in the pathway.

Sees sunburst
Pulls left lever   **CORRECT=**   **JUICE REWARD**

Sees cowboy
Pulls right lever   **CORRECT=**   **JUICE REWARD**

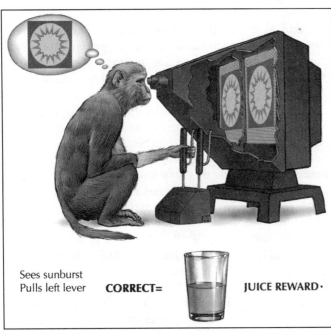

Sees sunburst
Pulls left lever   **CORRECT=**   **JUICE REWARD·**

Sees a jumble
but wants juice
Pulls any lever   **INCORRECT=**   **NO JUICE
REWARD**

MATT COLLINS

Currently it is not clear whether the activity of neurons in the very early areas is determined by their connections with other neurons in those areas or is the result of top-down, "feedback" connections emanating from the temporal or parietal lobes. Visual information flows from higher levels down to the lower ones as well as in the opposite direction. Theoretical studies indicate that systems with this kind of feedback can exhibit complicated patterns of behavior, including multiple stable states. Different stable states maintained by top-down feedback may correspond to different states of visual consciousness.

One important question is whether the activity of any of the neurons we have identified truly determine an animal's conscious perception. It is, after all, conceivable that these neurons are merely under the control of some other unknown part of the brain that actually determines conscious experience.

Elegant experiments conducted by William T. Newsome and his colleagues at Stanford University suggest that in area MT/V5, at least, neuronal activity can indeed determine directly what a monkey perceives. Newsome first identified neurons that selectively respond to a stimulus moving in a particular direction, then artificially activated them with small electric currents. The monkeys reported perceiving motion corresponding to the artificial activation even when stimuli were not moving in the direction indicated.

It will be interesting to see whether neurons of different types, in the ITC and possibly in lower levels, are also directly implicated in mediating consciousness. If they are, we would expect that stimulating or temporarily inactivating them would change an animal's reported perception during binocular rivalry.

A fuller account of visual awareness will also have to consider results from experiments on other cognitive processes, such as attention or what is termed working memory. Experiments by Robert Desimone and his colleagues at the National Institute of Mental Health reveal a remarkable resemblance between the competitive interactions observed during binocular rivalry and processes implicated in attention. Desimone and his colleagues train monkeys to report when they see stimuli for which they have been given cues in advance. Here, too, many neurons respond in a way that depends on what stimulus the animal expects to see or where it expects to see it. It is of obvious interest to know whether those neurons are the same ones as those firing only when a pattern reaches awareness during binocular rivalry.

The picture of the brain that starts to emerge from these studies is of a system whose processes create states of consciousness in response not only to sensory inputs but also to internal signals representing expectations based on past experiences. In principle, scientists should be able to trace the networks that support these interactions. The task is huge, but our success identifying neurons that reflect consciousness is a good start.

The Author

NIKOS K. LOGOTHETIS is director of the physiology of cognitive processes division of the Max Planck Institute for Biological Cybernetics in Tübingen, Germany. He received his Ph.D. in human neurobiology in 1984 from Ludwig-Maximillians University in Munich. In 1985 he moved to the brain and cognitive sciences department of the Massachusetts Institute of Technology, where he served as a postdoctoral fellow and research scientist. In 1990 he joined the faculty of the division of neuroscience at Baylor College of Medicine, where he conducted most of the research described in this article. He returned to Germany in 1997.

Further Reading

A VISION OF THE BRAIN. Semir Zeki. Blackwell Scientific Publications, 1993.

THE ASTONISHING HYPOTHESIS: THE SCIENTIFIC SEARCH FOR THE SOUL. Francis Crick. Scribner's, 1994.

EYE, BRAIN AND VISION. David H. Hubel. Scientific American Library, 1995.

THE VISUAL BRAIN IN ACTION. A. David Milner and Melvyn A. Goodale. Oxford University Press, 1996.

NOISE BUSTERS

TO DISSECT THE DIN THAT DAILY ASSAULTS OUR EARS,
RESEARCHERS FROM THE NOISE POLLUTION CLEARINGHOUSE
ARE TAKING TO THE STREETS

BY RICHARD & JOYCE WOLKOMIR

Secret laboratory of dr. decibel," reads the hand-lettered sign taped to Les Blomberg's office door at the Noise Pollution Clearinghouse, in Montpelier, Vermont. It was inspired by a Boston friend's telephone call, suggesting the organization create its own comic book superhero. College and high school interns put up the sign. Blomberg, the nonprofit organization's director, was inside his office at the time, oblivious to the tittering outside because he was fine-tuning sound levels on a CD recording he had made—ultra-large dump trucks, construction-site air compressors, jackhammers, that sort of thing. Blomberg's CDs go to noise-beset citizens so they can show officials their precise daily dose of acoustical irritant.

Combating noise is not the usual cartoon-hero derring-do. But in our society noise often is a protected monster. Regulations may be weak. Or noisemakers argue quieting down would be too costly. Sufferers desperately searching the Internet stumble upon the clearinghouse's site, www.nonoise.org. They call or write or e-mail—"I am writing to you at 2:30 A.M. because I was awakened by leaf blowers and I am so angry… " "I am dealing with a large lumber company which installed a new drying kiln a few months ago, and operates it 24 hours a day, 7 days a week. I live in a very rural area… " "Recently the level of airplane traffic over our home has increased to an intolerable level. I have become depressed… " "Now, the interstate has a constant roar that comes toward the school. We can't teach outside. The children seem to have trouble with attention. They also seem to be agitated all the time… " "Over the past four months our home has been assaulted by the throbbing bass of our downstairs neighbor's stereo. Asking, pleading, and mediation have not worked…"

The clearinghouse responds with data and noise-fighting information, such as how to approach officials, or how to organize a neighborhood. To the beleaguered, it seems as if a buff dude in blue tights flew in, red cape billowing. A typical reaction: "Just to know that someone has taken the time to do research such as this allows me to feel not so alone." So think of Les Blomberg as the brainy, physics-savvy, but vincible, protector of the noise oppressed. Think of him as that limited-budget battler of rogue sound waves, Dr. Decibel!

> Noise becomes really annoying at about the 55 to 65 decibel range. And every 10-decibel increase represents a doubling of the loudness.

Right now our superhero is standing at the corner of Lexington Avenue and 42nd Street, in Manhattan, aiming what looks like a TV remote control toward the Chrysler Building, more or less. It is smoggy and humid this afternoon, and wilted New Yorkers hurry by oblivious to Blomberg, although the sound meter he holds looks like, maybe, a detonator—hey, this is New York. And Blomberg, who is 39, his remaining dark-brown hair pulled back in a ponytail, wearing a pine-green shirt, khaki trousers and hiking boots, looks unthreatening. In fact, his trimmed beard and mustache frame an engaging grin that expresses the good-natured exuberance normally associated with, say, a Labrador retriever. He adjusts a knob as a corrections department bus with prisoners inside whooshes by, then peers appraisingly at a dial.

"OK, that was 78 decibels," he announces. Noise, most people find, becomes really annoying, he says, at about 55 to 65 decibels. Every 10-decibel increase represents a doubling of the loudness. So this Manhattan corner's loudness is four times the annoying level, a real pain in the tympanum.

Blomberg is counting decibels today in the city that is arguably our national noise-pollution capital. This corner's 78 decibels, for instance, makes it louder than most alarm clocks. But now a moving van's driver hits the brakes. Blomberg checks his meter: "That's over 90 decibels." It is like putting your ear next to an exceptionally loud vacuum cleaner. To be heard above the corner's engine whine and hissing air brakes and bicycle-tire hum and siren whoops, Blomberg finds he is compelled to raise his voice.

"We advise people every day, but usually from afar, so it's incredibly valuable to visit these people and experience their problems," he yells, somehow maintaining his benevolent grin. "Let's get on the subway downtown—I have to check on a new kind of noise pollution that we are calling Internet Buzz."

As the 7th Avenue Express rattles southward through its tunnel, Blomberg, hanging onto a metal strap, switches on his sound meter with his free hand. "It's 80 decibels, just riding along in here," he says. A passing train registers 85 decibels: sustained exposure at that level, he says, can induce hearing loss.

Blomberg can cite lots of unsettling noise data. According to the U.S. census, for instance, Americans' number one neighborhood complaint—above crime, traffic and poor public services—is noise. Every day more than 138 million Americans experience noise levels the U.S. Environmental Protection Agency (EPA) rates as annoying and disruptive. Among city dwelling Americans, 87 percent are exposed to noise so loud it has the potential to degrade hearing capacity over time. But you will not necessarily find peace in the suburbs or countryside either, not with the onslaught of leaf blowers, snow blowers, lawn mowers, chain saws, snowmobiles, powerboats and all-terrain vehicles. Because of airplane and helicopter overflights, the natural quiet is now preserved in only 7 percent of Arizona's Grand Canyon National Park and nowhere in Hawaii's Volcanoes National Park.

Meanwhile, researchers have demonstrated that noise can raise your blood pressure and change your blood chemistry. For instance, adrenaline levels can rise, indicating the imposition of stress. Noise is also the leading cause of hearing loss: in the United States, exposure to excessive noise has made some 10 million of us at least a little deaf. "Noise is unwanted sound," Blomberg points out. "And 'noise' comes from the Latin word for 'nausea.' "

Most sources of annoying noise are increasing. Blomberg cites recent U.S. Department of Transportation statistics. For instance, according to certain calculations, in 1997 personal automobile traffic was 360 percent of 1960 levels, and large truck traffic was 430 percent. Airliner travel in 1998 was 600 percent of 1960 levels, and air cargo was up a whopping 2,460 percent. Meanwhile, Blomberg says, we have new noise sources: "In 1960 there were no boom boxes, no boom cars, no leaf blowers, no jet skis, no car alarms and hardly any snowmobiles."

Vanished noise sources? "I can only think of the doorman's whistle," says Blomberg. America's revulsion with its own increasing racket, he says, led to his organization's founding in 1996, funded by such contributors as the Rockefeller Family Fund.

Blomberg exits the subway in lower Manhattan in his guise as Dr. Decibel, armed with a high-tech sound meter. "But I have to be Miss Manners too," he maintains. That is because he sees two underlying noise-pollution issues: "Sovereignty—who owns the air? And civility—how do we treat our neighbors?"

Internet Buzz straddles both issues. Blomberg strides along Hudson Street to a salmon-colored building. Last night he camped in an apartment facing this building to measure how much of its noise assaults neighbors. He also plotted strategy with neighborhood residents and their attorney, because this building emits a constant buzz.

"See, on the first and fourth floors, every window has been replaced by vents, all making noise," Blomberg says, aiming his sound meter. Inside the building, telecommunications multinationals and dot.coms have installed computers that control their operations. Each computer room requires a big cooling unit, which is blowing its exhaust—and its buzz—out the window. "It's 70 decibels here on the sidewalk, and that's how loud it is outside the apartments across the street, all day, all night," observes Blomberg. A normal home reading is about 25 decibels.

City ordinances are unclear. Do proscribed noise levels apply to individual cooling units? Or do they apply to the building's collective noise? Also, the banned decibel levels vary according to the sound's frequency. "People say, give me one number and tell me if it's a violation or not, but regulations often have variable numbers and different scales, and the complexity hinders enforcement," Blomberg notes. "Yet, if you had just one decibel level, you might have a buzz below that number, legal, but still unbearable."

Blomberg and his $10,000 noise meters are helping Hudson Street dwellers decide whom to file complaints against: Firms leasing space inside the building? Or the building's owners?

Next stop: the 7th Avenue and 14th Street apartment of author Tom Bernardin (*The Ellis Island Immigrant Cookbook*), founder of Friends Against Noisy New York (FANNY). Yesterday Blomberg affixed sound meters to the facade of Bernardin's building to record 24 hours of

New York noise. Now he peers at the digital readouts as Bernardin looks on. "The background here is 73.3 decibels," Blomberg says. That is about the level of a ringing telephone. Blomberg's meter has stored 24 hours of data in its built-in computer, both background noise and loud spikes. "Here's a spike of 104 decibels at 2:30 A.M., probably a siren or car alarm," Blomberg points out. "Here's one off my screen, louder than 100 decibels!"

Bernardin, who buys earplugs by the boxful, will present Blomberg's data to city officials. He wants to convince them to begin noise-cutting steps. For instance, the city could specify quieter buses. Blomberg notes that in Europe, trucks and buses can be only half as loud as vehicles conforming to U.S. regulations. Next on the agenda, he adds, should be noise limits for air conditioners. "If the background din dropped, police cruisers and fire trucks and ambulances wouldn't need such loud sirens," he says.

Bernardin, a former teacher who was a National Park Service guide at Ellis Island, where he relished the silence, gazes sadly out his windows at the Greenwich Village traffic roaring by. "This apartment has wraparound sound," he laments. In a guidebook, he finds a reference to an early 1900s socialite who founded the Society for the Suppression of Unnecessary Noise. "That was almost a century ago," he muses. "And the unnecessary noise is still unsuppressed."

Walking to a meeting, Blomberg and Bernardin spot a blue-suited executive clasping his hands over his ears. "Even in a wealthy neighborhood, we're creating acoustical slums," Blomberg says. Bernardin points out drivers operating remote car-door openers, making their cars toot. But here is a hitherto undiscovered noise source: a trailer truck offering curbside document shredding, accomplished via a churning and a thumping. "That's over 90 decibels," Blomberg announces. "It's louder than a… " But the churning drowns him out.

They arrive at the restaurant designated for the meeting Blomberg calls a New York Anti-Noise Summit. Economist Charles Komanoff, who coauthored a Noise Pollution Clearinghouse study on jet ski noise, reports he recently asked an audience: Noise pollution, or air pollution, from cars—if you could get rid of only one, which would it be? "A majority said noise," he says. "In my analyses, the costs from automobile air pollution are higher, but people are more bothered by noise from cars."

Also at the meeting is noise-consultant Arline Bronzaft, professor emerita of psychology at City University of New York and an adviser to the city's League of the Hard of Hearing. She authored a groundbreaking study on noise's impact on children's learning.

Bronzaft, appointed by the mayor's office to a committee on transit complaints, decided to test a public school next to the elevated train tracks at 212th Street and Broadway. "A train went by for 30 seconds every 45 minutes; the noise level in classrooms on that side of the building reached 89 decibels," Bronzaft recalls. By the sixth grade, students in these noisy classrooms, demographically identical to students on the school's opposite—quiet—side, lagged a year in reading ability. Bronzaft's report prompted the installation of noise-hushing rubber pads on tracks by the school and acoustical ceilings inside. Result: noise inside the affected classrooms was reduced by 6 to 8 decibels. "When we did the study again, to my great surprise and happiness, the children were all reading at the same level," reports Bronzaft. (Today noise levels at P. S. 98 again present problems: the trains, older by more than 20 years, have grown creakier, and noisier, over time.)

Two hot issues are on this meeting's agenda—Internet Buzz and proposed new federal airport noise policy. The discussion becomes—is it fair to say?—noisy.

A few hours later, en route to Grand Central Station and his train home, Les Blomberg stops for a soda. In mid-quaff, he says: "Make noise unto others as you would have others make noise unto you!"

Specialists who trek to remote sites to record phenomena such as birdcalls report that not even the North Pole or the Amazon is free of unnatural noise.

Even if the Noise Pollution Clearinghouse's three full-time staff members, and five part-time workers, and assorted interns, and all the noise-troubled people who call for help, actually wanted to move to a deserted area, they would be out of luck. Specialists who trek to remote sites to record birdcalls and other natural sounds report that not even the North Pole or Antarctica or the Amazon is now free of unnatural noise, such as the roar of airliners or the buzz of chain saws.

Les Blomberg, born in 1961, grew up in the suburbs of St. Paul, Minnesota, where his parents owned grocery stores. In high school, he recollects, he took "boom box speakers outside to entertain myself. I wasn't overly polite," he confesses. "I was a teenage boy, which shows there is hope, that people can learn."

He completed a degree in mathematics at the University of Minnesota and went on, graduating in 1993 from the University of Colorado with a master's degree in environmental ethics. In 1994 he and his partner, Brenda Hausauer, took on a joint assignment for the State of Vermont, writing a state energy plan. They were living in a downtown apartment in Vermont's tiny capital when Blomberg became a noise activist.

On many a morning at 4:00, down Blomberg's narrow lane, the town's solitary street sweeper roared. Blomberg campaigned to convince officials that a city of 8,000 did not need wee-hours downtown mechanized street sweeping. Marshaling volunteers, he proved brooms outperformed the machine. Finally—the clincher—he offered to record the downtown sweeper's noise and, at the appropriate hour, precisely reproduce it outside the officials' suburban homes.

News of Blomberg's work reached Harriet Barlow, director of the Blue Mountain Center, an artists' retreat in New York's Adirondack Mountains. She disliked noise. With a $50,000 grant, she started the Noise Pollution Clearinghouse. And she decided that Blomberg, trained in mathematics, physics and environmental philosophy, was just the fellow to head the new organization.

Dawn on Nantucket Island. Les Blomberg stands on a lawn, aiming his sound meter toward the Atlantic. He stands among gray saltbox cottages, some dating to the 1600s, buried in blue hydrangeas and yellow sunflowers, pink roses growing over their roofs. Nantucket is 16 miles long and about 6 miles wide, bigger than Manhattan. But its population is only 9,000, expanding to 60,000 in the summer. Noise? There is the ocean's rhythmic whoosh. Song sparrows. Goldfinches. Mourning doves. "OK," Blomberg says. "Here comes the first one."

At 6:03 A.M. an airplane flies over. "That's 58.4 decibels," Blomberg reports. At 6:07 A.M. another plane flies over, and another at 6:11 and again at 6:12, and at 6:16, 6:17, 6:18…

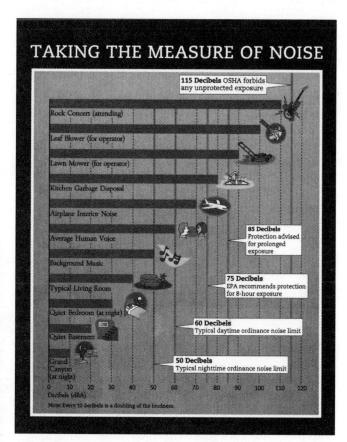

From the deep stillness of the Grand Canyon to the ear-assaulting din of a rock concert, a complex range of sounds underlies our everyday experience.

Later, Blomberg drives to the epidemic's source, the island's little airport, with his host, Wade Greene, formerly a *New York Times Magazine* editor, now an environmental

consultant to philanthropies. Greene also operates Wade Cottages, a vacation compound he created from his grandfather's summer home. He believes that airplane noise is going to hurt Nantucket tourism. Island stays are expensive. Vacationers value quiet. So do those who can afford a summer place here, where houses average $750,000 or more.

"Mainly we're dealing with two-engine Cessna 402 shuttle planes that fly to Hyannis, but there are private planes, too, and corporate jets," Greene is explaining. He points out a parked pickup's bumper sticker. "It Used To Be Nicer In Nantucket." Right now 26 airplanes are taxiing or waiting. Their noise is, literally, deafening. "You can get to this island only by ferry or by plane, and air traffic here is doubling every five years," says Greene. "This little airport is now the second busiest in all of New England, and sometimes the island of Nantucket has more flights coming and going than Boston's Logan Airport."

Blomberg is here to study Nantucket's noise dilemma. Greene contends many pilots ignore an agreement to fly one mile offshore. Blomberg shrugs. He calculates one mile is not enough: the planes should fly five to ten miles out.

Usually people affected by airliner noise have little political clout, Blomberg observes. "But here you can actually talk with aviation officials, and here the solution is simple—push the airplanes out to sea." He maintains: "If you can't do it on Nantucket, no place can do it."

Blomberg has also investigated the plight of the noise-beset residents of Loudon, New Hampshire. Today he sets up his equipment on a tripod in an immaculately kept gray ranch house's macadam driveway. "That's 78 decibels," he announces. Tom Early, the house's owner, a retired airline pilot, gray haired and gray mustached, looks on glumly. From his driveway you can see only his precisely trimmed lawn and white birches and one other home. But the roar from the New Hampshire International Speedway, a stock-car racetrack, seems to blot out everything. "That just hit 82 decibels," Les Blomberg says, eyeing his instruments. He notes that a typical city noise restriction for daytime is about 60 decibels, more than four times quieter. "At night they'll have rock bands," Tom Early says, shaking his head. "Louder than hell. And they have fireworks. And they fire off cannons."

Mufflers might be a solution. But Blomberg believes the real issue is that noise can increase the secretion of adrenaline in humans, perhaps because our distant ancestors associated loud sounds, like a lion's roar or a baby's scream, with danger. The greater the sound, the greater the adrenaline rush. Blomberg theorizes that racetracks prefer to be as loud as possible because it excites the fans. "That's why exercise classes crank up the decibels, and rock bands, and action movies," he observes. "In effect, noise becomes a drug they're pumping out and into you."

Later, Blomberg visits Daimon Meeh, 14, who shows him a letter he sent to New Hampshire's governor, along with a CD recording he made just outside his farmhouse of the racetrack's roar. "I don't remember a time when I didn't have to listen to the noise of New Hampshire International Speedway (NHIS) in Loudon," Daimon wrote, noting the track's growth: "As the noise of the racetrack grew increasingly louder, people in my town got more and more annoyed." He analyzed for the governor the noise's steady increase over the years and the economic effects. Despite his efforts, a solution has not yet been achieved.

Letters to the governor seem to be in the air. Stopping back at Tom Early's house, Blomberg finds the retired airline pilot irritated. "I'm just sending a letter off to the governor, and I told her I vote too," Early says. "Last night we were in here with the windows closed, trying to watch *My Fair Lady* on TV, and sometimes we couldn't hear it because the noise from the track was so loud."

When the Noise Pollution Clearinghouse's communications director, attorney Vicky Parra Tebbetts, checks the e-mail, mainly she finds messages like this: "Finally a thread of hope! Thank you so much for your help!" Or a New Jersey mayor seeks assistance deciding about 120-decibel alarms the volunteer fire company has set up in residential neighborhoods. From Japan comes a request for help—U.S. fighters flying low over Hiroshima suburbs. A musician writes from Hawaii: "It's the worst of situations—here in paradise! Five days a week we pay 2 gardeners to use an artillery of weed-wackers, lawn mowers and blowers, powered saws etc. to drive us nuts." From California, the Hollywood Heights Association seeks help dealing with news helicopters hovering overhead during movie premieres. And there is this: "We have been battling a neighborhood noise bully who has about 250 roosters on his 2 acre lot." As mottoes go, the watchword adopted by the clearinghouse seems benign: "Good Neighbors Keep their Noise To Themselves."

Richard and Joyce Wolkomir write from the peace and quiet of Vermont.

Originally from *Smithsonian*, March 2001, pp. 89-98. © 2001 by Smithsonian. Reprinted with permission of the authors, Richard and Joyce Wolkomir.

For Some, Pain Is
Orange

PERSONS WITH SYNESTHESIA
EXPERIENCE "EXTRA" SENSATIONS.
THE LETTER *T* MAY BE NAVY BLUE;
A SOUND CAN TASTE LIKE PICKLES

BY SUSAN HORNIK

WHEN NEW YORK ARTIST CAROL STEEN WAS 7 AND LEARNING to read, she exclaimed to a classmate as they walked home from school, " Isn't *A* the prettiest pink you've ever seen?" Her little chum responded with a withering look. "You're weird," she said.

Shabana Tajwar was a bit older when she discovered that her world was more colorful than most. In 1991, as a 20-year-old intern, she and a group of friends were trying to remember someone's name over lunch. "I knew the name was green. It started with *F* and *F* is green," says Tajwar, now an environmental engineer. "But when I mentioned that, everyone said, 'What are you talking about?'" She shrugs. "I was sort of in shock. I didn't know everyone didn't see things the same way."

While most of us experience the world through orderly, segregated senses, for some people two or more sensations are commingled. For Steen and Tajwar, hearing a name or seeing a letter or word in black and white causes an involuntary sensation of color. To Tajwar the letter *T* is always navy blue. "I don't see the actual letter as colored," she says. "I see the color flash, sort of in my mind's eye." Steen not only delights in pink *A*'s and gold

Y's, she experiences colored taste as well. "I see the most brilliant blue after I eat a salty pretzel," she says.

Others with synesthesia—from the Greek *syn*, meaning together, and *aisthesis*, perception—may feel or taste sounds, or hear or taste shapes. The chords of a strumming guitar may be a soft brushing sensation at the back of an ankle, a musical note may taste like pickles, a trumpet may sound "pointed," the taste of chicken may feel "round." A teenager once confessed that her boyfriend's kiss made her see "orange-sherbet foam."

Even more baffling to outsiders: while synesthetes' perceptions are consistent over time, they are not shared. Letters, for instance, don't evoke the same color for everyone. Steen jokes that her good friend and fellow synesthete Patricia Duffy is "great" but misguided. "She thinks *L* is pale yellow, not black with blue highlights," says Steen with a grin, as she pours a mug full of coffee in her downtown New York loft. Separately, over lunch in a sunny bistro, Duffy, a language instructor at the United Nations, confides, "Some of Carol's colors are so wrong!"

Even relatives who have synesthesia—it seems to run in families—see things differently. The Russian novelist Vladimir Nabokov tells in his memoirs about playing with a set of wooden blocks when he was 7 years old. He complained to his mother that the letters on the blocks weren't the right colors. She was sympathetic. She, too, objected to the shades—though she also disagreed with some of her son's color choices. According to one study, only one letter elicits consensus among a majority of synesthetes; apparently some 56 percent see *O* as a shade of white. For Nabokov, it radiated the hue of an "ivory-backed hand-mirror."

People with synesthesia have described their unusual perceptions to intrigued but baffled researchers for more than 200 years. At times they were viewed as mentally defective, at other times idealized as artistically gifted. Often, they weren't believed at all. Only in the past decade or so, using controlled studies, in-depth interviews and computer-aided visual tests, have scientists begun to identify and catalog the staggering variety of these automatically induced sensations. "We've gone to great lengths to identify the range of forms," says Peter Grossenbacher, a cognitive neuroscientist and one of the foremost U.S. researchers on synesthesia. "We understand it's a real experience. But we don't yet know how it comes to pass."

Already, scientists have discovered that synesthetes frequently have more than one form of the trait. Carol Steen's tall-windowed loft—part living space, part art studio—is jammed with her synesthesia-inspired paintings and sculptural models. Pulling letters painted on business-card-size pieces of paper off a shelf, she struggles to make clear the unique sensations that color her life and work. "It's like viewing the world in multimedia," she says. "I want to show other people what I'm seeing."

What Steen is seeing is not only color triggered by certain sounds, smells and flavors; when listening to music, she also sees shapes, which are reflected in her sculpture.

Steen also feels pain in color. When on vacation in British Columbia two years ago, she jumped down from a rock and tore a ligament. "All I saw was orange," she says. "It was like wearing orange sunglasses." In her paintings she depicts similar color sensations that she experiences during acupuncture. One abstract oil shows a green slash arcing through a field of red; in another a tiny red triangle drifts off into the distance on a sea of bright blue.

Researcher Peter Grossenbacher and a small cadre of scientists in this country, the United Kingdom, Canada, Germany and elsewhere are currently doing research with volunteers to try to figure out why Steen sees orange when the rest of us just ache. So far, they agree that synesthesia is more common in women than in men and is an international phenomenon. Grossenbacher primarily employs sophisticated screening and interviewing methods. Others, bolstered by dramatic advances in imaging techniques, are observing the neural activity of synesthetes and measuring the unique ways their brains respond to stimuli. In the process, they are shedding light on how we all perceive the world around us.

"It's the only way I know of perceiving," Steen points out. "If someone said they were going to take it away, it would be like saying they were going to cut off my leg." Although Steen delights in exploring her sensations, others remain ambivalent. When she was 20 and eating dinner with her family, Steen mentioned that the number 5 was yellow. "No," her father said. "It's yellow ocher." But after that evening, he refused to discuss it again.

Such embarrassment used to be the norm. In 1812, Dr. G. T. L. Sachs published the first scientific treatise on synesthesia. In it, he described how he and his sister experienced vivid color sensations when seeing, hearing or even thinking about various vowels, consonants, names and numbers. For the next 70 years, the only synesthetes to describe their symptoms publicly were doctors and researchers whose curiosity about their conditions outweighed their fear of being ridiculed or labeled insane.

Despite the obvious intelligence of the physician witnesses, most researchers viewed synesthesia as an illness. In 1864 Ernest Chabalier, a French doctor, described how a friend, who was also a physician, saw colors when he heard vowels, numbers, time periods and proper names. But Chabalier thought it significant that his friend had suffered hallucinations as a child. A decade later, when Dr. Jean Nussbaumer of Vienna vividly described his own and his brother's colored hearing, another Austrian physician suggested not too tactfully that the Nussbaumers were mentally unbalanced. Only in the late 1870s did George Henry Lewes offer a more sympathetic portrayal, comparing the twinned sensations of synesthetes to his own feeling of a chill in his legs when he witnessed an unpleasant sight.

Grossenbacher, who has studied synesthesia for the past seven years, says that for many of the dozens of people he and a team at the National Institutes of Health (NIH) have interviewed, "synesthesia doesn't present a problem, but in the back of their minds, some worry that they're mentally ill." In fact, synesthetes appear to be perfectly normal in every other way. Some even appear to have above average ability in recalling information, leading Grossenbacher and others to begin researching synesthesia's effect on memory.

Tajwar says synesthesia makes it easier for her to remember things like names. "When I meet someone, their name is a color, so I'll always associate that color with them," she says. (My nickname is Sue, which she says is "white"—primarily because the first letter, *S*, is white.) Michael Torke, a New York composer who associates colors with both letters and musical keys, also admits that synesthesia can serve as a memory aid.

In the 1980s Torke wrote a series of compositions inspired by synesthesia—including "Bright Blue Music," written in D major: "Green," written in E major; and "Ecstatic Orange," "Yellow Page," "Purple," "Rust" and others—all named for the shades Torke found himself "swimming in" when composing pieces in particular keys. The artist David Hockney has used synesthesia in his work as well—to paint the colors of music that he was listening to at the time. When designing sets for the Metropolitan Opera, he would listen to music and, inspired by the colors, paint the sets accordingly. "When it came time to paint the tree for Ravel," he told Richard Cytowic, a Washington, D.C. neurologist, "I put on the tree music for the opera, and it had a certain weight and color. The music would dictate the shape."

But for Torke, synesthesia became a mixed blessing. "The colors became all anyone wanted to talk or write about. I started to resent it."

Blame the cultural world's giddy love affair with "colored hearing" (and the notion that synesthetes are more artistically attuned), in part, on the French poet Arthur Rimbaud. In 1871 his sonnet "Voyelles" turned a medical curiosity and a seeming scientific rarity into an international cultural craze. "*A* black, *E* white, *I* red, *U* green, *O* blue…," read Rimbaud's much-debated verse. The idea of a melding of the senses fit perfectly with the Romantic view of the unity of man and nature. Overnight the fusion of color and sound showed up in Symbolist poetry, fin de siècle English literature, and French and Russian theater and music.

In his 1910 symphony Prometheus, Alexander Scriabin tried to meld music and color

American painter James McNeill Whistler said art should "appeal to the artistic sense of eye or ear." He titled the famous painting of his mother, *Arrangement in Black and Grey No. 1*, as though it were a musical composition. Russian abstract painter Wassily Kandinsky would later proclaim that for synesthetes, colors "call forth a vibration of the soul" like a violin at the touch of a bow.

In the decades surrounding the turn of the century, synesthetes came out of the closet and pseudo-synesthetes came out of the woodwork. Among the literati, having synesthesia became the yardstick for measuring an artist's genius. One enthusiast raved, "Color hearing marks for us a true progress in the perfection of our senses."

The fad reached a high-water mark of sorts with Russian composer Alexander Scriabin, a purported synesthete. In his 1910 symphony *Prometheus,* he ambitiously tried to meld music and color through the use of a mute "light organ" with which he intended to paint the concert hall with colored light in the form of beams, clouds and other shapes. It proved technically impossible at the time. When finally attempted at Carnegie Hall on March 20, 1915, only "a white sheet at the back of the platform… was illuminated by streaks and spots of light of various

colors," according to a critic who was dismissive of any meaningful connection between the colors and the music.

Regardless, the faddishness of synesthesia had already fostered a flurry of scientific interest—not lest because doctors suddenly had hundreds of self-confessed synesthetes willing to be interviewed. In 1893 some 26 articles were published on the phenomenon. But researchers had no way to differentiate between pretenders and true synesthetes. How could they identify—never mind study—a seemingly subjective experience? Largely abandoned by scientists, synesthesia increasingly became identified with decadent swooning artists, turbaned Spiritualists and, more recently, with LSD-enhanced psychedelic love-ins.

Battling those stereotypes, researchers have spent the past decade or so gathering tantalizing clues about the cluster of traits and brain anomalies that make up synesthesia. Thanks to their efforts, few now doubt that the phenomenon exists. "It's gone from complete disbelief to less of a disbelief," says Richard Cytowic, whose research and popular book, *The Man Who Tasted Shapes,* are credited with helping spark the current renewed interest in synesthesia. "People are aware now of the amazing things happening inside the brain, so this is less strange."

Carol Steen can remember the precise hour—one o'clock on August 31, 1993—when she heard Cytowic talking on National Public Radio about synesthesia as a real condition. "I burst into tears," Steen says. "I was no longer alone." She immediately got in touch with him. "I had so many questions. In a 20-minute phone call, I barely let him get a whole sentence out," says Steen (who has talked with Cytowic many times since). "That day changed my life."

On a steamy August afternoon at the NIH campus in Bethesda, Maryland, Peter Grossenbacher is drawing a web of circles and lines on a blackboard. There are several tentative theories about why synesthesia happens: one suggests that all infants may have it until about 6 months, but normally, as their brains develop and multisensory linkages die, their responses become segregated.

Grossenbacher offers a slightly different view. In all brains, he says, input goes from single-sense modules (he chalks in little circles representing hearing and sight on a blackboard) along a pathway into a multisensory region (a large circle that he draws with a flourish). There are also pathways leading back again, but for most of us those backward routes are inhibited. Grossenbacher thinks synesthetes may have an unusually strong feedback mechanism. Hallucinogenic drugs can produce synesthesia artificially, suggesting, in Grossenbacher's opinion, that we all have the feedback connections that make synesthesia possible. "The connections are normal," he conjectures. "They're just abnormal in the way they're used."

"We know synesthesia does happen," Grossenbacher says, "but scientists can't study the phenomenon without having ways of determining whether a particular person actually experiences it." Using a specially designed computer program with extremely specific color choice, the NIH team can precisely test the consistency of a synesthete's selections over time. Sitting at a computer in a white-walled windowless booth, Grossenbacher's colleague Carol Crane, a psychologist and synesthete, is staring at a color wheel on the screen and painstakingly selecting the precise shade and brightness of blue to match her number 2. "The first time I did this it was agonizing trying to find the exact color," says Crane. "I was so afraid there wouldn't be a color to match."

This intensity of association of a letter or word with a particular shade is a hallmark of "colored-language" synesthesia. "It's not enough to say it's orange," says Pat Duffy of her tangerine *A*. Her *G* is not just black, but black with glints of gold, and *Z* is a brownish black with bubbles. The initial letter of a word usually gives a cast to the entire word—but there are glints of the other letters. "It's like looking at a vase from a distance and thinking it's one color," says Duffy, "but when you're close-up you see it's really multicolored."

Reading a page of print, explains Carol Steen, can be like looking at a mosaic. "I 'see' the printed letter in black, or whatever color it's printed in," she says. "But I also see an overlay of my colors for those letters." Spoken words have the same colors as the words in print, but for some, the tone of a person's voice can add its own hues to the mix.

Accompanying the high degree of exactness is the consistency of the color choice over time. Dr. Simon Baron-Cohen, a psychologist at Cambridge University and the leading British researcher, conducted a landmark study in 1993 that convinced many skeptics of synesthesia's existence. He asked a group of colored-language synesthetes, and a control group, to describe the color or shape elicited by a list of 100 spoken words. Even a year and a half later, synesthetes gave the same answers 92 percent of the time. A week after the initial test, the group of non-synesthetes had an accuracy rate of only 37 percent.

Sitting in a noisy café in the Chelsea section of New York City, Pat Duffy, a petite and graceful 48-year-old, bristles at the thought of one of her numbers changing color. "It never changes," she insists, as she spears a lettuce leaf. "It can't. Can the shape of *V* change?"

Using Positron Emission Tomography (a PET scan), which shows patterns of cerebral blood flow and thus indicates neural activity, Baron-Cohen and his colleagues scanned the brains of synesthetes who link colors to spoken words. They also tested a control group. When the blindfolded volunteers listened to a tape of recorded words, they all showed activity in the language areas of their brains. But only in synesthetes did blood flow soar in areas of the visual cortex associated with such tasks as sorting images based on color. The implication is that "visual" information was being processed in the brains of synesthetes, even though they hadn't seen anything. Recently, those results were confirmed using functional Magnetic Resonance Imaging (fMRI), a newer technique for detecting changes in cerebral blood flow.

Many colored-language synesthetes share yet another "visual" aberration—a very concrete perception of time, numbers and the alphabet. Duffy has what she calls an "internal calendar," or "time landscape." When she wakes up in the morning thinking about the day or week ahead, she automatically sees a pathway of colored rectangles. Tuesday is dark blue. Her alphabet is a string of letters gradually sloping uphill. "I glide up the alphabet trail till I get the letter I need," she explains. Torke insists, "Numbers are like mountain peaks and valleys. At 20, there's a sharp turn to the right. At 100, they turn left."

A recent Canadian study of a synesthete doing arithmetic suggests how innate and spontaneous these traits are. Not just the sight of a number but the mere concept of a number can trigger color. When the subject was shown a math problem such as 5 + 2 =, followed by a patch of yellow (the color that corresponds to her number 7), she named the color and number faster than the control subjects. But when she was shown the "wrong" color as an answer, she took significantly longer than the control group to respond.

Depending on the circumstance, her color cue could be an aid or a hindrance. Such a strong association between colors and letters or numbers can easily cause confusion. Once when navigating Prague's subway system, Duffy saw that the *A* line was green and the *B* line yellow but found herself getting on the wrong line because they were nearly the reverse of her colors. "If the color coding doesn't match mine, it's a problem," she says. Admits Tajwar, "Because a number 2 and letter *S* are similar whites, I sometimes write 2 instead by *S* by mistake."

When Carol Steen stubbed her toe recently and let out a yelp, her husband dashed out of the bedroom to see what was wrong. It took a few moments for her to explain what had happened. "The first word out of my mouth was 'orange!' " she says, "then I managed to tell him I'd hurt my toe."

At times, all the additional stimuli can be distracting. Carol Steen laughs that she gets easily sidetracked when looking up a word in the dictionary. "I end up looking at all the colors," she says. Her friend Pat Duffy sometimes feels slightly overloaded. Duffy, who is currently working on a book about synesthesia, says: "I can't listen to music when I'm writing."

Despite the few negatives, synesthesia more often provides unequivocal pleasure. "It makes life more rich," says Michael Torke. An elderly English synesthete, who describes the word "emperor" as gray with silvery shimmers, says, "It enhances my ability to enjoy literature. I enjoy not only the sense of the word but the appearance."

For all the advances in understanding the condition, many fundamental questions remain. Even the number of synesthetes is under debate. Richard Cytowic once suggested that 10 people in a million have synesthesia. According to studies by Britain's Baron-Cohen, it's about 1 person in 2,000. But Grossenbacher suspects that the trait is more common—with maybe 1 person in 300 having had some form of synesthetic experience. On average, studies in England have shown about six females to every male. "That's not inconsistent with our findings," says Grossenbacher, who is continuing his NIH research with Carol Crane, in addition to other projects, as he takes up a new post at Naropa University in Boulder, Colorado.

Because the trait appears to run in families, researchers are now examining synesthetic family members and searching for a genetic factor. Their work may provide a missing piece of the puzzle. As Grossenbacher puts it, "Why does it happen in those brains and not others?"

When Michael Torke was in the second grade the teacher asked his class to imagine a useful machine and write a short story about it. Excited, he described a device that would show how different people experience similar sensations, like the color yellow. His parents and teacher were unenthusiastic. "They said, 'Why do you need it at all? Everyone experiences sensations the same,'" he remembers. "I really wanted to know how someone else tasted ice cream." As research into synesthesia continues, scientists are optimistic they can gain insight into human consciousness and perception in general. Their discoveries so far are a striking reminder that little Michael was right: reality isn't the same for everyone.

Susan Hornik last wrote about the barges that still ply the canals of Great Britain.

Originally from *Smithsonian*, February 2001, pp. 48-56. © 2001 by Smithsonian. Reprinted with permission of the author, Susan Hornik, a senior editor of Time Asia magazine.

dreamspeak

Dreams are a theater of the emotions,
where we play out the day's dramas that were left "to be continued."

By Milton Kramer, M.D.

We all go to bed with the problems of the day still on our minds. Unfortunately, a day is not like a play, which gets resolved by the time the final curtain falls. But dreams, with their colorful characters and settings, can play out that final scene while we sleep, processing the emotions we encounter in our waking lives.

Forty years of research on dreams suggests that they are not just the random firings of our brains. Neither are they highly symbolic visions that should chart the course of our lives. But dreams do, in fact, have meaning. And our research shows that the nature of that meaning helps determine our mood the next day. That, in turn, determines how we function and what we can accomplish. Quite simply, the dreams we have at night set the stage for our actions the following day, priming us to either rise and shine and conquer the world, or crawl back under the covers and duck the challenges that lie ahead.

Research has shown us that dreams are not just the machinations of the unconscious on random play.

For 13 nights, we monitored the dreams of Linda, 24, a volunteer, in our sleep laboratory. Whenever she was in rapid eye movement (REM) sleep—with her eyes darting from side to side, her brain waves speeded up and her pulse, breathing and blood pressure fluctuating—she was awakened and asked to report any dreams she had experienced. One night, she reported the following series of dreams.

1) "This little girl was asleep. She was being real cute, prolonging things for money or to stay in the hospital longer."

2) "I passed Frank's wife in the car. She saw me come…. She pulled away. I got kind of mad. I decided it didn't make any difference."

3) "I was playing tennis. I hit it back real hard. We won the game."

4) "A patient didn't need the doctor after all. She started out thinking she needed a doctor but she didn't. She had a big bandage on her stomach."

5) "Doctor was not able to treat the patient. He was not properly licensed. Patient is planning to use surgery against the doctor."

Although she had hit the sack feeling sleepy, a bit foggy, a little unhappy, and annoyed (she had mistakenly assumed the experiment was for one night and that she would be paid), Linda slept for her usual seven-and-a-half-hours and awakened refreshed, alert, happier and no longer irritable, ready to engage the day.

Was the change in Linda's mood a consequence of what went on during her sleep? My colleagues and I offer a resounding yes. Our work has led us to develop the Selective Mood Regulatory Theory of Dreams and Sleep. It holds that for Linda, as well as for everyone else, feeling better upon waking is a result of both getting uninterrupted sleep for an adequate length of time and of experiencing a series of otherwise unremembered dreams that engage disturbing feelings. (In our testing, the periodic awakenings were brief enough and the subjects young enough that sleep was not effectively interrupted.)

Linda's dreams were of a progressive nature. In them, she went from a clingy little girl to an assertive woman in charge of her life. It started with a dependent longing to be cared for by the doctor (father figure). This desire stirred the fear of being rejected by a married woman (mother figure). The tension between the desire to be cared for and the fear of rejection was resolved in the third dream, in which she had a victory with a partner of her own. In the fourth dream, she tried to reject the desire to be cared for, but the need for care still existed (the bandage). In the last dream, she asserted a more vigorous rejection of the doctor, serving to deny her need and the doctor's ability to meet that need.

We all have multiple dreams across the night, but not all of them succeed at untying our emotional knots. After examining a large number of dream series, my colleagues and I have discovered two modes of dream processing, two ways of responding to our unresolved problems. One mode, which we call a progressive sequence, resolves emotional problems by working through them step by step, and by comparing them to previous challenges that at some point or another we met successfully. The other, called a repetitive sequence, fails to resolve emotional problems but simply repeats them metaphorically over and over during the night's dreaming without charting any progress. With a repetitive sequence of dreams, we can awaken in a worse mood than when we went to bed.

dreams of glory

Western culture has privatized our dreams, regarding them solely as products of our innermost life. But certain dreams take us well beyond ourselves, tearing down the gated communities of our psyche.

By Marc Ian Barasch

There are dreams and there are *dreams*. Most of us have had—or will have—at least one dream that stops us in our tracks, when the evanescent wisps of the night gather the force of a Kansas tornado barreling straight for Oz. Such dreams are more than emotional coffee grounds and crumpled up impulses toward sex and violence that the waking mind nightly ditches down some inner disposal. Such dreams tell us that we are not who we think we are. They reveal dimensions beyond the everyday. People the world over have described such experiences. But we in the West have had only a sketchy understanding of what I call Healing Dreams—ones which, if we heed them, can guide us toward greater wholeness and have the power to transform our lives.

It has been standing policy in psychology that dreams are not meant to be enacted on the social stage; they are treated as personal creations that speak to the dreamer alone. But Healing Dreams chafe at such boundaries. They convey in symbolic terms surprisingly accurate images of disease and healing. They are also well-informed about our intimate relationships. But what is more, they are shrewd observers of our wider social backdrop. They are remarkably attuned to the clamor of community, to the nuances of the body politic, even to the fate of the earth. A Healing Dream wants to wriggle free of our solitary nets and head into open water, toward communion with the greater conclave of souls.

This may be a little frightening. Dreams are often socially transgressive. They champion the rude, lewd and wholly unacceptable.

People who act out their dreams on the social stage can be dangerous, becoming prey to delusions, dragging others along with them. When Julius Caesar dreamed he was sleeping with his mother, his royal dream interpreter told him he would soon possess Rome, the mother city. Caesar duly marched southward to take the capital. Would he and the world have been better off if, rather than setting out on the road to conquest, he had brought his dream to a therapist to work through his Oedipus complex?

In dreamwork, psychologists wisely counsel that we "keep the lid on the pot"; "withdraw the projections" back into the inner world. Our tradition of "psychologizing" the dream rather than, as in some cultures, acting upon it, is no small cultural achievement. But has Western psychology been too eager to bottle up the dream in the consulting room, forbidding it a wider life? Healing Dreams often speak to collective issues. They crave the give-and-take between the inner and outer worlds.

They confront us with our own unmet social potential, calling upon us each to know ourselves as part of the whole.

In *The Forgotton Language*, the neo-Freudian analyst Erich Fromm writes that in dreams, "we are con-

cerned exclusively with ourselves… in which 'I am' is the only system to which thoughts and feelings refer." Yet the privatization of the dream remains a peculiarly Western practice. Dreams in many cultures—the Plains Indians, for example—are a key component of social problem-solving, with vital public and even political implications.

The Zuni Indians of New Mexico have a custom of making public their "bad" dreams ("good" dreams, however, are sometimes withheld even from close relatives). Among the Quiche of Guatemala, all dreams, even small fragments, are shared immediately with family and tribe. An Australian aborigine told me, "We tell our dreams to the group because different people have different gifts and might help understand it. We have a saying, 'Share it out before the next sunrise.'" It sounded to me like the informal dream-sharing groups that have sprung up in Western societies over the past several decades—until, that is, he added a comment I found particularly intriguing: "We often meet each other while we're sleeping."

One society which reportedly followed a dream-sharing regimen was the Temiar Senoi, a jungle tribe of 10,000 living in the Cameron Highlands of Malaysia. Researcher Kilton Stewart reported in 1954 that if, for example, a child dreamed he had been attacked by a friend, his father would advise him to tell his friend about it. Then the friend would be advised by his father to give the dreamer a present and go out of his way to be friendly to him, in case he had offended the dreamer without wishing to.

"Thus," said Stewart, "the aggression building up around the image of the friend in the dreamer's mind thereby became the basis of a friendly exchange." Later in the day, dreams would be discussed by the entire community, and the messages and insights they contained would become part of the ritual and behavior of waking life.

Whether Stewart's Rousseauian portrait can be taken at face value or was a confabulation, remains an open question. Yet decades of research have revealed that tribal cultures the world over give dreams a central role in their collective lives. Barbara Tedlock reports that dreams are of such integral importance to Mexico's Quiche Maya that one out of four are initiated as "day-keepers," their term for dream interpreters. And the tales of the Temiar Senoi, whether apocryphal or historical, have been an inspiration to those seeking to bring dreams into the realm of social discourse.

One such person is the Unitarian minister Jeremy Taylor, who began running dream groups while performing civilian alternative service during the Vietnam War as a conscientious objector. He was assigned to do community organizing in Emeryville, California, an "all-black, working- and underclass" community. Tensions between blacks and whites in the group ran high, and meetings often degenerated into name-calling sessions.

One day Taylor suggested that they stop talking about waking life and instead start sharing their dreams. Many confessed they were having "nasty, racist dreams… of being attacked and menaced by sinister, hostile and dangerous people of other races." Though he feared such dreams could be like pouring gasoline on the fire, soon a more open form of dialogue began to emerge. It became clear to everyone, he says, that the "nasty" dream characters were unintegrated, undeveloped aspects of their own personalities, denied and projected onto others. They realized, writes Taylor, that "these ugly, scary, dark, powerful, sexy, violent, irresponsible, dangerous dream figures are vitally alive parts of my own authentic being." Gradually, he reports, "repressions were released, projections withdrawn.…"

He notes that cynicism, too, started to evaporate: "Authentic personal likes and dislikes began to replace ritual 'politeness,' blundering patronizing comments and repressed fear," Taylor writes. "The energy that had previously been squandered counterproductively in maintaining the repression and projection suddenly came welling up… as spontaneous surges of vitality and well-being… creative possibility and enthusiasm." The group dreamwork contributed to a style of interracial, grass-roots political organizing which eventually helped elect the first black public officials in what had been called "the most corrupt community in California."

The dreamer may be dismayed to find himself face to face with, even in thrall to, denizens of circles and rungs of society he in waking life tries to avoid. Dreams are the great leveler. But it is hard to avoid the fact—indeed, it is a little mortifying—that these images come close to cartoonish stereotypes. Even for those of us who pride ourselves on having a social conscience, our prejudices against the "other" have deep psychic roots. Such broad-stroke dream images function as emblems for what is ignored, repressed and denied—not just in my psyche, but in society at large.

Such images serve to undermine the ego's view of status and social position, its preposterous belief that we're not all in this together, that some of us are "above" others, that we can really wall ourselves off from our neighbors. The psyche has no such gated communities.

Though most of us are only too glad to see the upside-down world of the dream dissipate in the morning sun, these images are a potential source of social healing, telling us we cannot remain comfortably distanced from others' suffering. In our prejudices, fears and abdications of human connection, it is ourselves we are rejecting—the tender, wounded parts that contain our greatest wealth of soul.

Reprinted from Healing Dreams: Exploring the Dreams That Can Transform Your Life *by Marc Ian Barasch (Riverhead Books, Penguin Putnam Inc.). Copyright October 2000.*

If Linda had been more on edge, or if her problem had not been well-handled in the past, she might have experienced a repetitive sequence, the dream equivalent of just continuing to worry about a problem and not resolving it. On another night in the laboratory, she did have one such dream sequence:

1) "Somebody was lost. It was a dog and they were trying to find out where it lived. A little kid or somebody couldn't tell where he lives. It wasn't my dog though. I wasn't lost. The person who was lost was fumbling around leading everybody else around because he didn't know what he was doing. Somehow, we had phone numbers and we were trying to find the right one. It was supposed to be the little boy who was lost."

The individuals in the dream are unimportant. It is the roles they represent that carry meaning.

---

2) "They filled up the car. There wasn't enough room, unless I went back with the people we went back with before. I could go back with someone else. The place we were going was an orphanage someplace, some house, a place like that."

3) "I was dreaming about visiting. I think it was some EEG laboratory or something like that where the mothers could leave their children and go shopping. I doubt whether they could, though; there wouldn't be enough room for all these people."

In the dreams of this night, Linda illustrated a fear of being abandoned and an uncertainty as to whether her efforts to reconnect would work—calling on the telephone, riding in a car, or being picked up. It was no wonder she awakened disgruntled the following morning, having failed to engage her issues metaphorically during the night.

What determines whether we will have a helpful or unhelpful sequence of dreams? It depends on two factors: whether there is in our emotional arsenal a solution to the kind of problem at hand, and, whether we happen to be up to the task. Just as some days we are more productive than others, seemingly without rhyme or reason, so some of our dream experiences are more useful than others in solving life's quandaries.

Research has shown us that dreams are not just the machinations of the unconscious on random play. They have order, and they reflect important psychological aspects of our lives and personalities. When we examined the dream reports from a representative sample of people from Cincinnati, we found that there were similarities among the dreams of distinct groups—men and women, young and old, blacks and whites, married and single people, and between those of lower and middle social classes. If dreams were random, we would not have found any similarities.

We also have shown that dreams vary from person to person—they are individualized, like fingerprints—as well as from day to day, reinforcing the idea that the events of each day play out in the night's dreams.

These psychological regularities prove that the dream experience has order, and as we have seen in the laboratory, order paves the way for meaning. The nature of that meaning—how Linda interacted with Frank's wife, for example, and whether the outcome was favorable—can change our mood for better or worse from night to morning.

Changes in mood across the night turn out to be related to the people and activities that populate subjects' dreams. The production of a happy mood is particularly related to the types of people who appear in the intervening dreams.

In order to study the relationship between mood change and a night's dreams, we recruited 20 volunteers, both men and women, to sleep for 20 consecutive nights in the sleep laboratory. We had them rate their mood before and after going to sleep in terms of how friendly, aggressive, happy, clear-thinking, sleepy and anxious they felt. During the night, we awakened them at the end of each REM period and had them report their dreams. We found that their mood changed across the night along with changes in their dream content. And that as in Linda's case, the key to those mood changes was a matter of who starred in the dream and what scenes they acted out.

It is important to note that the specific individuals in the dream are unimportant. It is the roles they represent that carry the meaning. In Linda's dream, for example, Frank's wife was merely playing the role of wife, any wife. Rather than Jungian archetypes, the characters in our dreams—an older man, a female peer—are the vehicle for helping us deal with a central issue. They are actors in the theater of our unconscious, playing out the day's emotional dramas that have been left "to be continued."

Freud, a careful and astute observer of the manifestations of a variety of behavioral states, including sleep and depression, claimed that dreams are the guardians of sleep continuity. Since sleep can potentially be interrupted by emotional surges—from the day's unresolved issues bubbling up to the surface—the function of dreaming, Freud has suggested, is to contain or "diffuse" these emotional surges, which biological studies have confirmed exist.

We need sleep to be continuous if we are to improve our mood over the course of the night. In our experiments, we found a decrease in the capacity to contain the emotional surge among patients having nightmares. In other words, nightmares occur when dreams fail to blunt the body's emotional response, whereas successful dreaming controls and suppresses the feeling in dreams and protects the continuity of sleep.

REM-stage sleep, when the body undergoes changes in breathing, heart rate and blood pressure, presents the greatest risk for waking up. REM sleep is distributed during the night, with more in the second half, in such a way that as the likelihood of awakening increases, so increases the likelihood of the occurrence of REM sleep—and its protective dreams. Patients who report loss of dreaming after a brain injury experience poorer sleep than those who continue dreaming.

In another study—on the relationship between mood change and the physiology of sleep—we ruled out the possibility that the mood change was the result of other factors: the amount of sleep a person got during the night, the amount of REM sleep a person got during the night, or the mere passage of eight hours. We did this by depriving a group of individuals of sleep and seeing how their mood changed compared to those who had slept well. We found that, the following day, the sleep-deprived felt mentally foggy, more groggy and more aggressive—physiological conditions that sleep would have improved. Most importantly, they were also less happy, because they did not experience dreams, which would have regulated their mood. This mood alteration is one that anyone who has stayed up studying, working or partying knows well. (Interestingly, the group did feel more friendly, however, having spent the previous eight hours in a group, rather than alone.)

Although it has been a bone of contention among scientists, we believe our research shows that the change in the happy mood during the night is related to dream content and not just the fact of sleep.

Whether or not we are happy is not just a touchy-feely, quality-of-life issue. Employers have a tendency to say, "You may feel good but it's not going to produce more Nike sneakers or design a better building," but we believe it will. How we feel influences how well we function in waking life. Happiness affects performance.

Fortunately, most dream series are of the progressive type, repairing our mood from bedtime to morning. In our studies, such decreases in mood intensity occurred on about 60% of the 1,000 nights we studied. It's as if an emotional thermostat kicks in during the night to warm the mood that may have chilled during the day.

Our waking and dreaming lives have a great deal in common. With whom we spend the night and how well things work, awake or asleep, largely determine our happiness.

Milton Kramer, M.D., is Clinical Professor of Psychiatry at New York University School of Medicine and Director of their Sleep Consultation Service.

UNIT 4

Learning and Remembering

Unit Selections

Key Points to Consider

- What is learning? What is memory? How are the two linked? Are they necessarily always linked to each other?

- What are learning styles? Can you provide a concrete example of a learning style? Why are learning styles important? Does everyone have the same learning style? Should teachers try to match each child's style to the materials or to the teaching method? What does research suggest about the success of matching?

- What is a reward? What is punishment? Why is it better to reward than punish behaviors? How and when should rewards be utilized by parents? What are the downsides of using rewards?

- What is repression? What is the unconscious? Are there memories that we want to forget? Why? Which types of memories? Is there any evidence for the existence of repression and of the unconscious?

- Why is memory important? What is forgetting? Why do psychologists want to know about mechanisms that underlie learning and remembering? To what use can we put this information? Why do we forget? Are there methods we can use that can improve memory? What are they and can you give an example of each? What types of memory lapses are normal? What memory lapses signal problems? What are the seven sins of memory? Can you provide an example of each? What role does biology play in remembering, if any?

 **Links: www.dushkin.com/online/**
These sites are annotated in the World Wide Web pages.

The Opportunity of Adolescence
http://www.winternet.com/~webpage/adolescencepaper.html
Project Zero
http://pzweb.harvard.edu

Do you remember your first week of classes at college? There were so many new buildings and so many people's names to remember. And you had to recall accurately where all your classes were as well as your professors' names. Just remembering your class schedule was problematic enough. For those of you who lived in residence halls, the difficulties multiplied. You had to remember where your residence was, recall the names of individuals living on your floor, and learn how to navigate from your room to other places on campus, such as the dining halls and library. Then came examination time. Did you ever think you would survive college exams? The material in terms of difficulty level and amount was perhaps more than you thought you could manage.

What a stressful time you experienced when you first came to campus! Much of what created the stress was the strain on your learning and memory systems, two complicated processes. Indeed, most of you survived just fine and with your memories, learning strategies, and mental health intact.

The processes you depended on when beginning college were learning and memory, two of the oldest processes studied by psychologists. Today, with their sophisticated experimental techniques, psychologists have detected several types of memory processes and have discovered what makes learning more complete so that subsequent memory is more accurate. We also discovered that humans aren't the only organisms capable of these processes; all types of animals can learn, even an organism as simple as an earthworm or an amoeba.

Psychologists know, too, that rote learning and practice are not the only forms of learning. For instance, at this point in time in your introductory psychology class, you might be studying operant and classical conditioning, two very simple but nonetheless important forms of learning of which both humans and simple organisms are capable. Both types of conditioning can occur without our awareness or active participation in them. The

articles in this unit examine the processes of learning and remembering (or its reciprocal, forgetting) in some detail.

In "Memory and Learning," author Ruth Palombo Weiss reviews both processes and demonstrates their relationship to each other. She provides a good overview as background for the next articles as well as providing tips for improving each. The next two articles in this unit pertain to learning; the remaining articles relate to memory.

The second article examines learning styles, a subject that has long interested psychologists. Teachers today are often told that they should discover a child's learning style and then match teaching methods to it. In "Different Strokes for Different Folks: A Critique of Learning Styles," Steven Stahl examines this recommendation.

In "Regarding Rewards: Should You Be a Gold-Sticker Sticker?" learning is again examined. However, one simple form of learning, behavior modification, is emphasized. The author discusses the ramifications (such as bribery and manipulation) of the use of rewards by parents and concludes that this might not always be the best tactic for developing cooperative, well-behaved children. If rewards are to be used, then the author provides pointers as to how best to dispense them.

We next turn our attention to memory, because once something is learned, it needs to be remembered to be useful. There are certain types of memories we are motivated to forget, as in repressed memories. Bruce Bower explores Freud's notions of the unconscious and repressed memories. Modern scientists are indeed finding evidence for these two concepts.

The last article in this unit also pertains to memory. In "The Seven Sins of Memory," Daniel Schacter discusses common memory problems and what causes them. He also elucidates several memory techniques from which we can all benefit, even if we don't have serious memory disorders such as Alzheimer's disease.

Memory and Learning

So much learning, so little memory.

By Ruth Palombo Weiss

We take our memory for granted—until we can't recall someone's name, a word, or where we put our keys. Then we have a moment of panic: Are we losing our memory, or our mind?

Memory is essential for going about the daily business of our lives. We need memory for everything we do: perceiving the world, synethesizing and analyzing information, and applying knowledge to new situations. In fact, learning is the making of memory, which is laid down in our brains in chemical form. Chemical changes are created at the neuron level; without them, there's no substance for our minds to work with.

According to the current model of memory, input from our senses via the environment is processed through our perceptual memory in fractions of a second. If deemed important enough, either by one's unconscious or conscious mind, the input is put into the short-term memory. From there, it's either discarded or planted in the long-term memory.

Eric Jensen, educator and author of *Teaching With the Brain in Mind*, notes that "learning and memory are two sides of a coin. You can't talk about one without the other." He calls learning that lasts (information stored in our long-term memory) "long-term potentiation." When LTP occurs, "a cell is electrically stimulated over and over so that it excites a nearby cell. If a weaker stimulus is then applied to the neighboring cell a short time later, the cell's ability to get excited is enhanced."

Ken Kosik, professor of neurology at the Harvard Medical School and a co-founder of the Brigham and Women's Hospital Memory and Disorders Clinic, explains that our brain changes with learning in functional ways. When we learn something that stays with us for any length of time, it goes from the short-term into our medium- or long-term memory. When that occurs, certain genes in the brain turn on. When they turn on, new proteins are made and the connections between the axons and dendrites increase in complexity. In other words, new memories create new interconnecting pathways between neurons.

As we learn something new, each chemical message is laid down as a chain of neurons called a neural network. Those connections become stronger the more often our brains access the network. Synapses, or spaces between the neurons, also become stronger, says educator Marilee Sprenger in her book, *The Brain in Action*. She compares the process to creating a path in the woods: "The first time you create a path, it is rough and overgrown. The next time you use it, it's easier to travel because you have previously walked over the weeds and moved the obstacles. Each time thereafter, it gets smoother and smoother. In a similar fashion, the neural networks get more efficient, and messages travel more swiftly."

Neuroscientist Joseph LeDoux, author of *The Emotional Brain,* says that what we are conscious of at any given moment is what's in our short-term memory—especially our working memory, a special kind of short-term memory. Furthermore, only information that's registered in a person's short-term memory can eventually go into the long-term memory.

Jeb Schenck compares the short-term memory to a desktop: Once it's filled, if an additional item finds its way in, a pre-existing item will have to be pushed out.

Scientists agree that short-term memory capacity is limited to five to nine items, although it's capable of holding more information if packaged into chunks. Educator Jeb Schenck compares the short-term memory to a desktop: Once it's filled, if an additional item finds its way in, a pre-existing item will have to be pushed out. Moreover, with short-term memory, the more time that elapses between learning details and recalling them, the harder it is to access those details.

The hippocampus, a region deep within the brain, is the memory-staging area that connects stimuli and responses. It's vital for consolidation of memories. If we look at the cells in the hippocampus, we find a massive number of axons that move from deep within the brain as a two-way street. Hippocampal cells connect widely to many other regions in the brain, stopping at many way stations. Kosik explains that massive parallel processing takes place when we lay down or recall a memory, thus ensuring more flexibility in our ability to think in the sense that we can synthesize information from different sensory modalities.

Because new information builds on prior existing information, making new linkages and new insights is crucial to building up useful long-term memory. Each of us has thousands of feedback loops throughout our brains, all of which are cross-communicating and engaging the entire organ. In fact, the brain may discard unnecessary or useless information before we even known we've received it.

Kosik explains further that learning and experience can modify the number of neurons. The human brain has approximately 100 billion neurons, each with as many as 5,000 synaptic connections to other neurons. It's those synaptic

connections that are forged and reinforced by experience. Therefore, as a broad generalization, one can say that the more experience we have, the more connections are forged.

In her book *The Human Brain: A Guided Tour*, Susan A. Greenfield ponders how memories become consolidated in the cortex. No one knows exactly how the hippocampus and medial thalamus (vital for relaying incoming sensory information into the cortex) lay down memories.

Says Greenfield: "One attractive idea draws on memory being composed of otherwise arbitrary elements, brought together for the first time in the event or the fact to be remembered. The role of the hippocampus and medial thalamus would be to ensure that disparate, previously unassociated elements are now associated and thus somehow bound into a cohesive memory. One metaphor might be that of scaffolding: While a building is being established, the removal of the scaffolding would lead to collapse of the edifice. However, once the building is completed, the scaffolding is redundant."

Greenfield continues: "Memory can be subdivided into different processes, and each process will be served by different combinations of brain regions. But common to all these memory processes is perhaps the most mysterious issue of all: We know that some people can remember what happened to them 90 years ago, but by then every molecule in their bodies will have been turned over many times. If long-term changes mediating memories are occurring continuously in the brain, how are they sustained? How do neurons register more or less permanent change as a result of experience?"

Kosik admits that any answers to those questions are at the moment speculative. "The way in which we access long-term memory isn't well understood at all," he says.

Schenck says that teaching directs the making of memory. "As an instructor, you select different forms of memory and then teach to the creation of those memories. For example, if I'm teaching something that's in the form of visual recall, I'm aware that when I go to assess the learning, I'm going to have to ask for performances related to something visual. It's crucial to match the assessment with the types of memory used in instruction and

practice. In short, you're teaching the student how to find the memory."

Jensen echoes that thought when he says, "The variety of ways that we store and retrieve information tells us that we have to start thinking less of our memory in general and more of which kind of memory and how it can be retrieved."

Making a memory

One continual challenge to instructors is making sure participants perceive incoming information as important. A technique Schenck uses in the classroom to help that process is to make learners aware of how they are making a memory. He thinks it's necessary to bring to a conscious level how a person is learning, where he or she is storing the memory, and how to find it.

"In developing learners' skills in how to retrieve a specific memory when it's needed, it's crucial for them to become aware of how they are processing and accessing memory stores," says Schenck.

As each person learns in a unique way, it's vital for him or her to ask, "How do I learn?" That requires knowing how your own brain works. It means not only knowing conceptually how memory is built, but also being aware of when you are getting tired or when you're starting to loose track and drift away from the subject. To enhance one's focus, Schenck suggests having participants stand up and do some physical activity for several minutes to rev up their blood and circulation. Another tack is to change tasks for 15 to 20 minutes. "I tell my students to be alert to when they are learning," says Schenck, "but also to when they are not learning."

In order to create long-term memories, it's vital to be verbally explicit and to elaborate on any details. Creating personal linkages is an approach Schenck uses. He has participants make concept maps to show relationships between ideas. For those maps, he writes down a single key word or phrase. Then, participants provide everything that can be linked to the word or phrase. Each time a word is added, participants draw a line to the next word or concept. Some linkages may need an action verb to explain them.

For example, if the instructor gives the concept "Cells——>mitosis," then the line drawn by the learner would have "reproduce by" on top. As a concept map becomes progressively more intricate, it provides a visual map for learners of how the items or issues are related. Schenck says that technique improves memory for detail and the ability to make linkages to other topics.

> **The classic example is when we ask ourselves, "Where did I leave my keys? Mentally, we go through all the information we can recall before we blanked.**

Using multiple forms of review also enhances long-term memory. Rather than doing just a written review, educators who are using brain-based learning theory suggest also using drawings, pantomime, and role play to access memory stores through multiple modalities.

Another strategy to enhance the recall of stored information is to provide a framework of retrieval cues. By teaching key words, a procedure, or a sequence, learners have another tool to retrieve information. Say that a learner has a concept and understands it well, but in asking him or her to explain that idea, the instructor uses words differently from those the learner has been taught and has practiced. In such cases, the instructor is giving the wrong cues.

Says Schenck, "The learner won't be able to find the correct memory file because the wrong word has been typed in on the search mode. It's important to get

students to expand those cues while they're learning a concept or information."

Yet another idea for helping learners enhance memory is to give them external retrieval cues. The classic example is when we ask ourselves, "Where did I leave my keys?"

Mentally, we go through all of the information we can recall before we blanked. We often find that it helps to go to the room where we suspect the loss occurred so that the environment provides cues.

> **As you would imagine, the more active a students is in the learning process, the greater the long-term memory is.**

If you plan to test or assess a group in a particular type of room or facility, it will help if participants are taught or rehearsed in that facility at the same time of day and with the same noise and temperature range—just as basic military training replicates a combat environment as closely as possible.

Past perfection

Schenck talks about reviewing past perfection: "If students have successfully learned something, then make them rehearse it five to 10 times. They can further solidify the memory by reviewing again the next day. Often when learners

get something correct, the instructor stops, though the procedure or concept isn't yet stable in their minds. That's why it's necessary to practice it past perfection."

Schenck notes that after two to three weeks, memory decay stabilizes. "The greater the initial amount of information put into the long-term memory, the greater the final amount retained. As you would imagine, the more active a students is in the learning process, the greater the long-term memory is."

Research on the brain has proven to be a powerful factor in guiding learning specialists as they approach the complicated subject of learning and memory. Sprenger says, "Although nothing appears to remain constant in this field, I want teachers to know two things. One, the brain has everything to do with learning. Two, the more we know about brain science, the easier it will be to make the hundreds of decisions each day that affect students."

Says Kosik, "Ultimately the goal is not to give people photographic memories, but to learn how to improve intelligence, creativity, and imagination."

This is the third Training & Development article in a series by Weiss on learning and the brain. See "Brain-Based Learning" (July) and "Howard Gardner Talks About Technology" (September).

Ruth Palombo Weiss *is a freelance writer based in Potomac, Maryland; pivotal@erols.com. Many of the ideas in the article are from a paper by Kenneth S. Kosik, "Etching Memories in the Brain: The Reflection of Experience," given at the Brain-Based Learning Conference last April in Boston.*

DIFFERENT STROKES FOR DIFFERENT FOLKS?

A Critique of Learning Styles

BY STEVEN A. STAHL

I WORK WITH a lot of different schools and listen to a lot of teachers talk. Nowhere have I seen a greater conflict between "craft knowledge" or what teachers know (or at least think they know) and "academic knowledge" or what researchers know (or at least think they know) than in the area of learning styles. Over the years, my experience has told me to trust teachers; it has also taught me that teachers' craft knowledge is generally on target. I don't mean to say that teachers are always right, but they have learned a great deal from their thousands of observations of children learning in classrooms. So, when teachers talk about the need to take into account children's learning styles when teaching, and researchers roll their eyes at the sound of the term "learning styles," there is more to it than meets the eye.

The whole notion seems fairly intuitive. People are different. Certainly different people might learn differently from each other. It makes sense. Consider the following from the Web site of the National Reading Styles Institute, a major proponent of the application of learning styles to the teaching of reading:

We all have personal styles that influence the way we work, play, and make decisions. Some people are very analytical, and they think in a logical, sequential way. Some students are visual or auditory learners; they learn best by seeing or hearing. These students are likely to conform well to traditional methods of study.

Some people (we call them "global learners") need an idea of the whole picture before they can understand it, while "analytic learners" proceed more easily from the parts to the whole. Global learners also tend to learn best when they can touch what they are learning or move around while they learn. We call these styles of learning "tactile" and "kinesthetic." In a strictly tradi-

tional classroom, these students are often a problem for the teacher. She has trouble keeping them still or quiet. They seem unable to learn to read. (http://www.nrsi.com/about.html)

This all seems reasonable, but it isn't.

Research and Learning Styles

The reason researchers roll their eyes at learning styles is the utter failure to find that assessing children's learning styles and matching to instructional methods has any effect on their learning. The area with the most research has been the global and analytic styles referred to in the NRSI blurb above. Over the past 30 years, the names of these styles have changed—from "visual" to "global" and from "auditory" to "analytic"—but the research results have not changed.

In 1978, Tarver and Dawson reviewed 15 studies that matched visual learners to sight word approaches and auditory learners to phonics. Thirteen of the studies failed to find an effect, and the two that found the effect used unusual methodology. They concluded:

Modality preference has not been demonstrated to interact significantly with the method of teaching reading.[1]

One year later, Arter and Jenkins reviewed 14 studies (some of these are overlapping), all of which failed to find that matching children to reading methods by preferred modalities did any good. They concluded:

[The assumption that one can improve instruction by matching materials to children's modality strengths] appears to lack even minimal empirical support.[2]

Kampwirth and Bates, in 1980, found 24 studies that looked at this issue. Again, they concluded:

Matching children's modality strengths to reading materials has not been found to be effective.[3]

ILLUSTRATED BY BRU ASSOCIATES

In 1987, Kavale and Forness reviewed 39 studies using a meta-analysis technique that would be more sensitive to these effects. They found that matching children by reading styles had nearly no effect on achievement. They concluded:

Although the presumption of matching instruction strategies to individual modality preferences has great intuitive appeal, little empirical support for this proposition was found.... Neither modality testing nor modality teaching were shown to be [effective].[4]

A fifth review, in 1992, by Snider found difficulties in reliably assessing learning styles and a lack of convincing research that such assessment leads to improvement in reading.

Recognition of individuals' strengths and weaknesses is good practice; using this information,

however, to categorize children and prescribe methods can be detrimental to low-performing students. Although the idea of reading style is superficially appealing, critical examination should cause educators to be skeptical of this current educational fad.[5]

These five research reviews, all published in well-regarded journals, found the same thing: One cannot reliably measure children's reading styles and even if one could, matching children to reading programs by learning styles does not improve their learning. In other words, it is difficult to accurately identify children who are "global" and "analytic." So-called global children do not do better in whole language programs than they would in more phonics-based programs. And so-called analytic children do not do better in phonics programs than they do in whole language programs. In short, time after time, this notion of reading styles does not work.

This is an area that has been well researched. Many other approaches to matching teaching approaches to learning styles have not been well researched, if at all. I could not find studies in refereed journals, for example, documenting whether the use of Howard Gardner's Multiple Intelligences Model[6] improved instruction. This does not mean, of course, that the use of the model does not improve achievement, only that I could not find studies validating its use. The same is true of other learning style models.

One cannot prove a negative. Even if all of these studies failed to find that matching children by learning styles helps them read better, it is always possible that another study or another measure or another something will find that matching children to their preferred learning modality will produce results. But in the meantime, we have other things that we *know* will improve children's reading achievement. We should look elsewhere for solutions to reading problems.

Yet, the notion of reading styles (or learning styles) lingers on. This is true not only in my talks with teachers, but also in the literature that teachers read. The most recent issue of *Educational Leadership* included, as part of a themed issue on innovations, several articles on learning styles. *Phi Delta Kappan* also regularly contains articles on learning styles, as do other publications intended for teachers.

Research into Learning Styles

Among others, Marie Carbo claims that her learning styles work is based on research. [I discuss Carbo because she publishes extensively on her model and is very prominent on the workshop circuit. In the references for this article, I cite a few examples of her numerous writings on the topic.[7]] But given the overwhelmingly negative findings in the published research, I wondered what she was citing, and about a decade ago, I thought it would be interesting to take a look. Reviewing her articles, I found that out of 17 studies she had cited, only one was published.[8] Fifteen were doctoral dissertations and 13 of these came out of one university—St. John's University in New York, Carbo's alma mater. None of these had been in a peer-refereed journal. When I looked closely at the dissertations and other materials, I found that 13 of the 17 studies that supposedly support her claim had to do with learning styles based on something other than modality. In 1997, I found 11 additional citations. None of these was published, eight were dissertations, and six of these came from St. John's. In short, the research cited would not cause anyone to change his or her mind about learning styles.

What Do People Mean by Learning Styles?

Modality refers to one of the main avenues of sensation such as vision and hearing. I have only talked about modality-based reading styles because these are both the best researched and the most heavily promoted. The National Reading Styles Institute claims that it has worked with "over 150,000 teachers," and its advertisements seem to be everywhere. Furthermore, these notions of "visual" and "auditory" learners or "global" and "analytic" learners have been around for a long time and have found their way into a number of different programs, not just the NRSI programs.

There are other ways of looking at learning styles. People have proposed that children vary not only in perceptual styles, but on a host of different dimensions. To name a few, people have suggested that children are either two-dimensional/three-dimensional, simultaneous/sequential, connecting/compartmentalizing, inventing/reproducing, reflective/impulsive, field dependent/field independent, and so on.

Some of these are *learning preferences*, or how an individual chooses to work. These might include whether a person prefers to work in silence or with music playing, in bright light or dim light, with a partner or alone, in a warm room or a cool room, etc.

Some of these are *cognitive styles*, such as whether a person tends to reflect before making a choice or makes it impulsively, or whether a person tends to focus on details or sees the big picture.

Some of these are *personality types*, such as whether a person is introverted or extroverted.

Some of these are *aptitudes*, like many of Howard Gardner's multiple intelligences. Gardner suggests that people vary along at least seven different dimensions—*linguistic* or the ability to use language, *logico-mathematical* or the ability to use reasoning especially in mathematics, *spatial* or the ability to use images or pictures, *bodily-kinesthetic* or the ability to control movement, *musical, interpersonal* or the ability to work with people, and *intrapersonal*

or the thinking done inside oneself. The last two are more like personality types, rather than aptitudes or even learning styles. The others are Gardner's attempt to expand the notion of what we think is intelligent behavior to people who are skilled in music, or dance, or even in interpersonal relations. In contrast to the traditional vision of learning styles as either/or categories (either a person is visual or he or she is auditory), multiple intelligences are put forth by Gardner as separate abilities. A child may be strong in a few of these areas, or none of these areas.

What is a teacher to do with all this? If there are children who prefer to work with music, then the teacher might either provide Walkmans for those who prefer music or play music openly and provide earplugs for those who don't. If there are children who prefer to work in bright light, the teacher might seat those children over by the window. Children who like to snack while reading can be allowed to eat during class (healthy foods, of course). It would be easy to see how accommodating all of these preferences in a class could lead to chaos. How would a teacher lecture, give assignments, or even call to order a class in which a sizable proportion of the students was wearing earplugs? Or how does one regulate the temperature so part of the room is warm and part cool?

Others have used learning styles theory as a way of making sure that all the needs of diverse learners are being met. Marguerite Radenich used Gardner's model to examine literature study guides.[9] Her ideal was one that incorporated all of these ways of knowing into an integrated whole to be used to study adolescent literature. Thus, Gardner's model was used here to create more multidimensional instruction. This is very different from using these different styles to segregate children into groups where they would receive fairly one-dimensional instruction.

Thoughtful educators have tried to make this work, and perhaps it is workable, but trying to meet all of the preferences of a group of children would seem to take energy that would be better spent on other things. This is especially true since no one has proven that it works.

Learning Styles and Fortune Telling

Why does the notion of "learning styles" have such enduring popularity—despite the lack of supporting evidence? I believe that this phenomenon has a lot in common with fortune telling.

You go to see a fortune teller at a circus. She looks you over and makes some quick judgments—how young or old you are, how nicely you are dressed, whether you appear anxious or sad or lonely—and based on these judgments, tells your fortune. The fortune she tells may be full of simple and ambiguous statements—"you will be successful at your next venture," "you will be lucky at love," or may be more complex—"you are successful at home, but someone is jealous; make sure you watch yourself." Either way, the statements are specific enough so that they sound predictive, but ambiguous enough that they could apply to a number of situations.

When we read the statements on a Learning Style Inventory, they sound enough like us that we have a flash of recognition. These inventories typically consist of a series of forced choices, such as these from Marie Carbo's *Reading Style Inventory, Intermediate*, 1995.[10]

  a. I always like to be told exactly how I should do my reading work.
  b. Sometimes I like to be told exactly how I should do my reading work.
  c. I like to decide how to do my reading work by myself.
  Or
  a. I like to read in the morning.
  b. I don't like to read in the morning.
  a. I like to read after lunch.
  b. I don't like to read after lunch.
  a. I like to read at night.
  b. I don't like to read at night.
  Or
  a. I read best where it's quiet with no music playing.
  b. I read best where there is music playing.
  c. I read about the same where it's quiet or where there is music playing.

Since all of us have some preferences (my experience is that adults have clear preferences about music during reading, especially), these items tend to ring true. Like the fortunes told by the fortune teller, these statements at first light seem specific enough to capture real distinctions among people. But the problem with choices like these is that people tend to make the same choices. Nearly everybody would prefer a demonstration in science class to an uninterrupted lecture. This does not mean that such individuals have a visual style, but that good science teaching involves demonstrations. Similarly, nearly everybody would agree that one learns more about playing tennis from playing than from watching someone else play. Again, this does not mean that people are tactile/kinesthetic, but that this is how one learns to play sports. Many of these "learning styles" are not really choices, since common sense would suggest that there would not be much variance among people. In the class sample provided with the Reading Style Inventory above, for example, 96 percent of the fifth-graders assessed preferred quiet to working while other people were talking, 88 percent preferred quiet to music, 79 percent picked at least two times a day when they preferred to work, 71 percent had no preference about temperature, and so on. Virtually all of the questions had one answer preferred by a majority of the students.

The questions are just specific enough to sound like they mean something, but vague enough to allow different interpretations. For example, does "music" refer to Mozart or Rap? Obviously, one's choices would be different for different types of music. A more serious question would arise over the "teacher direction" item. Doesn't the amount of teacher direction needed depend on the difficulty of the assignment? There are some assignments that are self evident and do not need much teacher direction, but when work gets complex, students need more direction. This is not a matter of preference.

The other major problem with these inventories is that there are no questions about a child's reading ability. So children with reading problems are given the same measure as children who are doing well in reading. This has two effects. First, there is a bias on some items for children with different abilities. Consider these two items, also from the Carbo inventory:

  a. It's easy for me to remember rules about sounding out words.
  b. It's hard for me to remember rules about sounding out words.
  Or
  a. When I write words, I sometimes mix up the letters.
  b. When I write words, I almost never mix up the letters.

Children with reading problems are more likely to answer that they do not remember phonics rules and that they sometimes mix up the letters. According to the learning styles research reports, such children are likely to be considered as having a global (or visual) preference.[11] Actually, this may not be a preference at all, but a reflection of the child's current level of reading ability. The potential for harm occurs when children with reading problems are classified as "global" (visual) learners and thereby miss out on important instruction in decoding, or are classified as "analytic" (auditory) learners and miss out on opportunities to practice reading in connected text.

Not including information about reading ability also leads to some strange prescriptions. Adults attending learning styles workshops often get prescriptions for beginning reading instruction methods, such as the language experience approach or phonics/linguistic approaches, certainly not needed by competent readers. And for children, too, some of the approaches may be inappropriate. The language experience approach, for example, is best suited for children at the emergent literacy stage, when they need to learn about basic print concepts, one-to-one matching, letter identification, and so on.[12] For a second-grader, or even a newly literate adult, language experience may be appropriate (if they still have not mastered basic print concepts) or highly inappropriate (if they are already reading fluently). It depends on the readers' skill, not their learning styles.

Reliability

If you are to use a test, even an inventory like the one cited above, it should be reliable. If a test is reliable, that means you are going to get the same (or close to the same) results every time you administer it. If a test is 100 percent reliable (or has a reliability coefficient of 1.0), then a person will score exactly the same on Thursday as on Tuesday. Perfection is tough to come by, so we generally want a reliability coefficient to be .90 or higher.[13] If a test is not reliable, or trustworthy, then it is difficult to believe the results. This is a problem, not only with inventories, but with any measure that asks subjects to report about themselves.

Reliabilities of these measures are relatively low. The self-reported reliabilities of Carbo's Reading Style Inventory and Dunn and Dunn's Learning Style Inventories are moderate, especially for a measure of this kind—in the neighborhood of the .60s and the .70s. Similar reliabilities are reported for the Myers-Briggs Inventory, another learning styles assessment.[14] These are lower than one would want for a diagnostic measure. And, these scores are inflated, since for many items there is generally one answer that nearly everybody chooses. This would tend to make the reliabilities higher.

The vagueness in the items may tend to make the reliabilities low. Again, how a child interprets each item will influence how it is answered, as with the "teacher direction" and "music" examples discussed earlier.

Test-retest reliabilities are particularly important for a measure of learning styles. These moderate reliabilities could be interpreted in two ways. The test itself may not be a reliable measure of what it is supposed to measure—that is, a person has a stable learning style, but the test is not getting at it. If the test is not reliable, then the information it gives is not trustworthy.

The other possibility is that learning styles may change, from month to month, or even week to week. This is also problematic. If we are talking about matching a person to a situation using this instrument, this is a relatively long-term (semester or academic year) matching. If a person's style changes, then one either must measure learning styles frequently, or allow for more flexible assignments.

How Reading Develops

The Learning Style model assumes that different children need different approaches to learn to read. Children are different. They come to us with different personalities, preferences, ways of doing things. However, the research so far shows that this has little to do with how successful they will be as readers and writers. Children also come to us with different amounts of exposure to written text, with different skills and abilities, with different exposure to oral language. The research shows that these differences *are* important.

Rather than different methods being appropriate for different children, we ought to think about different methods being appropriate for children at different stages in their development. Children differ in their phonemic abilities, in their ability to recognize words automatically, in their ability to comprehend and learn from text, and in their motivation and appreciation of literature.[15] Different methods are appropriate for different goals. For example, approaches that involve the children in reading books of their own choice are important to develop motivated readers.[16] But whole language approaches, which rely largely on children to choose the materials they read, tend not to be as effective as more teacher-directed approaches for developing children's word recognition or comprehension.[17]

A language experience approach may be appropriate to help a kindergarten child learn basic print concepts. The child may learn some words using visual cues, such as might be taught through a whole word method. With some degree of phonological awareness, the child is ready to learn letters and sounds, as through a phonic approach. Learning about letters and sounds, in combination with practice with increasingly challenging texts, will develop children's ability to use phonetic cues in reading, and to cross-check using context. With additional practice in wide reading, children will develop fluent and automatic word recognition. None of this has anything to do with learning styles; it has to do with the children's current abilities and the demands of the task they have to master next.

What Do Teachers Get out of Learning Styles Workshops?

I have interviewed a number of teachers who have attended learning styles workshops. These were meetings of 200 to 300 teachers and principles, who paid $129 or so to attend a one-day workshop or up to $500 to attend a longer conference. They have found them to be pleasant experiences with professional presenters. The teachers also feel that they learned something from the workshops. After I pressed them, what it seemed that they learned is a wide variety of reading methods, a respect for individual differences among children, and a sense of possibilities of how to teach reading. This is no small thing. However, the same information, and much more, can be gotten from a graduate class in the teaching of reading.

These teachers have another thing in common—after one year, they had all stopped trying to match children by learning styles.

REFERENCES

1. Tarver, Sara, and M. M. Dawson. 1978. Modality preference and the teaching of reading. *Journal of Learning Disabilities* 11: 17–29.

2. Arter, J. A., and Joseph A. Jenkins. 1979. Differential diagnosis-prescriptive teaching: A critical appraisal. *Review of Educational Research* 49: 517–555.

3. Kampwirth, T. J., and M. Bates. 1980. Modality preference and teaching method. A review of the research. *Academic Therapy* 15: 597–605.

4. Kavale, Kenneth A., and Steven R. Forness. 1987. Substance over style: Assessing the efficacy of modality testing and teaching. *Exceptional Children* 54: 228–239.

5. Snider, Vicki E. 1992. Learning styles and learning to read: A critique. *Remedial and Special Education* 13: 6–18.

6. Gardner, Howard. 1993. *Frames of mind: The theory of multiple intelligences.* New York: Basic Books.

7. For example, Carbo, Marie. 1997. Reading styles times twenty. *Educational Leadership* 54 (6): 38–42; Carbo, Marie, Rita Dunn, and Kenneth Dunn. 1986. *Teaching students to read through their individual learning styles.* Englewood Cliffs, N.J.: Prentice-Hall.

8. See Stahl, Steven A. 1988. Is there evidence to support matching reading styles and initial reading methods? A reply to Carbo. *Phi Delta Kappan* 70 (4): 317–322.

9. Radenich, Marguerite Cogorno. 1997. Separating the wheat from the chaff in middle school literature study guides. *Journal of Adolescent and Adult Literacy* 41 (1): 46–57.

10. All examples are from Carbo, Marie. 1995. *Reading Style Inventory Intermediate (RSI-I)*; Author.

11. Carbo, M. 1988. Debunking the great phonics myth. *Phi Delta Kappan* 70: 226–240.

12. Stahl, Steven A., and Patricia D. Miller. 1989. Whole language and language experience approaches for beginning reading: A quantitative research synthesis. *Review of Educational Research* 59 (1): 87–116.

13. Harris, Albert J., and Edward Sipay. 1990. *How to increase reading ability.* 10th ed. White Plains, N.Y.: Longman.

14. Pittenger, David J. 1993. The utility of the Myers-Briggs Type Indicator. *Review of Educational Research* 63: 467–488.

15. Stahl, Steven A. 1998. Understanding shifts in reading and its instruction, *Peabody Journal of Education* 73 (3–4): 31–67.

16. Morrow, Lesley M., and Diane Tracey. 1998. Motivating contexts for young children's literacy development: Implications for word recognition development. In *Word recognition in beginning literacy*, edited by J. Metsala and L. Ehri. Mahwah, N.J.: Erlbaum; Turner, Julianne, and Scott G. Paris. 1995. How literacy tasks influence children's motivation for literacy. *The Reading Teacher* 48: 662–673.

17. Stahl and Miller, op. cit., Stahl, Steven A., C. William Suttles, and Joan R. Pagnucco. 1996. The effects of traditional and process literacy instruction on first-graders' reading and writing achievement and orientation toward reading. *Journal of Educational Research.* 89: 131–144.

Steven A. Stahl is professor of reading education at the University of Georgia and co-director of the Center for Improvement of Early Reading Achievement. His research interests are in beginning reading and vocabulary instruction.

From *American Educator*, Fall 1999, pp. 27-31. Reprinted with permission of the author and *American Educator*, the quarterly journal of American Federation of Teachers.

Regarding Rewards

Should you be a gold-sticker sticker?

By Teri Degler

One morning in the schoolyard I asked a group of parents if they ever used rewards—stickers, star charts and the like. Their responses were telling: "Well, yes, I hate to admit it, but I have." "Once I was so desperate I tried a star chart." "Don't tell anybody, but I used stickers to help wean my daughter from her nighttime bottle." The playground poll sums up how many of us react to tangible rewards: We feel guilty when we use them—and we thank our lucky (gold) stars when they work!

Perhaps we don't have to feel quite so conflicted about this, suggests David Factor, a Toronto psychologist and father of two. It helps, he says, if you understand that a reward is simply anything that follows a specific behaviour and makes that behaviour more likely to occur again. "Social rewards"—praise, encouragement and hugs—are a natural part of parenting and are often all that's needed in developing a new skill or improving a certain behaviour. But in cases where a pat on the back or an enthusiastic high-five isn't quite enough, tangible rewards can sometimes help.

"When my daughter, Tamara, was about three she was afraid to use the toilet for bowel movements," says Toronto mom Eileen Benson. "But she also disliked the feeling of having a messy diaper, so she would spend whole days holding everything in. She was really suffering, but nothing I tried worked. All I could do to keep things from getting worse was to make sure she was eating really healthy, high-fibre foods.

"Then one day when I was at my wit's end, a friend came over and brought Tamara one of those white-flour, sprinkle doughnuts. Tamara, of course, really wanted it. But I had to explain she couldn't eat anything like that when she wasn't having bowel movements. Immediately—even though this hadn't been my intention—she jumped up and ran to the potty."

This made Benson think a reward system might be the solution to their problem. With her daughter's help, Benson made a chart and put it on the fridge. Every time Tamara went to the potty, Benson praised her and let her pick a sticker to put on the chart. In less than two weeks, the problem was pretty well solved. "Some people might think this was manipulation," says Benson, "but I never saw it that way. The stickers just seemed to help Tamara redirect her energy or provide her with something else to focus on."

Probably the most common concern about rewards is that they are a form of bribery. Supporters of rewards counter this by saying a bribe is, by definition, an enticement to do something wrong ("I'll be your friend if you help me play this trick on the teacher"). Still, rewards can be manipulative. Edmonton family physician and mother of three Diana Andriashek says this is true "when parents use rewards to suit their own needs rather than the needs of the child"—such as when a father hands his daughter some money and tells her to go buy some ice cream and stop bugging him.

This is very different, Andriashek says, from using rewards to focus on the positive, the things your child is doing right instead of wrong. This, she says, is an acceptable way "to help shape a child's behaviour… and build feelings of competence and self-esteem." For example, when your daughter goes to bed by the 8:30 goal and gets to roll over and plunk the sticker on the chart, you comment on what a good job she's doing and this helps her feel good about herself. It's what you say, along with the reward, that makes it work.

Brenda Linn-Stringer, a Toronto mother and educator who has done doctoral studies on the effect of rewards on motivation, says that "tangible rewards should be used only with sensitivity and caution, and only in specific, limited situations"—not, she says, as an overall approach to parenting, as it is when families have charts, points or monetary rewards set all the time to elicit everything from compliant behaviour to the completion of chores.

A child can think "Well, if I'm not going to get a treat, I'm not going to behave."

"Human beings are complex creatures," says Linn-Stringer. "Children are naturally going to respond to positive reinforcement. But they are also going to think about why you're rewarding them—and they can come to two very different conclusions: One, that you really believe their accomplishment is worthwhile and you want to acknowledge it. Or two, that you think the task you're rewarding is boring or unpleasant in itself and requires some sugar coating—like practising scales on the piano.

"There's an old story," she says, "about a man who was being bothered by the noise a bunch of teenagers kept making, so he started to pay them to make the noise every day. Then, after a while, he stopped paying them—and they stopped making the noise!"

Ten Tips

If lots of love, attention and role-modelling don't seem to be enough to help your child master a particular skill or change a negative behaviour, and you decide tangible rewards are needed, here are a few tips that may help:

1. Pick one specific task or behaviour to work on—toilet training or aggression against a new sibling, for example.
2. Decide if you're going to reward the task itself (going to the potty), or a replacement behaviour (touching the baby gently).
3. Involve your child as much as possible—i.e. in making the chart and picking the reward. Be upfront about what you're doing and why. The more your child shares your goals and feels involved, the better.
4. Small rewards like stickers generally work better than big rewards like expensive toys. The fun of filling out a sticker chart often solves the problem before the chart is finished, and your child may completely forget about the larger toy he was promised.

5. When the desired behaviour occurs, let your child put on the sticker or drop the marble in the jar.
6. If you're not getting the desired behaviour, reward the closest thing to it, and gradually move towards your goal.
7. Be consistent and reward immediately or within a set time—an hour is forever for a two-year-old, so why would he bother?
8. Be sure you accompany the tangible reward with praise and encouragement, including information that helps your child see her progress: "Look how Michael smiles when you rub his back so gently!"
9. Gradually decrease the tangible rewards until you're using only praise and encouragement again.
10. Remember to use the reward system to train *yourself* to notice your child's good behaviour, and acknowledge it to him. See if you can do this daily without the reward system to remind you.

Several studies, adds Linn-Stringer, have shown that "unless tangible rewards somehow convey information—for example, your delight or appreciation or recognition of an accomplishment—their use can actually erode a child's intrinsic motivation."

One of the most significant factors in how a child perceives a reward is the relationship between the child and the adult who's offering it. Martha Massey, a Courtenay, B.C. teacher, recently saw an example of this. "I was observing several sixth-graders at the end of the day. They were all bursting with preadolescent energy but, instead of rushing outside, they were clamouring to help their teacher with chores. When they finished the chores, the teacher let them each pick a chocolate dollar from a bucket. Then they all ran off, pleased as punch. Watching this, it was so clear to me that the real reward for the kids was the wonderfully positive interaction they were having with their teacher while they were working. The chocolate was just a token—a little something that sweetened an already sweet relationship."

Eileen Benson points out that manipulation—and the perception of it—are also avoided when your child is involved and wants to solve the problem as much as you do. "Tamara and I recently set up a sticker chart to help her get to school on time. But

it didn't work. I'm the only one who wanted to get her to school in time for the bell. In the end, we found there were other things that were making her unhappy at school that needed to be dealt with."

As for rewarding daily tasks like picking up dirty socks or helping with the dishes (as opposed to extra jobs like cutting the grass that a child might reasonably earn money for), Linn-Stringer says this practice "can reduce what should be helpful family interactions into hard-core bargaining sessions. Remember, the reward game is a two-way street. The child can end up thinking, 'Well, if I'm not going to get a treat, I'm not going to behave.'"

Andriashek agrees with this warning but says, "For me, rewards and other forms of positive reinforcement are ways of helping parents find the child's strengths." This is particularly important, she says, "with strong-willed children who tend to respond to every form of discipline by saying things like 'Fine. Turn off the TV; I didn't want to watch it anyway.'

"This has certainly been true with my 13-year-old daughter. I realized early on that I could nag her into the ground to change behaviours, but if I did that, I'd lose her. And so I use positive reinforcement instead and focus on the things she does well."

Using rewards, says Andriashek, also helps stop a downward spiral of negativity. If, for example, you get angry and punish your five-year-old because she hits her little brother every time he frustrates her, you tend to increase her frustration and the likelihood of her striking out at him in some way. But if you focus on a behaviour that she exhibits instead of hitting, for instance being patient—first by using praise and other social rewards and then, if needed, moving on to tangible rewards—you break the cycle. And you help her *see* herself as a person who's patient instead of one who hits.

Even more importantly, says Andriashek, it helps you begin to notice how often she's kind and patient with him—something that may well have gone unnoticed while your attention was fixed so firmly on her misbehaviour. This means, Andriashek adds with a laugh, "it may well be the parent who's being 'trained' by the use of rewards as much as the child."

Resources

The Discipline Book: Everything You Need to Know to Have a Better-Behaved Child—From Birth to Age Ten, by William Sears, MD, and Martha Sears, RN, Little, Brown, 1995.

Repression tries for experimental comeback

Sigmund Freud and his theoretical heirs have held that people are capable of pushing unwanted memories into a kind of unconscious cold-storage, where they're gone but not forgotten. Many memory researchers view this mental process, called repression, as a fanciful idea lacking empirical support.

In the March 15 NATURE, researchers describe an everyday form of induced forgetting that may provide a scientific footing for Freudian repression.

When people consistently try to forget a memory in the face of reminders, they often succeed rather well at it, say psychologists Michael C. Anderson and Collin Green of the University of Oregon in Eugene. Successful forgetting increases with practice at avoiding a memory, Anderson and Green say.

"Everyday mechanisms of memory inhibition provide a viable model of repression," Anderson says. His view counters that of some clinicians, who hold that repression exists but only as a special process for dealing with traumas.

Anderson's work was inspired by the finding that kids who have been sexually abused by a trusted caregiver forget that experience far more often than do kids abused by a stranger. Children can willingly use indirect reminders, such as the abuser's presence, as cues to avoid thinking about the actual abuse, according to Anderson.

He and Green had 32 college students learn arbitrary word pairs, such as "ordeal-roach." Volunteers then saw a series of single words from those pairs. Words were shown once, eight times, 16 times, or not at all. On each presentation, participants saw a signal to either remember and say aloud the associated word or to avoid thinking about it.

On an ensuing memory test, students recalled nearly all of the words that they had tried to remember. Volunteers recalled progressively fewer other words, the more chances they had to try to forget them. On average, they recalled about 80 percent of words they tried to forget.

Similar findings emerged when participants saw new words and cues intended to jog their memories, such as "insect-r__" to spur recall of "roach." Again, memory suffered for words that students had tried to forget. These findings indicate that volunteers forgot specific words deliberately blocked, not word pairs.

Comparable memory losses emerged for students told that trying to forget a word would make them think about it more. For instance, people told not to think about, say, a white bear, can't think of anything but that white bear.

In Anderson's studies, however, volunteers used cues such as "ordeal" to anticipate and fend off unwanted memories. The white bear never showed its face.

The new data suggest that brain networks that restrain communication "could give rise to the type of repression proposed by Freud to underlie neuroses," says Martin A. Conway of the University of Bristol in England.

Elizabeth F. Loftus of the University of Washington in Seattle notes that memory was still pretty good for those who tried to forget words. She doesn't regard the study as evidence of repression.

Anderson's findings are "broadly consistent" with Freudian repression, remarks Daniel L. Schacter of Harvard University. Still, he cautions, it's too early to conclude that willful forgetting applies to emotionally sensitive experience.

—*B. Bower*

From *Science News*, March 17, 2001, p. 164. © 2001 by the Science Service, 1719 N Street, N.W., Washington, D.C. 20036; www.sciserv.org.
Reprinted by permission of Bruce Bower.

The Seven Sins of Memory:
How the Mind Forgets and Remembers

Memory's errors are as fascinating as they are important

By Daniel Schacter, Ph.D.

In Yasunari Kawabata's unsettling short story, "Yumiura," a novelist receives an unexpected visit from a woman who says she knew him 30 years earlier. They met when he visited the town of Yumiura during a harbor festival, the woman explains. But the novelist cannot remember her. Plagued recently by other troublesome memory lapses, he sees this latest incident as a further sign of mental decline. His discomfort turns to alarm when the woman offers more revelations about what happened on a day when he visited her room. "You asked me to marry you," she recalls wistfully. The novelist reels while contemplating the magnitude of what he had forgotten. The woman explains that she had never forgotten their time together and felt continually burdened by her memories of him.

After she finally leaves, the shaken novelist searches maps for the town of Yumiura with the hope of triggering recall of the place and the reasons why he had gone there. But no maps or books list a town called Yumiura. The novelist then realizes that he could not have been in the part of the country the woman described at the time she remembered. Her detailed, heart-felt and convincing memories were entirely false.

Kawabata's story dramatically illustrates different ways in which memory can get us into trouble. Sometimes we forget the past and at other times we distort it; some disturbing memories haunt us for years. Yet we also rely on memory to perform an astonishing variety of tasks in our everyday lives. Recalling conversations with friends or recollecting family vacations; remembering appointments and errands we need to run; calling up words that allow us to speak and understand others; remembering foods we like and dislike; acquiring the knowledge needed for a new job—all depend, in one way or another, on memory. Memory plays such a pervasive role in our daily lives that we often take it for granted until an incident of forgetting or distortion demands our attention.

Memory's errors have long fascinated scientists, and during the past decade they have come to occupy a prominent place in our society. Forgotten encounters, misplaced eyeglasses and failures to recall the names of familiar faces are becoming common occurrences for many adults who are busily trying to juggle the demands of work and family, and cope with the bewildering array of new communications technologies. How many passwords and "PINs" do you have to remember just to manage your affairs on the Internet, not to mention your voice mail at the office or on your cell phone?

In addition to dealing with the frustration of memory failures in daily life, the awful specter of Alzheimer's disease looms large on the horizon. As the general public becomes ever more aware of its horrors through such high-profile cases as Ronald Reagan's battle with the disorder, the prospects of a life dominated by catastrophic forgetting further increase our preoccupations with memory.

Although the magnitude of the woman's memory distortion in Yumiura seems to stretch the bounds of credulity, it has been equaled and even exceeded in everyday life. Consider the story of Binjimin Wikomirski, whose 1996 Holocaust memoir, *Fragments*, won worldwide acclaim for portraying life in a concentration camp from the perspective of a child. Wilkomirski presented readers with raw, vivid recollections of the unspeakable terrors he witnessed as a young boy. Even more remarkable, Wilkomirski had spent much of his adult life unaware of these traumatic childhood memories, only becoming aware of them in therapy. Because his story and memories inspired countless others, Wilkomirski became a sought-after international figure and a hero to Holocaust survivors.

The story began to unravel, however, in late August 1998, when Daniel Ganzfried, a Swiss journalist and himself the son of a Holocaust survivor, published a stunning article in a Zurich newspaper. Ganzfried revealed that Wilkomirski is actually Bruno Dossekker, a Swiss native born in 1941 to a young woman named Yvone Berthe Grosjean, who later gave him up for adoption to an orphanage. His foster parents, the Dossekkers, found him there. Young Bruno spent all of the war years in the safe confines of his native Switzerland. Whatever the basis for his traumatic "memories" of Nazi horrors, they did not come from childhood experiences in a concentration camp. Is Dossekker/Wilkomirski simply a liar? Probably not: he still strongly believes his recollections are real.

Memory's errors are as fascinating as they are important. They can be divided into seven fundamental transgressions or "sins," which I call transience, absent-mindedness, blocking, misattribution, suggestibility, bias and persistence. Just like the ancient seven deadly sins—pride, anger, envy, greed, gluttony, lust and sloth—the memory sins occur frequently in everyday life and can have serious consequences for all of us.

Transience, absentmindedness and blocking are sins of omission: we fail to bring to mind a desired fact, event or idea. Transience refers to a weakening or loss of memory over time. It is a basic feature of memory, and the culprit in many memory problems. Absentmindedness involves a breakdown at the interface between attention and memory. Absentminded memory errors—misplacing your keys or eyeglasses, or forgetting a lunch appointment—typically occur because we are preoccupied with distracting issues or concerns, and don't focus attention on what we need to remember.

The third sin, blocking, entails a thwarted search for information we may be desperately trying to retrieve. We've all had the experience of failing to produce a name to a familiar face. This frustrating experience happens even though we are attending carefully to the task at hand, and even though the desired name has not faded from our minds—as we become acutely aware when we unexpectedly retrieve the blocked name hours or days later.

The next four sins of misattribution, suggestibility, bias and persistence are all sins of commission: some form of memory is present, but it is either incorrect or unwanted. The sin of misattribution involves assigning a memory to the wrong source: mistaking fantasy for reality, or incorrectly remembering that a friend told you a bit of trivia that you actually read about in a newspaper. Misattribution is far more common than most people realize, and has potentially profound implications in legal settings. The related sin of suggestibility refers to memories that are implanted as a result of leading questions, comments or suggestions when a person is trying to call up a past experience. Like misattribution, suggestibility is especially relevant to—and sometimes can wreak havoc within—the legal system.

The sin of bias reflects the powerful influences of our current knowledge and beliefs on how we remember our pasts. We often edit or entirely rewrite our previous experiences—unknowingly and unconsciously—in light of what we now know or believe. The result can be a skewed rendering of a specific incident, or even of an extended period in our lives, that says more about how we feel now than about what happened then.

The seventh sin—persistence—entails repeated recall of disturbing information or events that we would prefer to banish from our minds altogether: remembering what we cannot forget, even though we wish that we could. Everyone is familiar with persistence to some degree: Recall the last time you suddenly awoke at 3 a.m., unable to keep out of your mind a painful blunder on the job or a disappointing result on an important exam. In more extreme cases of serious depression or traumatic experience, persistence can be disabling and even life-threatening.

"Two regions of the brain showed greater activity when people made abstract/concrete judgments about words they later remembered compared with those they later forgot."

New discoveries, some based on recent breakthroughs in neuroscience that allow us to see the brain in action as it learns and remembers, are beginning to illuminate the basis of the seven sins. These studies allow us to see in a new light what's going on inside our heads during the frustrating incidents of memory failure or error that can have a significant impact on our everyday lives. But to understand the seven sins more deeply, we also need to ask why our memory systems have come to exhibit these bothersome and sometimes dangerous properties: Do the seven sins represent mistakes made by Mother Nature during the course of evolution? Is memory flawed in a way that has placed our species at unnecessary risk? I don't think so. To the contrary, I contend that each of the seven sins is a byproduct of otherwise desirable and adaptive features of the human mind. Let's consider two of the most common memory sins: transience and absentmindedness.

TRANSIENCE

On October 3, 1995 the most sensational criminal trial of our time reached a stunning conclusion: a jury acquitted O. J. Simpson of murder. Word of the verdict spread quickly, nearly everyone reacted with either outrage or jubilation, and many people could talk about little else for days and weeks afterward. The Simpson verdict seemed like just the sort of momentous event that most of us would always remember vividly: how we reacted to it, and where we were when we heard the news.

Now, can you recall how you found out that Simpson had been acquitted? Chances are that you don't remember, or that what you remember is wrong. Several days after the verdict, a group of California undergraduates provided researchers with detailed accounts of how they learned about the jury's decision. When the researchers probed students' memories again 15 months later, only half recalled accurately how they found out about the decision. When asked again nearly three years after the verdict, less than 30% of students' recollections were accurate; nearly half were dotted with major errors.

The culprit in this incident is the sin of transience: forgetting that occurs with the passage of time. Research has shown that minutes, hours or days after an experience, memory preserves a relatively detailed record, allowing us to reproduce the past with reasonable if not perfect accuracy. But with the passing of time, the particulars fade and opportunities multiply for interference—generated by later, similar experiences—to blur our recollections.

Consider the following question: If I measure activity in your brain while you are learning a list of words, can I tell from this activity which words you will later remember having studied, and which words you will later forget? In other words, do measurements of brain activity at the moment when a perception is being transformed into a memory allow scientists to predict future remembering and forgetting of that particular event? If so, exactly which regions allow us to do the predicting?

In 1997, our group at the imaging center of Massachusetts General Hospital came up with an experiment to answer the question. Holding still in this cacophonous tunnel [the magnetic resonance imaging or MRI scanner], participants in our experiment saw several hundred words, one every few seconds, flashed to them from a computer by specially arranged mirrors. To make sure that they paid attention to every word, we asked our volunteers to indicate whether each word refers to something abstract, such as "thought," or concrete, such as "garden." Twenty minutes after the scan, we showed subjects the words they had seen in the scanner, intermixed with an equal number of words they hadn't seen, and asked them to indicate which ones they did and did not remember seeing in the scanner. We knew, based on preliminary work, that people would remember some words and forget others. Could we tell from the strength of the signal when participants were making abstract/concrete judgments which words they would later remember and which ones they would later forget?

We could. Two regions of the brain showed greater activity when people made abstract/concrete judgments about words they later remembered compared with those they later forgot. One was in the inner part of the temporal lobe, a part of the brain that, when damaged, can result in severe memory loss. The other region whose activity predicted subsequent memory was located further forward, in the lower left part of the vast territory known as the frontal lobes.

This finding was not entirely unexpected, because previous neuroimaging studies indicated that the lower left part of the frontal lobe works especially hard when people elaborate on incoming information by associating it to what they already know.

These results were exciting because there is something fascinating, almost science fiction-like, about peering into a person's brain in the present and foretelling what she will likely remember and forget in the future. But beyond an exercise in scientific fortune-telling, these studies managed to trace some of the roots of transience to the split-second encoding operations that take place during the birth of a memory. What happens in frontal and temporal regions during those critical moments determines, at least in part, whether an experience will be remembered for a lifetime, or drop off into the oblivion of the forgotten.

ABSENTMINDEDNESS

On a brutally cold day in February 1999, 17 people gathered in the 19th floor office of a Manhattan skyscraper to compete for a title known to few others outside that room: National Memory Champion. The winner of the U.S. competition would go on to challenge for the world memory championship several months later in London.

The participants were asked to memorize thousands of numbers and words, pages of faces and names, lengthy poems and decks of cards. The victor in this battle of mnemonic virtuosos, a 27-year-old administrative assistant named Tatiana Cooley, relied on classic encoding techniques: generating visual images, stories and associations that link incoming information to what she already knows. Given her proven ability to commit vast amounts of information to memory, one might also expect that Cooley's everyday life would be free from the kinds of memory problems that plague others. Yet this memory champion considers herself dangerously forgetful. "I'm incredibly absentminded," Cooley told a reporter. Fearful that she will forget to carry out everyday tasks. Cooley depends on to-do lists and notes scribbled on sticky pads. "I live by Post-its," she admitted ruefully.

The image of a National Memory Champion dependent on Post-its in her everyday life has a paradoxical, even surreal quality: Why does someone with a capacity for prodigious recall need to write down anything at all? Can't Tatiana Cooley call on the same memory abilities and strategies that she uses to memorize hundreds of words or thousands of numbers to help remember that she needs to pick up a jug of milk at the store? Apparently not: The gulf that separates Cooley's championship memory performance from her forgetful everyday life illustrates the distinction between transience and absentmindedness.

The kinds of everyday memory failures that Cooley seeks to remedy with Post-it notes—errands to run, appointments to keep and the like—have little to do with transience. These kinds of memory failures instead reflect the sin of absentmindedness: lapses of attention that result in failing to remember information that was either never encoded property (if at all) or is available in memory but is overlooked at the time we need to retrieve it.

To appreciate the distinction between transience and absentmindedness, consider the following three examples:

A man tees up a golf ball and hits it straight down the fairway. After waiting a few moments for his partner to hit, the man tees up his ball again, having forgotten that he hit the first drive.

A man puts his glasses down on the edge of a couch. Several minutes later, he realizes he can't find the glasses, and spends a half-hour searching his home before locating them.

"Memory's errors have long fascinated scientists, and during the past decade they have come to occupy a prominent place in our society."

A man temporarily places a violin on the top of his car. Forgetting that he has done so, he drives off with the violin still perched on the roof.

Superficially, all three examples appear to reflect a similar type of rapid forgetting. To the contrary, it is likely that each occurred for very different reasons.

The first incident took place back in the early 1980s, when I played golf with a patient who had been taking part in memory research conducted in my laboratory. The patient was in the early stage of Alzheimer's disease, and he had severe difficulties remembering recent events. Immediately after hitting his tee shot, the patient was excited because he had knocked it straight down the middle; he realized he would now have an easy approach shot to the green. In other words, he had encoded this event in a relatively elaborate manner that would ordinarily yield excellent memory. But when he started teeing up again and I asked him about his first shot, he expressed no recollection of it whatsoever. This patient was victimized by transience: he was incapable of retaining the information he had encoded, and no amount of cueing or prodding could bring it forth.

In the second incident, involving misplaced glasses, entirely different processes are at work. Sad to say, this example comes from my own experience—and happens more often than I would care to admit. Without attending to what I was doing, I placed my glasses in a spot where I usually do not put them. Because I hadn't fully encoded

this action to begin with—my mind was preoccupied with a scientific article I had been reading—I was at a loss when I realized that my glasses were missing. When I finally found them on the couch, I had no particular recollection of having put them there. But unlike the golfing Alzheimer's patient, transience was not the culprit: I never adequately encoded the information about where I put my glasses and so had no chance to retrieve it later.

The third example, featuring the misplaced violin, turned into far more than just a momentary frustration. In August 1967, David Margetts played second violin in the Roth String Quartet at UCLA. He had been entrusted with the care of a vintage Stradivarius that was owned by the department of music. After Margetts put the violin on his car's roof and drove off without removing it, UCLA made massive efforts to recover the instrument. Nonetheless, it went missing for 27 years before resurfacing in 1994 when the Stradivarius was brought in for repair and a dealer recognized the instrument. After a lengthy court battle, the violin was returned to UCLA in 1998.

There is, of course, no way to know exactly what Margetts was thinking about when he put the violin on his car's roof. Perhaps he was preoccupied with other things, just as I was when I misplaced my glasses. But because one probably does not set down a priceless Stradivarius without attending carefully to one's actions, I suspect that had Margetts been reminded before driving off, he would have remembered perfectly well where he had just placed the violin. In other words, Margetts was probably not sabotaged by transience, or even by failure to encode the event initially. Rather, forgetting in Margett's case was likely attributable to an absent-minded failure to notice the violin at the moment he needed to recall where he had put it. He missed a retrieval cue—the violin on the car's roof—which surely would have reminded him that he needed to remove the instrument.

Even though they often seem like our enemies, the seven sins are an integral part of the mind's heritage because they are so closely connected to features of memory that make it work well. The seven sins are not merely nuisances to minimize or avoid. They illuminate how memory draws on the past to inform the present, preserves elements of present experience for future reference, and allows us to revisit the past at will. Memory's vices are also its virtues, elements of a bridge across time that allows us to link the mind with the world.

Adapted from Daniel Schacter, Ph.D.'s *The Seven Sins of Memory: How the Mind Forgets and Remembers* (Houghton-Mifflin, 2001)

Daniel L. Schacter, Ph.D., is chairman of the psychology department at Harvard University and also author of "Searching for Memory" (HarperCollins, 1997).

From *Psychology Today*, May/June 2001, pp. 62-87. Excerpted from *The Seven Sins of Memory: How the Mind Forgets and Remembers*, by Daniel Schacter.

UNIT 5
Cognitive Processes

Unit Selections

Key Points to Consider

- Why study cognition? Why study the development of cognitive abilities; why would this be of interest to psychologists? What role does culture play in cognitive development? What aspects of culture most influence how we process incoming information about our world? Besides culture, can you think of other factors that influence our cognitive activity?

- Do you believe that animals can think? Can you offer anecdotal evidence? Can you offer scientific evidence? If animals think, how is their thinking similar to that of humans? How is it different?

- What is intelligence? Are learning and thinking central to our concepts of intelligence? How so? Why is the concept of intelligence so criticized? Why have IQ tests been criticized? Do you think the criticism is merited?

- What are some of the newer theories of intelligence? Can you think of people whom you would call "bright" by standards other than the traditional definitions of intelligence?

 **Links: www.dushkin.com/online/**
These sites are annotated in the World Wide Web pages.

Chess: Kasparov v. Deep Blue: The Rematch
  http://www.chess.ibm.com/home/html/b.html
Cognitive Science Article Archive
  http://www.helsinki.fi/hum/kognitiotiede/archive.html
Introduction to Artificial Intelligence (AI)
  http://www-formal.stanford.edu/jmc/aiintro/aiintro.html

As Rashad watches his 4-month old, he is convinced that the baby possesses a degree of understanding of the world around her. In fact, Rashad is sure he has one of the smartest babies in the neighborhood. Although he is indeed a proud father, he keeps these thoughts to himself so as not to alienate his neighbors whom he perceives as having less intelligent babies.

Jack lives in the same neighborhood as Rashad. However, Jack doesn't have any children, but he does own two fox terriers. Despite Jack's most concerted efforts, the dogs never come to him when he calls them. In fact, the dogs have been known to run in the opposite direction on occasion. Instead of being furious, Jack accepts his dogs' disobedience because he is sure the dogs are just dumb beasts and don't know any better.

Both of these vignettes illustrate important and interesting ideas about cognition or thought processes. In the first vignette, Rashad ascribes cognitive abilities and high intelligence to his child; in fact, Rashad perhaps ascribes too much cognitive ability to his 4-month-old child. On the other hand, Jack assumes that his dogs are incapable of thought, more specifically, incapable of premeditated disobedience, and therefore he forgives them.

Few adults would deny the existence of their cognitive abilities. Some adults, in fact, think about thinking, something which psychologists call metacognition. Cognition is critical to our survival as adults. But are there differences in mentation in adults? And what about other organisms? Can young children—infants for example—think? If they can, do they think like adults? And what about animals; can they think and solve problems? These and other questions are related to cognitive psychology and cognitive science, which is showcased in this unit.

Cognitive psychology has grown faster than most other specialties in psychology in the past 20 years. Much of this has occurred in response to new computer technology as well as to the growth of psycholinguistics. Computer technology has prompted an interest in artificial intelligence, the mimicking of human intelligence by machines. Similarly the study of psycholinguistics has prompted the examination of the influence of language on thought and vice versa.

While interest in these two developments has eclipsed interest in more traditional areas of cognition such as intelligence, we cannot ignore these traditional areas in this anthology. With regard to intelligence, one persistent problem has been the difficulty of defining just what intelligence is. David Wechsler, author of several of the most popular intelligence tests in current clinical use, defines intelligence as the global capacity of the individual to act purposefully, to think rationally, and to deal effectively with the environment. Other psychologists have proposed more complex definitions. The definitional problem arises when we try to develop tests that validly and reliably measure such concepts. Edward Boring once suggested that we define intelligence as whatever it is that an intelligence test measures.

The first article in this unit offers the reader a look into the world of cognitive development. Psychologist Mary Gauvain discusses how culture shapes cognitions and proclaims that psychologists have given the concept of culture short shrift in their theories and research on child development and cognition.

The discussion of intelligence continues in the next articles, which takes a new and broader approach to intelligence. Howard Gardner suggests that the traditional definition of intelligence is too narrow and should be expanded to include other measures. Gardner is highly critical, however, about the misuse of his theory and the attempts to expand the concept of intelligence too far.

The third article in this unit turns our attention to animals. Can animals think? Eugene Linden says yes. He alludes to special research on cognition in animals and concludes that animals can indeed think, but their thought processes certainly are not as rich or as complex as those of humans. Vivid examples of animal thought are provided.

We next continue with a discussion of intelligence. The third and final article takes a new and broader approach to intelligence. The author suggests that the traditional definition of intelligence is too narrow and should be expanded to include other features of intellect. Several theories of intelligence as well as methods for measuring intelligence are reviewed and critiqued.

Cognitive Development in Social and Cultural Context

Abstract

The development of thinking is discussed from a sociocultural perspective. Three features of the social and cultural context that play important roles in organizing and directing cognitive development are presented and illustrated empirically: (a) activity goals and values of the culture, (b) material and symbolic tools for satisfying cultural goals and values, and (c) higher level structures that instantiate cultural goals and values in everyday practices. The article concludes with a discussion of the utility of this approach for advancing understanding of human intellectual growth.

Keywords

cognitive development; sociocultural influences; sociohistorical approach

Mary Gauvain[1]
Department of Psychology, University of California at Riverside, Riverside, California

In all societies throughout the world, most children grow up to be competent members of their communities. This impressive phenomenon—and indeed it is impressive—relies on some inherent human ability to develop intellectual and social skills adapted to the circumstances in which growth occurs. It also relies on social and cultural practices that support and maintain desired patterns of development. This article focuses on two questions pertaining to this process. First, how do children develop the skills and knowledge to become competent members of their community? Second, how are cultures uniquely suited to support and lead this development? To address these questions, I discuss culturally devised ways for supporting the development and maintenance of valued cultural skills. Several areas of research are foundational to the ideas presented here.

The first influence is a cultural-practice view of cognition (Chaiklin & Lave, 1996), which includes research on situated learning, everyday cognition and practical intelligence. This work takes as a starting point the idea that people learn to think in specific contexts in which human activity is directed toward practical goals. An important contribution of this work is attention to the coordination between the thinker and the actions performed. The main limitation for present purposes is that it concentrates on learning rather than development. A second influence is the sociohistorical tradition (Cole, 1996), which emphasizes the role of material, symbolic, and social resources in organizing and supporting mental growth. The primary contribution of this approach is attention to the opportunities and constraints for cognitive development provided by the cultural community in which growth occurs. A practical limitation is that this idea, to date, has been broad in conception, touching on many aspects of psychological development. An organizational framework that links this approach more systematically to contemporary domains of research is needed for further examination and incorporation into the field. A

final influence is the concept of the *developmental niche* (Super & Harkness, 1986), which characterizes the psychological structure of the human ecosystem that guides children's development. The central idea is that it is not only the organism that provides structure and direction to development; rather, culture also possesses structure and direction, and it is through the conjoining of these two organized systems that human development unfolds. Super and Harkness proposed three subsystems of the developmental niche, physical and social settings, customs of child care, and psychology of the caregiver. These subsystems concentrate on social development. In this review, I extend this basic framework to the study of cognitive development.

THREE COGNITIVE SUBSYSTEMS OF THE DEVELOPMENTAL NICHE

Three subsystems of the developmental niche that connect cognitive development to culture are the activity goals and values of the culture and its members; historical means for satisfying cultural goals and values, especially the material and symbolic tools that support thinking and its development; and higher level structures that instantiate cultural goals and values in everyday practice and through which children become participants in the intellectual life of their community. These subsystems are hierarchically organized, from the microanalytic level (i.e., the level of individual psychological activity) to the broader social circumstances of development. A key point is the range of human experience represented: Culture penetrates human intellectual functioning and its development at many levels, and it does so through organized individual and social practices.

Activity Goals and Values of the Culture

Human behavior and thinking occur within meaningful contexts as people conduct purposeful, goal-directed activities (Vygotsky, 1978). The developmental implication is that children learn about and practice thinking in the course of participating in goal-directed activities—activities defined and organized by the cultural community in which development occurs. Much psychological research has focused on the organized, goal-directed nature of human activity (e.g., Duncker's classic studies of functional fixedness[2] and Bartlett's studies of memory), so this basic idea is not new. However, a cultural psychological approach offers two unique contributions: (a) an emphasis on the connection between activity structures (the means and goals that define human action) and the cultural practices from which they stem and (b) an examination of the relations among activity structures, cultural practices, and cognitive growth.

Research on children's everyday mathematics illustrates this linkage. Studies of the mathematical skills of Brazilian children who sell candy in the street (Carraher, Carraher, & Schliemann, 1985) indicate that mental activity reflects the practices that individuals engage in, that these practices are defined by cultural convention and routine, and that mathematical activities are handled differently, and more successfully, when the goal of the calculation is meaningful than when it is not. Another example

is found in how intelligent behavior changes following social reorganization. Inkeles and Smith (1974) observed industrialization in non-Western communities and found that one behavioral change was greater concern with time and planning activities in advance. The point is not that Westerners plan and non-Westerners do not. What occurred was a reorganization of cultural practices that, in turn, led to the reorganization of a cognitive behavior, planning.

The main point is that activities and the goals that guide them are expressions of culture. Focusing on the cultural context of human activity may advance understanding of how the human mind is organized over the course of development to fit with the requirements and opportunities of the culture. Incidentally, this point may offer insight into the issue of transfer or generalization of cognitive skills across different task contexts, a topic that has vexed psychologists for generations. Psychologists have often sought transfer by focusing on isomorphic tasks (i.e., tasks that are very similar in structure). However, the key psychological linkage supporting transfer may not be task properties per se, but may instead be the meaning and goals of an activity and how a culture has devised ways, such as problem-solving routines, to achieve these goals and connect human action over time and space.

Material and Symbolic Tools

Material and symbolic tools, or artifacts (Cole, 1996), are developed and used by cultural communities to support mental activity. Such tools not only enhance thinking but also transform it, and in so doing, they channel cognitive development in unique ways. Involvement with more experienced cultural members, who demonstrate and convey the use of these tools, is a critical part of this process. Through the use of such "tools for thinking," a person's mental functioning acquires an organized link to sociohistorically formulated means of thinking transmitted through these tools.

Research on the use of particular cultural tools and the development of mathematical thinking illustrates this point. Children who are skilled at using the abacus employ a "mental abacus" when calculating solutions in their heads (Hatano, Miyake, & Binks, 1977), and this skill enhances mental calculation. Historical examination lends further insight into this

process (Swetz, 1987). Late in the 12th century, a book by Leonardo of Pisa, who was also known as Fibonacci, introduced Hindu-Arabic notation and described the commercial applications of this system. This idea was picked up by Italian merchants in the next century and led to changes in conventions of calculating. At the time, Roman numerals were used, and large calculations were executed on the counting board, a form of abacus. These boards were very large, hard to transport, and difficult to use. Extensive training was needed to reach competence, and only a few people could do the calculations or check them for correctness. Hindu-Arabic numerals were entirely different. Far less equipment was needed to calculate with this system— ink and paper sufficed. This equipment was easy to transport, and, more important, it was easy to teach and learn. In a brief period of time, the long-established form of calculation was replaced. Although the Hindu-Arabic system limited the need for mental calculation, it helped lay the foundation for further developments in mathematics, especially in areas like number theory, in that calculations can be represented on paper and reexamined for patterns and structure (Swetz, 1987).

How does this historical case relate to the findings about skilled abacus users? Think again about mental calculation, a cognitive process that research indicates is aided by skill with the abacus. What this history tells us is that the shift from Roman to Hindu-Arabic numerals made mental calculation largely obsolete, as well as less valued, because calculating on paper allowed people to demonstrate their solution steps. It appears that differential skill of people who do and do not use the abacus may have origins in the notation shift introduced in the 13th and 14th centuries. The mathematical skills of experts are consistent with the requirements of the apparatus and the practice their notation systems afford.

The main point is that cultural tools and the thinking they support are not independent but merged. To describe thinking by concentrating on one and not the other is to ignore part of the problem-solving process. Too often in psychological research when tools of thinking are described, they are treated as entities outside the head, and therefore not part of, or at least not central to, the cognitive process being investigated. However, such thinking tools, both material and symbolic, are constituent elements of cognition and its development. The historical example suggests that many of the concepts considered fundamental to human cognition in the domains in which artifacts play important roles have not always been in place, at least not in the way they are conceptualized today. Certain tools of thought came into being at various points during human history, and these influenced thinking in extraordinary ways. These historical "changes of mind" may be illuminating for scholars interested in cognitive development. Although historical analysis is of limited use to psychologists for many reasons, such cases may be helpful for demonstrating an organized link among artifacts, social processes, and the mind that is often difficult to see in the more local, contemporary circumstances in which psychologists usually do their research.

Higher Level Structures and Practices

Organized social practices or conventions allow people to share their knowledge with one another. These structures help connect members of a community to each other and to a shared system of meaning. Examples of the connection between cognitive development and cultural ways of organizing and communicating knowledge exist in the developmental literature. Research on scripts, which are "outlines" of common, recurrent events (Nelson & Gruendel, 1981), treats the acquisition of culturally organized knowledge as a critical developmental achievement. Research on the development of other pragmatic conventions, such as skill at describing large-scale space (Gauvain & Rogoff, 1989) as if one is being taken on an imagined walk through it (a "mental tour"), also suggests that one important aspect of development is the increasing alignment of knowledge with the conventions of the community in which development occurs.

An intriguing question is whether these conventional forms influence the process of thinking and its development. There is far less data on this question. However, an interesting series of studies by Levinson (1996) in an Australian Aboriginal community, the Guugu Yimithirr, is relevant. To describe spatial location, the language used in this community does not rely on relativistic terms, like left and right, but on absolute or fixed directional terms, like north, south, windward, and upstream. How do these speakers encode spatial information? In one study, objects were positioned on a table in a windowless, nondescript room. Each participant studied these placements, was then taken to a similar room that was oriented differently, and asked to place the same set of objects on a table so as to duplicate the placements in the first room. Participants placed the items in ways that respected the cardinal directions of the original placements (i.e., an object placed on the north side of the table was placed on the north, even though this would mean that it would be on the "other side" of an object to an observer using relative position as a guide). Although these results do not specify the cognitive processes underlying this behavior, they suggest that performance on tasks involving spatial cognition involves the coordination of visual and linguistic encoding in ways related to practices of the cultural community.

Another set of higher level structures related to the development of thinking appears in practices of social interaction. In recent years, there has been extensive research on the influence of social interaction on cognitive development, with much of this work based on Vygotsky's (1978) notion of the zone of proximal development, which is defined as the distance between an individual's attained level of development and the individual's potential level of development that may be reached by guidance and support from others (see Rogoff, 1990). Results from this research support the claim that intelligence, especially in the early years, develops largely through social experiences. For example, when Tessler and Nelson (1994) tested the recall of 3- to 3-½-year-old children about a visit they took to a museum with their mothers, none of the children recalled any information that they had seen in the museum but not discussed with their mothers. Dyadic interaction with adults or peers is only one form of social exchange that may determine young children's opportunities for cognitive development in social context. Parents also influence children's learning via the practical routines they adopt to organize children's behaviors and by regulating the composition of children's social groups. Beyond the family and peer group, cognitive development is influenced by children's participation in more formal social institutions, especially school, and by opportunities to observe more competent cultural members as they engage in cognitive activities, a process Lave and Wenger (1991) call legitimate peripheral participation.

The point is that cognitive development occurs in and emerges from social situations. Conventions for organizing and conveying knowledge, as well as social practices within which knowledge is displayed and communicated, are an inherent aspect of thinking. For research to advance, these social systems need to be connected in a principled way to the developmental processes they help organize, as well as to the cultural system of meaning and practice they represent.

CONCLUSIONS

In summary, a sociocultural view of cognitive development enhances understanding of this psychological process. Dimensions of culture are realized in human action, and it is possible to specify and study these dimensions in relation to psychological development. They can bring the social and cultural character of intellectual development into relief. Understanding culture and cognitive development can be advanced via research designed for this purpose as well as by reexamining findings extant in the literature.

All this said, many hard questions remain. One concerns how to understand and describe individual skill that emerges in and is displayed in social situations. Psychologists have yet to devise a language for describing thinking that is not entirely in the head of the child or is only partially in place (i.e., evident only in some circumstances). Haith (1997) pointed out that many of the cognitive skills that children develop are defined in dichotomous terms. Consider mental representations. Representations are typically understood as something that a person either has or does not have (i.e., as states of understanding rather than as processes), and rarely as something that is partially or incompletely achieved. Such conceptualization may suffice in describing the mature thinker, though this is an open question. But it is surely inadequate for describing the development of knowledge that appears in the form of "partial understanding," such as that located in social performance. Thus, in order to incorporate the notion of partial or socially contextualized intellectual accomplishments into an understanding of cognitive development, we need a different conceptualization of many cognitive skills.

The analysis of culture in all aspects of psychological functioning is likely to increase dramatically in the next decade. How psychologists, especially those interested in intellectual development, will address this concern is unclear. Perhaps by developing conceptual frameworks, such as the one presented here, in which social and cultural systems of interacting and supporting psychological functions are an inextricable part of human behavior and development, this task may be eased.

Notes

1. Address correspondence to Mary Gauvain, Department of Psychology, University of California at Riverside, Riverside, CA 92521; e-mail: mary.gauvain@ucr.edu.
2. Functional fixedness is a problem-solving phenomenon in which people have difficulty seeing alternate uses for common objects.

Recommended Reading

Cole, M. (1996). (See References)
Gauvain, M. (1995). Thinking in niches: Sociocultural influences on cognitive development. *Human Development, 38*, 25–45.
Goodnow, J.J. (1990). The socialization of cognition. In J.W. Stigler, R.A. Schweder,

& G. Herdt (Eds.), *Cultural psychology* (pp. 259–286). New York: Cambridge University Press.
Nelson, K. (1996). *Language in cognitive development: The emergence of the mediated mind.* Cambridge, England: Cambridge University Press.
Rogoff, B. (1998). Cognition as a collaborative process. In W. Damon (Series Ed.) & D. Kuhn & R.S. Siegler (Vol. Eds.), *Handbook of child psychology: Vol. 2. Cognition, perception, and language* (pp. 679–744). New York: John Wiley and Sons.

References

Carraher, T.N., Carraher, D.W., & Schliemann, A.D. (1985). Mathematics in the streets and in schools. *British Journal of Developmental Psychology, 3*, 21–29.
Chaiklin, S., & Lave, J. (1996). *Understanding practice: Perspectives on activity and context.* Cambridge, England: Cambridge University Press.
Cole, M. (1996). *Cultural psychology.* Cambridge, MA: Harvard University Press.
Gauvain, M., & Rogoff, B. (1989). Ways of speaking about space: The development of children's skill at communicating spatial knowledge. *Cognitive Development, 4*, 295–307.
Haith, M.M. (1997, April). *Who put the cog in infant cognition? Is rich interpretation too costly?* Paper presented at the biennial meeting of the Society for Research in Child Development, Washington, DC.

Hatano, G., Miyake, Y., & Binks, M. (1977). Performance of expert abacus operators. *Cognition, 9*, 47–55.
Inkeles, A., & Smith, D.H. (1974). *Becoming modern.* Cambridge, MA: Harvard University Press.
Lave, J., & Wenger, E. (1991). *Situated learning: Legitimate peripheral participation.* New York: Cambridge University Press.
Levinson, S.C. (1996). Frames of reference and Molyneux's question: Crosslinguistic evidence. In P. Bloom, M.A. Peterson, L. Nadel, & M.F. Garrett (Eds.), *Language and space* (pp. 109–169). Cambridge, MA: MIT Press.
Nelson, K., & Gruendel, J. (1981). Generalized event representations: Basic building blocks of cognitive development. In M.E. Lamb & A.L. Brown (Eds.), *Advances in developmental psychology* (Vol. 1, pp. 131–158). Hillsdale, NJ: Erlbaum.
Rogoff, B. (1990). *Apprenticeship in thinking.* New York: Oxford University Press.
Super, C.M., & Harkness, S. (1986). The developmental niche: A conceptualization at the interface of child and culture. *International Journal of Behavioral Development, 9*, 545–569.
Swetz, F.J. (1987). *Capitalism and arithmetic.* La Salle, IL: Open Court.
Tessler, M., & Nelson, K. (1994). Making memories: The influence of joint encoding on later recall. *Consciousness and Cognition, 3*, 307–326.
Vygotsky, L.S. (1978). *Mind in society.* Cambridge, MA: Harvard University Press.

Who Owns Intelligence?

by *HOWARD GARDNER*

Three unresolved issues will dominate the discussion of intelligence: whether intelligence is one thing or many things; whether intelligence is inherited; and whether any of its elements can accurately be measured. The debate, a prominent psychologist argues, is really over proprietary rights to a fundamental concept of our age

ALMOST a century ago Alfred Binet, a gifted psychologist, was asked by the French Ministry of Education to help determine who would experience difficulty in school. Given the influx of provincials to the capital, along with immigrants of uncertain stock, Parisian officials believed they needed to know who might not advance smoothly through the system. Proceeding in an empirical manner, Binet posed many questions to youngsters of different ages. He ascertained which questions when answered correctly predicted success in school, and which questions when answered incorrectly foretold school difficulties. The items that discriminated most clearly between the two groups became, in effect, the first test of intelligence.

Binet is a hero to many psychologists. He was a keen observer, a careful scholar, an inventive technologist. Perhaps even more important for his followers, he devised the instrument that is often considered psychology's greatest success story. Millions of people who have never heard Binet's name have had aspects of their fate influenced by instrumentation that the French psychologist inspired. And thousands of psychometricians—specialists in the measurement of psychological variables—earn their living courtesy of Binet's invention.

Although it has prevailed over the long run, the psychologists' version of intelligence is now facing its biggest threat.

Many scholars and observers—and even some iconoclastic psychologists—feel that intelligence is too important to be left to the psychometricians. Experts are extending the breadth of the concept—proposing many intelligences, including emotional intelligence and moral intelligence. They are experimenting with new methods of ascertaining intelligence, including some that avoid tests altogether in favor of direct measures of brain activity. They are forcing citizens everywhere to confront a number of questions: What is intelligence? How ought it to be assessed? And how do our notions of intelligence fit with what we value about human beings? In short, experts are competing for the "ownership" of intelligence in the next century.

THE outline of the psychometricians' success story is well known. Binet's colleagues in England and Germany contributed to the conceptualization and instrumentation of intelligence testing—which soon became known as IQ tests. (An IQ, or intelligence quotient, designates the ratio between mental age and chronological age. Clearly we'd prefer that a child in our care have an IQ of 120, being smarter than average for his or her years, than an IQ of 80, being older than average for his or her intelligence.) Like other Parisian fashions of the period, the intelligence test migrated easily to the United States. First used to determine who was "feeble-minded," it was soon used to assess "normal" children, to identify the "gifted," and to determine who was fit to serve in the Army. By the 1920s the intelligence test had become a fixture in educational practice in the United States and much of Western Europe.

Early intelligence tests were not without their critics. Many enduring concerns were first raised by the influential journalist Walter Lippmann, in a series of published debates with Lewis Terman, of Stanford University, the father of IQ testing in America. Lippmann pointed out the superficiality of the questions, their possible cultural biases, and the risks of trying to determine a person's intellectual potential with a brief oral or paper-and-pencil measure.

Perhaps surprisingly, the conceptualization of intelligence did not advance much in the decades following Binet's and Terman's pioneering contributions. Intelligence tests came to be seen, rightly or wrongly, as primarily a tool for selecting people to fill academic or vocational niches. In one of the most famous—if irritating—remarks about intelligence testing, the influential Harvard psychologist E. G. Boring declared, "Intelligence is what the tests test." So long as these tests did what they were supposed to do (that is, give some indication of school success), it did not seem necessary or prudent to probe too deeply into their meaning or to explore alternative views of the human intellect.

> ## For the first time in many years the intelligence establishment is clearly on the defensive—and the new century seems likely to usher in quite different ways of thinking about intelligence.

Psychologists who study intelligence have argued chiefly about three questions. The first: Is intelligence singular, or does it consist of various more or less independent intellectual faculties? The purists— ranging from the turn-of-the-century English psychologist Charles Spearman to his latter-day disciples Richard J. Herrnstein and Charles Murray (of *The Bell Curve* fame)—defend the notion of a single overarching "g," or general intelligence. The pluralists—ranging from L. L. Thurstone, of the University of Chicago, who posited seven vectors of the mind, to J. P. Guilford, of the University of Southern California, who discerned 150 factors of the intellect—construe intelligence as composed of some or even many dissociable components. In his much cited *The Mismeasure of Man* (1981) the paleontologist Stephen Jay Gould argued that the conflicting

conclusions reached on this issue reflect alternative assumptions about statistical procedures rather than the way the mind is. Still, psychologists continue the debate, with a majority sympathetic to the general-intelligence perspective.

The public is more interested in the second question: Is intelligence (or are intelligences) largely inherited? This is by and large a Western question. In the Confucian societies of East Asia individual differences in endowment are assumed to be modest, and differences in achievement are thought to be due largely to effort. In the West, however, many students of the subject sympathize with the view—defended within psychology by Lewis Terman, among others—that intelligence is inborn and one can do little to alter one's intellectual birthright.

Studies of identical twins reared apart provide surprisingly strong support for the "heritability" of psychometric intelligence. That is, if one wants to predict someone's score on an intelligence test, the scores of the biological parents (even if the child has not had appreciable contact with them) are more likely to prove relevant than the scores of the adoptive parents. By the same token, the IQs of identical twins are more similar than the IQs of fraternal twins. And, contrary to common sense (and political correctness), the IQs of biologically related people grow closer in the later years of life. Still, because of the intricacies of behavioral genetics and the difficulties of conducting valid experiments with human child-rearing, a few defend the proposition that intelligence is largely environmental rather than heritable, and some believe that we cannot answer the question at all.

Most scholars agree that even if psychometric intelligence is largely inherited, it is not possible to pinpoint the sources of differences in average IQ between groups, such as the fifteen-point difference typically observed between African-American and white populations. That is because in our society the contemporary—let alone the historical—experiences of these two groups cannot be equated. One could ferret out the differences (if any) between black and white populations only in a society that was truly color-blind.

One other question has intrigued laypeople and psychologists: Are intelligence tests biased? Cultural assumptions are evident in early intelligence tests. Some class biases are obvious—who except the wealthy could readily answer a question about polo? Others are more subtle. Suppose the question is what one should do with money found on the street. Although ordinarily one might turn it over to the police, what if one had a hungry child? Or what if the police force were known to be hostile to members of one's ethnic group? Only the canonical response to such a question would be scored as correct.

Psychometricians have striven to remove the obviously biased items from such measures. But biases that are built into the test situation itself are far more difficult to deal with. For example, a person's background affects his or her reaction to being placed in an unfamiliar locale, being instructed by someone dressed in a certain way, and having a printed test booklet thrust into his or her hands. And as the psychologist Claude M. Steele has argued in these pages (see "Race and the Schooling of Black Americans," April, 1992), the biases prove even more acute when people know that their academic potential is being measured and that their racial or ethnic group is widely considered to be less intelligent than the dominant social group.

The idea of bias touches on the common assumption that tests in general, and intelligence tests in particular, are inherently conservative instruments—tools of the establishment. It is therefore worth noting that many testing pioneers thought of themselves as progressives in the social sphere. They were devising instruments that could reveal people of talent even if those people came from "remote and apparently inferior backgrounds," to quote from a college catalogue of the 1950s. And occasionally the tests did discover intellectual diamonds in the rough. More often, however, they picked out the privileged. The still unresolved question of the causal relationship between IQ and social privilege has stimulated many a dissertation across the social sciences.

Paradoxically, one of the clearest signs of the success of intelligence tests is that they are no longer widely administered. In the wake of legal cases about the propriety of making consequential decisions about education on the basis of IQ scores, many public school officials have become test-shy. By and large, the testing of IQ in the schools is restricted to cases involving a recognized problem (such as a learning disability) or a selection procedure (determining eligibility for a program that serves gifted children).

Despite this apparent setback, intelligence testing and the line of thinking that underlies it have actually triumphed. Many widely used scholastic measures, chief among them the SAT (renamed the Scholastic Assessment Test a few years ago), are thinly disguised intelligence tests that correlate highly with scores on standard psychometric instruments. Virtually no one raised in the developed world today has gone untouched by Binet's seemingly simple invention of a century ago.

Multiple Intelligences

THE concept of intelligence has in recent years undergone its most robust challenge since the days of Walter Lippmann. Some who are informed by psychology but not bound by the assumptions of the psychometricians have invaded this formerly sacrosanct territory. They have put forth their own ideas of what intelligence is, how (and whether) it should be measured, and which values should be invoked in considerations of the human intellect. For the first time in many years the intelligence establishment is clearly on the defensive—and the new century seems likely to usher in quite different ways of thinking about intelligence.

One evident factor in the rethinking of intelligence is the perspective introduced by scholars who are not psychologists. Anthropologists have commented on the parochialism of the Western view of intelligence. Some cultures do not even have a concept called intelligence, and others define intelligence in

terms of traits that we in the West might consider odd—obedience, good listening skills, or moral fiber, for example. Neuroscientists are skeptical that the highly differentiated and modular structure of the brain is consistent with a unitary form of intelligence. Computer scientists have devised programs deemed intelligent; these programs often go about problem-solving in ways quite different from those embraced by human beings or other animals.

Even within the field of psychology the natives have been getting restless. Probably the most restless is the Yale psychologist Robert J. Sternberg. A prodigious scholar, Sternberg, who is forty-nine, has written dozens of books and hundreds of articles, the majority of them focusing in one or another way on intelligence. Sternberg began with the strategic goal of understanding the actual mental processes mobilized by standard test items, such as the solving of analogies. But he soon went beyond standard intelligence testing by insisting on two hitherto neglected forms of intelligence: the "practical" ability to adapt to varying contexts (as we all must in these days of divorcing and downsizing), and the capacity to automate familiar activities so that we can deal effectively with novelty and display "creative" intelligence.

Sternberg has gone to greater pains than many other critics of standard intelligence testing to measure these forms of intelligence with the paper-and-pencil laboratory methods favored by the profession. And he has found that a person's ability to adapt to diverse contexts or to deal with novel information can be differentiated from success at standard IQ-test problems. His efforts to create a new intelligence test have not been crowned with easy victory. Most psychometricians are conservative—they like the tests that have been in use for decades, and if new ones are to be marketed, these must correlate well with existing instruments. So much for openness to novelty within psychometrics.

Others in the field seem less bound by its strictures. The psychologist and journalist Daniel Goleman has achieved worldwide success with his book *Emotional Intelligence* (1995). Contending that this new concept (sometimes nicknamed EQ) may matter as much as or more than IQ, Goleman draws attention to such pivotal human abilities as controlling one's emotional reactions and "reading" the signals of others. In the view of the noted psychiatrist Robert Coles, author of *The Moral Intelligence of Children* (1997), among many other books, we should prize character over intellect. He decries the amorality of our families, hence our children; he shows how we might cultivate human beings with a strong sense of right and wrong, who are willing to act on that sense even when it runs counter to self-interest. Other, frankly popular accounts deal with leadership intelligence (LQ), executive intelligence (EQ or ExQ), and even financial intelligence.

Like Coles's and Goleman's efforts, my work on "multiple intelligences" eschews the psychologists' credo of operationalization and test-making. I began by asking two questions: How did the human mind and brain evolve over millions of years? and How can we account for the diversity of skills and capacities that are or have been valued in different communities around the world?

Armed with these questions and a set of eight criteria, I have concluded that all human beings possess at least eight intelligences: linguistic and logical-mathematical (the two most prized in school and the ones central to success on standard intelligence tests), musical, spatial, bodily-kinesthetic, naturalist, interpersonal, and intrapersonal.

I make two complementary claims about intelligence. The first is universal. We all possess these eight intelligences—and possibly more. Indeed, rather than seeing us as "rational animals," I offer a new definition of what it means to be a human being, cognitively speaking: *Homo sapiens sapiens* is the animal that possesses these eight forms of mental representation.

My second claim concerns individual differences. Owing to the accidents of heredity, environment, and their interactions, no two of us exhibit the same intelligences in precisely the same proportions. Our "profiles of intelligence" differ from one another. This fact poses intriguing challenges and opportunities for our education system. We can ignore these differences and pretend that we are all the same; historically, that is what most education systems have done. Or we can fashion an education system that tries to exploit these differences, individualizing instruction and assessment as much as possible.

Intelligence and Morality

As the century of Binet and his successors draws to a close, we'd be wise to take stock of, and to anticipate, the course of thinking about intelligence. Although my crystal ball is no clearer than anyone else's (the species may lack "future intelligence"), it seems safe to predict that interest in intelligence will not go away.

> **Interest in the subject of intelligence is likely to be fed by the creation of machines that display intelligence and by the possibility that we can genetically engineer organisms of a specific intelligence or intelligences.**

To begin with, the psychometric community has scarcely laid down its arms. New versions of the standard tests continue to be created, and occasionally new tests surface as well. Researchers in the psychometric tradition churn out fresh evidence of the predictive power of their instruments and the correlations between measured intelligence and one's life chances. And some in the psychometric tradition are searching for the biological basis of intelligence: the gene or complex of genes that may affect intelligence, the neural structures that are crucial for intelligence, or telltale brain-wave patterns that distinguish the bright from the less bright.

Beyond various psychometric twists, interest in intelligence is likely to grow in other ways. It will be fed by the creation of machines that display intelligence and by the specific intelligence or intelligences. Moreover, observers as diverse as Richard Herrnstein and Robert B. Reich, President Clinton's first Secretary of Labor, have agreed that in coming years a large proportion of society's rewards will go to those people who are skilled symbol analysts—who can sit at a computer screen (or its technological successor), manipulate numbers and other kinds of symbols, and use the results of their operations to contrive plans, tactics, and strategies for enterprises ranging from business to science to war games. These people may well color how intelligence is conceived in decades to come—just as the need to provide good middle-level bureaucrats to run an empire served as a primary molder of intelligence tests in the early years of the century.

Surveying the landscape of intelligence, I discern three struggles between opposing forces. The extent to which, and the manner in which, these various struggles are resolved will influence the lives of millions of people. I believe that the three struggles are interrelated; that the first struggle provides the key to the other two; and that the ensemble of struggles can be resolved in an optimal way.

The first struggle concerns the breadth of our definition of intelligence. One camp consists of the purists, who believe in a single form of intelligence—one that basically predicts success in school and in school-like activities. Arrayed against the purists are the progressive pluralists, who believe that many forms of intelligence exist. Some of these pluralists would like to broaden the definition of intelligence considerably, to include the abilities to create, to lead, and to stand out in terms of emotional sensitivity or moral excellence.

The second struggle concerns the assessment of intelligence. Again, one readily encounters a traditional position. Once chiefly concerned with paper-and-pencil tests, the traditionally oriented practitioner is now likely to use computers to provide the same information more quickly and more accurately. But other positions abound. Purists disdain psychological tasks of any complexity, preferring to look instead at reaction time, brain waves, and other physiological measures of intellect. In contrast, simulators favor measures closely resembling the actual abilities that are prized. And skeptics warn against the continued expansion of testing. They emphasize the damage often done to individual life chances and self-esteem by a regimen of psychological testing, and call for less technocratic, more humane methods—ranging from self-assessment to the examination of portfolios of student work to selection in the service of social equity.

The final struggle concerns the relationship between intelligence and the qualities we value in human beings. Although no one would baldly equate intellect and human worth, nuanced positions have emerged on this issue. Some (in the *Bell Curve* mold) see intelligence as closely related to a person's ethics and values; they believe that brighter people are more likely to appreciate moral complexity and to behave judiciously. Some call for a sharp distinction between the realm of intellect on the one hand, and character, morality, or ethics on the other. Society's ambivalence on this issue can be discerned in the figures that become the culture's heroes. For every Albert Einstein or Bobby Fischer who is celebrated for his intellect, there is a Forrest Gump or a Chauncey Gardiner who is celebrated for human—and humane—traits that would never be captured on any kind of intelligence test.

Thanks to the work of the past decade or two, the stranglehold of the psychometricians has at last been broken. This is a beneficent development. Yet now that the psychometricians have been overcome, we risk deciding that anything goes—that emotions, morality, creativity, must all be absorbed into the "new (or even the New Age) intelligence." The challenge is to chart a concept of intelligence that reflects new insights and discoveries and yet can withstand rigorous scrutiny.

An analogy may help. One can think of the scope of intelligence as represented by an elastic band. For many years the definition of intelligence went unchallenged, and the band seemed to have lost its elasticity. Some of the new definitions expand the band, so that it has become taut and resilient; and yet earlier work on intelligence is still germane. Other definitions so expand the band that it is likely finally to snap—and the earlier work on intelligence will no longer be of use.

> # The concept of "intelligence" should not be expanded to include personality, motivation, will, character, creativity, and other important and significant human capacities. Such stretching is likely to snap the band.

Until now the term "intelligence" has been limited largely to certain kinds of problem-solving involving language and logic—the skills at a premium in the bureaucrat or the law professor. However, human beings are able to deal with numerous kinds of content besides words, numbers, and logical relations—for example, space, music, the psyches of other human beings. Like the elastic band, definitions of intelligence need to be expanded to include human skill in dealing with these diverse contents. And we must not restrict attention to solving problems that have been posed by others; we must consider equally the capacity of individuals to fashion products—scientific experiments, effective organizations—that draw on one or more human intelligences. The elastic band can accommodate such broadening as well.

So long as intelligences are restricted to the processing of contents in the world, we avoid epistemological problems—as we should. "Intelligence" should not be expanded to include personality, motivation, will, attention, character, creativity, and other important and significant human capacities. Such stretching is likely to snap the band.

Let's see what happens when one crosses one of these lines—for example, when one attempts to conflate intelligence and creativity. Beginning with a definition, we extend the descriptor "creative" to those people (or works or institutions) who meet two criteria: they are innovative, and their innovations are eventually accepted by a relevant community.

No one denies that creativity is important—and, indeed, it may prove even more important in the future, when nearly all standard (algorithmic) procedures will be carried out by computers. Yet creativity should not be equated with intelligence. An expert may be intelligent in one or more domains but not necessarily inclined toward, or successful in, innovation. Similarly, although it is clear that the ability to innovate requires a certain degree of intelligence, we don't find a significant correlation between measures of intellect and of creativity. Indeed, creativity seems more dependent on a certain kind of temperament and personality—risk-taking, tough-skinned, persevering, above all having a lust to alter the status quo and leave a mark on society—than on efficiency in processing various kinds of information. By collapsing these categories together, we risk missing dimensions that are important but separate; and we may think that we are training (or selecting) one when we are actually training (or selecting) the other.

Next consider what happens when one stretches the idea of intelligence to include attitudes and behaviors—and thus confronts human values within a culture. A few values can be expressed generically enough that they command universal respect: the Golden Rule is one promising candidate. Most values, however, turn out to be specific to certain cultures or subcultures—even such seemingly unproblematic ones as the unacceptability of killing or lying. Once one conflates morality and intelligence, one needs to deal with widely divergent views of what is good or bad and why. Moreover, one must confront the fact that people who score high on tests of moral reasoning may act immorally outside the test situation—even as courageous and self-sacrificing people may turn out to be unremarkable on formal tests of moral reasoning or intelligence. It is far preferable to construe intelligence itself as morally neutral and then decide whether a given use of intelligence qualifies as moral, immoral, or amoral in context.

As I see it, no intelligence is moral or immoral in itself. One can be gifted in language and use that gift to write great verse, as did Johann Wolfgang von Goethe, or to foment hatred, as did Joseph Goebbels. Mother Teresa and Lyndon Johnson, Mohandas Gandhi and Niccolò Machiavelli, may have had equivalent degrees of interpersonal intelligence, but they put their skills to widely divergent uses.

> I question the wisdom of searching for a "pure" intelligence. I do not believe that such alchemical intellectual essences actually exist; they are a product of our penchant for creating terminology.

Perhaps there is a form of intelligence that determines whether or not a situation harbors moral considerations or consequences. But the term "moral intelligence" carries little force. After all, Adolf Hitler and Joseph Stalin may well have had an exquisite sense of which situations contained moral considerations. However, either they did not care or they embraced their own peculiar morality, according to which eliminating Jews was the moral thing to do in quest of a pure Aryan society, or wiping out a generation was necessary in the quest to establish a communist state.

The Borders of Intelligence

WRITING as a scholar rather than as a layperson, I see two problems with the notion of emotional intelligence. First, unlike language or space, the emotions are not contents to be processed; rather, cognition has evolved so that we can make sense of human beings (self and others) that possess and experience emotions. Emotions are part and parcel of all cognition, though they may well prove more salient at certain times or under certain circumstances: they accompany our interactions with others, our listening to great music, our feelings when we solve—or fail to solve—a difficult mathematical problem. If one calls some intelligences emotional, one suggests that other intelligences are not—and that implication flies in the face of experience and empirical data.

The second problem is the conflation of emotional intelligence and a certain preferred pattern of behavior. This is the trap that Daniel Goleman sometimes falls into in his otherwise admirable *Emotional Intelligence*. Goleman singles out as emotionally intelligent those people who use their understanding of emotions to make others feel better, to solve conflicts, or to cooperate in home or work situations. No one would dispute that such people are wanted. However, people who understand emo-

tion may not necessarily use their skills for the benefit of society.

For this reason I prefer the term "emotional sensitivity"—a term (encompassing my interpersonal and intrapersonal intelligences) that could apply to people who are sensitive to emotions in themselves and in others. Presumably, clinicians and salespeople excel in sensitivity to others, poets and mystics in sensitivity to themselves. And some autistic or psychopathological people seem completely insensitive to the emotional realm. I would insist, however, on a strict distinction between emotional sensitivity and being a "good" or "moral" person. A person may be sensitive to the emotions of others but use that sensitivity to manipulate or to deceive them, or to create hatred.

I call, then, for a delineation of intelligence that includes the full range of contents to which human beings are sensitive, but at the same time designates as off limits such valued but separate human traits as creativity, morality, and emotional appropriateness. I believe that such a delineation makes scientific and epistemological sense. It reinvigorates the elastic band without stretching it to the breaking point. It helps to resolve the two remaining struggles: how to assess, and what kinds of human beings to admire.

Once we decide to restrict intelligence to human information-processing and product-making capacities, we can make use of the established technology of assessment. That is, we can continue to use paper-and-pencil or computer-adapted testing techniques while looking at a broader range of capacities, such as musical sensitivity and empathy with others. And we can avoid ticklish and possibly unresolvable questions about the assessment of values and morality that may well be restricted to a particular culture and that may well change over time.

Still, even with a limited perspective on intelligence, important questions remain about which assessment path to follow—that of the purist, the simulator, or the skeptic. Here I have strong views. I question the wisdom of searching for a "pure" intelligence—be it general intelligence, musical intelligence, or interpersonal intelligence. I do not believe that such alchemical intellectual essences actually exist; they are a product of our penchant for creating terminology rather than determinable and measurable entities. Moreover, the correlations that have thus far been found between supposedly pure measures and the skills that we actually value in the world are too modest to be useful.

What does exist is the use of intelligences, individually and in concert, to carry out tasks that are valued by a society. Accordingly, we should be assessing the extent to which human beings succeed in carrying out tasks of consequence that presumably involve certain intelligences. To be concrete, we should not test musical intelligence by looking at the ability to discriminate between two tones or timbres; rather, we should be teaching people to sing songs or play instruments or transform melodies and seeing how readily they master such feats. At the same time, we should abjure a search for pure emotional sensitivity—for example, a test that matches facial expressions to galvanic skin response. Rather, we should place (or observe) people in situations that call for them to be sensitive to the aspirations and motives of others. For example, we could see how they handle a situation in which they and colleagues have to break up a fight between two teenagers, or persuade a boss to change a policy of which they do not approve.

Here powerful new simulations can be invoked. We are now in a position to draw on technologies that can deliver realistic situations or problems and also record the success of subjects in dealing with them. A student can be presented with an unfamiliar tune on a computer and asked to learn that tune, transpose it, orchestrate it, and the like. Such exercises would reveal much about the student's intelligence in musical matters.

Turning to the social (or human, if you prefer) realm, subjects can be presented with simulated interactions and asked to judge the shifting motivations of each actor. Or they can be asked to work in an interactive hypermedia production with unfamiliar people who are trying to accomplish some sort of goal, and to respond to their various moves and countermoves. The program can alter responses in light of the moves of the subject. Like a high-stakes poker game, such a measure should reveal much about the interpersonal or emotional sensitivity of a subject.

A significant increase in the breadth—the elasticity—of our concept of intelligence, then, should open the possibility for innovative forms of assessment far more realistic than the classic short-answer examinations. Why settle for an IQ or an SAT test, in which the items are at best remote proxies for the ability to design experiments, write essays, critique musical performances, and so forth? Why not instead ask people actually (or virtually) to carry out such tasks? And yet by not opening up the Pandora's box of values and subjectivity, one can continue to make judicious use of the insights and technologies achieved by those who have devoted decades to perfecting mental measurement.

To be sure, one can create a psychometric instrument for any conceivable human virtue, including morality, creativity, and emotional intelligence in its several senses. Indeed, since the publication of Daniel Goleman's book dozens of efforts have been made to create tests for emotional intelligence. The resulting instruments are not, however, necessarily useful. Such instruments are far more likely to satisfy the test maker's desire for reliability (a subject gets roughly the same score on two separate administrations of the test) than the need for validity (the test measures the trait that it purports to measure).

Such instruments-on-demand prove dubious for two reasons. First, beyond some platitudes, few can agree on what it means to be moral, ethical, a good person: consider the differing values of Jesse Helms and Jesse Jackson, Margaret Thatcher and Margaret Mead. Second, scores on such tests are much more likely to reveal test-taking savvy (skills in language and logic) than fundamental character.

In speaking about character, I turn to a final concern: the relationship between intelligence and what I will call virtue—those qualities that we admire and wish to hold up as examples for our children. No doubt the desire to expand intelligence to encompass ethics and character represents a direct response to the general feeling that our society is lacking in these dimensions; the expansionist view of intelligence reflects the hope that if we transmit the technology of intelligence to these virtues, we might in the end secure a more virtuous population.

I have already indicated my strong reservations about trying to make the word "intelligence" all things to all people—the psychometric equivalent of the true, the beautiful, and the good. Yet the problem remains: how, in a post-Aristotelian, post-Confucian era in which psychometrics looms large, do we think about the virtuous human being?

My analysis suggests one promising approach. We should recognize that intelligences, creativity, and morality—to mention just three desiderata—are separate. Each may require its own form of measurement or assessment, and some will prove far easier to assess objectively than others. Indeed, with respect to creativity and morality, we are more likely to rely on overall judgments by experts than on any putative test battery. At the same time, nothing prevents us from looking for people who combine several of these attributes—who have musical and interpersonal intelligence, who are psychometrically intelligent and creative in the arts, who combine emotional sensitivity and a high standard of moral conduct.

Let me introduce another analogy at this point. In college admissions much attention is paid to scholastic performance, as measured by College Board examinations and grades. However, other features are also weighed, and sometimes a person with lower test scores is admitted if he or she proves exemplary in terms of citizenship or athletics or motivation. Admissions officers do not confound these virtues (indeed, they may use different scales and issue different grades), but they recognize the attractiveness of candidates who exemplify two or more desirable traits.

We have left the Eden of classical times, in which various intellectual and ethical values necessarily commingled, and we are unlikely ever to re-create it. We should recognize that these virtues can be separate and will often prove to be remote from one another. When we attempt to aggregate them, through phrases like "emotional intelligence," "creative intelligence," and "moral intelligence," we should realize that we are expressing a wish rather than denoting a necessary or even a likely coupling.

We have an aid in converting this wish to reality: the existence of powerful examples—people who succeed in exemplifying two or more cardinal human virtues. To name names is risky—particularly when one generation's heroes can become the subject of the next generation's pathographies. Even so, I can without apology mention Niels Bohr, George C. Marshall, Rachel Carson, Arthur Ashe, Louis Armstrong, Pablo Casals, Ella Fitzgerald.

In studying the lives of such people, we discover human possibilities. Young human beings learn primarily from the examples of powerful adults around them—those who are admirable and also those who are simply glamorous. Sustained attention to admirable examples may well increase the future incidence of people who actually do yoke capacities that are scientifically and epistemologically separate.

In one of the most evocative phrases of the century the British novelist E. M. Forster counseled us, "Only connect." I believe that some expansionists in the territory of intelligence, though well motivated, have prematurely asserted connections that do not exist. But I also believe that as human beings, we can help to forge connections that may be important for our physical and psychic survival.

Just how the precise borders of intelligence are drawn is a question we can leave to scholars. But the imperative to broaden our definition of intelligence in a responsible way goes well beyond the academy. Who "owns" intelligence promises to be an issue even more critical in the next century than it has been in this era of the IQ test.

Howard Gardner teaches human development at the Harvard Graduate School of Education. Among his books are *Multiple Intelligences* (1993), *Extraordinary Minds* (1997), and *The Disciplined Mind*.

From *The Atlantic Monthly*, February 1999, pp. 67–76. © 1999 by Howard Gardner. Reprinted by permission.

Can Animals Think?

In *The Parrot's Lament,* Eugene Linden reveals how animals demonstrate aspects of intelligence as they escape from, cheat and outfox humans

BY EUGENE LINDEN

THE FIRST TIME FU MANCHU BROKE OUT, zookeepers chalked it up to human error. On a balmy day, the orangutans at the Omaha Zoo had been playing in their big outdoor enclosure. Not long thereafter, shocked keepers looked up and saw Fu and his family hanging out in some trees near the elephant barn. Later investigation revealed that the door that connects the furnace room to the orangutan enclosure was open. Head keeper Jerry Stones chewed out his staff, and the incident was forgotten. But the next time the weather was nice, Fu Manchu escaped again. Fuming, Stones recalls, "I was getting ready to fire someone."

CHIMPS

WHAT THE SKEPTICS SAY Most feats of chimp "intelligence" can be explained as the learning of simple rules motivated by the desire for treats

WHAT CHIMPS DO In captivity, they have shown that they know when others have been misinformed—or can be fooled. Awareness of mental states is a key part of consciousness

The next nice day, alerted by keepers desperate to keep their jobs, Stones finally managed to catch Fu Manchu in the act. First, the young ape climbed down some air-vent louvers into a dry moat. Then, taking hold of the bottom of the furnace door, he used brute force to pull it back just far

enough to slide a wire into the gap, slip a latch and pop the door open. The next day, Stones noticed something shiny sticking out of Fu's mouth. It was the wire lock pick, bent to fit between his lip and gum and stowed there between escapes.

Fu Manchu's jailbreaks made headlines in 1968, but his clever tricks didn't make a big impression on the scientists who specialize in looking for signs of higher mental processes in animals. At the time, much of the action in animal intelligence was focused on efforts to teach apes to use human languages. No researcher cared much about ape escape artists.

And neither did I. In 1970, I began following studies of animal intelligence, particularly the early reports of chimpanzees who learned how to use human words. The big breakthrough in these experiments came when two psychologists, R. Allen and Beatrice Gardner, realized their chimps were having trouble forming word-like sounds and decided to teach a young female named Washoe sign language instead. Washoe eventually learned more than 130 words from the language of the deaf called American Sign Language.

Washoe's success spurred more language studies and created such ape celebrities as Koko the gorilla and Chantek the orangutan. The work also set off a fierce debate in scientific circles about the nature of animal intelligence—one that continues to this day. Indeed, it has been easier to defeat communism than to get scientists to agree on what Washoe meant three decades ago when she saw a swan on a pond and made the signs for "water bird." Was she inventing a phrase to describe water-

fowl, or merely generating signs vaguely associated with the scene in front of her?

Over the years I have written several articles and two books on animal-intelligence experiments and the controversy that surrounds them. I have witnessed at close range the problems scientists encounter when they try to examine phenomena as elusive as language and idea formation. Do animals really have thoughts, what we call consciousness? The very question offends some philosophers and scientists, since it cuts so close to what separates men from beasts. Yet, notes Harvard's Donald Griffin, to rule out the study of animal consciousness handicaps our understanding of other species. "If consciousness is important to us and it exists in other creatures," says Griffin, "then it is probably important to them."

DOLPHINS

WHAT THE SKEPTICS SAY The marine mammals may have big brains, but they're used to navigate, not cogitate

WHAT DOLPHINS CAN DO Marineland's Zippy would pick up objects before pool-cleaning divers saw them, then drop them behind the humans. The ruse suggests Zippy was not only playful but also keenly aware of human abilities and habits

Frustrated with what seemed like an endless and barren ideological debate, I began to wonder whether there might be better windows on animal minds than experiments designed to teach them human signs and symbols. When I heard about Fu Manchu, I realized what to me now seems obvious: if animals can think, they will probably do their best thinking when it serves their purposes, not when some scientist asks them to.

BEES

WHAT THE SKEPTICS SAY The insect may work hard, but it's essentially brainless

WHAT BEES DO They not only dance to tell others where to find pollen; there is also evidence that bees somehow realize when they are given a bum steer. When scientists fooled bee scouts by taking them to flowers in a boat in the middle of a lake, few bees flew out over water after the scouts danced

---

And so I started exploring the world of animal intelligence from the other side. I started talking to people who deal with animals professionally: veterinarians, animal researchers, zookeepers—people like Jerry Stones. Most are not studying animal intelligence per se, but they encounter it, and the lack of it, every day.

Get a bunch of keepers together and they will start telling stories about how their charges try to outsmart, beguile or otherwise astonish humans. They tell stories about animals that hoodwink or manipulate their keepers, stories about wheeling and dealing, stories of understanding and trust across the vast gulf that separates different species. And, if the keepers have had a few drinks, they will tell stories about escape.

Each of these narratives reveals another facet of what I have become convinced is a new window on animal intelligence: the kind of mental feats they perform when dealing with captivity and the dominant species on the planet—humanity.

What Do You Want for That Banana?

CAPTIVE ANIMALS OFTEN BECOME STUDENTS of the humans who control their lives. The great apes in particular are alert to situations that might temporarily give them the upper hand—for example, when some-

thing useful or valuable rolls into their exhibit or is left behind. The more worldly animals recognize the concept of value as meaning "something I have that you want," and they are not above exploiting such opportunities for all they are worth.

Consider the time that Charlene Jendry was in her office at the Columbus Zoo and word came to her that a male gorilla named Colo was clutching a suspicious object. Arriving on the scene, Charlene offered Colo some peanuts, only to be met with a blank stare. Realizing that they were negotiating, Charlene upped the ante and offered a piece of pineapple. At this point, without making eye contact with Charlene, Colo opened his hand and revealed that he was holding a key chain, much in the manner that a fence might furtively show a potential customer stolen goods on the street. Relieved that it was not anything dangerous or valuable, Charlene gave Colo the piece of pineapple. Astute bargainer that he was, Colo then broke the key chain and gave Charlene a link, perhaps figuring, "Why give her the whole thing if I can get a bit of pineapple for each piece?"

If an animal can show some skill in the barter business, why not in handling money? One ape, an orangutan named Chantek, did just that during his years as part of a study of sign language undertaken by psychologist Lyn Miles at the University of Tennessee. Chantek learned more than 150 words, but that wasn't all. He also figured out that if he did chores such as cleaning up his room, he could earn coins that he could later spend on treats and rides in Lyn's car.

Chantek's understanding of money seems to have extended far beyond simple transactions to such sophisticated concepts as inflation and counterfeiting. Lyn first used poker chips as the coin of the realm, but Chantek decided that he could expand the money supply by breaking the chips in two. When Lyn switched to using washers, Chantek found pieces of aluminum foil and tried to make imitation washers that he could pass off as the real thing. Lyn also tried to teach Chantek more virtuous habits such as saving, sharing and charity.

When I caught up with the orangutan at Zoo Atlanta, where he now lives, I did not see evidence of charity, but I did see an example of sharing that a robber baron might envy. When Lyn gave Chantek some grapes and asked him to share them with her, Chantek promptly ate all the fruit. Then, seemingly remembering that he'd been asked to share, handed Lyn the bare stem.

The Parrot's Lament

CAN ANIMALS HAVE A sense of humor? Sally Blanchard, publisher of a newsletter called the *Pet Bird Report*, thinks a pet parrot may have pulled her leg. That's one explanation for the time her African gray parrot, named Bongo Marie, seemed to feign distress at the possible demise of an Amazon parrot named Paco.

It happened one day when Blanchard was making Cornish game hen for dinner. As Blanchard lifted her knife, the African gray threw back its head and said, "Oh, no! Paco!" Trying not to laugh, Blanchard said, "That's not Paco," and showed Bongo Marie that the Amazon was alive and well. Mimicking a disappointed tone, Bongo Marie said, "Oh, no," and launched into a raucous laugh.

Was the parrot joking when it seemed to believe the other bird was a goner? Did Bongo Marie comprehend Blanchard's response? Studies of African grays have shown that they can understand the meaning of words—for example, that red refers to a color, not just a particular red object. Parrots also enjoy getting a reaction out of humans, and so, whether or not Bongo Marie's crocodile tears were intentional, the episode was thoroughly satisfying from the parrot's point of view.

What does this tell us? We have been equipped by nature for tasks like juggling numbers and assigning value to things, but these signal human abilities may also be present in more limited form in our closest relatives. Chimps engage in sharing, trading and gift giving in the wild, and they more than hold their own in the primitive bazaar of the zoo.

Lend a Helping Tail

WHY WOULD AN ANIMAL WANT TO COOPERATE with a human? The behaviorist would say that animals cooperate when, through reinforcement, they learn it is in their interest to cooperate. This is true as far as it goes, but I don't think it goes far enough. Certainly with humans, the intangible reinforcement that comes with respect, dignity and accomplishment can be far more motivating than material rewards.

Gail Laule, a consultant on animal behavior with Active Environments Inc., uses rewards to encourage an animal to do something, but also recognizes that animals are more than wind-up toys that blindly respond to tempting treats. "It's much easier to work with a dolphin if you assume that it is intelligent…. That was certainly the case with Orky," says Laule, referring to her work with one of the giant dolphins called orcas or killer whales. "Of all the animals I've worked with, Orky was the most intelligent… He would assess a situation and then do something based on the judgments he made."

Like the time he helped save a member of the family. Orky's mate Corky gave birth in the late 1970s, but the baby did not thrive at first, and the keepers took the little killer whale out of the tank by stretcher for emergency care and feeding. Things began to go awry when they returned the orca to the tank. The boom operator halted the stretcher when it was still a few feet above the water. Suddenly the baby began throwing up, through both its mouth and its blowhole. The keepers feared it would aspirate some vomit, which could bring on a fatal case of pneumonia, but they could not reach the baby dangling above.

Orky had been watching the procedure, and, apparently sizing up the problem, he swam under the stretcher and allowed one of the men to stand on his head. This was remarkable, says Tim, since Orky had never been trained to carry people on his head like Sea World's Shamu. Then, using the amazing power of his tail flukes to keep steady, Orky provided a platform that allowed the keeper to reach up and release the bridle so that the 420-lb. baby could slide into the water within reach of help.

The Keeper Always Falls for That One

A SAD FACT OF LIFE IS THAT IT IS EASIER TO spot evidence of intelligence in devious behavior than in acts of cooperation or love. Sophisticated acts of deception involve the conscious planting of false beliefs in others, which in turn implies awareness that others have mental states that can be manipulated. British psychologist Andrew Whiten of the University of St. Andrews in Scotland says this ability is a "mental Rubicon" dividing humans and at least the other great apes from the rest of the animal kingdom.

While psychologists have studied various forms of animal deception, zookeepers are its targets every day. Helen Shewman, of the Woodland Park Zoo in Seattle,

Wash., recalls that one day she dropped an orange through a feeding porthole for Meladi, one of the female orangutans. Instead of moving away, Meladi looked Helen in the eye and held out her hand. Thinking that the orange must have rolled off somewhere inaccessible, Helen gave her another one. When Meladi shuffled off Helen noticed that she had hidden the original orange in her other hand.

Tawan, the colony's dominant male, watched this whole charade, and the next day he too looked Helen in the eye and pretended that he had not yet received an orange. "Are you sure you don't have one?" Helen asked. He continued to hold her gaze and held out his hand. Relenting, she gave him another, then noticed that he had been hiding his orange under his foot.

LEOPARDS

WHAT THE SKEPTICS SAY Why should a leopard be smart? It's already perfect

WHAT LEOPARDS DO An orphaned cat that was returned to the wild in India moved her cubs from the jungle to her former house when floods neared. Later, she returned one cub to her den across a still swollen river. To ferry the second cub, she hopped in the prow of the owner's canoe and waited for him to take them across

---

We Gotta Get Outta This Place

WHILE ALL SORTS OF ANIMALS HAVE TRIED to break out of captivity, orangutans are the master escape artists of the menagerie. Besides picking locks, orangs have been known to make insulating mitts out of straw in order to climb over electric fences. Indeed, orangs have become design consultants: some zookeepers have used them to test new enclosures on the theory that if an orang can't find a way out, no other species of ape will. How do the orangs do it? One ingredient of success may be a patient, observing temperament. Zoologist Ben Beck once noted that if you give a screwdriver to a chimpanzee, it will try to use it for everything except its intended purpose. Give one to a gorilla, and it will first rear back in horror—"Oh, my God, it's going to hurt me!"—then try to eat it, and ultimately forget about it. Give it to an orangu-

tan, however, and the ape will first hide it and then, once you have gone, use it to dismantle the cage.

Along with Fu Manchu's crafty getaways, the most memorable orang escapes include a breakout at the Topeka Zoo. Jonathan, a young male, had been temporarily isolated in a holding area and resented it mightily. Keepers were not particularly worried because his cage was secured with an elaborate "guillotine" door that opened vertically and was remotely controlled by pneumatic pressure. When the door was closed, its top fit between two plates. As an extra precaution, a keeper would insert a pin through keyhole-like apertures in the plates and in the top of the door. The 5-in. pin would then be flopped over so that it could not be withdrawn without being flipped into the proper position. Taken together, these redundant security systems should have been able to contain most humans, much less an ape.

Nonetheless, a volunteer who regularly came to play with an infant orang in a neighboring cage began reporting that she could see Jonathan fiddling with something at the top of his cage. Geoff Creswell, a keeper, investigated, but when he looked in on the orang, Jonathan was always sitting quietly in a corner. Always, that is, until the day Creswell had a sudden, heart-stopping encounter with the big male outside his cage in a corridor of the holding area. After Jonathan had been put back behind bars, the keepers discovered that he had used a piece of cardboard to flip the pin into position so that it could be pushed out.

ELEPHANTS

WHAT THE SKEPTICS SAY Elephant communication consists of simple calls

WHAT ELEPHANTS DO At the Bronx Zoo, two elephants will take turns eating treats to foil keepers trying to lure them in for the night. The scheme requires the waiting elephant to trust the other not to eat the goodies

---

Jonathan's escape offered evidence of a panoply of higher mental abilities. He concealed his efforts from the humans in charge of him (but seemed not to realize that the person visiting the next cage might snitch on him); he figured out the workings of the locking mechanism and then fashioned a tool that enabled him to pick the lock. Perhaps most impressive was the planning and perseverance that went into this feat.

Sally Boysen, a psychologist at Ohio State University, probed the degree to which a chimp's ability to reason is subservient to the animal's desires. Her experiment involved two female chimps, Sheba and Sarah, and centered on a game in which Sheba would be shown two dishes filled with different amounts of treats. The first dish Sheba pointed to would be given to Sarah, meaning that Sheba had to think smaller to get larger. When she could actually see the treats, Sheba invariably pointed to the larger amount, only to see them given to Sarah. However, when tokens were substituted for real food, Sheba quickly realized that pointing to the smaller amount would get her the larger amount. It would seem that in the presence of real food, Sheba's appetites persistently overcame her ability to reason. When temptation was removed, Sheba could bring her cognitive abilities to bear and achieve her desired, albeit selfish, goal.

The same experiment was conducted with children. Four-year-olds realize that if they point to a smaller amount of food, they will be rewarded with more. Three-year-olds don't. This suggests that sometime during human maturation, children's cognitive abilities develop to the point that they realize they can be rewarded for restraint. The evidence also suggests that Sheba and other chimps are right on the cusp of that threshold. "In the course of an afternoon, we could toggle between Sheba reacting like a three-year-old and a four-year-old simply by switching what she was looking at," says Boysen.

Even if intelligence is shackled in animals, we can see it break out in flashes of brilliance. Countless creatures draw on their abilities not only to secure food and compete with their peers, but also to deal with, deceive and beguile the humans they encounter. Every so often, they do something extraordinary, and we gain insight into our own abilities, and what it's like to be an orangutan or an orca.

What is intelligence anyway? If life is about perpetuation of a species, and intelligence is meant to serve that perpetuation, then we can't hold a candle to pea-brained sea turtles who predated us and survived the asteroid impact that killed off the dinosaurs. As human history has shown, once minds break free of religious, cultural and physical controls, they burn hot and fast, consuming and altering everything around them. Perhaps this is why higher mental abilities, though present in other creatures, are more circumscribed. Still, it is comforting to realize that other species besides our own can stand back and appraise the world around them, even if their horizons are more constrained than the heady, perilous perspective that is our blessing and curse.

SCIENTIST AT WORK: ROBERT STERNBERG

His Goal: Making Intelligence Tests Smarter

By ERICA GOODE

Some people take their failures to heart. Dr. Robert J. Sternberg turns them into theories.

"I always seem to study the things I fail at," he said.

When his first marriage ended, for example, he set about developing a theory of love.

And when he was admitted to Yale as an undergraduate despite an unpleasant admissions interview (the interviewer noted in his file that he had "a flaky personality"), he theorized that interviews were not important predictors of college admissions and carried out a study to prove it.

In fact, Dr. Sternberg, a professor of psychology at Yale, a prolific researcher, a widely known expert on intelligence testing and the progenitor of his own theory of "successful" intelligence, in some ways owes his entire career to an early failure: hobbled by test anxiety, he scored poorly on an I.Q. test when he was 6 years old, the beginning of a lifelong obsession with developing his own measures of mental abilities.

Yet as the director of a new research center on the Yale campus, the Center for the Psychology of Abilities, Competencies and Expertise, or PACE, Dr. Sternberg—lanky,

intense and prone to jokes about space aliens—is more focused on success than failure: he hopes to change the way human potential is conceived of, identified and nurtured.

Supported by $7 million in grants from organizations like the National Science Foundation, the Army Research Institute and the W. T. Grant Foundation, the center, part of Yale's psychology department, is not the usual academic research institute: it has a mission, modestly stated as "to transform science, education and society."

"Our view is this country wastes a lot of talent," Dr. Sternberg said. "There are a lot of kids who have potential to be successful in their fields, but the way the system is set up, they never get the chance."

Working with a core group of about two dozen researchers from 10 countries, the center already has a variety of projects under way.

They include the testing of a novel curriculum, based on Dr. Sternberg's work, at the Sanger Academy, a charter school near Fresno, Calif.; a partnership with the University of Michigan School of Business to create a new test for screening future

corporate leaders; and studies on topics as diverse as leadership in the military and the psychology of wisdom, a quality Dr. Sternberg, 51, believes can be understood and eventually taught.

Efforts to define and assess the nature of human intelligence are as old as psychology itself.

But underlying the center's philosophy is its director's conviction that there is a great deal wrong with the way society now selects and educates the best and the brightest.

Like some other scholars, for example, Dr. Sternberg is critical of I.Q. tests, SAT's, Graduate Record Exams and other conventional assessment measures that form the bedrock of American education but have been the subject of increasing debate in recent years.

While supporters of such tests argue that they tap a general dimension of intelligence—usually referred to as "g"—and point to their power as predictors of future performance, Dr. Sternberg is among those who contend that the tests mainly measure the ability to succeed in a system that rewards the best test takers.

Conventional aptitude and achievement tests, he said, define intelligence narrowly and favor people who excel in certain types of mental abilities, mainly analytical thinking and memory skills. And the tests do, in fact, predict a variety of things, including school grades and performance on other similar tests.

But Dr. Sternberg argues that this is largely because those who get high scores on traditional tests receive "red carpet" treatment from early on: they are nurtured by secondary schoolteachers, accepted into prestigious colleges and then welcomed into good jobs or graduate schools once they get their degrees.

"It becomes a self-fulfilling prophecy," Dr. Sternberg said, fooling people into thinking that test performance is somehow ordained by God or nature as a marker of success, rather than simply reflecting society's chosen values.

More to the point, Dr. Sternberg adds, the gaps in a system that prizes conventional testing above all else are problematic. For one thing, some people who do well in school and on standardized tests founder later on in life, when a more well-rounded repertoire of skills is required.

For another, children whose strengths fall outside the "fixed spotlight" of the tests—who are adept, for example, at creative or practical abilities like those Dr. Sternberg stresses in his own intelligence tests and educational materials—are effectively locked out.

Schools make no effort to teach them in the ways they find easiest to learn. They quickly get the message that their skills are not valued, and start acting accordingly—and ultimately, Dr. Sternberg says, society is deprived of their contributions.

Nor does the narrow view of skills promoted by the tests, Dr. Sternberg believes, take into account the fact that "abilities are not something you're born with, that are etched in invisible ink on your forehead and cannot be changed."

Rather, he contends, research has demonstrated that abilities are mod-ifiable both in respect to level and kind.

"You can develop new kinds of abilities that you might not even have known you had," Dr. Sternberg said.

Like Dr. Howard Gardner, the author of "Frames of Mind: The Theory of Multiple Intelligences," Dr. Sternberg believes that society must broaden its lens, integrating a wider array of abilities into its conception of aptitude and achievement.

But while Dr. Gardner has posited seven types of intelligence, including spatial, musical, "interpersonal," and "bodily-kinesthetic" intelligence, Dr. Sternberg's own theory identifies a trio of mental abilities: analytical intelligence (the type measured by I.Q. tests), creative intelligence and practical intelligence.

All three types of abilities, he said, are often required to succeed in life.

"You need creative intelligence to come up with an idea, analytical intelligence to know if it's a good idea and practical intelligence to sell it," he said.

But people who have superior practical and creative skills often do not perform well on tests that reflect only analytical abilities, and thus are deprived of educational opportunities, Dr. Sternberg says. A disadvantaged teenager with strong leadership skills and "street smarts" well above average, for example, might perform poorly on the SAT. Or a "creative learner," who excels at open-ended assignments—Dr. Sternberg was such a student himself, he said—might be flummoxed by multiple-choice tests or memory tasks, ruining the chances for admission to a top-flight college.

Adding measures that tap creative and practical faculties to standard test batteries, the psychologist argues, could benefit everyone in the long run, and may even eliminate the need for what he sees as more flat-footed methods of broadening admissions policies, like affirmative action.

And, Dr. Sternberg said, his research suggests that when teachers balance analytical exercises—which often dominate class time—with creative and practical tasks, students' overall performance improves.

His own approach, being tested in several schools in a number of states, is intended to provide such a balance. In a unit on Bangladesh, for example, students may be asked not only to memorize facts about its history, but also spend equal time on an essay about what it would be like to live there.

Dr. Sternberg is known for his fondness for anecdote, and his voluminous output of books (he has written or edited 60) and papers (several hundred are listed on his vita). His background in testing and statistics, several colleagues said, allows him to challenge the testing establishment on its own terms.

"There aren't many people who have his insight and his flair," Dr. Stephen J. Ceci, a professor of psychology at Cornell. "He couples a high degree of creativity with all the core skills that unfortunately aren't always available to highly creative people: he has the right statistical abilities, good analytical abilities, great communication skills."

But Dr. Sternberg, the author of "Successful Intelligence: How Creative and Practical Intelligence Determine Success in Life" and "Love Is a Story: A New Theory of Relationships," also has his critics.

His views place him to the right of those who would throw out standardized tests altogether—he wants to add, not subtract, and well to the left of I.Q. devotees like Dr. Richard J. Herrnstein and Dr. Charles Murray, authors of the 1994 book "The Bell Curve." But some testing experts argue that Dr. Sternberg has yet to provide convincing evidence that the forms of intelligence he has identified are entirely distinct from what I.Q. tests measure.

"I think most traditional researchers would say, 'Sure, we have to broaden our conceptions and there's room to measure things beyond 'g,' " said Dr. Nat Brody, a professor of psychology at Wesleyan University and an expert on intelligence testing. "Bob is trying to seriously develop measures, collect data and try to get people to think in new ways. But I would say the jury is still out."

Perhaps Dr. Sternberg's harshest critic is Dr. Linda Gottfredson, a sociologist at the University of Delaware and the author of a critique of Dr. Sternberg's work on practical intelligence, to appear later this year in the journal Intelligence. "The bottom line for me is that he hasn't provided any good evidence to support his claim that there is a separate practical intelligence," Dr. Gottfredson said.

Dr. Sternberg, however, is rarely dispirited by such views. He is happy to spend hours rebutting them, and anyway, he has too much to do, a hundred projects to finish, another book to edit, another test to develop.

Not to mention the fact that he has always taken a kind of single-minded pleasure in systematically dismantling obstacles placed in his path..

In seventh grade, for example, he discovered a copy of the Stanford-Binet intelligence test in the adult section of the Maplewood, N.J., public library and decided to try it out on his classmates.

First he gave it to a girl he liked, hoping it would break the ice.

"She did very well on it," Dr. Sternberg recalled, "but the relationship did not get off the ground."

Then he gave it to a boy in his Scout troop. The boy, however, went home and told his mother, who called the school psychologist and complained. Young Robert was summoned to the principal's office and informed that if he ever brought the test to school again, it would be burned.

It was a devastating experience, Dr. Sternberg recalls. But it only made him more determined. He took to studying intelligence secretly, sending away for copies of tests by pretending to be a graduate student. By high school he was already something of an expert in the field.

And he did "quite well," he confesses, on his own SAT's.

"There is an advantage to feeling like a failure a lot of the time," Dr. Sternberg said. "It prevents you from getting too stuck."

UNIT 6
Emotion and Motivation

Unit Selections

Key Points to Consider

- What is motivation? What is an emotion? How are the two related to each other?

- What makes successful athletes and executives different from the rest of us? Are they just smarter? Do you think if you altered your focus or your motivational level, you would be a better athlete? A better student? A better business person? What is flow? Do you think you have "flow"; why?

- Why do people gain weight? What motivates them to overeat *or* to eat the wrong foods? What motivates individuals to lose weight? Why, in general, are Americans some of the most overweight people on the face of the earth? What can we do to lose weight and to maintain a healthy weight?

- From where do emotions originate, nature or nurture? Why did you give the answer you did? Do you think a person's level of emotionality or overall personality can change with time or is it somehow fixed early in life?

- Why is the face the key to understanding others' emotions? Are there any universally expressed facial emotions? What are the problems with studying universal emotions; in other words, does culture play a role in emotional expression? Are adult emotions similar to or different from emotions of younger individuals? How so?

- What is emotional intelligence? Why are individuals high in emotional intelligence successful? Can emotional intelligence be cultivated? Emotional intelligence is important on the job. Where else might emotional intelligence come in handy?

 **Links: www.dushkin.com/online/**
These sites are annotated in the World Wide Web pages.

CYFERNET-Youth Development
http://www.cyfernet.mes.umn.edu/youthdev.html
Nature vs. Nature: Gergen Dialogue With Winifred Gallagher
http://www.pbs.org/newshour/gergen/gallagher_5-14.html

Jasmine's sister was a working mother and always reminded Jasmine about how exciting her life was. Jasmine stayed home because she loved her children, 2-year-old Min, 4-year-old Chi'Ming, and newborn Yuan. One day Jasmine was having a difficult time with the children. The baby, Yuan, had been crying all day from colic. The other two children had been bickering over their toys. Jasmine, realizing that it was already 5:15 and her husband would be home any minute, frantically started preparing dinner. She wanted to fix a nice dinner so that she and her husband could eat after the children went to bed, then relax together.

This was not to be. Jasmine sat waiting. When her husband finally walked in the

door at 10:15, she was furious. His excuse, that his boss had invited the whole office for dinner, didn't reduce Jasmine's ire. She reasoned that her husband could have called to say that he wouldn't be home for dinner, could have taken 5 minutes to do that. Jasmine berated her husband. Her face was taut and red with rage and her voice wavered. Suddenly, bursting into tears, she ran into the living room. Her husband retreated to the safety of their bedroom.

Exhausted and disappointed, Jasmine sat alone and pondered why she was so angry with her husband. Was she just tired? Was she frustrated by negotiating with young children all day and simply wanted another adult around once in a while? Was she secretly worried and jealous that her husband was seeing another woman and had lied about his whereabouts? Was she combative because her husband's and her sister's lives seemed so much fuller than her own? Jasmine was unsure just how she felt and why she exploded in such rage at her husband, someone she loved dearly.

This story, while sad and gender-stereotyped, is not necessarily unrealistic when it comes to emotions. There are times when we are moved to deep emotion. On other occasions, we expect waterfalls of tears but find that our eyes are dry or simply a little misty. What are these strange things we call emotions? What motivates us to rage at someone we love?

These questions and others have inspired psychologists to study emotions and motivation. The above episode about Jasmine, besides introducing these topics to you, also illustrates why these two topics are usually interrelated in psychology. Some emotions, such as love, pride, and joy, are pleasant, so

pleasant that we are motivated to keep them going. Other emotions, such as anger, grief, and jealousy, are terribly draining and oppressive—so negative that we hope they will be over as soon as possible. Emotions and motivation and their relationship to each other are the focus of this unit.

The first two articles in this unit relate to motivation; the last two pertain to emotions. In "Into the Zone," Jay Tolson explores what motivates great athletes and executives. He notes that they are sometimes different from the rest of us. After careful consideration, he concludes that these successful individuals possess a certain mental ability—flow—that helps them to better tolerate stress and be more mentally tough than the rest of us.

In "The Weighting Game," Liz Brown ponders a perennial question for Americans. Why are so many Americans overweight? Are we more motivated to eat than we are to stay healthy? Brown helps us understand why we gain weight and what we can do to lose weight and maintain a healthier diet.

Two articles on emotions follow. The first, "What's in a Face," offers fascinating insight into emotional expressiveness. Beth Azar, a regular writer for the *APA Monitor,* discusses whether the face indeed mirrors our emotional states. She also argues that the face is important to social interactions because it tells us so much about another person's emotions and moods.

The final article on emotional intelligence (EQ) offers a description of this relatively new concept. EQ is the ability to recognize one's own or another's emotional states. Those high in EQ tend to be very successful regardless of intelligence level and other abilities. Schools, therefore, might want to foster EQ in children.

Into the Zone

The kind of mental conditioning that makes athletes into superstars also helps ordinary folks become extraordinary

BY JAY TOLSON

Sometimes you have to kill the thing you love. Pop-psych 101? To be sure. But Tiger Woods's Shermanesque march through the 2000 U.S. Open at Pebble Beach gave new force and meaning to the phrase. It's not just that Woods mowed down some of his nearest and dearest competitors, though that he certainly did. Nor is it only that he brought one of his favorite courses–and one of golf's hardest–to its knees. He also seemed to subdue the game itself: to beat it into submission.

"Kill them," Kultida Woods used to say when her young son went off to face the competition. It was oddly predatory counsel coming from a Thai-born mother who at other times imparted Buddhist wisdom about inner peace. But if Woods was ever confused by these seemingly dissonant messages, he didn't show it at the Open. He killed 'em, every one, with almost transcendent calm, posting the biggest margin of victory in the history of golf's four "major" annual tournaments. "He's so focused every time," said an amazed Ernie Els, who tied for a distant second place. "That hunger for winning a major championship, it's like 110 percent. To be honest with you, I don't feel like that every week when I'm playing. He's just differ-

ent. I'm not sure there's a lot of players out here like that."

Focus. Control. Flow. In the zone. Think of any other synonym for mental mastery, and it applies to the level of play that Woods achieved in the Open. And while this state of internal calm and power has different names, it boils down to this: When the body is brought to peak condition and the mind is completely focused, even unaware of what it's doing, an individual can achieve the extraordinary.

But this is not a game of chance. Psychologists and physiologists say ordinary people can achieve this state by inducing changes in physiology, including brain-wave patterns and even heart rates, through focusing and relaxation techniques. These might include breathing exercises or using verbal cues or developing rituals (bouncing the ball exactly three times before you take the foul shot). It also might involve visualizing successful outcomes before you make the swing or jump shot, without thinking about the mechanics of the action. The "stay in the present" focus that enables Woods to sink almost routinely those deadly 8- and 10-foot putts for par came in part from what his father, Earl Woods–his best personal sports psychol-

ogist–taught him about having a mental picture of the ball rolling into the hole.

Today, Americans of all stripes are using mental conditioning not just as a means to a better golf swing but also to make them better corporate competitors, more creative artists, and, some argue, better human beings. "When you're in the zone, it's so quiet, it's so peaceful," says Harriet Ross, a potter from Hartsdale, N.Y., who uses the lessons of Zen to relax and focus. Julio Bocca, who has been a ballet prodigy since he was 4 years old in Argentina, worried about a decline as his 30s approached. Instead, he has been dancing to acclaim around the world–an achievement reached, he believes, through mental focus.

Winning a high-speed car race or coming out on top in a corporate takeover isn't just a matter of skill; it's also about how people handle pressure. The intangible factor, not knowing who's going to buckle or who's going to hit the last-second field goal, is what makes these pursuits exciting–or terrifying. The same week that Woods breezed through the Open, for example, Yankee second baseman Chuck Knoblauch, who has become phobic about routine throws, made three errors in a single game. Golfer John Daly, whose physical gifts nearly match

Woods's, took 14 strokes on Pebble Beach's 18th hole and quit the Open after the first round.

Many athletes speak of choking as a failure to be "in the zone." That state is not unlike the "flow" defined by the Hungarian-American psychologist Mihaly Csikszentmihalyi. He began his career-long interest in the early 1960s studying a group of artists for his thesis on creativity. Struck by how so many became oblivious to their surroundings while they worked, he went on to investigate whether other activities and even jobs produced such absorption, such flow. What he found was that any pursuit was an "autotelic activity" if the doing, and not the goal, was the end in itself and if it involved such things as intense concentration, clarity of goals, quick feedback, and a fine balance of skills and challenges. Which is what works for Bocca. "When I do a solo–that's the moment you have to be 100 percent there– my mind is just in the character. I've been doing this for so many years, I don't have to think about what to do with my body. I don't think 'now is my pirouette, now is my jump.'"

Practitioners of Zen, yoga, and many Eastern forms of martial arts have experienced the truth behind these principles without having had them explained scientifically, as Csikszentmihalyi and other proponents of flow-and-peak states well realize. Indeed, the scientists have learned a great deal from those and other premodern disciplines. Folklore about the mental dimension of sport is as old as the games themselves, but the scientific study of that dimension did not begin until the late 19th century, primarily in Germany and France. Throughout most of the first half of the 20th century, researchers concentrated on the description of the character types and personalities of athletes and paid almost no attention to performance. A rare exception was German psychiatrist Johannes Heinrich Schultz (1884–1970), who developed "autogenic training," a form of self-hypnosis that was supposed to boost relaxation. Yet not even Schultz believed that his research into the links between emotional and bodily states should serve to enhance athletic performance.

The coaches of the East bloc nations, including East Germany, are often cred-

---

IN FINE FETTLE
Braving the 'bod pod'

ORLANDO—At LGE Performance Systems, the road to an "ideal performance state" starts with a 75-question survey: Are you pessimistic? Competitive? Do you think "me" or "we"? Self-introspection alone isn't enough: The questionnaire must also be completed by five people who know you best—a coach, say, or a secretary.

That heavy navel-gazing comes before you even arrive at the sprawling training camp. Which is good, because at LGE, it doesn't matter who you are—fine physical specimen of a professional football player, flabby *Fortune* 500 executive, or hard-bodied housewife. Everyone here is poked, prodded, and rebuilt from the outside in by an infuriatingly fit, impossibly relaxed team of psychologists, physiologists, trainers, and nutritionists. The three-day program, which runs around $4,000, begins with a battery of high-tech exams, including the terrifying "bod pod," an egg-shaped contraption that gauges body-fat percentage.

The goals here come straight from basic psychology: to unearth who you really are, to decide who you want to be, and to take action. Clients are taught to alternate periods of intense stress with periods of relaxation or release, in fitness and in life. "In the corporate world, people are trained to be linear," says Terry Lyles, a resident clinical psychologist. "They start the day and don't take breaks." He explains that an emotional and mental shift down—a rolling pattern as opposed to a straight line—will allow executives to come back and be totally refreshed.

"Last year, my mind was a barrier; it was holding me back," says Adrienne Johnson, 26, a guard for the Orlando Miracle, the local WNBA team, who found herself warming the bench all last season. She started working with LGE, and this season she's a starter, averaging 30 minutes a game—and double-digit points.
—*Carolyn Kleiner*

---

ited with being the first to use psychology to supercharge their athletes. (Sports historian John Hoberman contends this is largely a Cold War myth, based partly on a desire of Western observers to see athletes from communist countries as programmed robots.) The perception that psychology lay behind the success of East bloc athletes prompted curiosity in the West–and even, according to some leading American sports psychologists, a desire to venture into the field themselves.

Such was at least partly the case with Jim Loehr. Founder of a leading sports and motivational training center, LGE Performance Systems, in Orlando, Fla., Loehr began his career in the early 1970s as the head of a mental health center in southern Colorado. But the experience of successfully treating two professional athletes–albeit "under the cover of darkness"–changed his plans. It was not long before he decided to launch his own sports psychology practice in Denver, a decision greeted by derision from his peers.

Holy Grail. Some of the challenges he faced continue to plague the field. Prominent among them was Americans' tendency to associate psychology with the treatment of weakness or disorders, even though Loehr was concerned with improving performance, not in administering therapy. Undaunted, Loehr developed his own version of the peak performance state that has come to be the Holy Grail of the larger American sports psychology industry–the "ideal performance state" (IPS), he prefers to call it, or "mental toughness."

"The mind and the body are one," says Loehr. "Mental toughness is not just something you can sit in a room and visualize and all of a sudden you're mentally tough. The ability to handle physical stress takes us right into the ability to handle mental and emotional stress."

The center that he founded in Orlando in the early 1990s quickly became a mecca for a wide assortment of people who have one thing in common: the desire to be the best they can possibly be. Last week, for example, you could find retired tennis champ Jim Courier (getting in shape for his new career as a commentator), a dozen executives from Macy's department store, a 600-pound sumo wrestler, and various amateur athletes wandering the LGE grounds (box, Braving the 'bod pod'). They came to improve their performance on the playing field, in the boardroom, or in life in general–and what they got is an intense workout for both the mind and the muscles.

"When there's no time left on the clock, you're 2 points down and on the foul line, what is that person thinking about before they shoot the shot? If they have one mental thought that says, 'If I miss this shot we lose'… within moments, they are secreting negative brain chemistry," says Terry Lyles, LGE psychologist. It's all about taking yourself out of the moment, he explains, about using rituals to transport yourself before the shot or point. "They have to go from the mental side to tap into the emotional side next, which takes them to the physical part, which will be to shoot the foul shot. They've shot thousands of foul shots, but the issue is not shooting the foul shot, the issue is screaming fans, no time on the clock, and your whole team is looking for you to perform. The issue is focus."

"All of corporate America has its own form of stress, the same way the athlete has stress," says Rudy Borneo, vice chairman of Macy's West, who was visiting LGE last week. "It's really how you use that stress, how you build a format to make it positive rather than negative, how you can turn it into a growth factor."

Tony DiCicco became head of the U.S. Women's World Cup soccer team in 1994; a year later, he hired sports psychologist Colleen Hacker. He knew that coaches often talk about the importance of the mental game but rarely give it time commensurate with its importance. He is certain that hiring Hacker strengthened both individual and team performance. DiCicco points out that he is not alone in a growing appreciation of the value of sports psychologists: The U.S. Olympic team had only one in 1988, but it had 100 by 1996. There are now over 100 academic programs specializing in sports psychology, at least three academic journals, and over 1,000 members listed by the Association for the Advancement of Applied Sports Psychology. And elite

professional and amateur teams and athletes seem to be increasingly using their services.

The business. These specialists are taking the lessons of great athletes and coaches and shaping them into techniques that aspiring peak performers can learn to use. Sports Publishing Inc. of Champaign, Ill., whose books discuss how athletes get in the zone, plans to release 112 titles this year, about double last year's number. In the past few years, Simon & Schuster has published and reissued such titles as *Golf is a Game of Confidence* and *Executive Trap: How to Play Your Personal Best on the Golf Course and On the Job*. Many professional sports teams have psychologists on call, but that's a largely reactive, therapeutic approach. But another approach is spreading. Baseball's Cleveland Indians have a three-man performance-enhancement program that costs about $300,000 a year and deserves some credit for five straight American League Central Division titles since 1995, two of which led to World Series appearances.

Bob Troutwine, a psychologist in Liberty, Mo., has helped 18 NFL teams decide which players to recruit and how to use them. In 1998, Troutwine urged the Indianapolis Colts to draft Tennessee's Peyton Manning over another quarterback with similar statistics, Washington State's Ryan Leaf. A personality test showed that Manning was confident, but not brash, and Troutwine liked the fact that he was the son of former NFL quarterback Archie Manning. Troutwine was vindicated: Manning did well with the Colts, and Leaf, who was drafted by the San Diego Chargers, has flailed as a quarterback, insulted fans, and wants to leave the team. "In general you want competitive players," says Troutwine, who also consults for such corporate clients as Ford Motor Co. and Sprint Co., "but if a team is in a building phase, a hypercompetitive player may not handle losing very well."

The trend in hiring sports psychologists has yet to trickle down to the lower levels of sport, according to Albert J. Figone of California's Humboldt State University. But that's in large part because coaches view motivation and the

mental game as their prerogative, even if they usually give it too little attention. Stanford University's Jim Thompson, director of the Positive Coaching Alliance, thinks it's absurd to use this stuff on kids. "All the sports psychology in the world isn't going to help the average kid unless he has tremendous skills as well," Thompson points out. "The danger is that parents might think, gee, if I could get my kid a good sports psychologist, he could be Tiger Woods. Well, no."

Kid stuff. But back in Orlando, Neil Clausen is on the court for his daily tennis lesson, nailing one perfect backhand after another. Just 10 years old, this pint-size player already has a clear idea of his goals ("I'm here because I'm trying to go to Wimbledon") and an even more pronounced conception of what it's going to take to get there: "I need to work on my racket preparation, but things like concentration are very important [too]. I see players throwing their racket around… and I just don't think it really works, I don't think its very nice." His mother brings him to LGE six days a week. "We will go to matches and whether it's professionals or 12-year-olds, you have some incredible athletes, physically blessed people, who are just not able to pull it off during a match, all because their mental strength lets them down, or they couldn't focus, or they got distracted," she says. Neil is a quick study. In a pretend match, in between points, he quietly, solemnly goes through his own rituals: He adjusts strings on his racket, for one thing, and works on his breathing.

In an interview last year with *Psychology Today*, Richard Suinn, who in 1972 became the first sports psychologist to serve on the U.S. Olympic sports medicine team, listed the mental skills that modern sports psychology focuses on, including "stress management, self-regulation, visualization, goal setting, concentration, focus, even relaxation." Sound good? It's clear why so many who are outside sports respond to what sports psychology offers. "If you attack work, family, spiritual life the way you attack a game, it all works the same way," says Peter Cathey, chief operating officer of XPO Network Inc., a start-up interactive marketing company. Cathey has faced several challenges recently–moving across the country to start a new company, dealing with his mother's death, and putting his father in the hospital. But he says he's never felt more mentally fit, thanks to skills acquired at LGE. "There's no emotional hit in the face I can't deal with."

"If Tiger goes out to play and doesn't take a good relaxing breath or relax once in two hours, then that tension shows up as a bogey," explains stay-at-home mother Caryn Rohrbaugh, of Lemoyne, Pa. Rohrbaugh went through LGE so that she could perform better in the home and enjoy her time there. "For me, two hours of not taking a breath, not eating right, not being in the right mind-set turns up as impatience, forgetting to schedule something, a general feeling of being overwhelmed. It's still a bogey, though."

There is no question that the mental toughness developed by world-class athletes has pulled them through trials off the playing field as well as on–another reason why so many people are drawn to the peak performance ideal. Perhaps no sport is more mentally demanding than competitive cycling, and champion Lance Armstrong demonstrated some of the mental grit he acquired over years of fierce competitive racing by struggling back from testicular cancer. Diagnosed with the disease in 1996, he not only survived the surgery and debilitating chemo treatments but came back to win the Tour de France in 1999, a story recounted in his book, *It's Not About the Bike*.

The most honest, articulate, and (not coincidentally) influential specialists will tell you forthrightly that they are drawing on the collective wisdom of the best proven minds in the field–the great coaches of past and present. Many of them are or have been coaches themselves, and most are athletes, former or active. Bob Rotella, former director of the sports psychology program at the University of Virginia and now a full-time consultant to golf professionals and other athletes, says that so much of the formal psychology that he read in graduate school focused on dysfunction and

problems that he "turned to people like Vince Lombardi or [UCLA's] John Wooden and studied their philosophies."

Rotella has taught what he calls "learned effectiveness" for years, which means, he says, "teaching about being in the best state of mind, basing your thinking on where you want to go, not where you've been." Doing so, Rotella found himself in strong sympathy with the work of at least one theoretical psychologist, the great turn-of-the-century thinker William James. James, whose work is making a strong comeback these days because of its emphasis on the conscious mind and the will, spoke clearly to Rotella. "He seemed to fit with what I learned from the coaches." That might sound like a dubious distinction to some intellectuals, but James probably would have taken it as a compliment. The power of the mind to shape reality was one of his lasting beliefs.

Just as James is the quintessential American thinker for having created a serious philosophy of human potential, so the best sports psychologists, and not just Rotella, extend that philosophy in popular form, often in an eloquent popular literature that includes books by Rotella himself (many written with Bob Cullen) and such modern classics as Michael Murphy's *Golf in the Kingdom*.

Obsession. Proponents of peak performance see it as laudably consistent with the American dream of self-betterment and the pursuit of happiness. "To me, pursuing excellence is why we came to America," says Rotella. But John Hoberman, a University of Texas professor who has written often about the dehumanization of sports, sees the emphasis on performance as part of the contemporary obsession with competitiveness, an obsession that crowds out other human and civilized values, "including," he says, "moderation and balance."

But do critics like Hoberman ignore the possibility that peak performance might entail leading a richer, more balanced life, one that can allow more attention to others, including family, friends, and community? Being in the zone or the

flow may be in fact a supremely human value, particularly if it is, as many sports psychologists contend, a state in which our peak capacities are exercised almost without thinking. After all, competition is a reality that cannot be wished away; why not learn to manage it as best as one can? As Woods commented after he'd won, "I had a–a weird feeling this week–it's hard to describe–a feeling of tranquillity, calmness."

Csikszentmihalyi, who now directs the Quality of Life Research Center at Claremont Graduate University, sees peak performance state as a concept or ideal that can approach his notion of flow, but only with difficulty. "In my work," he explains, "I'm trying to understand how to make life better as it goes. The question is, why are you experiencing the peak performance state–for its own sake or in order to win? If winning, the goal, takes over, the pleasure of the doing fades."

In other words, if the peak performance state becomes merely an instrument, its resemblance to true flow will vanish. But there is no guarantee, of course, that this will not happen in any discipline or undertaking that one pursues, whether it be the making of pottery in the spirit of Zen or the playing of the piano in the spirit of the heck of it. When and if peak performance ceases to be the kind of activity that another quintessential American, Robert Frost, writes about in his poem "Two Tramps in Mud Time," then it might well become a lesser thing. Listen to the poet describe the state that he aimed for, and consider its possible relevance to our peak performance culture:

But yield who will to their separation,
My object in living is to unite
My avocation and my vocation
As my two eyes make one in sight.
Only where love and need are one,
And the work is play for mortal stakes,
Is the deed ever really done
For Heaven and the future's sakes.

With Carolyn Kleiner and David L. Marcus

the weighting game

8 MUST-HAVE TIPS FOR WEIGHT-MANAGEMENT SUCCESS

by liz brown

did you know that there are 30 to 40 billion fat cells in that body of yours? At times, they may seem like an army of enemies out to sabotage your appearance in a swimsuit, but they saved our ancestors from starving by storing fat to get them through lean times. Trouble is, we have more than enough food available in America in this day and age, and we're usually not trekking across frozen tundra or arid steppes in search of the next encampment.

Pair our hefty calorie intakes with generally sedentary lives—sitting in front of the computer all day, driving from office to home, plopping down on the couch with the remote control to unwind—and it's easy to see why 97 million Americans weigh more than they should.

more than just bikini avoidance

Being overweight can damage much more than your poolside self-confidence. According to the authors of *Mayo Clinic on Healthy Weight*, overweight people have increased risks of developing high blood pressure, high triglycerides and low HDL ("good") cholesterol, type 2 diabetes mel-litus, coronary artery disease, gallbladder disease, stroke, respiratory problems, osteoarthritis and various kinds of cancer. Due to these problems, overweight people may have a substandard quality of life and possibly die sooner than their healthy counterparts.

There is good news, however. Even a five to 10 percent weight loss can lower your health risks. If you are overweight, you might find your energy level and confidence increasing as the pounds come off, too. It's true that genetics play a role in how your body deals with calories. A family history of obesity increases your odds of ending up obese by 25 to 30 percent, but that just means you may have to work a little harder than those without such a history to achieve and maintain a healthy weight. You're not doomed. You can choose to adopt healthy habits.

Better Nutrition spoke with nutrition and exercise experts to learn their recipes for healthy weight loss and maintenance. Here, along with tips from the *Mayo Clinic on Healthy Weight* book, are some important ingredients for success.

1. REALITY CHECK

Before you set any weight loss goals, be realistic. Are you truly overweight, or are you striving to be as unrealistically thin as a supermodel? One good way to find out is to measure your Body Mass Index, or BMI. It's better at estimating body fat and health risks than other methods—including that dreaded bathroom scale. (To calculate your BMI, see box at right.) If your BMI is 19 to 24, there's probably not a health advantage to losing weight. Keep up healthy habits to stay in this ideal range. If your BMI is 25 or more, losing weight might improve your health. If your BMI is under 19, you're most likely underweight.

Fat around the middle is associated with a higher risk of heart disease, diabetes, cancer and other health problems, so determining whether or not you have too much weight here is also important. From the highest point on each hip-bone, measure across the abdomen just above these points. If this is over 35 inches in women or 40 inches in men, you are at increased health risk. Combined with a BMI of 25 or more, the risk increases. A good rule of thumb is this: The bigger the waist, the bigger the health risk.

2. TAKE A LONG, HARD LOOK

If you are overweight, look deep inside yourself to try to find out why. Is there some emotional reason why you overeat? Do you seek comfort in food? If you're overeating for emotional reasons, counseling might help get to the root of your problem so you no longer need food as a Band-Aid.

3. STOCK THE PANTRY WITH HEALTHY FOODS

Instead of jumping on the diet-of-the-week bandwagon, experts advise eating a diet with 50 to 65 percent carbohydrates (emphasizing whole grains, legumes, fruits and veggies); 20 to 25 percent protein; and the remainder from mostly unsaturated fat (olive oil over butter or meat fat, for example). High-fiber foods will fill you up and are not very calorie-dense. They also take a while to chew, giving your body time to signal you that it's time to put your fork down after you've had enough.

Instead of potato chips or crackers containing hydrogenated oils, opt for almonds, peanuts, soy nuts, air-popped popcorn sprinkled with nutritional yeast or mixed seasonings, carrots, grapes, pretzels or other non-fried snacks.

4. EAT WITH INTENTION

This one seems easy, yet few of us do it in our multi-tasking frenzy. For many people, eating while driving, watching TV or working at the computer is practically second nature. But these distractions take away from our enjoyment and awareness of what we're eating, often contributing to eating too fast and overeating. Make a point of sitting at the table, turning off the TV and computer and setting aside your work for mealtimes.

5. GIVE UP YOUR MEMBERSHIP TO THE CLEAN PLATE CLUB

As a child, you may have been encouraged to finish every last morsel of food on your plate. While we certainly don't want kids in China to go hungry, stuffing yourself to the brink of exploding won't help anyone, including you. Get used to pushing your plate aside when you've had enough.

6. PORTIONS

In this age of super-size everything, it's easy to lose sight of what a portion of food actually looks like. Here are a few guidelines:

- Two tablespoons of peanut butter is the size of a ping pong ball
- 1 teaspoon of butter or margarine is the size of a stamp and the thickness of a thumb tip, and the normal serving size of butter is a tablespoon, which is about a 1/2-inch pat
- 1 ounce of nuts is one handful
- 1/2 cup of chips or popcorn is a large handful
- 1 serving of bread is one slice or 1/4 of a standard sized bagel
- 1 cup of ice cream is a scoop the size of a baseball

To keep portion sizes in check, use small dishes to serve meals and desserts. Instead of a cereal bowl, use a dessert dish for ice cream. Put your pasta in a cereal bowl instead of loading it onto a gargantuan plate.

7. PLAN AHEAD

The amount of planning you do for the week ahead can make or break healthy eating patterns. Have healthy snacks on hand and bring sandwiches if you'll be away from home at lunch or staying late at the office. Determine whether you'll be walking by a store where you can buy yogurt and/or fruit during a snack or lunch break.

8. LOOK FORWARD TO YOUR WORKOUT

It's not always easy to drag yourself out of bed for a morning jog. If that's the case, find some other aerobic activity that you enjoy enough to keep doing. Walking is one easy option.

WHY BMI IS NOT THE ABBREVIATION FOR A FOREIGN CAR:

To calculate your BMI, follow these steps, from *Mayo Clinic on Healthy Weight*:
1. Multiply your weight in pounds by .45
2. Multiply your height in inches by .025.
3. Square the answer from step 2.
4. Divide the answer from step 1 by the answer from step 3. The result is your BMI.

Take a dance or yoga class, or sign up at a gym and ask a trainer to help you use the weights. Find out if there's a local indoor pool for lap swimmers; it's easy on the joints and a darn good workout. Aim for 30 minutes of cardiovascular exercise most days of the week—getting your heart pumping is important. (If you have health problems, be sure to ask your doctor to help you devise an exercise program that is safe, and before beginning an exercise program, become familiar with your maximum heart rate so you don't put unnecessary stress on your heart.)

weight matters

Clearly, weight management is all about health. In the culture that has produced Barbie and a media filled with waiflike images of women and men who often look anorexic and cadaverous, we're not advocating blanket weight loss at all. In fact, in some situations, weight gain is indicated (in cases of an overactive thyroid, recovery from surgery or illness, etc.). What's needed is an accurate BMI, a realistic assessment of our body-image goals and the fortitude to carry out a healthy weight management plan. We don't need an obsession with calories or pounds; what we do need is the right attitude that eliminates the need for deprivation or "dieting."

From *Better Nutrition,* June 2001, pp. 48-52. © 2001 by Better Nutrition. Reprinted by permission.

What's in a face?

**Do facial expressions reflect inner feelings?
Or are they social devices for influencing others?**

BY BETH AZAR
Monitor staff

After 30 years of renewed interest in facial expression as a key clue to human emotions, frowns are appearing on critics' faces. The face, they say, isn't the mirror to emotions it's been held out to be.

The use of facial expression for measuring people's emotions has dominated psychology since the late 1960s when Paul Ekman, PhD, of the University of California, San Francisco, and Carroll Izard, PhD, of the University of Delaware, reawakened the study of emotion by linking expressions to a group of basic emotions.

Many took that work to imply that facial expressions provided the key to people's feelings. But in recent years the psychology literature has been sprinkled with hotly worded attacks by detractors who claim that there is no one-to-one correspondence between facial expressions and emotions. In fact, they argue, there's no evidence to support a link between what appears on someone's face and how they feel inside.

But this conflict masks some major areas of agreement, says Joseph Campos, PhD, of the University of California at Berkeley. Indeed, he says, "there is profound agreement that the face, along with the voice, body posture and hand gestures, forecast to outside observers what people will do next."

The point of contention remains in whether the face also says something about a person's internal state. Some, such as Izard, say, "Abso-

lutely." Detractors, such as Alan Fridlund, PhD, of the University of California, Santa Barbara, say an adamant "No." And others, including Campos and Ekman, land somewhere in the middle. The face surely can provide important information about emotion, but it is only one of many tools and should never be used as a "gold standard" of emotion as some researchers, particularly those studying children, have tended to do.

"The face is a component [of emotion]," says Campos. "But to make it the center of study of the human being experiencing an emotion is like saying the only thing you need to study in a car is the transmission. Not that the transmission is unimportant, but it's only part of an entire system."

WHERE IT ALL BEGAN

Based on findings that people label photos of prototypical facial expressions with words that represent the same basic emotions—a smile represents joy, a scowl represents anger—Ekman and Izard pioneered the idea that by carefully measuring facial expression, they could evaluate people's true emotions. In fact, since the 1970s, Ekman and his colleague Wallace Friesen, PhD, have dominated the field of emotion research with their theory that when an emotion occurs, a cascade of electrical impulses, emanating from emotion centers in the brain, trigger specific facial expressions and other physio-

logical changes—such as increased or decreased heart rate or heightened blood pressure.

If the emotion comes on slowly, or is rather weak, the theory states, the impulse might not be strong enough to trigger the expression. This would explain in part why there can sometimes be emotion without expression, they argue. In addition, cultural "display rules"—which determine when and whether people of certain cultures display emotional expressions—can derail this otherwise automatic process, the theory states. Facial expressions evolved in humans as signals to others about how they feel, says Ekman.

> **"The face is like a switch on a railroad track. It affects the trajectory of the social interaction the way the switch would affect the path of the train."**
>
> *Alan Fridlund*
> *University of California, Santa Barbara*

"At times it may be uncomfortable or inconvenient for others to know how we feel," he says. "But in the long run, over the course of evolution, it was useful to us as signalers. So, when you see an angry look on my face, you know that I may be preparing to respond in an angry fashion, which means that I may attack or abruptly withdraw."

THE FACE IS LIKE A SWITCH

Although Fridlund strongly disagrees with Ekman in his writings, arguing that expressions carry no inherent meaning, the two basically agree that facial expressions forecast people's future actions. But instead of describing expressions from the point of view of the expresser, as Ekman tends to do, Fridlund thinks more in terms of people who perceive the expressions.

Expressions evolved to elicit behaviors from others, says Fridlund. So, a smile may encourage people to approach while a scowl may impel them to stay clear, and a pout may elicit words of sympathy and reassurance. And, he contends, expressions are inherently social. Even when people are alone they are holding an internal dialogue with another person, or imagining themselves in a social situation.

"The face is like a switch on a railroad track," says Fridlund. "It affects the trajectory of the social interaction the way the switch would affect the path of the train."

Thinking of facial expressions as tools for influencing social interactions provides an opportunity to begin predicting when certain facial expressions will occur and will allow more precise theories about social interactions, says Fridlund. Studies by him and others find that expressions occur most often during pivotal points in social interactions—during greetings, social crisis or times of appeasement, for example.

"At these pivotal points, where there's an approach, or proximity, or more intimacy, the face as well as the gestures form a kind of switching station for the possibilities of social interactions," says Fridlund.

The University of Amsterdam's Nico Frijda, PhD, agrees that expressions are a means to influence others. They also, he believes, occur when people prepare to take some kind of action whether there are others present or not. For example, if you're scared and want to protect yourself, you frown and draw your brows in preparation—what Ekman would call a "fear" expression. But there is no one-to-one correspondence between the face and specific emotions, Frijda contends.

"There is some affinity between certain emotions and certain expressions," he says, "if only because some emotions imply a desire for vigorous action, and some facial expressions manifest just that."

NOT A 'GOLD STANDARD'

Herein lies the major point of contention within the facial expression community, says Berkeley's Campos.

"All sides agree that the face—and voice and posture, for that matter—forecast what a person will do next," he says. "But over and above that, is feeling involved?"

Although much work in the emotion literature relies on a link between facial expression and emotions, there's a paucity of evidence supporting it.

"There's some sense in which faces express emotion, but only in the sense that everything expresses emotion," says psychologist James Russell, PhD, of the University of British Columbia, a long-time critic of the expression-emotion link. "Music does, posture does, words do, tone of voice does, your behavior does. The real question is, 'Is there anything special about faces?' And there we really don't know much."

What's more likely, argues Russell, is that facial expressions tell others something about the overall character of a person's mood—whether it's positive or negative—and context then provides details about specific emotions.

Others, including Ekman and Campos, contend that the face can display information about emotions. But, they admit, it is by no means a "gold standard." The face is only one of many measures researchers can use to infer emotion. And those who only examine faces when trying to study emotion will jump to false conclusions.

"There is a link between facial expression and emotion," explains developmental psychologist Linda Camras, PhD, of DePaul University. "But it's not a one-to-one kind of relationship as many once thought. There are many situations where emotion is experienced, yet no prototypic facial expression is displayed. And there are times when a facial expression appears with no corresponding emotion."

In a classic set of experiments with infants, Camras found that some facial expressions can occur in the absence of the emotions they supposedly represent.

"An emotion has to be plausible [for the situation you're examining]," she says. "You can't do blind coding of facial expression and necessarily be on the right track, even for infants."

But to say, as Fridlund does, that there's no connection between some facial expressions and some emotions is simply wrong, says Ekman. When we look at people's expressions, he says, we don't receive direct information about their heart rate or other physiological changes that accompany emotions. We might even think, "He's going to whack me" rather than "He's angry," says Ekman.

"But these signals—facial expressions and physiological changes associated with internal emotions—can't exist independently," he contends.

FURTHER REFERENCE

Ekman, P., & Rosenberg, E. (1997). *What the Face Reveals*. New York: Oxford University Press.

Fridlund, A. (1994). *Human Facial Expression: An Evolutionary View*. San Diego, CA: Academic Press.

Russell, J., & Fernandez-Dols, J. M. (Eds.) (1997). *The Psychology of Facial Expression*. New York: Cambridge University Press.

Emotional Intelligence: What the Research Says

When integrating the concept of emotional intelligence into curriculum practice, educators need to understand the models, rely on solid research, and—as always—tread carefully.

Casey D. Cobb and John D. Mayer

Emotional intelligence was popularized by Daniel Goleman's 1995 best-selling book, *Emotional Intelligence.* The book described emotional intelligence as a mix of skills, such as awareness of emotions; traits, such as persistence and zeal; and good behavior. Goleman (1995) summarized the collection of emotional intelligence qualities as "character."

The public received the idea of emotional intelligence enthusiastically. To some, it de-emphasized the importance of general IQ and promised to level the playing field for those whose cognitive abilities might be wanting. To others, it offered the potential to integrate the reasoning of a person's head and heart. Goleman made strong claims: Emotional intelligence was "as powerful," "at times more powerful," and even "twice as powerful" as IQ (Goleman, 1995, p. 34; Goleman, 1998, p. 94). On its cover, *Time* magazine declared that emotional IQ "may be the best predictor of success in life, redefining what it means to be smart" (Gibbs, 1995). Goleman's book became a *New York Times*—and international—best-seller.

The claims of this science journalism extended easily to the schools. *Emotional Intelligence* concluded that developing students' emotional competencies would result in a "'caring community,' a place where students feel respected, cared about, and bonded to classmates" (Goleman, 1995, p. 280). A leader of the social and emotional learning movement referred to emotional intelligence as "the integrative concept" underlying a curriculum for emotional intelligence (Elias et al., 1997, pp. 27, 29). And the May 1997 issue of *Educational Leadership* extensively covered the topic of emotional intelligence.

Two Models

This popular model of emotional intelligence was based on, and added to, a 1990 academic theory and subsequent publications now referred to as the *ability* approach to emotional intelligence. The logic behind the ability model was that emotions are signals about relationships. For example, sadness signals loss. We must process emotion—perceive, understand, manage, and use it—to benefit from it; thus, emotional processing—or emotional intelligence—has great importance (Mayer & Salovey, 1997; Salovey & Mayer, 1990).

The concept of emotional intelligence legitimates the discussion of emotions in school.

The ability model argued for an emotional intelligence that involves perceiving and reasoning abstractly with information that emerges from feelings. This argument drew on research findings from areas of nonverbal perception, empathy, artificial intelligence, and brain research. Recent empirical demonstrations have further bolstered the case (Mayer, Caruso, & Salovey, 1999; Mayer, DiPaolo, & Salovey, 1993; 1990; Mayer & Salovey, 1993; Salovey & Mayer, 1990).

The ability model made no particular claims about the potential predictive value of emotional intelligence. In fact, even several years after the publication of Goleman's book, psychologists view the popular claims about predicting success as ill-defined, unsupported, and implausible (Davies, Stankov, & Roberts, 1998; Epstein, 1998). Rather, the ability version emphasizes that emotional intelligence exists. If emotional intelligence exists and qualifies as a traditional or standard intelligence (like general IQ), people who are labeled *bleeding hearts* or *hopeless romantics* might be actually engaged in sophisticated information processing. Moreover, the concept of emotional intelligence legitimates the discussion of emotions in schools and other organizations because emotions reflect crucial information about relationships.

Two models of emotional intelligence thus developed. The first, the ability model, defines emotional intelligence as a set of abilities and makes claims about the importance of emotional information and the potential uses of reasoning well with that information. The second, which we will refer to as the mixed model, is more popularly oriented. It mixes emotional intelligence as an ability with social competencies, traits, and behaviors, and makes wondrous claims about the success this intelligence leads to.

Educational leaders have experimented with incorporating emotional learning in schools. For the most part, emotional intelligence is finding its way into schools in small doses, through socioemotional learning and character education programs. But examples of grander plans are evolving, with a few schools organizing their entire curriculums around emotional intelligence. One state even attempted to integrate emotional learning into all its social, health, and education programs (Elias et al., 1997; Rhode Island Emotional Competency Partnership, 1998).

Educational practices involving emotional intelligence should be based on solid research, not on sensationalistic claims.

The problem is that some educators have implemented emotional intelligence programs and policies without much sensitivity to the idea that there is more than one emotional intelligence model. We have expressed concern that school practices and policies on emotional intelligence relied on popularizations that were, in some instances, far ahead of the science on which they were presumably based (Mayer & Cobb, 2000). The early claims of the benefits of emotional intelligence to students, schools, and beyond were made without much empirical justification.

We hope that emotional intelligence is predictive of life success or that it leads to good behavior, but we recognize that it is fairly early in the game. We are also wary of the sometimes faddish nature of school reform and the grave fate of other hastily implemented curricular innovations. Consider the rush by California to

implement self-esteem programs into its schools in the late 1980s (Joachim, 1996). Substantial resources were exhausted for years before that movement was deemed a failure. The construct of emotional intelligence comes at a time when educators are eager to find answers to problems of poor conduct, interpersonal conflict, and violence plaguing schools; however, educational practices involving emotional intelligence should be based on solid research, not on sensationalistic claims. So, what *does* the research say?

Identifying emotions in faces, pictorial designs, music, and stories are typical tasks for assessing the emotional perception area of emotional intelligence.

Measuring Emotional Intelligence

Emotional intelligence, whether academically or popularly conceived, must meet certain criteria before it can be labeled a psychological entity. One criterion for an intelligence is that it can be operationalized as a set of abilities. Ability measures—measures that ask people to solve problems with an eye to whether their answers are right or wrong—are the sine qua non of assessing an intelligence. If you measure intelligence with actual problems (such as, What does the word *season* mean?), you can assess how well a person can think. If you simply ask a student how smart she is (for example, How well do you solve problems?)—a so-called self-report—you cannot be certain that you are getting an authentic or genuine answer. In fact, the correlation between a person's score on an intelligence test and self-reported intelligence is almost negligible. Early evidence suggests that self-reported emotional intelligence is fairly unrelated to actual ability (Mayer, Salovey, & Caruso, 2000).

Ability-based testing of emotional intelligence has centered on the Mayer-Salovey-Caruso Emotional Intelligence Test (MSCEIT) and its precursor, the Multifactor Emotional Intelligence Scale (MEIS). Both tests measure the four areas of emotional intelligence: perception, facilitation of thought, understanding, and management (Mayer, Caruso, & Salovey, 1999). For example, look at the pictures of the faces on this page. Is the person happy? Sad? Are other emotions expressed? Identifying emotions in faces, pictorial designs, music, and stories are typical tasks for assessing the area of emotional intelligence called emotional perception.

Another type of MSCEIT question asks, When you are feeling slow and sour, which of the following emotions does this most closely resemble: (A) frustration, (B) jealousy, (C) happiness, or (D) joy? Most people would probably choose *frustration* because people become frustrated when they move too slowly and are disappointed (or sour) that things aren't going as planned. This kind of question measures the second area of emotional intelligence: emotional facilitation of thought.

A third type of MSCEIT question tests individuals' knowledge about emotions: Contempt is closer to which combination of emotions: *anger and fear* or *disgust and anger?* Such a question assesses emotional understanding.

The final type of MSCEIT questions measures emotional management. These questions describe a hypothetical situation that stirs the emotions (such as the unexpected break-up of a long-term relationship) and then ask how a person should respond to obtain a given outcome (for example, staying calm).

One crucial aspect of assessing emotional intelligence lies in the method by which answers are scored. Scoring a standard IQ test is fairly straightforward, with clear-cut, defensible answers for every item. The responses on a test of emotional intelligence are better thought of as *fuzzy sets*—certain answers are more right or plausible than others, and only some answers are absolutely wrong all the time. To assess the relative correctness of an answer, we can use consensus, expertise or target criteria (or some combination). A correct response by way of the consensus approach is simply the answer most frequently selected by test-takers. Answers can also be deemed correct by such experts as psychologists or other trained professionals. Finally, correct responses can be validated using a target criterion. For instance, the actual emotional reaction of an anonymously depicted spouse facing a difficult decision could serve as the targeted response in a test item that described his or her situation.

The MSCEIT and MEIS are undergoing considerable scrutiny from the scientific community. Although not everyone is convinced yet of their validity, the tests do provide the most dramatic evidence thus far for the existence of an emotional intelligence. Early findings provide strong evidence that emotional intelligence looks and behaves like other intelligences, such as verbal intelligence, but remains distinct enough to stand alone as a separate mental ability. Like other intelligences, emotional intelligence appears to develop with age (Mayer, Caruso, & Salovey, 1999).

Predictive Value

The first emotional intelligence tests were used two years *after* the popular claims of 1995, so the actual findings lag behind the popular perception of a well-established area of research. One important pattern is emerging, however. Preliminary research (primarily from unpublished studies and dissertations) from the MEIS suggests a modest relationship between emotional intelligence and lower levels of "bad" behaviors.

In one study, high scores in emotional intelligence moderately predicted the absence of adult bad behavior,

such as getting into fights and arguments, drinking, smoking, and owning firearms (Mayer, Caruso, Salovey, Formica, & Woolery, 2000). In a dissertation study, the MEIS-A measured the emotional intelligence of fifty-two 7th and 8th graders in an urban school district (Rubin, 1999). Analyses indicated that higher emotional intelligence was inversely related to teacher and peer ratings of aggression among students. In another study, researchers reported that higher MEIS-A scores among 200 high school students were associated with lower admissions of smoking, intentions to smoke, and alcohol consumption (Trinidad & Johnson, 2000). The conclusion suggested by such research is that higher emotional intelligence predicts lower incidences of "bad" behavior. As for the claims about success in life—those studies have yet to be done.

What Can Schools Do?

Educators interested in emotional intelligence of either the ability or mixed type are typically directed to programs in social and emotional learning (Goleman, 1995; Goleman, 1996; Mayer & Salovey, 1997). These programs had been around for years before the introduction of the emotional intelligence concept. Some aspects of the programs overlap with the ability approach to emotional intelligence. This overlap occurs when programs ask early elementary children to "appropriately express and manage" various emotions and "differentiate and label negative and positive emotions in self and others," or call for students to integrate "feeling and thinking with language" and learn "strategies for coping with, communicating about, and managing strong feelings" (Elias et al., 1997, p. 133–134). Other aspects of these programs are specifically more consistent with the mixed (or popular) models than the ability approach in that they include distinct behavioral objectives, such as "becoming assertive, self-calming, cooperative," and "understanding responsible behavior at social events" (p. 135). There is also an emphasis on such values as honesty, consideration, and caring.

What may work better, at least for some students, is helping them develop the capacity to make decisions on their own in their own contexts.

What would a curriculum based on an ability model look like? Basically, it would drop the behavioral objectives and values and focus on emotional reasoning.

Choosing Approaches

The emotional intelligence curriculum (or ability model) and the social and emotional learning curriculum (or mixed model) both overlap and diverge. The emotional ability approach focuses only on teaching emotional reasoning. The social and emotional learning curriculum mixes emotional skills, social values, and behaviors. In the case of these two approaches, less—that is, the pure ability model—may be better. What troubles us about the broader social and emotional learning approach is that the emphasis on students getting along with one another could stifle creativity, healthy skepticism, or spontaneity—all valued outcomes in their own right. Teaching people to be tactful or compassionate as full-time general virtues runs counter to the "smart" part of emotional intelligence, which requires knowing when to be tactful or compassionate and when to be blunt or even cold and hard.

Moreover, a social and emotional approach that emphasizes positive behavior and attitudes can be a real turn-off for a negative thinker—often the very student that the teacher is trying to reach. Research supports this concern: Positive messages appear less believable and less sensible to unhappy people than sad messages do (Forgas, 1995). We suspect that troubled students will be alienated by insistent positivity. There may be nothing wrong with trying such approaches, but they may not work.

Correctly perceiving emotional information is part of the way that children make sense of things.

What may work better at least for some students, is helping them develop the capacity to make decisions on their own in their own contexts. This type of education is knowledge-based and is more aligned with an ability model of emotional intelligence. It involves teaching students emotional knowledge and emotional reasoning, with the hope that this combination would lead children to find their own way toward making good decisions.

Most children will require gentle guidance toward the good. We wonder, however, whether we can achieve this goal better by example and indirect teaching than by the direct, uniform endorsement of selected values in the curriculum.

How Might the Ability Curriculum Work?

The teaching of emotional knowledge has been a facet of some curriculums for years. For example, educators can help children perceive emotions in several ways. Elementary teachers could ask the class to name the feelings that they are aware of and then show what they look or feel like (for example, Show me sad). Similarly, teachers could ask students to identify the emotions depicted by various pictures of faces. Children can also learn to read more subtle cues, such as the speed and intonation of voice, body posture, and physical gestures.

Correctly perceiving emotional information is one way children make sense of things. The ability to perceive emotions can be further fine-tuned as a student ages. Consider the level of sophistication required for an actor to put on a convincing expression of fear—and for the audience to recognize it as such.

Students can also learn to use emotions to create new ideas. For instance, asking students in English class to write about trees as if they were angry or delighted facilitates a deeper understanding of these emotions.

Understanding emotions should also be a goal of the curriculum. For example, social studies expert Fred Newmann (1987) has suggested that higher-order thinking can be enhanced through empathic teaching. A social studies teacher could show images of the Trail of Tears, the forced exodus of the Cherokee from their homeland, and have students discuss the feelings involved. This could help students vicariously experience what those perilous conditions were like. In literature courses, teachers who point out the feelings of a story character, such as a triumphant figure skater or a despairing widow, can teach a great deal about what emotions tell us about relationships. Because the ability version of emotional intelligence legitimizes discussing emotions by considering them to convey information, it also supports emotionally evocative activities—such as theater, art, and interscholastic events—that help kids understand and learn from personal performance.

Emotional Intelligence in Schools

Educators looking to incorporate emotional intelligence into their schools should be aware that the two different models of emotional intelligence suggest two somewhat different curricular approaches. The model of emotional intelligence that makes its way into schools should be empirically defensible, measurable, and clear enough to serve as a basis for curriculum development. We believe that an ability-based curriculum, which emphasizes emotional knowledge and reasoning, may have advantages because it reaches more students.

References

Davies, M., Stankov, L., & Roberts, R. D. (1998). Emotional intelligence: In search of an elusive construct. *Journal of Personality & Social Psychology, 75*, 989–1015.

Elias, M. J., Zins, J. E., Weissberg, R. P., Frey, K. S., Greenberg, M. T., Haynes, N. M., Kessler, R., Schwab-Stone, M. E., & Schriver, T. P. (1997). *Promoting social and emotional learning: Guidelines for educators.* Alexandria, VA: ASCD.

Epstein, S. (1998). *Constructive thinking: The key to emotional intelligence.* Westport, CT: Praeger.

Forgas, J. P. (1995). Mood and judgement: The affect infusion model (AIM). *Psychological Bulletin, 117*(1), 39–66.

Gibbs, N. (1995, October 2). The EQ factor. *Time, 146*(14), 60–68.

Goleman, D. (1995). *Emotional intelligence.* New York: Bantam.

Goleman, D. (1996). *Emotional intelligence: A new vision for educators* [Videotape]. Port Chester, NY: National Professional Resources.

Goleman, D. (1998, November/December). What makes a leader? *Harvard Business Review, 76,* 93–102.

Joachim, K. (1996). The politics of self-esteem. *American Educational Research Journal, 33,* 3–22.

Mayer, J. D., Caruso, D. R., & Salovey, P. (1999). Emotional intelligence meets standards for a traditional intelligence. *Intelligence, 27,* 267–298.

Mayer, J. D., Caruso, D. R., Salovey, P., Formica, S., & Woolery, A. (2000). Unpublished raw data.

Mayer, J. D., & Cobb, C. D. (2000). Educational policy on emotional intelligence: Does it make sense? *Educational Psychology Review, 12*(2), 163–183.

Mayer, J. D., DiPaolo, M. T., & Salovey, P. (1990). Perceiving affective content in ambiguous visual stimuli: A component of emotional intelligence. *Journal of Personality Assessment, 54,* 772–781.

Mayer, J. D., & Salovey, P. (1993). The intelligence of emotional intelligence. *Intelligence, 17*(4), 433–442.

Mayer, J. D., & Salovey, P. (1997). What is emotional intelligence? In P. Salovey & D. Sluyter (Eds.), *Emotional development and emotional intelligence: Implications for educators* (pp. 3–31). New York: BasicBooks.

Mayer, J. D., Salovey, P., & Caruso, D. R. (2000). Models of emotional intelligence. In R. J. Sternberg (Ed.), *Handbook of Intelligence* (pp. 396–420). Cambridge: Cambridge University Press.

Newmann, F. M. (1987). *Higher order thinking in the teaching of social studies: Connections between theory and practice.* Madison, WI: National Center on Effective Secondary Schools. (ERIC Document Reproduction Service No. 332 880)

Rhode Island Emotional Competency Partnership. (1998). *Update on emotional competency.* Providence, RI: Rhode Island Partners.

Rubin, M. M. (1999). *Emotional intelligence and its role in mitigating aggression: A correlational study of the relationship between emotional intelligence and aggression in urban adolescents.* Unpublished manuscript, Immaculata College, Immaculata, PA.

Salovey, P., & Mayer, J. D. (1990). Emotional intelligence. *Imagination, Cognition, & Personality, 9*(3), 185–211.

Trinidad, D. R., & Johnson, A. (2000). *The association between emotional intelligence and early adolescent tobacco and alcohol use.* Unpublished manuscript, University of Southern California, Los Angeles, CA.

Casey D. Cobb (casey.cobb@unh.edu) is Assistant Professor of Education and **John D. Mayer** is Professor of Psychology at the University of New Hampshire, 62 College Rd., Durham, NH 03824.

UNIT 7
Development

Unit Selections

Key Points to Consider

- What are the various milestones or developmental landmarks that mark human development? What purpose do various developmental events serve? Can you give examples of some of these events?

- Why is embryonic and fetal life so important? How do the experiences of the fetus affect the child after it is born? What factors deter the fetus from achieving its full potential?

- Do parents matter or do you think that child development is mostly dictated by genes? Do you think that both nature and nurture affect development? Do you think one of these factors is more important than the other? Which one and why? Do you think it is important for both parents to be present during their child's formative years? Do you think fathers and mothers differ in their interactions with their children? How so? Why do some claim that parenting is a "lost art"? How and why are parents and schools at odds with each other?

- What is puberty? What is adolescence? How are today's teens different from teens in the past, for example their parents' generation? What societal factors are influencing teens today? If you had to rank these factors, which are most influential, which are least influential? Which are positive influences and which are negative?

- Why do we age? Can we stay younger longer? What do Americans say is more important—a high quality but shorter life or a poor quality and longer life? Why do you think they answered the way they did? How would you answer and why? Would you want to live to 100?

- Why is death a stigmatized topic in America? Do you think people should discuss it more often and more openly? Do you think they ever will? How can we make dying easier for the dying person and for those close to the dying person? What can be done to help those with terminal illnesses?

 **Links: www.dushkin.com/online/**
These sites are annotated in the World Wide Web pages.

American Association for Child and Adolescent Psychiatry
http://www.aacap.org
Behavioral Genetics
http://www.uams.edu/department_of_psychiatry/slides/html/genetics/index.htm

The Garcias and the Szubas are parents of newborns. Both sets of parents wander down to the hospital's neonatal nursery where both babies, José Garcia and Kimberly Szuba, are cared for by pediatric nurses when the babies are not in their mothers' rooms. Kimberly is alert, active, and often crying and squirming when her parents watch her. José is quiet, often asleep, and less attentive to external stimuli when his parents watch him.

Why are these babies so different? Are the differences gender-related? Will these differences disappear as the children develop or will the differences become exaggerated? What does the future hold for each child? Will Kimberly excel at sports and José excel at English? Can Kimberly overcome her parents' poverty and succeed in a professional career? Will José become a doctor like his mother or a pharmacist like his father? Will both of these children escape childhood disease, abuse, and the other misfortunes sometimes visited upon children?

Developmental psychologists are concerned with all of the Kimberlys and Josés of our world. Developmental psychologists study age-related changes in language, motoric and social skills, cognition, and physical health. They are interested in the com-

mon skills shared by all children as well as the differences between children and the events that create these differences.

In general, developmental psychologists are concerned with the forces that guide and direct development. Some developmental theorists argue that the forces that shape a child are found in the environment in such factors as social class, quality of available stimulation, parenting style, and so on. Other theorists insist that genetics and related physiological factors, such as hormones, underlie the development of humans. A third set of psychologists believe that some combination or interaction of both factors, physiology and environment (or nature and nurture), are responsible for development.

In this unit, we are going to look at issues of development in a chronological fashion. The first article pertains to fetal development, which is crucial to the development of the child after it is born. Various environmental factors can deter development of or even damage the fetus. Janet Hopson reviews these in "Fetal Psychology."

In the next article, "Parenting: The Lost Art," Kay Hymowitz discusses children's misconduct and academic failure. She attempts to disentangle the blaming that occurs by schools and parents so as to discover the real cause. Part of the problem, she advises, is that today's parents want to be friends rather than parents to their children.

We move next to some information about adolescence. In "A World of Their Own," Sharon Begley suggests that teens today are very different from teens of past generations. While their peers are still very influential, there are a number of other societal influences that were not experienced by past teens. The Internet, for example, is a powerful influence on today's teens. Begley interviewed teens and reveals what they say and think about these societal changes and the impacts on their lives.

The next article is about adulthood and aging. The American Association of Retired Persons conducted a recent poll to determine whether quality of life or quantity (age) is more important to its members. Most elderly opted for a shorter life with better quality rather than a longer life with poor quality.

The final article in this series looks at the ultimate stage in development—death. Death is stigmatized in America; few people openly discuss it. There is much information contained in the article about issues surrounding death, such as hospice care, how to be with a dying person, and so forth. The article claims that we ought to be more open and is therefore designed to stimulate dialogue on this topic.

FETAL PSYCHOLOGY

Behaviorally
speaking, there's little
difference between a newborn
baby and a 32-week-old fetus.
A new wave of research suggests
that the fetus can feel, dream, even
enjoy *The Cat in the Hat*. **The
abortion debate may never
be the same.**

By Janet L. Hopson

The scene never fails to give goose bumps: the baby, just seconds old and still dewy from the womb, is lifted into the arms of its exhausted but blissful parents. They gaze adoringly as their new child stretches and squirms, scrunches its mouth and opens its eyes. To anyone watching this tender vignette, the message is unmistakable. Birth is the beginning of it all, ground zero, the moment from which the clock starts ticking. Not so, declares Janet DiPietro. Birth may be a grand occasion, says the Johns Hopkins University psychologist, but "it is a trivial event in development. Nothing neurologically interesting happens."

Armed with highly sensitive and sophisticated monitoring gear, DiPietro and other researchers today are discovering that the real action starts weeks earlier. At 32 weeks of gestation—two months before a baby is considered fully prepared for the world, or "at term"—a fetus is behaving almost exactly as a newborn. And it continues to do so for the next 12 weeks.

A fetus spends hours in the rapid eye movement sleep of dreams.

As if overturning the common conception of infancy weren't enough, scientists are creating a startling new picture of intelligent life in the womb. Among the revelations:

- By nine weeks, a developing fetus can hiccup and react to loud noises. By the end of the second trimester it can hear.

- Just as adults do, the fetus experiences the rapid eye movement (REM) sleep of dreams.

- The fetus savors its mother's meals, first picking up the food tastes of a culture in the womb.

- Among other mental feats, the fetus can distinguish between the voice of Mom and that of a stranger, and respond to a familiar story read to it.

- Even a premature baby is aware, feels, responds, and adapts to its environment.

- Just because the fetus is responsive to certain stimuli doesn't mean that it should be the target of efforts to enhance development. Sensory stimulation of the fetus can in fact lead to bizarre patterns of adaptation later on.

The roots of human behavior, researchers now know, begin to develop early—just weeks after conception, in fact. Well before a woman typically knows she is pregnant, her embryo's brain has already begun to bulge. By five weeks, the organ that looks like a lumpy inchworm has already embarked on the most spectacular feat of human development: the creation of the deeply creased and convoluted cerebral cortex, the part of the brain that will eventually allow the growing person to move, think, speak, plan, and create in a human way.

At nine weeks, the embryo's ballooning brain allows it to bend its body, hiccup, and react to loud sounds. At week ten, it moves its arms, "breathes" amniotic fluid in and out, opens its jaw, and stretches. Before the first trimester is over, it yawns, sucks, and swallows as well as feels and smells. By the end of the second trimester, it can hear; toward the end of pregnancy, it can see.

FETAL ALERTNESS

Scientists who follow the fetus' daily life find that it spends most of its time not exercising these new abilities but sleeping. At 32 weeks, it drowses 90 to 95% of the day. Some of these hours are spent in deep sleep, some in REM sleep, and some in an indeterminate state, a product of the fetus' immature brain that is different from sleep in a baby, child, or adult. During REM sleep, the fetus' eyes move back and forth just as an adult's eyes do, and many researchers believe that it is dreaming. DiPietro speculates that fetuses dream about what they know—the sensations they feel in the womb.

Closer to birth, the fetus sleeps 85 to 90% of the time, the same as a newborn. Between its frequent naps, the fetus seems to have "something like an awake alert period," according to developmental psychologist William Fifer, Ph.D., who with his Columbia University colleagues is monitoring these sleep and wakefulness cycles in order to identify patterns of normal and abnormal brain development, including potential predictors of sudden infant death syndrome. Says Fifer, "We are, in effect, asking the fetus: 'Are you paying attention? Is your nervous system behaving in the appropriate way?' "

FETAL MOVEMENT

Awake or asleep, the human fetus moves 50 times or more each hour, flexing and extending its body, moving its head, face, and limbs and exploring its warm wet compartment by touch. Heidelise Als, Ph.D., a developmental psychologist at Harvard Medical School, is fascinated by the amount of tactile stimulation a fetus gives itself. "It touches a hand to the face, one hand to the other hand, clasps its feet, touches its foot to its leg, its hand to its umbilical cord," she reports.

Als believes there is a mismatch between the environment given to preemies in hospitals and the environment they would have had in the womb. She has been working for years to change the care given to preemies so that they can curl up, bring their knees together, and touch things with their hands as they would have for weeks in the womb.

By 15 weeks, a fetus has an adult's taste buds and may be able to savor its mother's meals.

Along with such common movements, DiPietro has also noted some odder fetal activities, including "licking the uterine wall and literally walking around the womb by pushing off with its feet." Laterborns may have more room in the womb for such maneuvers than first babies. After the initial pregnancy, a woman's uterus is bigger and the umbilical cord longer, allowing more freedom of movement. "Second and subsequent children may develop more motor experience in utero and so may become more active infants," DiPietro speculates.

Fetuses react sharply to their mother's actions. "When we're watching the fetus on ultrasound and the mother starts to laugh, we can see the fetus, floating upside down in the womb, bounce up and down on its head, bum-bum-bum, like it's bouncing on a trampoline," says DiPietro. "When mothers watch this on the screen, they laugh harder, and the fetus goes up and down even faster. We've wondered whether this is why people grow up liking roller coasters."

FETAL TASTE

Why people grow up liking hot chilies or spicy curries may also have something to do with the fetal environment. By 13 to 15 weeks a fetus' taste buds already look like a mature adult's, and doctors know that the amniotic fluid that surrounds it can smell strongly of curry, cumin, garlic, onion and other essences from a mother's diet. Whether fetuses can taste these flavors isn't yet known, but scientists have found that a 33-week-old preemie will suck harder on a sweetened nipple than on a plain rubber one.

"During the last trimester, the fetus is swallowing up to a liter a day" of amniotic fluid, notes Julie Mennella, Ph.D., a biopsychologist at the Monell Chemical Senses Center in Philadelphia. She thinks the fluid may act as a "flavor bridge" to breast milk, which also carries food flavors from the mother's diet.

FETAL HEARING

Whether or not a fetus can taste, there's little question that it can hear. A very premature baby entering the world at 24 to 25 weeks responds to the sounds around it, observes Als, so its auditory apparatus must already have been functioning in the womb. Many pregnant women report a fetal jerk or sudden kick just after a door slams or a car backfires.

Even without such intrusions, the womb is not a silent place. Researchers who have inserted a hydrophone into the uterus of a pregnant woman have picked up a noise level "akin to the background noise in an apartment," according to DiPietro. Sounds include the whooshing of blood in the mother's vessels, the gurgling and rumbling of her stomach and intestines, as well as the tones of her voice filtered through tissues, bones, and fluid, and the voices of other people coming through the amniotic wall. Fifer has found that fetal heart rate slows when the mother is speaking, suggesting that the fetus not only hears and recognizes the sound, but is calmed by it.

FETAL VISION

Vision is the last sense to develop. A very premature infant can see light and shape; researchers presume that a fetus has the same ability. Just as the womb isn't com-

What's the Impact on Abortion?

Though research in fetal psychology focuses on the last trimester, when most abortions are illegal, the thought of a fetus dreaming, listening and responding to its mother's voice is sure to add new complexity to the debate. The new findings undoubtedly will strengthen the convictions of right-to-lifers—and they may shake the certainty of pro-choice proponents who believe that mental life begins at birth.

Many of the scientists engaged in studying the fetus, however, remain detached from the abortion controversy, insisting that their work is completely irrelevant to the debate.

"I don't think that fetal research informs the issue at all," contends psychologist Janet DiPietro of Johns Hopkins University. "The essence of the abortion debate is: When does life begin? Some people believe it begins at conception, the other extreme believes that it begins after the baby is born, and there's a group in the middle that believes it begins at around 24 or 25 weeks, when a fetus can live outside of the womb, though it needs a lot of help to do so.

"Up to about 25 weeks, whether or not it's sucking its thumb or has personality or all that, the fetus cannot survive outside of its mother. So is that life, or not? That is a moral, ethical, and religious question, not one for science. Things can behave and not be alive. Right-to-lifers may say that this research proves that a fetus is alive, but it does not. It cannot."

"Fetal research only changes the abortion debate for people who think that life starts at some magical point," maintains Heidelise Als, a psychologist at Harvard University. "If you believe that life begins at conception, then you don't need the proof of fetal behavior." For others, however, abortion is a very complex issue and involves far more than whether research shows that a fetus hiccups. "Your circumstances and personal beliefs have much more impact on the decision," she observes.

Like DiPietro, Als realizes that "people may use this research as an emotional way to draw people to the pro-life side, but it should not be used by belligerent activists." Instead, she believes, it should be applied to helping mothers have the healthiest pregnancy possible and preparing them to best parent their child. Columbia University psychologist William Fifer, Ph.D., agrees. "The research is much more relevant for issues regarding viable fetuses—preemies."

Simply put, say the three, their work is intended to help the babies that live—not to decide whether fetuses should.—*Camille Chatterjee*

pletely quiet, it isn't utterly dark, either. Says Fifer: "There may be just enough visual stimulation filtered through the mother's tissues that a fetus can respond when the mother is in bright light," such as when she is sunbathing.

A fetus prefers hearing Mom's voice over a stranger's—speaking in her native, not a foreign tongue—and being read aloud familiar tales rather than new stories.

Japanese scientists have even reported a distinct fetal reaction to flashes of light shined on the mother's belly. However, other researchers warn that exposing fetuses (or premature infants) to bright light before they are ready can be dangerous. In fact, Harvard's Als believes that retinal damage in premature infants, which has long been ascribed to high concentrations of oxygen, may actually be due to overexposure to light at the wrong time in development.

A six-month fetus, born about 14 weeks too early, has a brain that is neither prepared for nor expecting signals from the eyes to be transmitted into the brain's visual cortex, and from there into the executive-branch frontal lobes, where information is integrated. When the fetus is forced to see too much too soon, says Als, the accelerated stimulation may lead to aberrations of brain development.

FETAL LEARNING

Along with the ability to feel, see, and hear comes the capacity to learn and remember. These activities can be rudimentary, automatic, even biochemical. For example, a fetus, after an initial reaction of alarm, eventually stops responding to a repeated loud noise. The fetus displays the same kind of primitive learning, known as habituation, in response to its mother's voice, Fifer has found.

But the fetus has shown itself capable of far more. In the 1980s, psychology professor Anthony James De-Casper, Ph.D., and colleagues at the University of North Carolina at Greensboro, devised a feeding contraption that allows a baby to suck faster to hear one set of sounds through headphones and to suck slower to hear a different set. With this technique, DeCasper discovered that within hours of birth, a baby already prefers its mother's voice to a stranger's, suggesting it must have learned and remembered the voice, albeit not necessarily consciously, from its last months in the womb. More recently, he's found that a newborn prefers a story read to it repeatedly in the womb—in this case, *The Cat in the Hat*—over a new story introduced soon after birth.

DeCasper and others have uncovered more mental feats. Newborns can not only distinguish their mother from a stranger speaking, but would rather hear Mom's voice, especially the way it sounds filtered through amniotic fluid rather than through air. They're xenophobes, too: they prefer to hear Mom speaking in her native language than to hear her or someone else speaking in a foreign tongue.

By monitoring changes in fetal heart rate, psychologist Jean-Pierre Lecanuet, Ph.D., and his colleagues in Paris have found that fetuses can even tell strangers' voices apart. They also seem to like certain stories more than others. The fetal heartbeat will slow down when a familiar French fairy tale such as *La Poulette* ("The Chick") or *"Le Petit Crapaud"* ("The Little Toad"), is read near the mother's belly. When the same reader delivers another unfamiliar story, the fetal heartbeat stays steady.

The fetus is likely responding to the cadence of voices and stories, not their actual words, observes Fifer, but the conclusion is the same: the fetus can listen, learn, and remember at some level, and, as with most babies and children, it likes the comfort and reassurance of the familiar.

FETAL PERSONALITY

It's no secret that babies are born with distinct differences and patterns of activity that suggest individual temperament. Just when and how the behavioral traits originate in the womb is now the subject of intense scrutiny.

In the first formal study of fetal temperament in 1996, DiPietro and her colleagues recorded the heart rate and movements of 31 fetuses six times before birth and compared them to readings taken twice after birth. (They've since extended their study to include 100 more fetuses.) Their findings: fetuses that are very active in the womb tend to be more irritable infants. Those with irregular sleep/wake patterns in the womb sleep more poorly as young infants. And fetuses with high heart rates become unpredictable, inactive babies.

"Behavior doesn't begin at birth," declares DiPietro. "It begins before and develops in predictable ways." One of the most important influences on development is the fetal environment. As Harvard's Als observes, "The fetus gets an enormous amount of 'hormonal bathing' through the mother, so its chronobiological rhythms are influenced by the mother's sleep/wake cycles, her eating patterns, her movements."

The hormones a mother puts out in response to stress also appear critical. DiPietro finds that highly pressured mothers-to-be tend to have more active fetuses—and more irritable infants. "The most stressed are working pregnant women," says DiPietro. "These days, women tend to work up to the day they deliver, even though the implications for pregnancy aren't entirely clear yet. That's our cultural norm, but I think it's insane."

Als agrees that working can be an enormous stress, but emphasizes that pregnancy hormones help to buffer both mother and fetus. Individual reactions to stress also matter. "The pregnant woman who chooses to work is a different woman already from the one who chooses not to work," she explains.

She's also different from the woman who has no choice but to work. DiPietro's studies show that the fetuses of poor women are distinct neurobehaviorally—less active, with a less variable heart rate—from the fetuses of middle-class women. Yet "poor women rate themselves as less stressed than do working middle-class women," she notes. DiPietro suspects that inadequate nutrition and exposure to pollutants may significantly affect the fetuses of poor women.

Stress, diet, and toxins may combine to have a harmful effect on intelligence. A recent study by biostatistician Bernie Devlin, Ph.D., of the University of Pittsburgh, suggests that genes may have less impact on IQ than previously thought and that the environment of the womb may account for much more. "Our old notion of nature influencing the fetus before birth and nurture after birth needs an update," DiPietro insists. "There is an antenatal environment, too, that is provided by the mother."

Parents-to-be who want to further their unborn child's mental development should start by assuring that the antenatal environment is well-nourished, low-stress, drug-free. Various authors and "experts" also have suggested poking the fetus at regular intervals, speaking to it through a paper tube or "pregaphone," piping in classical music, even flashing lights at the mother's abdomen.

Does such stimulation work? More importantly: Is it safe? Some who use these methods swear their children are smarter, more verbally and musically inclined, more physically coordinated and socially adept than average. Scientists, however, are skeptical.

"There has been no defended research anywhere that shows any enduring effect from these stimulations," asserts Fifer. "Since no one can even say for certain when a fetus is awake, poking them or sticking speakers on the mother's abdomen may be changing their natural sleep patterns. No one would consider poking or prodding a newborn baby in her bassinet or putting a speaker next to her ear, so why would you do such a thing with a fetus?"

Als is more emphatic: "My bet is that poking, shaking, or otherwise deliberately stimulating the fetus might alter its developmental sequence, and anything that affects the development of the brain comes at a cost."

Gently talking to the fetus, however, seems to pose little risk. Fifer suggests that this kind of activity may help parents as much as the fetus. "Thinking about your fetus, talking to it, having your spouse talk to it, will all help prepare you for this new creature that's going to jump into your life and turn it upside down," he says—once it finally makes its anti-climactic entrance.

Reprinted with permission from *Psychology Today*, September/October 1998, pp. 44–48, 76. © 1998 by Sussex Publishers, Inc.

PARENTING:
THE LOST ART

BY KAY S. HYMOWITZ

LAST FALL the Federal Trade Commission released a report showing what most parents already knew from every trip down the aisle of Toys R Us and every look at prime time television: Entertainment companies routinely market R-rated movies, computer games, and music to children. The highly publicized report detailed many of the abuses of these companies—one particularly egregious example was the use of focus groups of 9- and 10-year-olds to test market violent films—and it unleashed a frenzied week of headlines and political grandstanding, all of it speaking to Americans' alarm over their children's exposure to an increasingly foul-mouthed, vicious, and tawdry media.

But are parents really so alarmed? A more careful reading of the FTC report considerably complicates the fairy tale picture of big, bad wolves tempting unsuspecting, innocent children with ads for *Scream* and *Doom* and inevitably raises the question: "Where were the parents?" As it turns out, many youngsters saw the offending ads not when they were reading *Nickelodeon Magazine* or watching *Seventh Heaven* but when they were leafing through *Cosmo Girl*, a junior version of Helen Gurley Brown's sex manual *Cosmopolitan*, or lounging in front of *Smackdown!*—a production of the World Wrestling Federation where wrestlers saunter out, grab their crotches, and bellow "Suck It!" to their "ho's" standing by. Other kids came across the ads when they were watching the WB's infamous teen sex soap opera *Dawson's Creek* or MTV, whose most recent hit, "Undressed," includes plots involving whipped cream, silk teddies, and a tutor who agrees to strip every time her student gets an answer right. All of these venues, the report noted without irony, are "especially popular among 11- to 18-year-olds." Oh, and those focus groups of 9- and 10-year-olds? It turns out that all of the children who attended the meetings had permission from their parents. To muddy the picture even further, only a short time before the FTC report, the Kaiser Family Foundation released a study entitled *Kids and Media: The New Millennium*

showing that half of all parents have no rules about what their kids watch on television, a number that is probably low given that the survey also found that two-thirds of American children between the ages of eight and eighteen have televisions in their bedrooms; and even more shocking, one-third of all under the age of seven.

In other words, one conclusion you could draw from the FTC report is that entertainment companies are willing to tempt children with the raunchiest, bloodiest, crudest media imaginable if it means expanding their audience and their profits. An additional conclusion, especially when considered alongside *Kids and the Media*, would be that there are a lot of parents out there who don't mind enough to do much about it. After all, protesting that your 10-year-old son was subjected to a trailer for the R-rated *Scream* while watching *Smackdown!* is a little like complaining that he was bitten by a rat while scavenging at the local dump.

Neither the FTC report nor *Kids and the Media* makes a big point of it, but their findings do begin to bring into focus a troubling sense felt by many Americans—and no one more than teachers—that parenting is becoming a lost art. This is not to accuse adults of being neglectful or abusive in any conventional sense. Like always, today's boomer parents love their children; they know their responsibility to provide for them and in fact, as *Kids and the Media* suggests, they are doing so more lavishly than ever before in human history. But throughout that history adults have understood something that perplexes many of today's parents: That they are not only obliged to feed and shelter the young, but to teach them self-control, civility, and a meaningful way of understanding the world. Of course, most parents care a great deal about their children's social and moral development. Most are doing their best to hang on to their sense of what really matters while they attempt to steer their children through a dizzyingly stressful, temptation-filled, and in many ways unfamiliar world. Yet these parents know they often cannot count on the support of their peers. The parents of their 10-year-old's friend let the girls watch an R-rated movie until 2 a.m. during a sleepover; other parents are nowhere to be found when beer is passed around at a party attended by their 14-year-old. These AWOL parents have redefined the meaning of the term. As their children gobble down their own microwaved dinners, then go on to watch their own televisions or surf the Internet on their own computers in wired bedrooms where they set their own bedtimes, these parents and their children seem more like housemates and friends than experienced adults guiding and shaping the young. Such parent-peers may be warm companions and in the short run effective advocates for their children, but they remain deeply uncertain about how to teach them to lead meaningful lives.

If anyone is familiar with the fallout from the lost art of parenting, it is educators. About a year ago, while researching an article about school discipline, I spoke to teachers, administrators, and school lawyers around the country and asked what is making their job more difficult today. Their top answer was almost always the same: parents. Sometimes they describe overworked, overburdened parents who have simply checked out: "I work 10 hours a day, and I can't come home and deal with this stuff. He's *your* problem," they might say. But more often teachers find parents who rather than accepting their role as partners with educators in an effort to civilize the next generation come in with a "my-child-right-or-wrong" attitude. These are parent-advocates.

Everyone's heard about the growing number of suspensions in middle and high schools around the country. Now the state of Connecticut has released a report on an alarming increase in the number of young children—first-graders, kindergartners, and *preschoolers*—suspended for persistent biting, kicking, hitting, and cursing. Is it any wonder? Parent-advocates have little patience for the shared rules of behavior required to turn a school into a civil community, not to mention those who would teach their own children the necessary limits to self-expression. "'You and your stupid rules.' I've heard that a hundred times," sighs Cathy Collins, counsel to the School Administrators of Iowa, speaking not, as it might sound, of 16-year-olds, but of their parents. Even 10 years ago when a child got into trouble, parents assumed the teacher or principal was in the right. "Now we're always being second-guessed," says a 25-year veteran of suburban New Jersey elementary schools. "I know my child, and he wouldn't do this," or, proudly, "He has a mind of his own," are lines many educators repeat hearing.

In the most extreme cases, parent-advocates show (and teach their children) their contempt for school rules by going to court. Several years ago, a St. Charles, Mo., high schooler running for student council was suspended for distributing condoms on the day of the election as a way of soliciting votes. His family promptly turned around and sued on the grounds that the boy's free speech rights were being violated because other candidates had handed out candy during student council elections without any repercussions. Sometimes principals are surprised to see a lawyer trailing behind an angry parent arriving for a conference over a minor infraction. Parents threaten teachers with lawsuits, and kids repeat after them: "I'll sue you," or "My mother's

going to get a lawyer." Surveys may show a large number of parents in favor of school uniforms, but for parent-advocates, dress codes that limit their child's self-expression are a particular source of outrage. In Northumberland County, Pa., parents threatened to sue their children's *elementary* school over its new dress code. "I have a little girl who likes to express herself with how she dresses," one mother of a fourth-grader said. "They ruined my daughter's first day of school," another mother of a kindergartner whined.

Parent-advocates may make life difficult for teachers and soccer coaches. But the truth is things aren't so great at home either. Educators report parents of second- and third-graders saying things like: "I can't control what she wears to school," or "I can't make him read." It's not surprising. At home, parent-advocates aspire to be friends and equals, hoping to maintain the happy affection they think of as a "good relationship." It rarely seems to happen that way. Unable to balance warmth with discipline and affirmation with limit-setting, these parents are puzzled to find their 4-year-old ordering them around like he's Louis XIV or their 8-year-old screaming, "I hate you!" when they balk at letting her go to a sleepover party for the second night in a row. These buddy adults are not only incapable of helping their children resist the siren call of a sensational, glamorous media; in a desperate effort to confirm their "good relationship" with their kids, they actively reinforce it. They buy them their own televisions, they give them "guilt money," as market researchers call it, to go shopping, and they plan endless entertainments. A recent article in *Time* magazine on the Britney Spears fad began by describing a party that parents in Westchester, N.Y., gave their 9-year-old complete with a Britney impersonator boogying in silver hip-huggers and tube top. Doubtless such peer-parents tell themselves they are making their children happy and, anyway, what's the harm. They shouldn't count on it. "When one of our teenagers comes in looking like Britney Spears, they carry with them an attitude," one school principal was quoted as saying. There's a reason that some of the clothing lines that sell the Britney look adopt names such as "Brat" or "No Boundaries."

Of course, dressing like a Las Vegas chorus girl at 8 years old does not automatically mean a child is headed for juvenile hall when she turns 14. But it's reasonable to assume that parent-friends who don't know how to get their third-graders to stop calling them names, never mind covering their midriffs before going to school, are going to be pretty helpless when faced with the more serious challenges of adolescence. Some parents simply give up. They've done all they can, they say to themselves; the kids have to figure it out for themselves. "I feel if [my son] hasn't learned the proper values by 16, then we haven't done our job," announces the mother of a 16-year-old in a fascinating 1999 *Time* magazine series, "Diary of a High School." Others continue the charade of peer friendship by endorsing their adolescent's risk-taking as if they were one of the in-crowd. In a recent article in *Education Week*, Anne W. Weeks, the director of college guidance at a Maryland high school, tells how when police broke up a party on the field of a nearby college, they discovered that most of the kids were actually local high schoolers. High school officials called parents to express their concern, but they were having none of it; it seems parents were the ones providing the alcohol and dropping their kids off at what they knew to be a popular (and unchaperoned) party spot. So great is the need of some parents to keep up the pretense of their equality that they refuse to heed their own children's cry for adult help. A while back, the *New York Times* ran a story on Wesleyan University's "naked dorm" where, as one 19-year-old male student told the reporter: "If I feel the need to take my pants off, I take my pants off," something he evidently felt the need to do during the interview. More striking than the dorm itself—after all, when kids are in charge, as they are in many colleges, what would we expect?—was the phone call a worried female student made to her parents when she first realized she had been assigned to a "naked dorm." She may have been alarmed, but her father, she reports, simply "laughed."

Perhaps more common than parents who laugh at naked dorms or who supply booze for their kids' parties, are those who dimly realize the failure of their experiment in peer-parenting. These parents reduce their role to exercising damage control over kids they assume "are going to do it anyway." For them, there is only one value left they are comfortable fighting for: safety. One mother in *Time*'s "Diary of a High School" replenishes a pile of condoms for her own child and his friends once a month, doubtless congratulating herself that she is protecting the young. Safety also appears to be the logic behind the new fad of co-ed sleepover parties as it was described recently in the *Washington Post*. "I just feel it's definitely better than going to hotels, and this way you know all the kids who are coming over, you know who they are with," explains the mother of one high schooler. Kids know exactly how to reach a generation of parents who, though they waffled on whether their 8-year-old could call them "idiot," suddenly became tyrants when it came to seat belts and helmets. The article describes how one boy talked his parents into allowing him to give a co-ed sleepover party. "It's too dangerous for us to be out late at night with all the drunk drivers. Better that we are home. It's better than us lying about where we are and renting some sleazy motel room." The father found the "parental logic," as the reporter puts it, so irresistible that he allowed the boy to have not one, but two co-ed sleepover parties.

Nothing gives a better picture of the anemic principles of peer-parenting—and their sorry impact on kids—than a 1999 PBS *Frontline* show entitled "The Lost Children of Rockdale County." The occasion for the show was an outbreak of syphilis in an affluent Atlanta suburb that ultimately led health officials to treat 200 teenagers. What was so remarkable was not that 200 teenagers in a large suburban area were having sex and that they have overlapping partners. It was the way they were having sex. This was teen sex as *Lord of the Flies* author William Golding might have imagined it—a heart of darkness tribal rite of such degradation that it makes a collegiate "hook up" look like splendor in the grass. Group sex was commonplace, as were 13-year-old participants. Kids would gather together after school and watch the Playboy cable TV channel, making a game of imitating everything they saw. They tried almost every permutation of

sexual activity imaginable—vaginal, oral, anal, girl-on-girl, several boys with a single girl, or several girls with a boy. During some drunken parties, one boy or girl might be "passed around" in a game. A number of the kids had upwards of 50 partners.

To be sure, the Rockdale teens are the extreme case. The same could not be said of their parents. As the *Frontline* producers show them, these are ordinary, suburban soccer moms and dads, more affluent than most, perhaps, and in some cases overly caught up in their work. But a good number were doing everything the books tell you to do: coaching their children's teams, cooking dinner with them, going on vacations together. It wasn't enough. Devoid of strong beliefs, seemingly bereft of meaningful experience to pass on to their young, these parents project a bland emptiness that seems the exact inverse of the meticulous opulence of their homes and that lets the kids know there are no values worth fighting for. "They have to make decisions, whether to take drugs, to have sex," the mother of one of the boys intones expressionlessly when asked for her view of her son's after-school activity. "I can give them my opinion, tell them how I feel. But they have to decide for themselves." These lost adults of Rockdale County have abdicated the age-old distinction between parents and children, and the kids know it. "We're pretty much like best friends or something," one girl said of her parents. "I mean I can pretty much tell 'em how I feel, what I wanna do and they'll let me do it." Another girl pretty well sums up the persona of many contemporary parents when she says of her own mother. "I don't really consider her a mom all that much. She takes care of me and such, but I consider her a friend more."

So what happened to the lost art of parenting? Why is it that so many adults have reinvented their traditional role and turned themselves into advocates, friends, and copious providers of entertainment?

For one thing, this generation of parents has grown up in a culture that devotedly worships youth. It's true that America, a nation of immigrants fleeing the old world, has always been a youthful country with its eye on the future. But for the "I-hope-I-die-before-I-get-old" generation, aging, with its threat of sexual irrelevance and being out of the loop, has been especially painful. Boomers are the eternal teenagers—hip, sexy, and aware—and when their children suggest otherwise, they're paralyzed with confusion. In an op-ed published in the *New York Times* entitled "Am I a Cool Mother?" Susan Borowitz, co-creator of *Fresh Prince of Bel-Air*, describes her struggle with her role as parent-adult that one suspects is all too common. On a shopping expedition, she is shocked when her 10-year-old daughter rolls her eyes at the outfits she has chosen for her. "There is nothing more withering and crushing," she writes. "I stood there stunned. 'This can't be happening to me. I'm a cool mom.'" Determined to hang on to her youthful identity, she buys a pair of bell-bottom pants to take her daughter to DJ Disco Night at her school where she spots other "cool moms... pumping their fist and doing the Arsenio woof." Finally Borowitz comes to her senses. "This was a party for the kids. I am not a kid. I am a mom." No one could quarrel with her there, but the telling point is that it took 10 years for her to notice.

The Parent as Career Coach

There is one exception to today's parents' overall vagueness about their job description: They *know* they want their children to develop impressive résumés. This is what William Doherty, professor of family science at the University of Minnesota, calls "parenting as product development."

As early as the preschool years, parent-product developers begin a demanding schedule of gymnastics, soccer, language, and music lessons. In New York City, parents take their children to "Language for Tots," beginning at six months—that is, before they can even speak. Doherty cites the example of one Minnesota town where, until some cooler—or more sleep-deprived—heads prevailed, a team of 4-year-olds was scheduled for hockey practice the only time the rink was available—at 5 A.M. By the time children are ready for Little League, some parents hire hitting and pitching coaches from companies like Grand Slam USA. So many kids are training like professionals in a single sport instead of the more casual three or four activities of childhood past that doctors report a high rate of debilitating and sometimes even permanent sports injuries.

Of course, there's nothing wrong with wanting to enrich your children's experience by introducing them to sports and the arts. But as children's list-worthy achievements take on disproportionate and even frenzied significance, parents often lose sight of some of the other things they want to pass down—such as kindness, moral clarity, and a family identity. One Manhattan nursery school director reports that if a child receives a high score on the ERB (the IQ test required to get into private kindergarten), parents often conclude that the child's brilliance excuses him or her from social niceties. "If he can't pass the juice or look you in the eye, it's 'Oh, he's bored.'" Douglas Goetsch, a teacher at Stuyvesant High School, the ultra-competitive school in New York City, recently wrote an article in the school newspaper about the prevalence of cheating; in every case, he says, cheating is related to an "excessively demanding parent." Other educators are seeing even young children complaining about stress-related headaches and stomachaches.

Katherine Tarbox, a Fairfield, Conn., teen, describes all this from the point of view of the child-product in her recently published memoir *Katie.com*. At 13, Katie was an "A" student, an accomplished pianist who also sang with the school choir, and a nationally ranked swimmer. Impressive as they were, Katie's achievements loomed too large. "I always felt like my self-worth was determined by how well I placed. And I think my parents felt the same way—their status among the team parents depended on how well their child placed." Like many middle-class children today, the combination of school, extracurricular activities, and her parents' work schedule reduced family time so much that, "Home was a place I always felt alone." Aching to be loved for herself rather than her swim times and grade point average, she develops an intense relationship with a man on the Internet who very nearly rapes her when they arrange to meet at an out-of-town swim meet.

Even after their daughter's isolation stands revealed, Katie's parents are so hooked on achievement they still don't really notice their daughter. Katie complains to her therapist that her mother is always either at the office or working on papers at home. The woman has a helpful suggestion that epitomizes the overly schematized, hyper-efficient lives that come with parenting as product development: She suggests that Katie schedule appointments with her mother.

Related to this youth worship is the boomer parents' intense ambivalence about authority. The current generation of parents came of age at a time when parents, teachers, the police, and the army represented an authority to be questioned and resisted. Authority was associated with *Father Knows Best*, the Vietnam War, Bull Connor, and their own distant fathers. These associations linger in boomer parents' subconscious minds and make them squirm uncomfortably when their own children beg for firm guidance. Evelyn Bassoff, a Colorado therapist, reports that when she asks the women in her mothers' groups what happens when they discipline their daughters, they give answers such as "I feel mean," "I feel guilty," and "I quake all over; it's almost like having dry heaves inside." A survey by Public Agenda confirms that parents feel "tentative and uncertain in matters of discipline and authority." And no wonder. Notice the way *Time* describes the dilemma faced by parents of Britney Spears wannabes; these parents, the writers explain, are "trying to walk the line between fashion and fascism." The message is clear; the opposite of letting your child do what she wants is, well, becoming Hitler.

It would be difficult to overstate how deep this queasiness over authority runs in the boomer mind. Running so hard from outmoded models of authority that stressed absolute obedience, today's parents have slipped past all recognition of the child's longing for a structure he can believe in. In some cases, their fear not only inhibits them from disciplining their children, it can actually make them view the rebellious child as a figure to be respected. (Oddly enough, this is true even when, as is almost always the case these days, that rebellion takes the form of piercings and heavy metal music vigorously marketed by entertainment companies.) It's as if parents believe children learn individuality and self-respect in the act of defiance, or at the very least through aggressive self-assertion. Some experts reinforce their thinking. Take Barbara Mackoff, author of *Growing a Girl* (with a chapter tellingly entitled "Make Her the Authority"). Mackoff approvingly cites a father who encourages a child "to be comfortable arguing or being mad at me. I figure if she has lots of practice getting mad at a six-foot-one male, she'll be able to say what she thinks to anyone." The author agrees; the parent who tells the angry child "calm down, we don't hit people," she writes, "is engaging in silencing." In other words, to engage in civilization's oldest parental task—teaching children self-control—is to risk turning your child into an automaton ripe for abuse.

But the biggest problem for boomer peer-parents is that many of them are not really sure whether there are values important enough to pursue with any real conviction. In his book *One Nation After All*, the sociologist Alan Wolfe argues that although Americans are concerned about moral decline, they are also opposed to people who get too excited about it. This inherent contradiction—people simultaneously judge and refuse to judge—explains how it is that parents can both dislike their children watching *Smackdown!* on TV, talking back to them, drinking, or for that matter, engaging in group sex, but also fail to protest very loudly. Having absorbed an ethos of nonjudgmentalism, the parents' beliefs on these matters have been drained of all feeling and force. The Rockdale mother who blandly repeats "her opinion" about drugs and sex to her son is a perfect example; perhaps she is concerned about moral decline, but because her concern lacks all gravity or passion, it can't possibly have much effect. All in all, Wolfe seems to find the combination of concern and nonjudgmentalism a fairly hopeful state of affairs—and surely he is right that tolerance is a key value in a pluralistic society—but refusing to judge is one thing when it comes to your neighbor's divorce and quite another when it comes to your 13-year-old child's attitudes toward, say, cheating on a test or cursing out his soccer coach.

WHEN PARENTS fail to firmly define a moral universe for their children, it leaves them vulnerable to the amoral world evoked by their peers and a sensational media. As the Rockdale story makes clear, the saddest consequences appear in the sex lives of today's teenagers. Recently in an iVillage chat room, a distraught mother wrote to ask for advice after she learned that her 15-year-old daughter had sex with a boy. The responses she got rehearsed many of the principles of peer-parenting. Several mothers stressed safety and told the woman to get her daughter on the pill. Others acted out the usual boomer uneasiness over the power they have with their children. "Let your daughter know you trust her to make the 'right' decision when the time comes," wrote one. "Tell her that you are not 'giving your permission,'" another suggested, "but that you are also very aware that she will not 'ask for permission' either when the time comes." But it was the one teenager who joined in that showed how little these apparently hip mothers understood about the pressures on kids today; when she lost her virginity at 14, the girl writes: "it was because of a yearning to be loved, to be accepted." Indeed, the same need for acceptance appears to be driving the trend among middle-schoolers as young as seventh grade engaging in oral sex. According to the December 2000 *Family Planning Perspectives*, some middle school girls view fellatio as the unpleasant price they have to pay to hang on to a boyfriend or to seem hip and sophisticated among their friends. The awful irony is that in their reluctance to evoke meaningful values, parent advocates and peers have produced not the free-thinking, self-expressive, confident children they had hoped, but kids so conforming and obedient they'll follow their friends almost anywhere.

And so in the end, it is children who pay the price of the refusal of parents to seriously engage their predicament in a media-saturated and shadowy adult world. And what a price it is. When parenting becomes a lost art, children are not only deprived of the clarity and sound judgment they crave. They are deprived of childhood.

Kay S. Hymowitz, a senior fellow at the Manhattan Institute and contributing editor at City Journal, *is the author of* Ready or Not: What Happens When We Treat Children as Small Adults *(Encounter Books, 2000).*

A World of Their Own

**They're spiritual, optimistic and ambitious.
How teens want to shape the future.**

By Sharon Begley

THE TEMPTATION, OF COURSE, IS to seek The Teen, the one who can stand as a symbol of this generation, who exemplifies in a single, still-young life the aspirations, the values, the habits and outlook of the 22 million other Americans 13 to 19. Who, then, shall we offer up? Perhaps Vanesa Vathanasombat, 17, of Whittier, Calif., who spends her free time going to the beach and hanging at malls with friends. "You are who you hang around with," she says. "Before, parents made you who you are. Now, teens are pretty much defined by their friends. I see my mom maybe an hour a day and not at all on weekends." Or maybe Zoe Ward, 15, of Shoreline, Wash., who takes road trips with a friend (they sleep in the car) and sells her poetry on the street: "I can't decide if I want to be famous or if I want to go live in the mountains. That's what it's like for a lot of high-school kids: we don't know how to get there, what it's really going to be like." Or, finally, Marcus Ruopp, 16, of Newton, Mass., who would like to be an engineer or maybe a teacher after the Peace Corps, in order to "give back to the community."

No one teen incorporates all the attitudes and characteristics that the teachers who teach them, the parents who raise them, the researchers who study them and the kids who *are* them name as the identifying marks of this generation. In large part that is because "today's teens may have less in common with each other than those in generations past," says psychologist William Damon of Stanford University. "[Some] are absolutely on track: they're bright-eyed, genuine and ambitious. But a significant number are drifting or worse." Innumerable teens, then, will not recognize themselves in the portraits that follow. Yes, of course there are teens for whom adults are a strong presence, and teens who seldom volunteer. There are teens who are emotional wrecks, or even mentally ill. There are teens to whom "Instant Message" means Mom's telling them right away who phoned while they were out. And there are teens who belong to no clique—or "tribe." But, according to a new NEWSWEEK Poll as well as sociologists who have studied tens of thousands of the kids born between 1981 and 1987, those teens are the exceptions. As much as is possible when you are talking about 22 million human beings, a portrait of the millennial generation is emerging.

Style counts
Teen cliques are more fluid than adults think, but each has its own distinctive tribal markings, from hippie chic to body art to buttoned-down prep

They were born at a time when the very culture was shifting to accommodate them—changing tables in restrooms, BABY ON BOARD signs and minivans. Yet, as a group, they lead lives that are more "adult-free" than those of previous generations. "Adolescents are not a tribe apart because *they* left *us*, as most people assume," says Patricia Hersch, author of the 1998 book "A Tribe Apart." "We left them. This generation of kids has spent more time on their own than any other in recent history."

When today's teens are not with their friends, many live in a private, adult-free world of the Web and videogames. Aminah McKinnie, 16, of Madison, Miss., attends church, loves gospel hip-hop and hopes to work in the computer industry. She doesn't "hang out," she says. "I shop on the Internet and am looking for a job on the Internet. I do homework, research, e-mail and talk to my friends on the Internet." She is not unusual. Data released last year from the Alfred P. Sloan Study of Youth and Social Development found that teens spend 9 percent of their waking hours outside school with friends. They spend 20 percent of their waking hours alone. "Teens are isolated to an extent that has never been possible before," says Stanford's Damon. "There is an ethic among adults that says, 'Kids want to be autonomous; don't get in their face.' "

A Snapshot of a Generation

In the Internet age, teens seem to be coming of age ever earlier. A recent NEWSWEEK Poll explores what concerns today's youth and asks if their parents have a clue.

• Stress: Do teens today face more problems than their parents did as teens?		• Family: Do your parents spend enough time with you?	
	TEENS		TEENS
More	70%	Enough	61%
Fewer	5	Too little	24
Same	24	Too much	5

• **48% of teens say they use a computer almost every day at home**

• **21% have looked at something on the Internet that they wouldn't want their parents to know about**

• **Identity: How much peer pressure from friends do you feel (does your teen feel) today to do the following?**

THOSE RESPONDING A LOT	TEENS	PARENTS
Have sex	10%	20%
Grow up too fast	16	34
Steal or shoplift	4	11
Use drugs or abuse alcohol	10	18
Defy parents or teachers	9	16
Be mean to kids who are different	11	14

• **If you had to choose between fitting in with friends or becoming outstanding in some way, which would you (your teen) choose?**

	TEENS	PARENTS
Fitting in	26%	43%
Becoming outstanding	69	50

• **Worries: How concerned are you about the following?**

THOSE RESPONDING A LOT	TEENS	PARENTS
Not having enough money to buy the things you (they) want	34%	35%
The cost of your (their) college education	54	68
Violence in society	59	82
Not being sure about your (their) future job opportunities	43	49
Your (their) getting into trouble with drugs	25	66
Your (their) drinking or abusing alcohol	26	64
Sexual permissiveness in society	33	72
Sexually transmitted diseases	58	75

• Hostility: Many teens these days feel a lot of anger. How angry are you?		• Faith: How important is religion in your life today?	
	TEENS		TEENS
Very	3%	Very	43%
Somewhat	25	Somewhat	35
Not too	43	Not too	14
Not at all	29	Not at all	8

• **17% of teens and 37% of parents say they worry a lot about safety at school**

• **21% of teenagers polled say that most of the teens they know have already had sex**

FOR THIS SPECIAL NEWSWEEK POLL, PRINCETON SURVEY RESEARCH ASSOCIATES INTERVIEWED A NATIONAL SAMPLE OF TEENS 13–19 AND 509 PARENTS OF SUCH TEENS BY TELEPHONE APRIL 20–28. THE MARGIN OF ERROR IS +/–5 PERCENTAGE POINTS FOR PARENTS; +/– 6 FOR ALL TEENS; COPYRIGHT 2000 BY NEWSWEEK, INC.

This generation is strongly peer-driven. "This is much more a team-playing generation," says William Strauss, coauthor of the 1997 book "The Fourth Turning." "Boomers may be bowling alone, but Millennials are playing soccer in teams." That makes belonging so crucial that it can be a matter of life and death. In Littleton, Colo., a year ago, the two teenage shooters stood apart, alienated from the jock culture that infused Columbine High School. Yet in a landmark study of 7,000 teens, researchers led by Barbara Schneider of the University of Chicago found that teen social groups are as fluid and hard to pin down as a bead of mercury. "Students often move from one group to another, and friendships change over a period of a few weeks or months," they write in "The Ambitious Generation." "Best friends are few." As a group, today's teens are also infused with an optimism not seen among kids in decades (it doesn't hurt to have grown up in a time of relative peace and the longest economic expansion in U.S. history). "I think a lot of adolescents now are being taught that they can make a difference," says Sophie Mazuroski, 15, of Portland, Maine. "Children of our generation want to. I am very optimistic." Still the law of teenage angst is still on the books: 4.3 percent of ninth graders make suicide attempts serious enough to require medical treatment.

Sound and Fury
"There's a lot of anger in my generation. You can hear it in the music. Kids are angry for a lot of reasons, but mostly because parents aren't around."

Robertino Rodriquez, 17

This generation of teens is more spiritual than their parents, but often less conventionally so. Many put together their own religious canon as they would a salad from a salad bar. Yet despite their faith, teens, as well as those who study them, say that "lying and cheating are standard behavior," as Trisha Sandoval, 17, of Santa Fe Springs, Calif., puts it—more so than for earlier generations. Elsewhere on the values front, teens today are less likely than those in 1992 "to get somebody pregnant, drive drunk or get into fights," says Kevin Dwyer, president of the National Association of School Psychologists. And teens, says Strauss, "had harsher opinions about the Clinton-Lewinsky scandal than any other group." Coming of age in a time of interracial marriages, many eschew the old notions of race; maturing at Internet speed, they are more connected than any generation. Both may bode well for tolerance. "Prejudice against homosexuals, bisexuals, African-Americans, Latinos—this is a big issue," says Kathryn Griffin, 18, of Palo Alto, Calif., who hopes to make a career in advertising or marketing. "It's insane that people have these feelings [about other people] when they don't even know them."

What do they want out of life? Schneider and coauthor David Stevenson found that today's teens "are the most occupationally

and educationally ambitious generation" ever. Most plan to attend college, and many aspire to work as professionals. A majority identify "happiness" as a goal, along with love and a long and enjoyable life. But many doubt that marriage and career will deliver that, so they channel their energies more broadly. About half of teens perform community service once a month by, for instance, delivering meals to the homeless or reading to the elderly. But does their volunteer work reflect real compassion, or meeting a school requirement?

In Living Colors
"We don't care about skin, man. I know a lot about my heritage, about who I am. I'm more than just some black dude who is good at sports. I'm the future."

Marcus Robinson, 17

Regardless of what their terrified parents suspect, the belief that today's teens "are more sexual, rebellious and inebriated is flat-out wrong," says pediatrician Victor Strasburger of the University of New Mexico. In 1997, 48 percent of high-school students had had sexual intercourse, compared with 54 percent in 1991, according to the CDC. More are smoking (36 percent, compared with 28 percent in 1991), but the percentage who are drinking alcohol remains at 51 percent. The social surround, though, may be different now. "A lot of my friends are into drinking a lot," says Marcus Ruopp. "Kids don't see it as a big problem. It's a regular thing, not like they're rebelling. There is no pressure to drink."

Some sociologists believe that each generation assumes the societal role of the generation that is dying, as if something in the Zeitgeist whispers to the young what is being lost, what role they can fill. Those now passing away are the children of the Depression and of World War II. They were tested, and they emerged with optimism, and purpose, and a commitment to causes larger than themselves. As Trisha Sandoval puts it, "We want to accomplish something with our lives." Teens today, with their tattoos and baggy shorts, could not seem more different from their grandparents. But every generation has a chance at greatness. Let this one take its shot.

With PAT WINGERT *in Washington,* HOPE WHITE SCOTT *in Boston,* ANA FIGUEROA *in Los Angeles and* DEVIN GORDON, SUSANNAH MEADOWS *and* MICHAEL CRONIN *in New York*

Live to 100? No thanks

Most people opt for quality, not quantity, in later years

BY SUSAN L. CROWLEY

Despite stunning medical advances that can extend life, most Americans do not want to live to be 100. They fear the disabilities, impoverishment and isolation commonly thought to accompany old age.

The finding emerged in a wide-ranging AARP survey on attitudes toward longevity. When asked how long they want to live, 63 percent of the 2,032 respondents opted for fewer than 100 years.

"What this says to me," notes Constance Swank, director of research at AARP, "is that people are more interested in the quality of their lives than the length. They don't want to be encumbered by poor health and financial worries in their older years."

Survey respondents reported they would like to live to an average of about 91 years, but expect to live to 80. According to the U.S. Census Bureau, the life expectancy for a child born in 1997 is 76.5 years. A person turning 65 in 1997 could expect to live another 17.6 years.

The telephone survey, conducted from April 9 to 14 for AARP by Market Facts, Inc. of McLean, Va., also found that a huge majority of people are aware that their behavior and habits can affect how well they age.

This was "the real take-home message for me," says Terrie Wetle, deputy director of the National Institute on Aging. "It was very good news that more than 90 percent recognized that they had some control over how they age."

Harvard neuropsychologist Margery Hutter Silver, who is associate director of the New England Centenarian Study, agrees: "Just the fact of thinking you have control is going to have tremendous impact."

Over eight out of 10 respondents reported doing things to stay healthy. Seventy percent said they exercise, 33 percent watch their diets, 10 percent watch their weight and 10 percent maintain a positive attitude.

Most Americans are also optimistic that life will be better for the typical 80-year-old in 2050 and that medical advances will lead to cures for cancer, heart disease, AIDS and Alzheimer's disease.

Yet, even though they are taking steps to age well and are upbeat about the future, most people are still leery of what might befall them if they live to be 100.

That shouldn't come as a surprise, people of all ages told the Bulletin. "Our society bases its economy on young stars and young entrepreneurs," says Lynda Preble, 28, who works for a public relations firm in San Francisco. "I'm sure most people don't understand where they fit in once they are older."

"I was not surprised," says writer and publicist Susan Hartt, 57, of Baltimore. "As the saying goes, 'Old age is not for sissies.'"

Even though disability rates among the old are declining, chronic health problems and poverty are still more likely to appear in advanced age, Wetle says, and "people know that."

"I'm going to hang it up when I'm restricted to bed," say Marion Ballard, 59, a former software company owner in Bethesda, Md.

"A slow mental decline scares me the most," says Lilavati Sinclair, a 32-year-old mother in Bothell, Wash. For Peter Winkert, 47, a sales executive in Cazenovia, N.Y., "running out of income is my biggest concern."

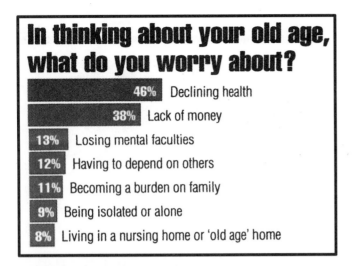

In thinking about your old age, what do you worry about?

- 46% Declining health
- 38% Lack of money
- 13% Losing mental faculties
- 12% Having to depend on others
- 11% Becoming a burden on family
- 9% Being isolated or alone
- 8% Living in a nursing home or 'old age' home

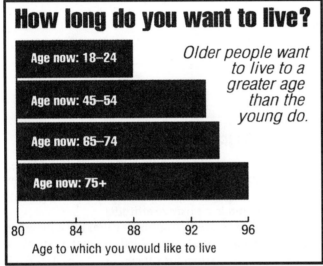

How long do you want to live?

Age now: 18–24

Age now: 45–54

Age now: 65–74

Age now: 75+

Older people want to live to a greater age than the young do.

80   84   88   92   96
Age to which you would like to live

AARP SURVEY BY MARKET FACTS, INC. MCLEAN, VA.

Others express fear of being alone, burdening their families, living in a nursing home or, as one person puts it, "losing my joy and will to keep on living."

How old a person is tends to influence his or her views on age and aging. Among those ages 18 to 24, a person is "old" at 58, according to the survey, while those 65 or older think "old" starts at 75.

"I used to think I would be dead at 30," jokes one woman who just turned 30. "Now that I know I'll be around a while, I want to enjoy life as long as possible."

Not unexpectedly, older people hope and expect to live to greater ages than the young. Survey respondents 75 and older want to live to 96, but for 18- to 24-year-olds, 88 is enough.

Julie Vermillion, 24, who is a public affairs assistant in Washington, D.C., and Erin Laughlin, 23, a dog trainer in Sebastopol, Calif., say that living to 85 is about right.

Yet 85-year-old Lucille Runkel of Cochranton, Pa., is still in good shape and still active. "I wouldn't mind living to be 100 if I'm in good health," she says, "but I don't want to be dependent on my children."

"If I feel well enough," says lawyer Lester Nurick, 84, of Potomac, Md., "I could go on forever…but I would never put a number on it."

"Young people deal with the mythology instead of the reality of aging," says AARP's Swank. "Older people are living it, and many embrace the challenges, the joys. No one wants to be debilitated, but for many, the later years are highly satisfying. So why walk away from it?"

Older people have also witnessed the development of life-saving vaccines, drugs and surgical techniques and are more confident of continuing medical breakthroughs. "What we see here," Swank says, "is the wisdom of age."

Writer Hartt says she wouldn't mind putting up with some infirmities to achieve such wisdom. "So what was adolescence—a day at the beach?"

Lack of information helps fuel the myths of old age. For example, only 28 percent of survey respondents know that the 85-plus age group is the fastest-growing segment of the population.

And many people don't know that most Americans over 65 live independently, with fewer than 5 percent in nursing homes, adds Harvard's Silver.

Other survey highlights:

•On average, people with a college education hope to live longer (to age 92) than those with a high-school education (to 89).

•Fifty-two percent of those with a yearly household income of over $50,000 worry about poor health in old age, compared to 41 percent among those with incomes lower than $50,000.

•Those who say they are doing things to stay healthy and active expect to live to 81, while others expect to live to 76.

Given new findings about centenarians—whose numbers in the United States grew to more than 62,000 by 1998 and by some estimates could reach 1 million by 2050—aiming for the century mark is not unreasonable.

Living to 100 doesn't mean you'll be in poor health, says Silver, who is co-author with Thomas T. Perls, M.D., of "Living to 100" (Basic Books, 1999). To the contrary, centenarians are often healthier than people in their 80s.

But there's a trick, according to their book: "One must stay healthy the vast majority of one's life in order to live to 100."

Some think it's a worthy goal.

"It would be cool to live for over a century, just because of the history involved," says one 30-something. "I can't even guess what will come."

From the *AARP Bulletin*, July/August 1999, pp. 6-7. © 1999 by the American Association of Retired Persons. Reprinted by permission.

Start the Conversation

The MODERN MATURITY guide to end-of-life care

The Body Speaks

Physically, dying means that "the body's various physiological systems, such as the circulatory, respiratory, and digestive systems, are no longer able to support the demands required to stay alive," says Barney Spivack, M.D., director of Geriatric Medicine for the Stamford (Connecticut) Health System. "When there is no meaningful chance for recovery, the physician should discuss realistic goals of care with the patient and family, which may include letting nature take its course. Lacking that direction," he says, "physicians differ in their perception of when enough is enough. We use our best judgment, taking into account the situation, the information available at the time, consultation with another doctor, or guidance from an ethics committee."

Without instructions from the patient or family, a doctor's obligation to a terminally ill person is to provide life-sustaining treatment. When a decision to "let nature take its course" has been made, the doctor will remove the treatment, based on the patient's needs. Early on, the patient or surrogate may choose to stop interventions such as antibiotics, dialysis, resuscitation, and defibrillation. Caregivers may want to offer food and fluids, but those can cause choking and the pooling of dangerous fluids in the lungs. A dying patient does not desire or need nourishment; without it he or she goes into a deep sleep and dies in days to weeks. A breathing machine would be the last support: It is uncomfortable for the patient, and may be disconnected when the patient or family finds that it is merely prolonging the dying process.

The Best Defense Against Pain

Pain-management activists are fervently trying to reeducate physicians about the importance and safety of making patients comfortable. "In medical school 30 years ago, we worried a lot about creating addicts," says Philadelphia internist Nicholas Scharff. "Now we know that addiction is not a problem: People who are in pain take

pain medication as long as they need it, and then they stop." Spivack says, "We have new formulations and delivery systems, so a dying patient should never have unmet pain needs."

In Search of a Good Death

If we think about death at all, we say that we want to go quickly, in our sleep, or, perhaps, while flyfishing. But in fact only 10 percent of us die suddenly. The more common process is a slow decline with episodes of organ or system failure. Most of us want to die at home; most of us won't. All of us hope to die without pain; many of us will be kept alive, in pain, beyond a time when we would choose to call a halt. Yet very few of us take steps ahead of time to spell out what kind of physical and emotional care we will want at the end.

The new movement to improve the end of life is pioneering ways to make available to each of us a good death—as we each define it. One goal of the movement is to bring death through the cultural process that childbirth has achieved; from an unconscious, solitary act in a cold hospital room to a situation in which one is buffered by pillows, pictures, music, loved ones, and the solaces of home. But as in the childbirth movement, the real goal is choice—here, to have the death you want. Much of death's sting can be averted by planning in advance, knowing the facts, and knowing what options we all have. Here, we have gathered new and relevant information to help us all make a difference for the people we are taking care of, and ultimately, for ourselves.

In 1999, the Joint Commission on Accreditation of Healthcare Organizations issued stern new guidelines about easing pain in both terminal and nonterminal patients. The movement intends to take pain seriously:

to measure and treat it as the fifth vital sign in hospitals, along with blood pressure, pulse, temperature, and respiration.

The best defense against pain, says Spivack, is a combination of education and assertiveness. "Don't be afraid to speak up," he says. "If your doctor isn't listening, talk to the nurses. They see more and usually have a good sense of what's happening." Hospice workers, too, are experts on physical comfort, and a good doctor will respond to a hospice worker's recommendations. "The best situation for pain management," says Scharff, "is at home with a family caregiver being guided by a hospice program."

The downsides to pain medication are, first, that narcotics given to a fragile body may have a double effect: The drug may ease the pain, but it may cause respiratory depression and possibly death. Second, pain medication may induce grogginess or unconsciousness when a patient wants to be alert. "Most people seem to be much more willing to tolerate pain than mental confusion," says senior research scientist M. Powell Lawton, Ph.D., of the Philadelphia Geriatric Center. Dying patients may choose to be alert one day for visitors, and asleep the next to cope with pain. Studies show that when patients control their own pain medication, they use less.

Final Symptoms

Depression This condition is not an inevitable part of dying but can and should be treated. In fact, untreated depression can prevent pain medications from working effectively, and antidepressant medication can help relieve pain. A dying patient should be kept in the best possible emotional state for the final stage of life. A combination of medications and psychotherapy works best to treat depression.

Anorexia In the last few days of life, anorexia—an unwillingness or inability to eat—often sets in. "It has a protective effect, releasing endorphins in the system and contributing to a greater feeling of well-being," says Spivack. "Force-feeding a dying patient could make him uncomfortable and cause choking."

Dehydration Most people want to drink little or nothing in their last days. Again, this is a protective mechanism, triggering a release of helpful endorphins.

Drowsiness and Unarousable Sleep In spite of a coma-like state, says Spivack, "presume that the patient hears everything that is being said in the room."

Agitation and Restlessness, Moaning and Groaning The features of "terminal delirium" occur when the patient's level of consciousness is markedly decreased; there is no significant likelihood that any pain sensation can reach consciousness. Family members and other caregivers may interpret what they see as "the patient is in pain" but as these signs arise at a point very close to death, terminal delirium should be suspected.

Hospice: The Comfort Team

Hospice is really a bundle of services. It organizes a team of people to help patients and their families, most often in the patient's home but also in hospice residences, nursing homes, and hospitals:

- Registered nurses who check medication and the patient's condition, communicate with the patient's doctor, and educate caregivers.
- Medical services by the patient's physician and a hospice's medical director, limited to pain medication and other comfort care.
- Medical supplies and equipment.
- Drugs for pain relief and symptom control.
- Home-care aides for personal care, homemakers for light housekeeping.
- Continuous care in the home as needed on a short-term basis.
- Trained volunteers for support services.
- Physical, occupational, and speech therapists to help patients adapt to new disabilities.
- Temporary hospitalization during a crisis.
- Counselors and social workers who provide emotional and spiritual support to the patient and family.
- Respite care—brief noncrisis hospitalization to provide relief for family caregivers for up to five days.
- Bereavement support for the family, including counseling, referral to support groups, and periodic check-ins during the first year after the death.

Hospice Residences Still rare, but a growing phenomenon. They provide all these services on-site. They're for patients without family caregivers; with frail, elderly spouses; and for families who cannot provide at-home care because of other commitments. At the moment, Medicare covers only hospice services; the patient must pay for room and board. In many states Medicaid also covers hospice services (see How Much Will It Cost?). Keep in mind that not all residences are certified, bonded, or licensed; and not all are covered by Medicare.

Getting In A physician can recommend hospice for a patient who is terminally ill and probably has less than six months to live. The aim of hospice is to help people cope with an illness, not to cure it. All patients entering hospice waive their rights to curative treatments, though only for conditions relating to their terminal illness. "If you break a leg, of course you'll be treated for that," says Karen Woods, executive director of the Hospice Association of America. No one is forced to accept a hospice referral, and patients may leave and opt for curative care at any time. Hospice programs are listed in the Yellow Pages. For more information, see Resources.

The Ultimate Emotional Challenge

A dying person is grieving the loss of control over life, of body image, of normal physical functions, mobility and strength, freedom and independence, security, and the illusion of immortality. He is also grieving the loss of an earthly future, and reorienting himself to an unknowable destiny.

At the same time, an emotionally healthy dying person will be trying to satisfy his survival drive by adapting to this new phase, making the most of life at the moment, calling in loved ones, examining and appreciating his own joys and accomplishments. Not all dying people are depressed; many embrace death easily.

Facing the Fact

Doctors are usually the ones to inform a patient that he or she is dying, and the end-of-life movement is training physicians to bring empathy to that conversation in place of medspeak and time estimates. The more sensitive doctor will first ask how the patient feels things are going. "The patient may say, 'Well, I don't think I'm getting better,' and I would say, 'I think you're right,' " says internist Nicholas Scharff.

At this point, a doctor might ask if the patient wants to hear more now or later, in broad strokes or in detail. Some people will need to first process the emotional blow with tears and anger before learning about the course of their disease in the future.

"Accept and understand whatever reaction the patient has," says Roni Lang, director of the Geriatric Assessment Program for the Stamford (Connecticut) Health System, and a social worker who is a longtime veteran of such conversations. "Don't be too quick with the tissue. That sends a message that it's not okay to be upset. It's okay for the patient to be however she is."

Getting to Acceptance

Some patients keep hoping that they will get better. Denial is one of the mind's miracles, a way to ward off painful realities until consciousness can deal with them. Denial may not be a problem for the dying person, but it can create difficulties for the family. The dying person could be leaving a lot of tough decisions, stress, and confusion behind. The classic stages of grief outlined by Elisabeth Kübler-Ross—denial, anger, bargaining, depression, and acceptance—are often used to describe post-death grieving, but were in fact delineated for the process of accepting impending loss. We now know that these states may not progress in order. "Most people oscillate between anger and sadness, embracing the prospect of death and unrealistic episodes of optimism," says Lang. Still, she says, "don't place demands on them

Survival Kit for Caregivers

A study published in the March 21, 2000, issue of **Annals of Internal Medicine** shows that caregivers of the dying are twice as likely to have depressive symptoms as the dying themselves.

No wonder. Caring for a dying parent, says social worker Roni Lang, "brings a fierce tangle of emotions. That part of us that is a child must grow up." Parallel struggles occur when caring for a spouse, a child, another relative, or a friend. Caregivers may also experience sibling rivalry, income loss, isolation, fatigue, burnout, and resentment.

To deal with these difficult stresses, Lang suggests that caregivers:

• Set limits in advance. How far am I willing to go? What level of care is needed? Who can I get to help? Resist the temptation to let the illness always take center stage, or to be drawn into guilt-inducing conversations with people who think you should be doing more.

• Join a caregiver support group, either disease-related like the Alzheimer's Association or Gilda's Club, or a more general support group like The Well Spouse Foundation. Ask the social services department at your hospital for advice. Telephone support and online chat rooms also exist (see Resources).

• Acknowledge anger and express it constructively by keeping a journal or talking to an understanding friend or family member. Anger is a normal reaction to powerlessness.

• When people offer to help, give them a specific assignment. And then, take time to do what energizes you and make a point of rewarding yourself.

• Remember that people who are critically ill are self-absorbed. If your empathy fails you and you lose patience, make amends and forgive yourself.

to accept their death. This is not a time to proselytize." It is enough for the family to accept the coming loss, and if necessary, introduce the idea of an advance directive and health-care proxy, approaching it as a "just in case" idea. When one member of the family cannot accept death, and insists that doctors do more, says Lang, "that's the worst nightmare. I would call a meeting, hear all views without interrupting, and get the conversation around to what the patient would want. You may need another person to come in, perhaps the doctor, to help 'hear' the voice of the patient."

What Are You Afraid Of?

The most important question for doctors and caregivers to ask a dying person is, What are you afraid of? "Fear aggravates pain," says Lang, "and pain aggravates fear." Fear of pain, says Spivack, is one of the most common problems, and can be dealt with rationally. Many people do not know, for example, that pain in dying is not inevitable. Other typical fears are of being separated from loved ones, from home, from work; fear of being a burden, losing control, being dependent, and leaving things undone. Voicing fear helps lessen it, and pinpointing fear helps a caregiver know how to respond.

How to Be With a Dying Person

Our usual instinct is to avoid everything about death, including the people moving most rapidly toward it. But, Spivack says, "In all my years of working with dying people, I've never heard one say 'I want to die alone.' " Dying people are greatly comforted by company; the benefit far outweighs the awkwardness of the visit. Lang offers these suggestions for visitors:

• Be close. Sit at eye level, and don't be afraid to touch. Let the dying person set the pace for the conversation. Allow for silence. Your presence alone is valuable.

• Don't contradict a patient who says he's going to die. Acceptance is okay. Allow for anger, guilt, and fear, without trying to "fix" it. Just listen and empathize.

• Give the patient as much decision-making power as possible, as long as possible. Allow for talk about unfinished business. Ask: "Who can I contact for you?"

• Encourage happy reminiscences. It's okay to laugh.

• Never pass up the chance to express love or say goodbye. But if you don't get the chance, remember that not everything is worked through. Do the best you can.

Taking Control Now

Sixty years ago, before the invention of dialysis, defibrillators, and ventilators, the failure of vital organs automatically meant death. There were few choices to be made to end suffering, and when there were—the fatal dose of morphine, for example—these decisions were made privately by family and doctors who knew each other well. Since the 1950s, medical technology has been capable of extending lives, but also of prolonging dying. In 1967, an organization called Choice in Dying (now the Partnership for Caring: America's Voices for the Dying; see Resources) designed the first advance directive—a document that allows you to designate under what conditions you would want life-sustaining treatment to be continued or terminated. But the idea did not gain popular understanding until 1976, when the parents of Karen Ann Quinlan won a long legal battle to disconnect her from respiratory support as she lay for months in a vegetative state. Some 75 percent of Americans are in favor of advance directives, although only 30–35 percent actually write them.

Designing the Care You Want

There are two kinds of advance directives, and you may use one or both. A Living Will details what kind of life-sustaining treatment you want or don't want, in the event of an illness when death is imminent. A durable power of attorney for health care appoints someone to be your decision-maker if you can't speak for yourself. This person is also called a surrogate, attorney-in-fact, or health-care proxy. An advance directive such as Five Wishes covers both.

Most experts agree that a Living Will alone is not sufficient. "You don't need to write specific instructions about different kinds of life support, as you don't yet know any of the facts of your situation, and they may change," says Charles Sabatino, assistant director of the American Bar Association's Commission on Legal Problems of the Elderly.

The proxy, Sabatino says, is far more important. "It means someone you trust will find out all the options and make a decision consistent with what you would want." In most states, you may write your own advance directive, though some states require a specific form, available at hospital admitting offices or at the state department of health.

When Should You Draw Up a Directive?

Without an advance directive, a hospital staff is legally bound to do everything to keep you alive as long as possible, until you or a family member decides otherwise. So advance directives are best written before emergency status or a terminal diagnosis. Some people write them at the same time they make a will. The process begins with discussions between you and your family and doctor. If anybody is reluctant to discuss the subject, Sabatino suggests starting the conversation with a story. "Remember what happened to Bob Jones and what his family went through? I want us to be different...." You can use existing tools—a booklet or questionnaire (see Resources)—to keep the conversation moving. Get your doctor's commitment to support your wishes. "If you're asking for something that is against your doctor's conscience" (such as prescribing a lethal dose of pain medication or removing life support at a time he considers premature), Sabatino says, "he may have an obligation to transfer you to another doctor." And make sure the person you name as surrogate agrees to act for you and understands your wishes.

Filing, Storing, Safekeeping...

An estimated 35 percent of advance directives cannot be found when needed.

• Give a copy to your surrogate, your doctor, your hospital, and other family members. Tell them where to find the original in the house—not in a safe deposit box where it might not be found until after death.

Five Wishes

Five Wishes is a questionnaire that guides people in making essential decisions about the care they want at the end of their life. About a million people have filled out the eight-page form in the past two years. This advance directive is legally valid in 34 states and the District of Columbia. (The other 16 require a specific state-mandated form.)

The document was designed by lawyer Jim Towey, founder of Aging With Dignity, a nonprofit organization that advocates for the needs of elders and their caregivers. Towey, who was legal counsel to Mother Teresa, visited her Home for the Dying in Calcutta in the 1980s. He was struck that in that haven in the Third World, "the dying people's hands were held, their pain was managed, and they weren't alone. In the First World, you see a lot of medical technology, but people die in pain, and alone." Towey talked to MODERN MATURITY about his directive and what it means.

What are the five wishes? Who do I want to make care decisions for me when I can't? What kind of medical treatment do I want toward the end? What would help me feel comfortable while I am dying? How do I want people to treat me? What do I want my loved ones to know about me and my feelings after I'm gone?

Why is it so vital to make advance decisions now? Medical technology has extended longevity, which is good, but it can prolong the dying process in ways that are almost cruel. Medical schools are still concentrating on curing, not caring for the dying. We can have a dignified season in our life, or die alone in pain with futile interventions. Most people only discover they have options when checking into the hospital, and often they no longer have the capacity to choose. This leaves the family members with a guessing game and, frequently, guilt.

What's the ideal way to use this document? First you do a little soul searching about what you want. Then discuss it with people you trust, in the livingroom instead of the waiting room—before a crisis. Just say, "I want a choice about how I spend my last days," talk about your choices, and pick someone to be your health-care surrogate.

What makes the Five Wishes directive unique? It's easy to use and understand, not written in the language of doctors or lawyers. It also allows people to discuss comfort dignity, and forgiveness, not just medical concerns. When my father filled it out, he said he wanted his favorite afghan blanket in his bed. It made a huge difference to me that, as he was dying, he had his wishes fulfilled.

For a copy of Five Wishes in English or Spanish, send a $5 check or money order to Aging With Dignity, PO Box 1661, Tallahassee, FL 32302. For more information, visit www.agingwithdignity. org.

- Some people carry a copy in their wallet or glove compartment of their car.
- Be aware that if you have more than one home and you split your time in several regions of the country, you should be registering your wishes with a hospital in each region, and consider naming more than one proxy.
- You may register your Living Will and health-care proxy online at uslivingwillregistry.com (or call 800-548-9455). The free, privately funded confidential service will instantly fax a copy to a hospital when the hospital requests one. It will also remind you to update it: You may want to choose a new surrogate, accommodate medical advances, or change your idea of when "enough is enough." M. Powell Lawton, who is doing a study on how people anticipate the terminal life stages, has discovered that "people adapt relatively well to states of poor health. The idea that life is still worth living continues to readjust itself."

Assisted Suicide: The Reality

While advance directives allow for the termination of life-sustaining treatment, assisted suicide means supplying the patient with a prescription for life-ending medication. A doctor writes the prescription for the medication; the patient takes the fatal dose him- or herself. Physician-assisted suicide is legal only in Oregon (and under consideration in Maine) but only with rigorous preconditions. Of the approximately 30,000 people who died in Oregon in 1999, only 33 received permission to have a lethal dose of medication and only 26 of those actually died of the medication. Surrogates may request an end to life support, but to assist in a suicide puts one at risk for charges of homicide.

Good Care: Can You Afford It?

The ordinary person is only one serious illness away from poverty," says Joanne Lynn, M.D., director of the Arlington, Virginia, Center to Improve Care of the Dying. An ethicist, hospice physician, and health-services researcher, she is one of the founding members of the end-of-life-care movement. "On the whole, hospitalization and the cost of suppressing symptoms is very easy to afford," says Lynn. Medicare and Medicaid will help cover that kind of acute medical care. But what is harder to afford is at-home medication, monitoring, daily help with eating and walking, and all the care that will go on for the rest of the patient's life.

"When people are dying," Lynn says, "an increasing proportion of their overall care does not need to be done by doctors. But when policymakers say the care is nonmedical, then it's second class, it's not important, and nobody will pay for it."

Bottom line, Medicare pays for about 57 percent of the cost of medical care for Medicare beneficiaries.

Another 11 percent is paid by Medicaid, 20 percent by the patient, 10 percent from private insurance, and the rest from other sources, such as charitable organizations.

Medi-what?

This public-plus-private network of funding sources for end-of-life care is complex, and who pays for how much of what is determined by diagnosis, age, site of care, and income. Besides the private health insurance that many of us have from our employers, other sources of funding may enter the picture when patients are terminally ill.

•**Medicare** A federal insurance program that covers health-care services for people 65 and over, some disabled people, and those with end-stage kidney disease. Medicare Part A covers inpatient care in hospitals, nursing homes, hospice, and some home health care. For most people, the Part A premium is free. Part B covers doctor fees, tests, and other outpatient medical services. Although Part B is optional, most people choose to enroll through their local Social Security office and pay the monthly premium ($45.50). Medicare beneficiaries share in the cost of care through deductibles and co-insurance. What Medicare does not cover at all is outpatient medication, long-term nonacute care, and support services.

•**Medicaid** A state and federally funded program that covers health-care services for people with income or assets below certain levels, which vary from state to state.

•**Medigap** Private insurance policies covering the gaps in Medicare, such as deductibles and co-payments, and in some cases additional health-care services, medical supplies, and outpatient prescription drugs.

Many of the services not paid for by Medicare can be covered by private long-term-care insurance. About 50 percent of us over the age of 65 will need long-term care at home or in a nursing home, and this insurance is an extra bit of protection for people with major assets to protect. It pays for skilled nursing care as well as non-health services, such as help with dressing, eating, and bathing. You select a dollar amount of coverage per day (for example, $100 in a nursing home, or $50 for at-home care), and a coverage period (for example, three years—the average nursing-home stay is 2.7 years). Depending on your age and the benefits you choose, the insurance can cost anywhere from around $500 to more than $8,000 a year. People with pre-existing conditions such as Alzheimer's or MS are usually not eligible.

How Much Will It Cost?

Where you get end-of-life care will affect the cost and who pays for it.

•**Hospital** Dying in a hospital costs about $1,000 a day. After a $766 deductible (per benefit period), Medicare reimburses the hospital a fixed rate per day, which varies by region and diagnosis. After the first 60 days in a hospital, a patient will pay a daily deductible ($194) that goes up (to $388) after 90 days. The patient is responsible for all costs for each day beyond 150 days. Medicaid and some private insurance, either through an employer or a Medigap plan, often help cover these costs.

•**Nursing home** About $1,000 a week. Medicare covers up to 100 days of skilled nursing care after a three-day hospitalization, and most medication costs during that time. For days 21–100, your daily co-insurance of $97 is usually covered by private insurance—if you have it. For nursing-home care not covered by Medicare, you must use your private assets, or Medicaid if your assets run out, which happens to approximately one-third of nursing-home residents. Long-term-care insurance may also cover some of the costs.

•**Hospice care** About $100 a day for in-home care. Medicare covers hospice care to patients who have a life expectancy of less than six months. (See Hospice: The Comfort Team.) Such care may be provided at home, in a hospice facility, a hospital, or a nursing-home. Patients may be asked to pay up to $5 for each prescription and a 5 percent co-pay for in-patient respite care, which is a short hospital stay to relieve caregivers. Medicaid covers hospice care in all but six states, even for those without Medicare.

About 60 percent of full-time employees of medium and large firms also have coverage for hospice services, but the benefits vary widely.

•**Home care without hospice services** Medicare Part A pays the full cost of medical home health care for up to 100 visits following a hospital stay of at least three days. Medicare Part B covers home health-care visits beyond those 100 visits or without a hospital stay. To qualify, the patient must be homebound, require skilled nursing care or physical or speech therapy, be under a physician's care, and use services from a Medicare-participating home-health agency. Note that this coverage is for medical care only; hired help for personal nonmedical services, such as that often required by Alzheimer's patients, is not covered by Medicare. It is covered by Medicaid in some states.

A major financial disadvantage of dying at home without hospice is that Medicare does not cover out-patient prescription drugs, even those for pain. Medicaid does cover these drugs, but often with restrictions on their price and quantity. Private insurance can fill the gap to some extent. Long-term-care insurance may cover payments to family caregivers who have to stop work to care for a dying patient, but this type of coverage is very rare.

Resources

MEDICAL CARE

For information about pain relief and symptom management:
Supportive Care of the Dying (503-215-5053; careofdying.org).

For a comprehensive guide to living with the medical, emotional, and spiritual aspects of dying:

Handbook for Mortals by Joanne Lynn and Joan Harrold, Oxford University Press.

For a 24-hour hotline offering counseling, pain management, downloadable advance directives, and more:

The Partnership for Caring (800-989-9455; www.partnershipforcaring.org).

EMOTIONAL CARE

To find mental-health counselors with an emphasis on lifespan human development and spiritual discussion:
American Counseling Association (800-347-6647; counseling.org).

For disease-related support groups and general resources for caregivers:
Caregiver Survival Resources (caregiver911.com).

For AARP's online caregiver support chatroom, access **America Online** every Wednesday night, 8:30–9:30 EST (keyword: AARP).

Education and advocacy for family caregivers:
National Family Caregivers Association (800-896-3650; nfcacares.org).

For the booklet,
Understanding the Grief Process (D16832, EEO143C), e-mail order with title and numbers to member@aarp.org or send postcard to AARP Fulfillment, 601 E St NW, Washington DC 20049. Please allow two to four weeks for delivery.

To find a volunteer to help with supportive services to the frail and their caregivers:
National Federation of Interfaith Volunteer Caregivers (816-931-5442; nfivc.org).

For information on support to partners of the chronically ill and/or the disabled:
The Well Spouse Foundation (800-838-0879; www.wellspouse.org).

LEGAL HELP

AARP members are entitled to a free half-hour of legal advice with a lawyer from **AARP's Legal Services Network**. (800-424-3410; www.aarp.org/lsn).

For **Planning for Incapacity**, a guide to advance directives in your state, send $5 to Legal Counsel for the Elderly, Inc., PO Box 96474, Washington DC 20090-6474. Make out check to LCE Inc.

For a **Caring Conversations** booklet on advance-directive discussion:
Midwest Bioethics Center (816-221-1100; midbio.org).

For information on care at the end of life, online discussion groups, conferences:
Last Acts Campaign (800-844-7616; lastacts.org).

HOSPICE

To learn about end-of-life care options and grief issues through videotapes, books, newsletters, and brochures:
Hospice Foundation of America (800-854-3402; hospice-foundation.org).

For information on hospice programs, FAQs, and general facts about hospice:
National Hospice and Palliative Care Organization (800-658-8898; nhpco.org).

For **All About Hospice: A Consumer's Guide** (202-546-4759; www.hospice-america.org).

FINANCIAL HELP

For **Organizing Your Future**, a simple guide to end-of-life financial decisions, send $5 to Legal Counsel for the Elderly, Inc., PO Box 96474, Washington DC 20090-6474. Make out check to LCE Inc.

For **Medicare and You 2000** and a **2000 Guide to Health Insurance for People With Medicare** (800-MEDICARE [633-4227]; medicare.gov).

To find your State Agency on Aging: **Administration on Aging, U.S. Department of Health and Human Services** (800-677-1116; aoa.dhhs.gov).

GENERAL

For information on end-of-life planning and bereavement: (www.aarp.org/endoflife/).

For health professionals and others who want to start conversations on end-of-life issues in their community:
Discussion Guide: On Our Own Terms: Moyers on Dying, based on the PBS series, airing September 10–13. The guide provides essays, instructions, and contacts. From PBS, www.pbs.org/onourownterms Or send a postcard request to On Our Own Terms Discussion Guide, Thirteen/WNET New York, PO Box 245, Little Falls, NJ 07424-9766.

Funded with a grant from The Robert Wood Johnson Foundation, Princeton, N.J. *Editor* Amy Gross; *Writer* Louise Lague; *Designer* David Herbick

UNIT 8
Personality Processes

Unit Selections

31. **Making Sense of Self-Esteem**, Mark R. Leary
32. **Nurturing Empathy**, Julia Glass
33. **Secrets of Happiness**, Stephen Reiss

Key Points to Consider

- What is the study of personality; what is the definition of personality? What are some of the major tenets of personality theories? Do you know any personality theories? Can you differentiate one theory from another?

- What is self-esteem? Why is it such an important concept? Do you think self-esteem comes exclusively from appraisals by others? If not, from where else does it originate? How can we raise children with high self-esteem? What do you think are the consequences of low self-esteem? Why might the concept of self-esteem as currently defined in psychology be inadequate?

- What is empathy? Can you provide some concrete examples of empathic behavior? Why is empathy an important characteristic? Can empathy be cultivated in children? If yes, how?

- What is happiness? What do most people think are the roots of happiness? What does Stephen Reiss, author of "Secrets of Happiness," believe creates happiness? What are the six basic values that need to be satisfied in order for people to feel happy?

- What other personality traits do you think would be important to measure besides empathy and happiness?

 **Links: www.dushkin.com/online/**
These sites are annotated in the World Wide Web pages.

The Personality Project
http://personality-project.org/personality.html

Sabrina and Sadie are identical twins. When the girls were young children, their parents tried very hard to treat them equally. Whenever Sabrina received a present, Sadie received one. Both girls attended dance school and completed early classes in ballet and tap dance. In elementary school, the twins were both placed in the same class with the same teacher. The teacher also tried to treat them the same.

In junior high school, Sadie became a tomboy. She loved to play rough-and-tumble sports with the neighborhood boys. On the other hand, Sabrina remained indoors and practiced on her piano. Sabrina was keenly interested in the domestic arts, such as sewing, needlepoint, and crochet. Sadie was more interested in reading novels, especially science fiction, and in watching adventure programs on television.

As the twins matured, they decided it would be best to attend different colleges. Sabrina went to a small, quiet college in a rural setting, and Sadie matriculated at a large public university. Sabrina majored in English, with a specialty in poetry; Sadie switched majors several times and finally decided on communications.

Why, when these twins were exposed to the same early childhood environment, did their interests and paths diverge later? What makes people, even identical twins at times, so unique, so different from one another?

The study of individual differences is the domain of personality. The psychological study of personality has included two major thrusts. The first has focused on the search for the commonalties of human life and development. Its major question would be: How are humans, especially their personalities, affected by specific events or activities? Personality theories are based on the assumption that a given event, if it is important, will affect almost all people in a similar way, or that the processes by which events affect people are common across events and people. Most psychological research into personality variables has made this assumption. Failures to replicate a research project are often the first clues that differences in individual responses require further investigation.

While some psychologists have focused on personality-related effects that are presumed to be universal among humans, others have devoted their efforts to discovering the bases on which individuals differ in their responses to environmental events. In the beginning, this specialty was called genetic psychology, because most people assumed that individual differences resulted from differences in genetic inheritance. By the 1950s the term genetic psychology had given way to the more current term: the psychology of individual differences.

Does this mean that genetic variables are no longer the key to understanding individual differences? Not at all. For a time, psychologists took up the philosophical debate over whether genetic or environmental factors were more important in determining behaviors. Even today, behavior geneticists compute the heritability coefficients for a number of personality and behavior traits, including intelligence. This is an expression of the degree to which differences in a given trait can be attributed to differences in inherited capacity or ability. Most psychologists, however, accept the principle that both genetic and environmental determinants are important in any area of behavior. These researchers are devoting more of their efforts to discovering how

the two sources of influence interact to produce the unique individual. Given the above, the focus of this unit is on personality characteristics and the differences and similarities among individuals.

What is personality? Most researchers in the area define personality as patterns of thoughts, feelings, and behaviors that persist over time and over situations, are characteristic or typical of the individual, and usually distinguish one person from another.

We first examine a concept crucial to personality. In our first article we will take a general look at self-esteem or the way we perceive our own self-worth. In "Making Sense of Self-Esteem," Mark Leary takes an empirical approach to the study of this all-important concept. Leary believes that the concept of self-esteem needs to be redefined and expanded within the field of psychology if the concept is to have any real utility.

We next look at several important personal attributes or personality traits. In "Nurturing Empathy," Julia Glass discusses what empathy is and why it is an important human trait. She also provides tips for parents on how to foster it in children.

The second personality attribute we examine is happiness. Some people are generally happy while others are not. Psychology is turning its focus away from negative traits, such as jealousy and anxiety, to more positive traits, such as optimism and happiness. In fact this "new" psychology is called "positive psychology." Thus, here we explore happiness and what it takes to be happy. The answers might surprise you.

Making Sense of Self-Esteem

Mark R. Leary[1]
Department of Psychology, Wake Forest University, Winston-Salem, North Carolina

Abstract
Sociometer theory proposes that the self-esteem system evolved as a monitor of social acceptance, and that the so-called self-esteem motive functions not to maintain self-esteem per se but rather to avoid social devaluation and rejection. Cues indicating that the individual is not adequately valued and accepted by other people lower self-esteem and motivate behaviors that enhance relational evaluation. Empirical evidence regarding the self-esteem motive, the antecedents of self-esteem, the relation between low self-esteem and psychological problems, and the consequences of enhancing self-esteem is consistent with the theory.
Keywords
self-esteem; self; self-regard; rejection

Self-esteem has been regarded as an important construct since the earliest days of psychology. In the first psychology textbook, William James (1890) suggested that the tendency to strive to feel good about oneself is a fundamental aspect of human nature, thereby fueling a fascination—some observers would say obsession—with self-esteem that has spanned more than a century. During that time, developmental psychologists have studied the antecedents of self-esteem and its role in human development, social psychologists have devoted attention to behaviors that appear intended to maintain self-esteem, personality psychologists have examined individual differences in the trait of self-esteem, and theorists of a variety of orientations have discussed the importance of self-regard to psychological adjust-

ment. In the past couple of decades, practicing psychologists and social engineers have suggested that high self-esteem is a remedy for many psychological and social problems.

Yet, despite more than 100 years of attention and thousands of published studies, fundamental issues regarding self-esteem remain poorly understood. Why is self-esteem important? Do people really have a need for self-esteem? Why is self-esteem so strongly determined by how people believe they are evaluated by others? Is low self-esteem associated with psychological difficulties and, if so, why? Do efforts to enhance self-esteem reduce personal and social problems as proponents of the self-esteem movement claim?

PERSPECTIVES ON THE FUNCTION OF SELF-ESTEEM

Many writers have assumed that people seek to maintain their self-esteem because they possess an inherent "need" to feel good about themselves. However, given the apparent importance of self-esteem to psychological functioning, we must ask why self-esteem is so important and what function it might serve. Humanistic psychologists have traced high self-esteem to a congruency between a person's real and ideal selves and suggested that self-esteem signals people as to when they are behaving in self-determined, autonomous ways. Other writers have proposed that people seek high self-esteem because it facilitates goal achievement. For example, Bednar, Wells, and Peterson (1989) proposed that self-esteem is subjective feedback about the adequacy of the self. This feedback—self-esteem—is positive when the individual copes well with circumstances

but negative when he or she avoids threats. In turn, self-esteem affects subsequent goal achievement; high self-esteem increases coping, and low self-esteem leads to further avoidance.

The ethological perspective (Barkow, 1980) suggests that self-esteem is an adaptation that evolved in the service of maintaining dominance in social relationships. According to this theory, human beings evolved mechanisms for monitoring dominance because dominance facilitated the acquisition of mates and other reproduction-enhancing resources. Because attention and favorable reactions from others were associated with being dominant, feelings of self-esteem became tied to social approval and deference. From this perspective, the motive to evaluate oneself positively reduces, in evolutionary terms, to the motive to enhance one's relative dominance.

One of the more controversial explanations of self-esteem is provided by terror management theory, which suggests that the function of self-esteem is to buffer people against the existential terror they experience at the prospect of their own death and annihilation (Solomon, Greenberg, & Pyszczynski, 1991). Several experiments have supported aspects of the theory, but not the strong argument that the function of the self-esteem system is to provide an emotional buffer specifically against death-related anxiety.

All of these perspectives offer insights into the nature of self-esteem, but each has conceptual and empirical difficulties (for critiques, see Leary, 1999; Leary & Baumeister, in press). In the past few years, a novel perspective—sociometer theory—has cast self-esteem in a somewhat different light as it attempts to address lingering questions about the nature of self-esteem.

SOCIOMETER THEORY

According to sociometer theory, self-esteem is essentially a psychological meter, or gauge, that monitors the quality of people's relationships with others (Leary, 1999; Leary & Baumeister, in press; Leary & Downs, 1995). The theory is based on the assumption that human beings possess a pervasive drive to maintain significant interpersonal relationships, a drive that evolved because early human beings who belonged to social groups were more likely to survive and reproduce than those who did not (Baumeister & Leary, 1995). Given the disastrous implications of being ostracized in the ancestral environment in which human evolution occurred, early human beings may have developed a mechanism for monitoring the degree to which other people valued and accepted them. This psychological mechanism—the *sociometer*—continuously monitors the social environment for cues regarding the degree to which the individual is being accepted versus rejected by other people.

The sociometer appears to be particularly sensitive to changes in relational evaluation—the degree to which others regard their relationship with the individual as valuable, important, or close. When evidence of low relational evaluation (particularly, a decrement in relational evaluation) is detected, the sociometer attracts the person's conscious attention to the potential threat to social acceptance and motivates him or her to deal with it. The affectively laden self-appraisals that constitute the "output" of the sociometer are what we typically call self-esteem.

Self-esteem researchers distinguish between *state self-esteem*—momentary fluctuations in a person's feelings about him- or herself—and *trait self-esteem*—the person's general appraisal of his or her value; both are aspects of the sociometer. Feelings of state self-esteem fluctuate as a function of the degree to which the person perceives others currently value their relationships with him or her. Cues that connote high relational evaluation raise state self-esteem, whereas cues that connote low relational evaluation lower state self-esteem. Trait self-esteem, in contrast, reflects the person's general sense that he or she is the sort of person who is valued and accepted by other people. Trait self-esteem may be regarded as the resting state of

the sociometer in the absence of incoming information relevant to relational evaluation.

SELF-ESTEEM AND ITS RELATIONSHIP TO BEHAVIOR

Sociometer theory provides a parsimonious explanation for much of what we know about self-esteem. Here I examine how sociometer theory answers four fundamental questions about self-esteem raised earlier.

The Self-Esteem Motive

As noted, many psychologists have assumed that people possess a motive or need to maintain self-esteem. According to sociometer theory, the so-called self-esteem motive does not function to maintain self-esteem but rather to minimize the likelihood of rejection (or, more precisely, relational devaluation). When people behave in ways that protect or enhance their self-esteem, they are typically acting in ways that they believe will increase their relational value in others' eyes and, thus, improve their chances of social acceptance.

The sociometer perspective explains why events that are known (or potentially known) by other people have much greater effects on self-esteem than events that are known only by the individual him- or herself. If self-esteem involved only private self-judgments, as many psychologists have assumed, public events should have no greater impact on self-esteem than private ones.

Antecedents of Self-Esteem

Previous writers have puzzled over the fact that self-esteem is so strongly tied to people's beliefs about how they are evaluated by others. If self-esteem is a *self*-evaluation, why do people judge themselves by *other* people's standards? Sociometer theory easily explains why the primary determinants of self-esteem involve the perceived reactions of other people, as well as self-judgments on dimensions that the person thinks are important to significant others. As a monitor of relational evaluation, the self-esteem system is inherently sensitive to real and potential reactions of other people.

Evidence shows that state self-esteem is strongly affected by events

that have implications for the degree to which one is valued and accepted by other people (Leary, Haupt, Strausser, & Chokel, 1998; Leary, Tambor, Terdal, & Downs, 1995). The events that affect self-esteem are precisely the kinds of things that, if known by other people, would affect their evaluation and acceptance of the person (Leary, Tambor, et al., 1995). Most often, self-esteem is lowered by failure, criticism, rejection, and other events that have negative implications for relational evaluation; self-esteem rises when a person succeeds, is praised, or experiences another's love—events that are associated with relational appreciation. Even the mere possibility of rejection can lower self-esteem, a finding that makes sense if the function of the self-esteem system is to warn the person of possible relational devaluation in time to take corrective action.

The attributes on which people's self-esteem is based are precisely the characteristics that determine the degree to which people are valued and accepted by others (Baumeister & Leary, 1995). Specifically, high trait self-esteem is associated with believing that one possesses socially desirable attributes such as competence, personal likability, and physical attractiveness. Furthermore, self-esteem is related most strongly to one's standing on attributes that one believes are valued by significant others, a finding that is also consistent with sociometer theory.

In linking self-esteem to social acceptance, sociometer theory runs counter to the humanistic assumption that self-esteem based on approval from others is false or unhealthy. On the contrary, if the function of self-esteem is to avoid social devaluation and rejection, then the system must be responsive to others' reactions. This system may lead people to do things that are not always beneficial, but it does so to protect their interpersonal relationships rather than their inner integrity.

Low Self-Esteem and Psychological Problems

Research has shown that low self-esteem is related to a variety of psychological difficulties and personal problems, including depression, loneliness, substance abuse, teenage pregnancy, academic failure, and criminal behavior. The evidence in support of the link between low self-esteem and psychological problems has often been overstated; the relationships are weaker and more scattered than typically assumed (Mecca, Smelser, & Vasconcellos, 1989). Moreover, high self-esteem also has notable drawbacks. Even so, low self-esteem tends to be more strongly associated with psychological difficulties than high self-esteem.

From the standpoint of sociometer theory, these problems are caused not by low self-esteem but rather by a history of low relational evaluation, if not outright rejection. As a subjective gauge of relational evaluation, self-esteem may parallel these problems, but it is a coeffect rather than a cause. (In fact, contrary to the popular view that low self-esteem causes these problems, no direct evidence exists to document that self-esteem has any causal role in thought, emotion, or behavior.) Much research shows that interpersonal rejection results in emotional problems, difficulties relating with others, and maladaptive efforts to be accepted (e.g., excessive dependency, membership in deviant groups), precisely the concomitants of low self-esteem (Leary, Schreindorfer, & Haupt, 1995). In addition, many personal problems lower self-esteem because they lead other people to devalue or reject the individual.

Consequences of Enhancing Self-Esteem

The claim that self-esteem does not cause psychological outcomes may appear to fly in the face of evidence showing that interventions that enhance self-esteem do, in fact, lead to positive psychological changes. The explanation for the beneficial effects of programs that enhance self-esteem is that these interventions change people's perceptions of the degree to which they are socially valued individuals. Self-esteem programs always include features that would be expected to increase real or perceived social acceptance; for example, these programs include components aimed at enhancing social skills and interpersonal problem solving, improving physical appearance, and increasing self-control (Leary, 1999).

CONCLUSIONS

Sociometer theory suggests that the emphasis psychologists and the lay public have placed on self-esteem has been somewhat misplaced. Self-esteem is certainly involved in many psychological phenomena, but its role is different than has been supposed. Subjective feelings of self-esteem provide ongoing feedback regarding one's relational value vis-à-vis other people. By focusing on the monitor rather than on what the monitor measures, we have been distracted from the underlying interpersonal processes and the importance of social acceptance to human well-being.

Recommended Reading

Baumeister, R. F. (Ed.). (1993). *Self-esteem: The puzzle of low self-regard.* New York: Plenum Press.
Colvin, C. R., & Block, J. (1994). Do positive illusions foster mental health? An examination of the Taylor and Brown formulation. *Psychological Bulletin, 116,* 3–20.
Leary, M. R. (1999). (See References)
Leary, M. R., & Downs, D. L. (1995). (See References)
Mecca, A. M., Smelser, N. J., & Vasconcellos, J. (Eds.). (1989). (See References)

Note

1. Address correspondence to Mark Leary, Department of Psychology, Wake Forest University, Winston-Salem, NC 27109; e-mail: leary@wfu.edu.

References

Barkow, J. (1980). Prestige and self-esteem: A biosocial interpretation. In D. R. Omark, F. F. Strayer, & D. G. Freedman (Eds.), *Dominance relations: An ethological view of human conflict and social interaction* (pp. 319–332). New York: Garland STPM Press.

Baumeister, R. F., & Leary, M. R. (1995). The need to belong: Desire for interpersonal attachments as a fundamental human motivation. *Psychological Bulletin, 117,* 497–529.
Bednar, R. L., Wells, M. G., & Peterson, S. R. (1989). *Self-esteem: Paradoxes and innovations in clinical theory and practice.* Washington, DC: American Psychological Association.
James, W. (1890). *The principles of psychology* (Vol. 1). New York: Henry Holt.
Leary, M. R. (1999). The social and psychological importance of self-esteem. In R. M. Kowalski & M. R. Leary (Eds.), *The social psychology of emotional and behavioral problems: Interfaces of social and clinical psychology* (pp. 197–221). Washington, DC: American Psychological Association.
Leary, M. R., & Baumeister, R. F. (in press). The nature and function of self-esteem: Sociometer theory. *Advances in Experimental Social Psychology.*
Leary, M. R., & Downs, D. L. (1995). Interpersonal functions of the self-esteem motive: The self-esteem system as a sociometer. In M. H. Kernis (Ed.), *Efficacy, agency, and self-esteem* (pp. 123–144). New York: Plenum Press.
Leary, M. R., Haupt, A. L., Strausser, K. S., & Chokel, J. L. (1998). Calibrating the sociometer: The relationship between interpersonal appraisals and state self-esteem. *Journal of Personality and Social Psychology, 74,* 1290–1299.
Leary, M. R., Schreindorfer, L. S., & Haupt, A. L. (1995). The role of self-esteem in emotional and behavioral problems: Why is low self-esteem dysfunctional? *Journal of Social and Clinical Psychology, 14,* 297–314.
Leary, M. R., Tambor, E. S., Terdal, S. J., & Downs, D. L. (1995). Self-esteem as an interpersonal monitor. The sociometer hypothesis. *Journal of Personality and Social Psychology, 68,* 518–530.
Mecca, A. M., Smelser, N. J., & Vasconcellos, J. (Eds.). (1989). *The social importance of self-esteem.* Berkeley: University of California Press.
Solomon, S., Greenberg, J., & Pyszczynski, T. (1991). A terror management theory of social behavior: The psychological functions of self-esteem and cultural worldviews. *Advances in Experimental Social Psychology, 24,* 93–159.

nurturing
empathy

How seeing the world through another's eyes not only makes a child compassionate but helps him learn right from wrong

BY JULIA GLASS

On mellow summer evenings, my neighbor Holly Lance and I used to get our 2-year-old sons together outside for "run them bone tired" playdates. One evening, as they were sprinting and cavorting with typical pinball momentum, Holly's son, Stefan, burst into tears. Holding his elbow in obvious pain, he collapsed in his mother's arms. My son approached his inconsolable playmate with a look of alarm. He watched Stefan cry for a few seconds, then walked to a nearby wall, bumped his head against it, and erupted into sobs to rival Stefan's.

I had never seen Alec do anything so peculiar. Was he trying to upstage his friend? It was Holly who said, "What a sweet thing to do!" And then I saw that Alec had clearly been attempting—if somewhat clownishly—to comfort someone he loved. I'd long since begun to encourage Alec's verbal, physical, and musical abilities, but what about his emotional abilities? Should I be nurturing this flair for compassion? I wondered.

"At its simplest, empathy means feeling the same thing another person's feeling; at its most sophisticated, it's understanding his entire life situation," says Martin Hoffman, Ph.D., professor of psychology at New York University and author of *Empathy and Moral Development: Implications for Caring and Justice.*

It's empathy that leads us, as adults, not just to help out friends and family but also to stop for a driver stranded by the side of the road, point a bewildered tourist in the right direction, even water a thirsty tree. Without it, our species would probably be extinct, says Hoffman. It is also a key to moral internalization—our children's increasing ability, as they grow, to make decisions by themselves that weigh others' needs and desires against their own.

The root of empathy is linking what an emotion feels like for you with what it feels like for others.

Given the importance of this attribute, here's how to recognize empathy's earliest signs and encourage it to blossom.

Born to Connect

There you are squeezing melons in the produce aisle, your 1-year-old babbling blissfully away, when a baby over in the snack-foods section starts to wail. All too predictably, so does yours. Experts believe that such copycat grief may be an emotional reflex that helps "train" our nature toward a more genuine form of compassion.

"The root of empathy is being able to recognize a link between what it feels like for you to be in a particular emotional state and what that feels like for another person, and it looks as if we're born with a primitive form of that kind of identification," says Alison Gopnik, Ph.D., a psychology professor at the University of California at Berkeley and coauthor of *The Scientist in the Crib.* "Even within an hour of birth, babies will try to make the same facial expression they see someone else making." Over the next few months, infants strive to coordinate their gestures and vocalizations as well as their expressions with those of adults around them.

At about 9 months, a baby begins to pay attention to how others feel about things. Confronted with an unfamiliar object—a toy robot or pureed squash—he'll instantly look at Mom to read her take. If she looks apprehensive, he'll hold back; if she looks pleased, he'll probably dive right in. While this reveals a new depth of perception, it also shows that babies have yet to grasp the most fundamental principle of civilized society: Each of us is a separate being with individual proclivities and feelings. You can't comprehend the feelings of another person until you grasp the concept that there is such a thing as another person.

You Are You, I Am I: Discovering Others

"For most of the first year, babies are pretty confused about what's going on around them," says Hoffman. "If they see another baby fall down and need comfort from his mother, they'll cry and need comfort too."

About midway through the second year, most toddlers begin to recognize themselves in a mirror—seeing themselves as unique, distinct objects. They now see other people as separate—but only physically. They have yet to learn that different people have different inner states as well. So when one toddler sees another in distress, her instinct is to fetch her own mother rather than her playmate's, to placate the child with her own favorite toy. She'll recognize the suffering as belonging to someone else but can't imagine any appropriate remedy other than the one that would suit her. This impulse is one of the most common early signs of what we recognize as genuine empathy, and it may continue even after kids gain a greater sense of what makes other people tick.

When 4-year-old Shai Karp's mother was rushed to the hospital for an appendectomy, he went along and sat with her as she was being checked in for surgery. "He'd brought his favorite stuffed animal, Tumby—short for the 'tumble dry low' on its label," says his mother, Judy

Wilner. "As I sat there, feeling miserable, Shai insisted I keep Tumby with me that night."

---

3 empathy busters

"Empathy is innate, but you can stunt its development," says psychologist Martin Hoffman, Ph.D. Try not to:

Overindulge. Just as an authoritative, "because I said so" style of parenting may prevent children from understanding the whys and wherefores of considerate behavior, so may overly permissive parenting. Kids raised without enough limits may come to feel very entitled—and entitlement, which focuses on the self, is anything but empathic.

Smother. Empathizing with another's strong feelings sometimes requires keeping a respectful distance, especially when a child needs to retreat for a time with a difficult emotion, such as shame or guilt. Resist the urge to try to protect kids from such strong emotions.

Stress competition. "In middle-class America, consideration of others is valued very highly," says Hoffman, "but so is individual achievement." For the first few years of life, those two values rarely collide; mothers may compare kids' developmental milestones, for instance, but such competition takes place mainly between parents. Come the school years, that changes.

"If a kid does excel, it's normal to feel some empathic distress for friends who don't do as well," says Hoffman, but many parents just want their kids to feel good about succeeding and don't acknowledge their empathy. Likewise, students who perform poorly need a more compassionate response than a dose of tutoring and a well-meant "You'll do better next time." The competition won't go away; what's important is to recognize its dark side and discuss how it affects your child's feelings toward peers.

Somewhat ironically, the age at which this type of generosity arises is exactly when, behaviorally speaking, the Tubby custard hits the fan. Because just as toddlers are trying to learn how to make other people feel better, they're also learning how to make other people—most notably, their parents—feel decidedly worse. And it's not just, as I used to think, that Mother Nature throws in these random adorable moments to pacify our rage; the two tendencies are closely intertwined.

The Altruistic Twos?

Toward the end of the second year, children begin to understand that other people have thoughts, feelings, and wants different from their own—often through a process of trial and error. When a toddler trying to comfort his friend sees that his own favorite toy doesn't do the trick, he'll try the friend's favorite toy instead or he'll fetch the friend's mom.

Preschoolers begin to perceive subtler feelings, such as that a classmate may be sad because he misses his parents.

This stage marks a primitive but true form of empathy, says Hoffman, one when children not only start to recognize the different experiences of other people but also, when necessary, reach out to them. "Empathy isn't just a feeling; it's a motive," he stresses. Whether we're throwing a bridal shower or helping a friend cope with a death in the family, empathy spurs us to partake in someone else's experience. We don't always act on the urge, but when we do, it often makes us feel good.

This eventful early age is also a period of intensive experimenting to find out what makes people different from one another. "It's around age two that we begin to see children perform these lovely altruistic acts—and do things precisely because we don't want them to," says Gopnik. "The same impulse that leads a child to think, 'Mom's crying, I'm not; I can comfort her,' also leads to 'Mom doesn't want me to touch that lamp; I can touch that lamp, I'm going to touch it.' If you think about what we want to encourage—understanding how other people feel—the 'terrible twos' is a part of that." (For more on promoting this understanding, see "Encouraging Compassion," at right.)

Toward a More Mature Compassion

From this point on, children refine and enlarge their perspective on other people's inner lives. In the preschool years, says Hoffman, they begin to perceive more subtle, removed feelings—such as that a classmate may be sad because he misses his parents. They also learn that a single event can lead to different reactions from different people. Sometime between ages 5 and 8—having grasped their own gender and ethnic identity—they begin to look at each person around them as having a distinct personal history and to consider its influences on that person's experiences and feelings. "They also start to see how having different personalities makes people react differently, and they begin to take that into account when dealing with people," adds Gopnik.

Children are now on the threshold of what Hoffman says is a highly sophisticated form of empathy—empathy for another's experience beyond the immediate situation, a skill that we work on for the rest of our lives. They can

encouraging compassion

"Showing affection to kids helps them feel secure and loved," says psychologist Hoffman, "and that contributes to their ability to feel consideration for others. Being a model of empathy—actively helping others—is also important." Beyond these fairly obvious gestures, you can encourage compassion if you:

• **Discipline in ways that invoke natural empathy.** By the end of the second year, scoldings constitute some two-thirds of all parent-child interactions, says Hoffman. And much of the offending behavior involves situations in which the child hurts or upsets someone else.

When your child is the transgressor, it's important not just to let him know he was wrong but also to be specific about the consequences of his actions. Saying, "You made me angry when you poured your milk on the table because now I have to mop it up and we don't have any more" or "You hurt his feelings when you grabbed that airplane—how would you feel if he grabbed it from you?" is an essential step toward making a child feel both guilt for the behavior and responsibility for how other people feel. In time, the ability to anticipate that guilt can motivate kids to "do the right thing."

• **Encourage conciliatory gestures.** Ask your child to apologize or give the person he hurt a hug, pat, or kiss.

• **Don't stifle his emotions.** Adults may try too quickly to "fix" a child's bad feelings—to distract him from sadness with treats, negotiate to thwart his anger, or otherwise derail an emotion that may help teach him the less pleasant aspect of human nature. This doesn't mean you have to accept misbehavior in the name of letting your child "feel"; part of learning to be empathic is learning that we can't act on every emotion we have.

• **Make feelings a topic of discussion.** When you see other people in different situations, ask your child to imagine what those people might be feeling. And don't limit yourself to real life. Talk about your child's emotional response to books, TV shows, and videos.

• **Revel in role-playing games.** "They let kids feel what it's like to be somebody else—a daddy, a baby," says psychologist Alison Gopnik, Ph.D. "That's important to empathy. When my son was three, I'd say, 'I'm going to be Alexei, and you be Mommy.' I'd be difficult and carry on, and he'd say things like 'You can't do that! It's going to be a big mess and I'm going to have to clean it up!' It was a great way to work out some of our conflicts."—J.G.

see that some people have generally happy or sad lives, and they can begin to empathize with entire groups of people (the homeless, earthquake victims, firefighters battling an inferno).

Last Thanksgiving a friend's 4-year-old daughter had a poignant moment. "AnnaBess walked into the kitchen when her father was dressing the turkey," recalls her mother, Wendy Greenspun. "She started crying and said, 'Daddy, that turkey doesn't want to be dead! He wants to be alive! He wants to be with his friends.' She was extremely upset for almost an hour." Whether or not AnnaBess was expressing an unusually precocious empathy, this much is clear: She was saddened by another creature's hardship, and her outrage occurred spontaneously—without prompting by anyone else.

For when it comes to raising empathic children, says Hoffman, parents need not fret about following some rule book or missing a narrow window of opportunity. "The beauty of empathy," he says, "is that it comes naturally. It doesn't have to be forced. You need only nourish it."

JULIA GLASS *recently won her third Nelson Algren Fiction Award and a fellowship in writing from the New York Foundation for the Arts.*

From *Parenting* magazine, June/July 2001, p. 72. © 2001 by The Parenting Group. Reprinted by permission.

Secrets of Happiness

**After psychologist Steven Reiss survived a life-threatening illness,
he took a new look at the meaning of life. Now, based on a survey of more than 6,000 people,
Reiss offers new insights about what it really takes to be happy.**

By Steven Reiss, Ph.D.

Sometimes we are so consumed with our daily lives that we forget to look at the larger picture of who we are and what we need to be happy. We work, raise our children, and manage our chores, but it takes an extraordinary event such as a life-threatening illness, or the death of a loved one, to focus our attention on the meaning of our lives.

I faced death for the first time when I was told I needed a liver transplant a few years ago. I thought about the meaning in my life and why I lived the way I did. I started to question the Pleasure Principle, which says that we are motivated to maximize pleasure and minimize pain. When I was ill, I discovered exactly why I wanted to get better and continue living, and it had little to do with pleasure or pain.

Pleasure theory has been around since the days of ancient Greece and is well-represented in modern-day society and academic psychology. Socrates pondered the idea that pleasure is the basis of morality; he wondered if pleasure indicates moral good and pain indicates evil. Epicurus, the greatest of all pleasures theorists, believed that the key to a happy life was to minimize stomach distress, or anxiety, by changing one's attitudes and beliefs. His rational-emotive philosophy was popular for 700 years in ancient Greece and Rome.

More recently, *Playboy* founder Hugh Hefner used pleasure theory to justify the sexual revolution of the 1960s. Psychologist N. M. Bradburn said that the quality of a person's life can be measured by the excess of positive over negative feelings. So is maximizing pleasure and minimizing pain the ultimate key to human happiness? No. When I was in the hospital analyzing what made my life satisfying, I didn't focus on the parties. In fact, pleasure and pain were not even considerations.

If pleasure is not what drives us, what does? What desires must we fulfill to live a happy life? To find out what *really* drives human behavior, my graduate students and I asked more than 6,000 people from many stations in life which values are most significant in motivating their behavior and in contributing to their sense of happiness. We analyzed the results to learn how different motives are related and what is behind their root meanings.

The results of our research showed that nearly everything we experience as meaningful can be traced to one of 16 basic desires or to some combination of these desires. We developed a standardized psychological test, called the Reiss Profile, to measure the 16 desires. (See box "The 16 Keys to Happiness."

Happiness defined

Harvard social psychologist William McDougall wrote that people can be happy while in pain and unhappy while experiencing pleasure. To understand this, two kinds of happiness must be distinguished: feel-good and value-based. Feel-good happiness is sensation-based pleasure. When we joke around or have sex, we experience feel-good happiness. Since feel-good happiness is ruled by the law of diminishing returns, the kicks get harder to come by. This type of happiness rarely lasts longer than a few hours at a time.

Value-based happiness is a sense that our lives have meaning and fulfill some larger purpose. It represents a spiritual source of satisfaction, stemming from our deeper purpose and values. We experience value-based happiness when we satisfy any of the 16 basic desires—the more desires we satisfy, the more value-based happiness we experience. Since this form of happiness is not ruled by the law of diminishing returns, there is no limit to how meaningful our lives can be.

Malcolm X's life is a good example of both feel-good and value-based happiness. When racial discrimination denied him the opportunity to pursue his childhood ambition of becoming a lawyer, he turned to a life of partying, drugs and sex. Yet this pleasure seeking produced little happiness—by the age of 21, he was addicted to cocaine and sent to jail for burglary. He had experienced a lot of pleasure, yet he was unhappy because his life was inconsistent with his own nature and deeper values. He had known feel-good happiness but not value-based happiness.

After reaching rock bottom, he embraced the teachings of the Nation of Islam and committed himself to his most fundamental values. He led his followers toward greater social justice, married, had a family of his own and found happiness. Although he experienced less pleasure and more anxiety as a leader, he was much happier because he lived his life in accordance with his values.

The 16 basic desires make us individuals. Although everybody embraces these desires, individuals prioritize them differently. Al Gore, for example, has a very strong desire for power. This desire makes him happy when he is in a leadership role, when he gives advice to others, or when he shows how competent and smart he is. George W. Bush has a strong desire for social contact. This desire makes him happy when he socializes and unhappy when he spends a lot of time alone. The two politicians place very different values on the basic desires of power and social contact, which is reflected in their personalities—Gore tends to be overbearing and overeager to get ahead, and Bush tends to be a good ol' boy.

Although everybody wants to attain a certain status, individuals differ in how motivated they are to obtain it. Jackie Kennedy Onassis, for example, had a passion for status—she needed to be wealthy to be truly happy. By obtaining wealth, she thought that she could satisfy her deep desire for respect from her upper-class peers. She spent much of her life pursuing wealth by marrying two multimillionaires. In contrast, Howard Hughes did not care much about status—he didn't care about what people thought of him and spent little time trying to earn their respect. While Jackie Kennedy Onassis placed high value on gaining status and the respect of her social peers, Howard Hughes had both but neither made him happy.

Revenge is another goal that motivates people differently. Now that Regis Philbin has hit the big time with his show "Who Wants To Be A Millionaire," why does he keep reminding us of the times he had been passed over earlier in his career? By embarrassing those who lacked faith in him, Philbin is gaining a measure of revenge. In comparison, John F. Kennedy Jr. did not go after people who criticized him or his family. Revenge can be fun, but it is more motivating for some than for others.

The 16 basic desires

You cannot find enduring happiness by aiming to have more fun or by seeking pleasure. What you need to do, as the 19th-century philosopher J. S. Mill observed, is to satisfy your basic desires and take happiness in passing. First, use the quiz to figure out who you are (see quiz, "The 16 keys to happiness"). Find out which of the 16 desires provide the most meaning in your life. How strongly are you motivated

to obtain a successful marriage, career or family? Do you love a good meal and dining out? Must you be physically fit to be happy? Fortunately, you do not have to satisfy all 16 desires, only the five or six most important to you.

After you identify your most important desires, you need to find effective ways to satisfy them. There is a catch, however. Shortly after you satisfy a desire, it reasserts itself, motivating you to satisfy the desire all over again. After a career success, for example, you feel competent, but only for a period of time. Therefore, you need to satisfy your desires repeatedly.

How can we repeatedly satisfy our most important basic desires and find value-based happiness? Most people turn to relationships, careers, family, leisure and spirituality to satisfy their most important desires.

Since we have the potential to satisfy our basic desires through relationships, we can find greater happiness by finding new relationships or by improving the ones we already have. After looking at the 16 basic desires and estimating the five or six most important to you, do the same for your partner, or have your partner take the quiz. Compare the two lists—the strengths of your relationship are indicated by similar desires, and the weaknesses are indicated by disparate desires.

Shelly and Sam are a good case in point. Before they married, both placed value on romance, fitness and socializing, but they differed on whether or not they should have children. Shelly secretly thought she could change Sam's mind. When Sam still did not want children after a few years of marriage, Shelly did not take her birth control pills one night and ended up having a baby boy. Sam loved his boy, but he didn't enjoy raising him.

What can Shelly and Sam do to improve their relationship and regain happiness? Counseling is worth a try, but even with the best counselor it will be difficult for them to resolve their differences. Their problem is that they prioritize the basic desire for family differently—one enjoys raising children, the other doesn't. The desire for family, which is not easily changed, has pulled them in different directions, turning a happy marriage into an unhappy one. Their best bet to improve their relationship may be to set aside time for activities that satisfy the desires that bind them. If they set aside time to put the romance back in their lives, maybe the strong points in the relationship will outweigh the weak ones. Ultimately, that is

the judgment we all must make, because few relationships are perfect.

Our basic desires can also be satisfied through work. Steven Spielberg, for example, honored his Jewish heritage when he made the movie *Schindler's List,* the Academy award-winning film about the Holocaust. When Spielberg thinks about his accomplishment, he feels a sense of loyalty to his Jewish heritage, an intrinsically valued feeling that satisfies the desire for honor.

Rocky Graziano also found value-based happiness through his career. Graziano was a fighter—that was who he was and who he wanted to be. He was an unhappy juvenile delinquent who got himself into fistfights. But when he became a boxer—rising to the rank of middleweight champion—he finally found work that provided a socially acceptable means for him to satisfy his passion for vengeance. Fighting had gone from a source of displeasure to a source of happiness in his life.

One way to become happier is to find a job or career that is more fulfilling than the one you have now. To do this, you need to analyze how you can use work to better satisfy your five or six most important basic desires. If you have a high desire for acceptance, for example, you need work that exposes you to little evaluation and potential criticism. If you have a high desire for order, you need work that involves minimal ambiguity and exposes you to few changes. If you are a curious person, you need a job that makes you think.

Our basic desires can also be satisfied through leisure activities. Watching sports, for example, provides us with opportunities to repeatedly experience the intrinsically valued feelings of competition, loyalty, power and revenge. When Brandi Chastain kicked the winning field goal and the United States won the 1999 World Cup in women's soccer, a surge of power went through the nation like a bolt of lightning—the crowd roared and people thrust their fists powerfully into the air. Sports produces more or less the same range of intrinsically valued feelings in fans as they do in players, which is why so many people watch.

One of the deepest ways to satisfy our desires is through spirituality. We can satisfy the desire for honor by embracing the religious denomination of our parents. A psychologically important attribute of religion is the emphasis given to the desire for unity, or to open one's heart to God. At least for some, faith is a path toward greater value-based happiness.

the 16 keys to happiness

To increase your value-based happiness, first read the following statements and mark whether they describe you strongly (+), somewhat (0), or very little (-). The ones that describe you strongly show the keys to your happiness--you should aim to satisfy these to increase your happiness. Some tips to help you do this can be found in the main article, and more can be found in the author's book, *Who Am I: The 16 Basic Desires That Motivate Our Happiness and Define Our Personalities.*

DESIRE	STATEMENT	SELF-RATING
CURIOSITY	I have a thirst for knowledge.	_____
ACCEPTANCE	I have a hard time coping with criticism.	_____
ORDER	It upsets me when things are out of place.	_____
PHYSICAL ACTIVITY	Physical fitness is very important to me.	_____
HONOR	I am a highly principled and loyal person.	_____
POWER	I often seek leadership roles.	_____
INDEPENDENCE	Self-reliance is essential to my happiness.	_____
SOCIAL CONTACT	I am known as a fun-loving person.	_____
FAMILY	My children come first.	_____
STATUS	I am impressed by people who own expensive things.	_____
IDEALISM	Compared with most people, I am very concerned with social causes.	_____
VENGEANCE	It is very important to me to get even with those who insult or offend me.	_____
ROMANCE	Compared with my peers, I spend much more time pursuing or having sex.	_____
EATING	I love to eat and often fantasize about food.	_____
SAVING	I hate throwing things away.	_____
TRANQUILITY	It scares me when my heart beats rapidly.	_____

Value-based happiness is the great equalizer in life. You can find value-based happiness if you are rich or poor, smart or mentally challenged, athletic or clumsy, popular or socially awkward. Wealthy people are not necessarily happy, and poor people are not necessarily unhappy. Values, not pleasure, are what bring true happiness, and everybody has the potential to live in accordance with their values.

READ MORE ABOUT IT

Who Am I: The 16 Basic Desires That Motivate Our Happiness and Define Our Personalities, Steven Reiss, Ph.D. (Tarcher/Putnam, 2000)

The Art of Happiness: A Handbook for Living, His Holiness the Dalai Lama and Howard C. Cutler, M. D. (Riverhead Books, 1998)

Steven Reiss, Ph.D., is a professor of psychology and psychiatry at Ohio State University, where he directs the university's Nisonger Center.

UNIT 9
Social Processes

Unit Selections

Key Points to Consider

- What is bullying? What causes bullying? Why is bullying so deleterious to its victim? What can schools and parents do to reduce or prevent bullying? How is bullying related to violence? Is the violence done only to others?

- What is prejudice? Can you differentiate it from stereotyping? Is prejudice only negative; can we have positive biases, too? If prejudice is so pervasive, should we give up and let prejudice exist? Why or why not? What is the jigsaw classroom? How does the jigsaw room change school climate? Is it effective in reducing racial prejudice?

- What is culture? What is cultural diversity? Why is there a push in U.S. schools to teach about culture? How should we teach about other cultures? How might plans to teach appreciation of other cultures backfire?

- Is love always a positive emotion? How is love for another related to love for parents? How and why do we sabotage some of our most intimate relationships?

 **Links: www.dushkin.com/online/**
These sites are annotated in the World Wide Web pages.

National Clearinghouse for Alcohol and Drug Information
http://www.health.org

Everywhere we look there are groups of people. Your general psychology class is a group. It is what social psychologists would call a secondary group, a group which comes together for a particular, somewhat contractual reason and then disbands after its goals have been met. Other secondary groups include athletic teams, church associations, juries, committees, and so forth.

There are other types of groups, too. One other type is a primary group. A primary group has much face-to-face contact, and there is often a sense of "we-ness" (cohesiveness as social psychologists would call it) in the group. Examples of primary groups include families, suite mates, sororities, and fraternities.

Collectives are loosely knit, large groups of people. A bleacher full of football fans would be a collective. A line of people waiting to get into a rock concert would also be a collective. As you might guess, collectives behave differently from primary and secondary groups.

Mainstream American society and any other large group that shares common rules and norms is also a group, albeit an extremely large group. While we might not always think about our society and how it shapes our behavior and our attitudes, society and culture nonetheless have a measureless influence on us. Psychologists, anthropologists, and sociologists alike are all interested in studying the effects of a culture on its members.

In this unit we will look at both positive and negative forms of social interaction. We will move from a focused form of social interaction to broader forms of social interaction, from interpersonal to group to societal processes.

In the first article, "Disarming the Rage," Richard Jerome and his colleagues discuss the all-important and timely topic of bullying. Bullying, they say, leads to self-inflicted violence or to other-directed violence by the victims. How parents and schools can guard against bullying and therefore prevent violence are highlighted in this article.

Then, Erica Goode, in "Rational and Irrational Fears Combine in Terrorism's Wake," investigates the intense fears and other reactions that Americans are exhibiting in the wake of the September 11, 2001, attacks.

We next move to another lingering societal problem in the United States—prejudice. Hate groups and white supremacy groups are active in many communities. Minority school children feel the sting of prejudice in their classrooms and on the playgrounds. A prominent psychologist in the field of prejudice discusses his creative solution to the prejudice problem in American schools. By using the jigsaw classroom, Elliott Aronson is able to reduce prejudice as well as alter the school climate.

In the next article of this unit on social interaction, we explore the largest social issue of all—culture. There is a push in the United States to teach about other cultures. In "Merits and Perils of Teaching About Other Cultures," Walter McDougall investigates the trend of teaching about cultural diversity in public schools and universities. He suggests that some of the best-laid plans go asunder and that we need to rethink how, when, and what we teach about other cultures.

The final selection in this unit moves us to a smaller level of analysis—intimate relationships. The article "Finding Real Love" describes how and why some of us sabotage our most intimate relationships. The author suggests that we become defensive with our intimate partners, especially when they remind us of a difficult parent.

DISARMING THE RAGE

Across the country, thousands of students stay home from school each day, terrified of humiliation or worse at the hands of bullies. In the wake of school shootings—most recently in California and Pennsylvania—parents, teachers and lawmakers are demanding quick action

Richard Jerome

In the rigid social system of Bethel Regional High School in Bethel, a remote town in the tundra of southwest Alaska, Evan Ramsey was an outcast, a status earned by his slight frame, shy manner, poor grades and broken family. "Everybody had given me a nickname: Screech, the nerdy character on *Saved by the Bell*," he recalls. "I got stuff thrown at me, I got spit on, I got beat up. Sometimes I fought back, but I wasn't that good at fighting." Taunted throughout his years in school, he reported the incidents to his teachers, and at first his tormentors were punished. "After a while [the principal] told me to just start ignoring everybody. But then you can't take it anymore."

On the morning of Feb. 19, 1997, Ramsey, then 16, went to school with a 12-gauge shotgun, walked to a crowded common area and opened fire. As schoolmates fled screaming, he roamed the halls shooting randomly—mostly into the air. Ramsey would finally surrender to police, but not before killing basketball star Josh Palacios, 16, with a blast to the stomach, and principal Ron Ed-

wards, 50, who was shot in the back. Tried as an adult for murder, Ramsey was sentenced to 210 years in prison after a jury rejected a defense contention that he had been attempting "suicide by cop," hoping to be gunned down but not intending to kill anyone. Still, Ramsey now admits in his cell at Spring Creek Correctional Center in Seward, Alaska, "I felt a sense of power with a gun. It was the only way to get rid of the anger."

Unfortunately Ramsey is not alone. Children all over the country are feeling fear, hopelessness and rage, emotions that turn some of them into bullies and others into their victims. Some say that is how it has always been and always will be—that bullying, like other adolescent ills, is something to be endured and to grow out of. But that view is changing. At a time when many parents are afraid to send their children to school, the wake-up call sounded by the 13 killings and 2 suicides at Columbine High School in Colorado two years ago still reverberates. It is now clear that Columbine shooters Dylan Klebold and

Eric Harris felt bullied and alienated, and in their minds it was payback time.

In recent months there have been two other horrifying shooting incidents resulting, at least in part, from bullying. On March 5, 15-year-old Charles "Andy" Williams brought a .22-cal. pistol to Santana High School in Santee, Calif., and shot 15 students and adults, killing 2. He was recently certified to stand trial for murder as an adult. His apparent motive? Lethal revenge for the torment he had known at the hands of local kids. "We abused him pretty much, I mean verbally," concedes one of them. "I called him a skinny faggot one time."

Two days after the Williams shooting, Elizabeth Bush, 14, an eighth grader from Williamsport, Pa., who said she was often called "idiot, stupid, fat, ugly," brought her father's .22-cal. pistol to school and shot 13-year-old Kimberly Marchese, wounding her in the shoulder. Kimberly, one of her few friends, had earned Elizabeth's ire by allegedly turning on her and joining in with the taunters. Bush admitted her guilt and offered apologies. A ward of the court until after she turns 21, she is now in a juvenile psychiatric facility. Kimberly, meanwhile, still has bullet fragments in her shoulder and is undergoing physical therapy.

As school enrollment rises and youths cope with the mounting pressures of today's competitive and status-conscious culture, the numbers of bullied children have grown as rapidly as the consequences. According to the National Education Association, 160,000 children skip school each day because of intimidation by their peers. The U.S. Department of Education reports that 77 percent of middle and high school students in small midwestern towns have been bullied. And a National Institutes of Health study newly released in the *Journal of the American Medical Association* reveals that almost a third of 6th to 10th graders—5.7 million children nationwide—have experienced some kind of bullying. "We are talking about a significant problem," says Deborah Prothrow-Stith, professor of public health practice at Harvard, who cites emotional alienation at home as another factor in creating bullies. "A lot of kids have grief, loss, pain, and it's unresolved."

Some experts see bullying as an inevitable consequence of a culture that rewards perceived strength and dominance. "The concept of power we admire is power over someone else," says Jackson Katz, 41, whose Long Beach, Calif., consulting firm counsels schools and the military on violence prevention. "In corporate culture, in sports culture, in the media, we honor those who win at all costs. The bully is a kind of hero in our society." Perhaps not surprisingly, most bullies are male. "Our culture defines masculinity as connected to power, control and dominance," notes Katz, whose work was inspired in part by the shame he felt in high school when he once stood idly by while a bully beat up a smaller student.

As for the targets of bullying, alienation runs like a stitch through most of their lives. A study last fall by the U.S. Secret Service found that in two-thirds of the 37 school shootings since 1974, the attackers felt "persecuted, bullied, threatened, attacked or injured." In more than three-quarters of the cases, the attacker told a peer of his violent intentions. William Pollack, a clinical psychologist and author of *Real Boys' Voices*, who contributed to the Secret Service study, said that several boys from Columbine described bullying as part of the school fabric. Two admitted to mocking Klebold and Harris. "Why don't people get it that it drives you over the edge?" they told Pollack. "It isn't just Columbine. It is everywhere."

That sad fact is beginning to sink in, as the spate of disturbing incidents in recent years has set off desperate searches for answers. In response, parents have begun crusades to warn and educate other families, courts have seen drawn-out legal battles that try to determine who is ultimately responsible, and lawmakers in several states—including Texas, New York and Massachusetts—have struggled to shape anti-bullying legislation that would offer remedies ranging from early intervention and counseling to the automatic expulsion of offenders.

One of the most shocking cases of victimization by bullies took place near Atlanta on March 28, 1994. That day, 15-year-old Brian Head, a heavyset sophomore at suburban Etowah High School, walked into his economics class, pulled out his father's 9-mm handgun and pressed it to his temple. "I can't take this anymore," he said. Then he squeezed the trigger. Brian had been teased for years about his weight. "A lot of times the more popular or athletic kids would make him a target," his mother, Rita, 43, says of her only child, a sensitive boy with a gift for poetry [see box at right]. "They would slap Brian in the back of the head or push him into a locker. It just broke him." Not a single student was disciplined in connection with his death. After his suicide, Rita, a magazine copy editor, and her husband, Bill, 47, counseled other parents and produced a video for elementary school students titled *But Names Will Never Hurt Me* about an overweight girl who suffers relentless teasing.

Georgia residents were stunned by a second child's death on Nov. 2, 1998. After stepping off a school bus, 13-year-old Josh Belluardo was fatally punched by his neighbor Jonathan Miller, 15, who had been suspended in the past for bullying and other infractions. In that tragedy's wake Georgia Gov. Roy Barnes in 1999 signed an anti-bullying law that allows schools to expel any student three times disciplined for picking on others.

On the other side of the continent, Washington Gov. Gary Locke is pressing for anti-bullying training in schools, following two high-profile cases there. Jenny Wieland of Seattle still cannot talk of her only child, Amy Ragan, shot dead at age 17 more than eight years ago, without tearing up. A soccer player and equestrian in her senior year at Marysville-Pilchuck High School, Amy was heading to the mall on the night of Nov. 20, 1992, when she stopped at a friend's apartment. There, three schoolmates had gathered by the time Trevor Oscar Turner showed up. Then 19, Turner was showing off a .38-cal. revolver, holding it to kids' heads, and when he got to Amy, the weapon went off. Turner pleaded guilty to first-degree manslaughter and served 27 months of a 41-month sentence.

"I can't help but wonder what Amy's life would be like if she was still alive," says Wieland today. "I wonder about her career and if she'd be in love or have a baby." Wieland turned her grief into action. In 1994 she helped start Mothers Against Violence in America (MAVIA), an activist group patterned after Mothers Against Drunk Driving. She left her insurance job to become the program's director and speaks annually at 50 schools. In 1998 she became the first director of SAVE (Students Against Violence Everywhere), which continues to grow, now boasting 126 student chapters nationwide that offer schools anti-harassment and conflict-resolution programs. "People ask how I can stand to tell her story over and over," she says. "If I can save just one child, it's well worth the pain."

Not long after Amy Ragan's death, another bullying scenario unfolded 50 miles away in Stanwood, Wash. Confined to a wheelchair by cerebral palsy, Calcutta-born Taya Haugstad was a fifth grader in 1993, when a boy began calling her "bitch" and "retard." The daily verbal abuse led to terrible nightmares. By middle school, according to a lawsuit Taya later filed, her tormentor—a popular athlete—got physical, pushing her wheelchair into the wall and holding it while his friends kicked the wheels. Eventually Taya was diagnosed with posttraumatic stress disorder. "Imagine that you can't run away or scream," says her psychologist Judith McCarthy. "Not only was she traumatized, she's handicapped. She felt terribly unsafe in the world." Her adoptive parents, Karrie and Ken Haugstad, 48 and 55, complained to school authorities and went to court to get a restraining order against the bully, but it was never issued. Taya sued the school district and the boy in 1999. The judge awarded her $300,000 last year, ruling that the school was negligent in its supervision, thus inflicting emotional distress. (The ruling is under appeal.) Taya, now 19 and a high school junior, hopes to study writing in college. She says she holds no grudge against her nemesis, who received undisclosed punishment from the school. "I don't think about him," she says.

But Josh Sneed may never forgive the boys he refers to as the Skaters. It was in 1996, late in his freshman year at Powell High School in Powell, Tenn., when, he says, a group of skateboarders began to terrorize him. With chains clinking and baseball bats pounding the pavement, he claims, they chased him and threatened to beat him to death. Why Josh? He was small and "a country boy," says his homemaker mother, Karen Grady, 41. "They made fun of him for that. They told him he was poor and made fun of him for that."

Then on Oct. 17, 1996, "I just snapped," her son says. As Jason Pratt, known as one of the Skaters, passed him in the cafeteria, Sneed whacked him on the head with a tray. "I figured if I got lucky and took him out, all the other non-

Lost in the Shadows

BRIAN HEAD, 15

After years of being tormented at school, this Georgia teen who loved music and video games ended his life with a gunshot. Later, his parents found this poem among his belongings.

As I walk in the light, the shadow draws me closer,
with the ambition and curiosity of a small boy
and the determination of a man.
The shadow is sanctuary, a place to escape the light.
In the light they can see me,
in the light they can see all.
Although the light is wide in its spread,
they still cannot see the pain in my face.
The pain that their eyes bring to bear when
they look upon me.
They see me as an insignificant "thing,"
Something to be traded, mangled and mocked.
But in the shadows I know they would not,
nor could not, see such a lie.
In the shadows, their evil eyes cannot stare
my soul into oblivion.
In the dark, I am free to move without their
judgmental eyes on me.
In the shadows, I can sleep without dreams of
despair and deception.
In the shadows I am home.

sense would stop." But after a few punches, Josh slipped on a scrap of food, hit his head on the floor and lost consciousness as Pratt kneed him in the head several times. Finally a football player leapt over two tables and dragged Sneed away, likely saving his life. Four titanium plates were needed to secure his shattered skull, and he was so gravely injured that he had to relearn how to walk and talk. Home-schooled, Sneed eventually earned his GED, but he hasn't regained his short-term memory. Assault charges against both him and Pratt were dismissed, but Pratt (who declined to comment) was suspended from school for 133 days.

Grady sued the county, claiming that because the school knew Josh was being terrorized but never disciplined the tormentors, they effectively sanctioned the conditions that led to the fight. Her attorney James A. H. Bell hopes the suit will have national implications. "We tried to make a statement, holding the school system accountable for its failure to protect," he says. In February Sneed and Grady were awarded $49,807 by a judge who found the county partly at fault. A tractor buff who once aspired to own a John Deere shop, Josh now lives on his grandfather's farm, passing his days with cartoons, video games and light chores. "Everybody's hollering that they need to get rid of guns, but it's not that," he says. "You need to find out what's going on in school."

Around the country, officials are attempting to do precisely that, as many states now require a safe-school plan that specifically addresses bullying. Most experts agree that metal detectors and zero-tolerance expulsions ignore the root of the problem. Counseling and fostering teamwork seem most effective, as evidenced by successful programs in the Cherry Creek, Colo., school district and DeKalb County, Ga. "We create an atmosphere of caring—it's harder to be a bully when you care about someone," says John Monferdini, head counselor at the DeKalb Alternative School, which serves 400 county students, most of whom have been expelled for bullying and violent behavior. Apart from academics, the school offers conflict-resolution courses and team-oriented outdoor activities that demand cooperation. "Yeah, I'm a bully," says Chris Jones, 15. "If I'm with friends and we see someone coming along we can jump on, we do it. It's like, you know, an adrenaline rush." But a stint in DeKalb is having a transformative effect. "When I came here, it was because we beat up a kid so badly—sticking his head in the bleachers—and the only thing I wished was that we'd had a chance to hurt him worse before we got caught. That's not the way I am now."

One wonders if intervention might have restrained the bullies who tormented Evan Ramsey. Ineligible for parole until 2066, when he'll be 86, Ramsey, now 20, spends most days working out, playing cards, reading Stephen King novels and studying for his high school diploma. He also has plenty of time to reflect on the horrible error in judgment he made. "The worst thing is to resort to violence," he says. "I'd like to get letters from kids who are getting problems like I went through. I could write back and help them." His advice: "If they're being messed with, they have to tell someone. If nothing's done, then they have to go [to] higher and higher [authority] until it stops. If they don't get help, that's when they'll lose it and maybe do something bad—really bad. And the pain of doing that never really stops."

Ron Arias in Seward, **Mary Boone** in Seattle, **Lauren Comander** in Chicago, **Joanne Fowler** in New York City, **Maureen** Harrington in Stanwood, **Ellen Mazo** in Jersey Shore, Pa., **Jamie Reno** in Santee, **Don Sider** in West Palm Beach and **Gail Cameron Wescott** in Atlanta

BULLIES 101

How can parents tell when their child is being bullied—or bullying others?

In 1993 a panel of experts in the Cherry Creek School District in Englewood, Colo., published Bully-Proofing Your School, *a manifesto designed to stop bullying at an early age. One of its coauthors, Dr. William Porter, 55, a clinical psychologist, offers the following guidelines for parents.*

•What is a bully?
A bully is a child who takes repeated hostile actions against another child and has more power than the individual he targets. Bullies tend to be very glib and don't accept responsibility for their behavior.

•How do I know if my child is being bullied?
He or she may show an unwillingness to go to school and may have bruises or damage to belongings that can't be explained. Children who are being bullied tend to keep silent about it and may become withdrawn, depressed and feel no one can help.

•What do I do if my child is being bullied?
Listen to your child and express confidence that the problem can be solved. Keep trying until you find someone at the school to help. Practice with your child such protective skills as avoiding the confrontation or using humor to deflate a tense moment.

•What if my child is a bully?
Set clear and consistent expectations of behavior, and work with the school on follow-up. Don't let the child talk his or her way out of the behavior, and find positive ways for him or her to get attention.

Rational and Irrational Fears Combine in Terrorism's Wake

By ERICA GOODE

The familiar became strange, the ordinary perilous.

On Sept. 11, Americans entered a new and frightening geography, where the continents of safety and danger seemed forever shifted.

Is it safe to fly? Will terrorists wage germ warfare? Where is the line between reasonable precaution and panic?

Jittery, uncertain and assuming the worst, many people have answered these questions by forswearing air travel, purchasing gas masks and radiation detectors, placing frantic calls to pediatricians demanding vaccinations against exotic diseases or rushing out to fill prescriptions for Cipro, an antibiotic most experts consider an unnecessary defense against anthrax.

Psychologists who study how people perceive potential hazards say such responses are not surprising, given the intense emotions inspired by the terrorist attacks.

"People are particularly vulnerable to this sort of thing when they're in a state of high anxiety, fear for their own well-being and have a great deal of uncertainty about the future," said Dr. Daniel Gilbert, a professor of psychology at Harvard.

"We don't like that feeling," Dr. Gilbert said. "We want to do something about it. And, at the moment, there isn't anything particular we can do, so we buy a gas mask and put an American decal on our car and take trains instead of airplanes."

But, he added, "I'll be very surprised if five years from now even one life was saved by these efforts."

Still, many psychologists said avoiding flying might be perfectly reasonable if someone is going to spend the entire flight in white-knuckled terror. And though experts say gas masks will offer dubious protection in a chemical attack, if buying them helps calm people down, it can do no harm.

"The feelings may be irrational, but once you have the feelings, the behavior is perfectly rational," said Dr. George Lowenstein, a professor of economics and psychology at Carnegie Mellon University. "It doesn't make sense to take a risk just because it's rational if it's going to make you miserable. The rational thing is to do what makes you comfortable."

The public's fears may be heightened, he and other experts said, by the sense that the government failed to predict or prevent the Sept. 11 attacks, making people less trusting of the reassurances offered by the authorities, who have said that biological attacks are unlikely and, with vastly heightened security, air travel is safe.

The vivid, the involuntary and the unfamiliar seem to be more threatening.

Checkpoints on highways, closed parking structures at airports, flyovers by military aircraft and other security measures, they added, while reassuring many people, may for others increase anxiety by providing a constant reminder of danger.

In fact, the threats now uppermost in many people's minds, Dr. Lowenstein and other psychologists said, are examples of the kinds of risks that people find most frightening.

"All the buttons are being pushed here," said Dr. Paul Slovic, a professor of psychology at the University of Oregon and the author of "The Perception of Risk." Threats posed by terrorism, he said, "are horrific to contemplate, seem relatively uncontrollable and are catastrophic."

He and other researchers have found that risks that evoke vivid images, that are seen as involuntary, that are unfamiliar or that kill many people at once are often perceived as more threatening than risks that are voluntary, familiar and less extreme in their effects. For example, in studies, people rank threats like plane crashes and nuclear accidents higher than dangers like smoking or car accidents, which actually cause many more deaths each year.

This fact is a source of endless frustration to some scientists, who cannot understand why people panic over almost undetectable quantities of pesticides on vegetables but happily devour charcoal-broiled hamburgers and steaks, which contain known carcinogens formed in grilling. And, when asked to rank the relative dangers of a variety of potential hazards, scientific experts routinely give lower ratings to things like nuclear power and pesticides than do laypeople, researchers have found.

"Everything in some sense is dangerous, in some concentration and some place, and usually not in others," said Dr. James Collman, a chemistry professor at Stanford and the author of "Naturally Dangerous: Surprising Facts About Food, Health and the Environment."

He said his daughter called him after the terrorist attacks to ask if she should buy a gas mask.

"I told her not to panic," he said. "I thought it was sort of statistically a silly thing to do, and were there ever any toxic gases out there, whatever mask she had might or might not be effective anyway."

Yet psychologists say the average person's responses make sense if one realizes that human beings are not the cool, rational evaluators that economists and other social scientists once assumed them to be.

Rather, the human brain reacts to danger through the activation of two systems, one an instant, emotional response, the other a higher level, more deliberate reaction.

The emotional response to risk, Dr. Lowenstein said, is deeply rooted in evolution and shared with most other animals. But rationality—including the ability to base decisions about risk on statistical likelihood—is unique to humans.

Yet the two responses, he said, often come into conflict, "just as the experts clash with the laypeople."

"People often even within themselves don't believe that a risk is objectively that great, and yet they have feelings that contradict their cognitive evaluations," Dr. Lowenstein said.

For example, he said, "The objective risk of driving for four or five hours at high speeds still has got to be way higher than the risk of flying."

What You Don't Know . . .

Whether people fear something depends not only on how dangerous it actually is, but also on how much they know about it and how much control they believe they have over their exposure to it. Researchers use diagrams like this to chart perceptions of risk.

UNKNOWN RISKS

Less risky, less frightening
- Marijuana
- Aspirin
- Sunbathing

Most frightening
- Terrorism
- Nuclear weapons
- Nuclear power
- Nerve gas

VERTICAL AXIS
At bottom, risks that subjects view as known and observable; at top, those whose effects are hardest to observe.

CONTROLLABLE RISKS   UNCONTROLLABLE RISKS

HORIZONTAL AXIS ▶
At left, things described as controllable. At right, things that seem beyond one's control.

Least frightening
- Surfing
- Motorcycles
- Alcoholic beverages
- Hunting

More risky, more frightening
- Smoking
- Heroin
- Crime
- Open-heart surgery

KNOWN RISKS

Items are shown in no special order.

Source: "The Perception of Risk," by Paul Slovic

The New York Times

Yet Dr. Lowenstein added that a group of his colleagues, all academic experts on risk assessment, chose to drive rather than fly to a conference after the terrorist attacks.

"If you ask them which is objectively more dangerous, they would probably say that driving is," Dr. Lowenstein said. And though his colleagues cited potential airport delays, he said he suspected fear might also have played into their decision.

President Bush and other policy makers in Washington, Dr. Lowenstein said, must contend with a similar struggle between reason and emotion in shaping their response to the attacks.

"A lot of what's going on is this battle where the emotions are pushing us to respond in a way that would give us quick release but would have all sorts of long-term consequences," Dr. Lowenstein said.

In fact, studies show that once awakened, fear and other emotions heighten people's reactions to other potential hazards. In one study, for example, students shown sad films perceived a variety of risks as more threatening than students who saw emotionally neutral films.

Fear can also spread from person to person, resulting in wild rumors and panic.

One example often cited by sociologists who study collective behavior is the so-called Seattle windshield pitting epidemic, which occurred in 1954, a time when cold war fears ran high and the United States was testing the hydrogen bomb.

That year, tiny holes in car windshields were noticed in Bellingham, Wash., north of Seattle. A week later, similar pitting was seen by residents of towns south of Bellingham. Soon, people in Seattle and all over the state were reporting mysterious damage to their windshields. Many speculated that fallout from the H-bomb tests was the cause. Others blamed cosmic rays from the sun. At the height of the panic, the mayor of Seattle even called President Dwight D. Eisenhower for help.

But eventually, a more mundane explanation revealed itself: In the usual course of events, people did not examine their windshields that closely. The holes, pits and dings turned out to be a result of normal wear and tear, which few had noticed until it was drawn to their attention.

The antidote to such fears, psychologists say, is straightforward information from trustworthy sources.

"Trustworthiness has two elements," said Dr. Baruch Fischhoff, a psychologist in Carnegie Mellon's department of social and decision sciences. "One is honesty and the other is competence."

Attempts by the authorities to use persuasion often fall flat, Dr. Fischhoff said, because "if people feel they have to peel away the agenda of the communicator in order to understand the content of the message, that's debilitating."

"Give me the facts in a comprehensible way, and leave it to me to decide what's right for me," he said.

Yet what psychologists can say with some certainty is that, if no further attacks occur in the near future, people's fears are likely to fade quickly—even faster than the fearful themselves would predict.

Studies suggest, Dr. Gilbert said, that "people underestimate their resilience and adaptiveness."

We have remarkable both psychological and physiological mechanisms to adapt to change," he said. "I guarantee you that in six months whatever New Yorkers are feeling will seem pretty normal to them, even if it is not exactly what they were feeling before."

Nobody Left to Hate

by Elliot Aronson

In 1971 a highly explosive situation had developed in Austin, Texas—one that has played out in many cities across the United States. Austin's public schools had recently been desegregated and, because the city had always been residentially segregated, white youngsters, African American youngsters, and Mexican-American youngsters found themselves sharing the same classroom for the first time in their lives. Within a few weeks, long-standing suspicion, fear, distrust, and antipathy among the groups produced an atmosphere of turmoil and hostility, exploding into interethnic fistfights in corridors and schoolyards across the city.

The school superintendent called me in to see if I could do anything to help students learn to get along with one another. After observing what was going on in classrooms for a few days, my graduate students and I concluded that intergroup hostility was being exacerbated by the competitive environment of the classroom.

Let me explain. In every classroom we observed, the students worked individually and competed against one another for grades. Here is a description of a typical fifth-grade classroom we observed:

> The teacher stands in front of the class, asks a question, and waits for the children to indicate that they know the answer. Most frequently, six to ten youngsters raise their hands. But they do not simply raise their hands, they lift themselves a few inches off their chairs and stretch their arms as high as they can in an attempt to attract the teacher's attention. To say they are eager to be called on is an incredible understatement. Several other students sit quietly with their eyes averted, as if trying to make themselves invisible. These are the ones who don't know the answer. Understandably, they are trying to avoid eye contact with the teacher because they do not want to be called on.
>
> When the teacher calls on one of the eager students, there are looks of disappointment, dismay, and unhappiness on the faces of the other students who were avidly raising their hands but were not called on. If the selected student comes up with the right answer, the teacher smiles, nods approvingly, and goes on to the next question. This is a great reward for the child who happens to be called on. At the same time that the fortunate student is coming up with the right answer and being smiled upon by the teacher, an audible groan can be heard coming from the children who were striving to be called on but were ignored. It is obvious they are disappointed because they missed an opportunity to show the teacher how smart and quick they are. Perhaps they will get a chance next time. In the meantime, the students who didn't know the answer breathe a sigh of relief. They have escaped being humiliated this time.

The teacher may have started the school year with a determination to treat every student equally and encourage all of them to do their best, but the students quickly sorted themselves into different groups. The "winners" were the bright, eager, highly competitive students who fervently raised their hands, participated in discussions, and did well on tests. Understandably, the teacher felt gratified that these students responded to her teaching. She praised and encouraged them, continued to call on them, and depended on them to keep the class going at a high level and at a reasonable pace.

Then there were the "losers." At the beginning, the teacher called on them occasionally, but they almost invariably didn't know the answer, were too shy to speak, or couldn't speak English well. They seemed embarrassed to be in the spotlight; some of the other students made snide comments—sometimes under their breath, occasionally out loud. Because the schools in the poorer section of town were substandard, the African American and Mexican-American youngsters had received a poorer education prior to desegregation. Consequently, in Austin it was frequently these students who were among the "losers." This tended unfairly to confirm the unflattering stereotypes that the white kids had about minorities. The "losers" were considered stupid or lazy.

The minority students also had preconceived notions about the white kids: they considered them pushy show-offs and teachers' pets. These stereotypes were seemingly confirmed by the way most of the white students behaved in the competitive classroom.

After a while, the typical classroom teacher stopped trying to engage the students who weren't doing well. She or he felt it was kinder not to call on them and expose them to ridicule by the other students. In effect, a silent pact was made with the losers: to leave them alone as long as they weren't disruptive. Without really meaning to, the teacher gave up on these students—and so did the rest of the class. Without really meaning to, the teacher contributed to the difficulty the students were experiencing. After a while, these students tended to give up on themselves as well—perhaps believing that they *were* stupid—because they sure weren't getting it.

The jigsaw classroom facilitates interaction among all students in the class, leading them to value one another as contributors to their common task.

It required only a few days of intensive observation and interviews for us to have a pretty good idea of what was going on in these classrooms. We realized we needed to do something drastic to shift the emphasis from a relentlessly competitive atmosphere to a more cooperative one. It was in this context that we invented the *jigsaw strategy.*

THE JIGSAW CLASSROOM

Jigsaw is a specific type of group learning experience that requires everyone's cooperative effort to produce the final product. Just as in a jigsaw puzzle, each piece—each student's part—is essential for the production and full understanding of the final product. If each student's part is essential, then each student is essential. That is precisely what makes this strategy so effective.

Here's how it works. The students in a history class, for example, are divided into small groups of five or six students each. Suppose their task is to learn about World War II. In one jigsaw group, let us say that Sara is responsible for researching Hitler's rise to power in prewar Germany. Another member of the group, Steven, is assigned to cover concentration camps; Pedro is assigned Britain's role in the war; Lin is to research the contribution of the Soviet Union; Babu will handle Japan's entry into the war; and Monique will read about the development of the atom bomb. Eventually each student will come back to

her or his jigsaw group and will try to present a vivid, interesting, well-organized report to the group. The situation is specifically structured so that the only access any member has to the other five assignments is by listening intently to the report of the person reciting. Thus, if Babu doesn't like Pedro or he thinks Sara is a nerd, if he heckles them or tunes out while they are reporting, he cannot possibly do well on the test that follows.

To increase the probability that each report will be factual and accurate, the students doing the research do not immediately take it back to their jigsaw group. After completing their research, they must first meet with the students from each of the jigsaw groups who had the identical assignment. For example, those students assigned to the atom bomb topic meet together to work as a team of specialists, gathering information, discussing ideas, becoming experts on their topic, and rehearsing their presentations. This is called the "expert" group. It is particularly useful for those students who might have initial difficulty learning or organizing their part of the assignment for it allows them to benefit from listening to and rehearsing with other "experts," to pick up strategies of presentation, and generally to bring themselves up to speed.

After this meeting, when each presenter is up to speed, the jigsaw groups reconvene in their initial heterogeneous configuration. The atom bomb expert in each group teaches the other group members what she or he has learned about the development of the atom bomb. Each student in each group educates the whole group about her or his specialty. Students are then tested on what they have learned from their fellow group members about World War II.

What is the benefit of the jigsaw classroom? First and foremost it is a remarkably efficient way to learn the material. But even more important, the jigsaw process encourages listening, engagement, and empathy by giving each member of the group an essential part to play in the academic activity. Group members must work together as a team to accomplish a common goal—each person depends on all the others. No student can achieve her or his individual goal (learning the material, getting a good grade) unless everyone works together as a team. Group goals and individual goals complement and bolster each other. This "cooperation by design" facilitates interaction among all students in the class, leading them to value one another as contributors to their common task.

Our first intervention was with fifth graders. First we helped several fifth-grade teachers devise a cooperative jigsaw structure for the students to learn about the life of Eleanor Roosevelt. We divided the students into small groups—diversified in terms of race, ethnicity, and gender—and made each student responsible for a certain portion of Roosevelt's biography. Needless to say, at least one or two of the students in each group were already viewed as losers by their classmates.

Carlos was one such student. Carlos was very shy and felt insecure in his new surroundings. English was his second language. He spoke it quite well but with a slight accent. Try to imagine his experience: After attending an inadequately funded, substandard neighborhood school consisting entirely of Mexican-American students like himself, he was suddenly bussed across town to the middle-class area of the city and catapulted into a class with Anglo students who spoke English fluently and seemed to know much more than he did about all the subjects taught in the school—and were not reluctant to let him know it.

When we restructured the classroom so that students were now working together in small groups, this was terrifying to Carlos at first. He could no longer slink down in his chair and hide in the back of the room. The jigsaw structure made it necessary for him to speak up when it was his turn to recite. Carlos gained a little confidence by rehearsing with the others who were also studying Roosevelt's work with the United Nations, but he was understandably reticent when it was his turn to teach the students in his jigsaw group. He blushed, stammered, and had difficulty articulating the material he had learned. Skilled in the ways of the competitive classroom, the other students were quick to pounce on Carlos' weakness and began to ridicule him.

One of my research assistants was observing that group and heard some of its members make comments such as, "Aw, you don't know it, you're dumb, you're stupid. You don't know what you're doing. You can't even speak English." Instead of admonishing them to "be nice" or "try to cooperate," she made one simple but powerful statement. It went something like this: "Talking like that to Carlos might be fun for you to do, but it's not going to help you learn anything about what Eleanor Roosevelt accomplished at the United Nations—and the exam will be given in about fifteen minutes." What my assistant was doing was reminding the students that the situation had changed. The same behavior that might have seemed useful to them in the past, when they were competing against each other, was now going to cost them something very important: the chance to do well on the upcoming exam.

Old, dysfunctional habits do not die easily, but they do die. Within a few days of working with jigsaw, Carlos' groupmates gradually realized that they needed to change their tactics. It was no longer in their own best interest to rattle Carlos; he wasn't the enemy—he was on their team. They needed him to perform well in order to do well themselves. Instead of taunting him and putting him down, they started to gently ask him questions. The other students began to put themselves in Carlos' shoes so they could ask questions that didn't threaten him and would help him recite what he knew in a clear and understandable manner.

After a week or two, most of Carlos' groupmates had developed into skillful interviewers, asking him relevant questions to elicit the vital information from him. They became more patient, figured out the most effective way to work with him, helped him out, and encouraged him. The more they encouraged Carlos, the more he was able to relax; the more he was able to relax, the quicker and more articulate he became. Carlos' groupmates began to see him in a new light. He became transformed in their minds from a "know-nothing loser who can't even speak English" to someone they could work with, someone they could appreciate, maybe even someone they could like.

Moreover, Carlos began to see himself in a new light: as a competent, contributing member of the class who could work with others from different ethnic groups. His self-esteem grew, and as it grew his performance improved even more; and as his performance continued to improve, his groupmates continued to view him in a more and more favorable light.

Within a few weeks, the success of the jigsaw was obvious to the classroom teachers. They spontaneously told us of their great satisfaction over the way the atmosphere of their classrooms had been transformed. Adjunct visitors (such as music teachers and the like) were little short of amazed at the dramatically changed atmosphere in the classrooms. Needless to say, this was exciting to my graduate students and me. But, as scientists, we were not totally satisfied; we were seeking firmer, more objective evidence—and we got it.

Jigsaw students from poorer neighborhoods showed enormous academic improvement; they scored significantly higher on objective exams than the poorer students in traditional classes.

Because we had randomly introduced the jigsaw intervention into some classrooms and not others, we were able to compare the progress of the jigsaw students with that of the students in traditional classrooms in a precise, scientific manner. After only eight weeks there were clear differences, even though students spent only a small portion of their classtime in jigsaw groups. When tested objectively, jigsaw students expressed significantly less prejudice and negative stereotyping, showed more self-confidence, and reported that they liked school better than children in traditional classrooms.

Moreover, this self-report was bolstered by hard behavioral data. For example, the students in jigsaw classrooms were absent less often than those in traditional classrooms. In addition, the jigsaw students from poorer neighborhoods showed enormous academic improvement over the course of eight weeks; they scored significantly higher on objective exams than the poorer students in traditional classes, while those students who were already doing well continued to do well—as well as their counterparts in traditional classes.

Jigsaw and Basketball

You might have noticed a rough similarity between the kind of cooperation that goes on in a jigsaw group and the kind of cooperation that is necessary for the smooth functioning of an athletic team. Take a basketball team, for example. If the team is to be successful, each player must play her or his role in a cooperative manner. If each player is hellbent on being the highest scorer on the team, then each will shoot whenever the opportunity arises.

In contrast, on a cooperative team, the idea is to pass the ball crisply until one player manages to break clear for a relatively easy shot. If I pass the ball to Sam, and Sam whips a pass to Jameel, and Jameel passes to Tony, who breaks free for an easy lay-up, I'm elated even though I didn't receive credit for either a field goal or an assist. This is true cooperation.

As a result of this cooperation, athletic teams frequently build a cohesiveness that extends to their relationship off the court. They become friends because they have learned to count on one another. There is one difference between the outcome of a typical jigsaw group and that of a typical high-school basketball team, however, and it is a crucial difference. In high school, athletes tend to hang out with each other and frequently exclude nonathletes from their circle of close friends. In short, the internal cohesiveness of an athletic team often goes along with the exclusion of everyone else.

In the jigsaw classroom, we circumvented this problem by the simple device of shuffling groups every eight weeks. Once a group of students was functioning well together—once the barriers had been broken down and the students showed a great deal of liking and empathy for one another—we would re-form the groupings. At first the students would resist this re-forming of groups. Picture the scene: Debbie, Carlos, Tim, Patty, and Jacob have just gotten to know and appreciate one another and they are doing incredibly good work as a team. Why should they want to leave this warm, efficient, and cozy group to join a group of relative strangers?

Why, indeed? After spending a few weeks in the new group, the students invariably discover that the new people are just about as interesting, friendly, and wonderful as their former group. The new group is working well together and new friendships form. Then the students move on to their third group, and the same thing begins to happen. As they near the end of their time in the third group, it begins to dawn on most students that they didn't just luck out and land in groups with four or five terrific people. Rather, they realize that just about *everyone* they work with is a good human being. All they need to do is pay attention to each person, to try to understand her or him, and good things will emerge. That is a lesson well worth learning.

Encouraging General Empathy

Students in the jigsaw classroom become adept at empathy. When we watch a movie, empathy is what brings tears or joy in us when sad or happy things happen to a character. But why should we care about a character in a movie? We care because we have learned to feel and experience what that character experiences—as if it were happening to us. Most of us don't experience empathy for our sworn enemies. So most moviegoers watching *Star Wars*, for example, will cheer wildly when the Evil Empire's spaceships are blown to smithereens. Who cares what happens to Darth Vader's followers.

Is empathy a trait we are born with or is it something we learn? I believe we are born with the capacity to feel for others. It is part of what makes us human. I also believe that empathy is a skill that can be enhanced with practice. It I am correct, then it should follow that working in jigsaw groups would lead to a sharpening of a youngster's general empathic ability, because to do well in the group the child needs to practice feeling what her or his groupmates feel.

To test this notion, one of my graduate students, Diane Bridgeman, conducted a clever experiment in which she showed a series of cartoons to ten-year-old children. Half of the children had spent two months participating in jigsaw classes; the others had spent that time in traditional classrooms. In one series of cartoons, a little boy is looking sad as he waves goodbye to his father at the airport. In the next frame, a letter carrier delivers a package to the boy. When the boy opens the package and finds a toy airplane inside, he bursts into tears. Diane asked the children why they thought the little boy burst into tears at the sight of the airplane. Nearly all of the children could answer correctly: because the toy airplane reminded him of how much he missed his father.

Then Diane asked the crucial question: "What did the letter carrier think when he saw the boy open the package and start to cry?" Most children of this age make a consistent error: they assume that everyone knows what they know. Thus, the youngsters in the control group thought the letter carrier would know the boy was sad because the gift reminded him of his father leaving.

But the children who had participated in the jigsaw classroom responded differently. They were better able to take the perspective of the letter carrier—to put themselves in his shoes. They realized that he would be confused at seeing the boy cry over receiving a nice present because the letter carrier hadn't witnessed the farewell scene at the airport. Offhand, this might not seem very important. After all, who cares whether kids have the ability to figure out what is in the letter carrier's mind? In point of fact, we should all care—a great deal.

165

Here's why: the extent to which children can develop the ability to see the world from the perspective of another human being has profound implications for empathy, prejudice, aggression, and interpersonal relations in general. When you can feel another person's pain, when you can develop the ability to understand what that person is going through, it increases the probability that your heart will open to that person. Once your heart opens to another person, it becomes virtually impossible to bully that other person, to taunt that other person, to humiliate that other person—and certainly to kill that other person. If you develop the general ability to empathize, then your desire to bully or taunt anyone will decrease. Such is the power of empathy.

This isn't a new idea. We see it, for example, in William Wharton's provocative novel *Birdy*. One of the protagonists, Alphonso, a sergeant in the army, takes an immediate dislike for an overweight enlisted man, a clerk typist named Ronsky. There are a great many things that Alphonso dislikes about Ronsky. At the top of his list is Ronsky's annoying habit of continually spitting—he spits all over his desk, his typewriter, and anyone who happens to be in the vicinity. Alphonso cannot stand the guy and has fantasies of punching him out. Several weeks after meeting him, Alphonso learns that Ronsky had earlier taken part in the Normandy invasion and had watched in horror as several of his buddies were cut down before they even had a chance to hit the beach. It seems that his constant spitting was a concrete manifestation of his attempt to get the bad taste out of his mouth. Upon learning this, Alphonso sees his former enemy in an entirely different light. He sighs with regret and says to himself, "Before you know it, if you're not careful, you can get to feeling for everybody and there's nobody left to hate."

Who can benefit?

We now have almost thirty years of scientific research demonstrating that carefully structured cooperative learning strategies are effective. Students learn material as well as, or better than, students in traditional classrooms. The data also show that through cooperative learning the classroom becomes a positive social atmosphere where students learn to like and respect one another and where taunting and bullying are sharply reduced. Students involved in jigsaw tell us that they enjoy school more and show us that they do by attending class more regularly.

It goes without saying that the scientific results are important. But on a personal level, what is perhaps even more gratifying is to witness, firsthand, youngsters actually going through the transformation. Tormentors evolve into supportive helpers and anxious "losers" begin to enjoy learning and feel accepted for who they are.

The jigsaw classroom has shown us the way to encourage children to become more compassionate and empathic toward one another. Accordingly, it stands to reason that this technique could provide a simple, inexpensive, yet ideal solution to the recent epidemic of school shootings that is plaguing the United States.

However, it can be misleading to suggest that jigsaw sessions always go smoothly. There are always problems, but most can be prevented or minimized. And I don't mean to imply that competition, in and of itself, is evil; it isn't. But, at any age, a general atmosphere of exclusion that is ruthless and relentless is unpleasant at best and dangerous at worst.

The poet W. H. Auden wrote, "We must love one another or die." It is a powerful statement, but perhaps too powerful. Ideally, it's best to bring people together in cooperative situations before animosities develop. In my judgment, however, although loving one another is very nice, it isn't essential. What is essential is that we learn to *respect* one another and to feel empathy and compassion for one another—even those who seem very different from us in race, ethnicity, interests, appearance, and so on.

In Austin our goal was to reduce the bigotry, suspicion, and negative racial stereotyping that was rampant among the city's public school students. We didn't try to persuade students with rational or moral arguments, nor did we declare National Brotherhood Week. Such direct strategies have proven notoriously ineffective when it comes to changing deep-seated emotional attitudes of any kind.

Rather, we engaged the scientifically proven mechanism of self-persuasion: we placed students in a situation where the only way they could hope to survive was to work with and appreciate the qualities of others who were previously disliked. Self-interest may not be the prettiest of motives for changing behavior, but it is an opening—and an open door is better than one that is bolted shut.

Elliot Aronson is a distinguished social psychologist and fellow of the American Academy of Arts and Sciences. He has received a variety of national and international awards for his teaching, scientific research, and writing, including the American Psychological Association's highest award in 1999 for a lifetime of scientific contributions. This article is adapted from his new book, Nobody Left to Hate: Teaching Compassion After Columbine (*W. H. Freeman and Company, April 2000).*

From *The Humanist*, May/June 2000, pp. 17-21. © 2000 by The Humanist. Reprinted by permission.

Merits and Perils of Teaching About Other Cultures

BY WALTER A. MCDOUGALL

NOTHING IN my experience sums up the merits and perils of studying other cultures better than an appalling week I spent at Fort Sill in February 1969. Almost all of us recent graduates from artillery school had orders for Vietnam, and so we were subjected to a week of what the army called "In-Country Orientation." A model Vietnamese fortified hamlet had been constructed there on the Oklahoma plains, and our instructor, a butter-bar lieutenant no older than I, insisted that its defenses were impregnable, as if none of us had ever heard the frequent news reports of villages overrun. We were also told what to do in case of an ambush: which is not to get pinned down, but charge right into the enemy's guns. And we learned all about the poisonous serpents and insects we could expect to encounter. In sum, far from boosting our morale and making us gung-ho, the course left us feeling utterly terrified and unprepared. But worst of all was when they herded hundreds of us into an auditorium to hear a lecture on Vietnamese culture and society. The instructor was not a scholarly expert, or a native Vietnamese, or perhaps a Green Beret who knew Vietnamese and had lived with the people. Rather, the teacher was a grizzled drill sergeant who paraphrased a manual, stumbling over his words. "Awright, you mens, listen up! You will now git orientated into Vit-mese society. Da mostly thing y'all gots to know is dat Vit-nam is a Confusion society. Dat means that ever'body is in a kind of high-arky: like the chillun obey deir parents, and the womens obey deir mens, and ever'body obeys the guv-ment. It's sorta like da army chain o' command."

I must have stopped listening, because that is all I remember. But looking back, I can imagine that orientation as a metaphor of the whole U.S. enterprise in Southeast Asia. As our current fiasco in the Balkans demonstrates anew, Americans make a habit of declaring a war, sending over massive firepower, then expressing amazement when the locals do not bend at once to our will. Only then do we finally decide that it might be a good idea to learn something about the history and culture of the people we are trying to bludgeon, help, and change. Not that a common soldier needs an advanced degree in multicultural studies, but it would help if our policymakers took time to study the world over which they profess to exercise a benevolent hegemony.

The value of studying other cultures is not something we Americans, or Westerners in general, discovered only recently, as a consequence of having our consciousness raised by the multiculturalists. Medieval Christians were fascinated by their Muslim adversaries. The Age of Exploration inspired Europeans to collect information about the strange lands they discovered, think of themselves as one civilization among many, and ask what caused the differences, as well as similarities, among cultures. The Enlightenment systematized the study of non-Western peoples, giving birth eventually to world history (Voltaire), encyclopedias (Diderot), and comparative politics (Montesquieu). In the 19th century, archaeology, cultural anthropology, comparative religion, and a new burst of European imperialism enriched the study of other civilizations, however much solipsistic Westerners took for granted the superiority of their own ways and assumed that all other peoples must inevitably follow in their path. As Walt Whitman wrote,

> One thought ever at the fore
> That in the Divine Ship, breasting time and space
> All peoples of the globe together sail,
>   sail the same voyage
> Are bound to the same destination.

Today's radical multiculturalists accordingly disparage what they call Europe's "Enlightenment Project" as a campaign to explore, subdue, and study the whole world for the purpose of controlling it, exploiting it, and ultimately making it an extension of Western civilization. That is highly tendentious, but does have a measure of truth. At Amherst College in 1964, all of us freshmen were obliged to take History 1, a course that developed themes in world history rather than Western Civ, and as such was very progressive. But the themes chosen were invariably Western themes projected onto the history of other civilizations. One early block of material dealt with the conquest of Mexico by Cortes. To be sure, we were taught about pre-Columbian cultures, but whereas I remember a good deal about the Spanish side of this culture clash, literally all I remember about the Aztec side was their belief that a hummingbird on the left was an omen of good luck—or was it bad luck? Anyway, "hummingbird-on-the-left" became a stock laugh line for Amherst students.

Only multicultural history can teach students the ways all human beings are alike.

A later instruction block compared the Mexican, Chinese, and Young Turk revolutions of the early 20th century, a truly interesting exercise. But the theme uniting them was "paths to modernization," so it was not the essence of historic Mexican, Chinese, or Islamic culture that was at issue, but rather the struggles of those civilizations to come to grips with their backwardness and adopt Western ways. Indeed, I do not think I ever studied other cultures on their own terms—independent of Western intrusions—until my graduate years at Chicago, when I read the books of William H. McNeill, beginning with *The Rise of the West: A History of the Human Community*. To be sure, Amherst and Chicago had many professors who specialized in other cultures and offered courses on them. But those of us in mainstream fields such as European and American history were not exposed to true multicultural education in the survey courses of high school and college.

McNeill was a tireless advocate for the study of world history and other cultures long before it became fashionable. But alas, no sooner did his campaign for world history, as opposed to Western Civ surveys, begin to gain ground than the whole movement was captured by the ideological multiculturalists, Afrocentrists, ethnic lobbies, and victim groups who substituted curricula that depicted Western Civ as a story of progress for curricula that damned Western Civ as a story of plunder, rapine, imperialism, exploitation, and slavery. In other words, the focus was *still* on the West, with other cultures appearing mostly as virginal victims.

Another expression of the multicultural trend is less subjective, but anodyne, and that is the "non-Western" requirement that so many college majors, including the International Relations program I direct, impose on their students. We feel we must make a bow toward multiculturalism, so we just insist that students take one or two courses that are non-Western in focus. The implicit purpose would seem to be to sensitize students to other cultural traditions and alert them to the astonishing fact that there is a whole world out there beyond Great Neck, Long Island, and Newport Beach, California. (I recently asked an I.R. major if he had any experience traveling abroad. He proudly said yes, he had been to Cancun.) But what good does one course on sub-Saharan Africa or Ming China really achieve? It is not enough to make one really conversant in African or Chinese history, religion, and society, and it certainly tells one nothing about the variety of human cultures. Ultimately, instead of acquiring new categories to use in thinking about human nature and history, the student merely receives a smattering of knowledge that is *hors de categorie:* outside Western norms, and therefore just strange. Rather, it is like the high school athletic program that—in between major sports—schedules two days of lacrosse and handball just to let students know that those games exist.

Should we teach our students about other cultures? Absolutely! But do we succeed? I think most of us do not. First, because few of us are qualified to teach about Islam, or India, or traditional China or Japan. We may do better than that drill sergeant, but do we risk just conveying new stereotypes to students, rather than getting beyond stereotypes? And how do we integrate non-Western material into existing courses? The recent debate over the National History Standards reveals the difficulty in doing this, even leaving aside all political controversy. The easiest way is to retain the old Western Civ chronology, but to insert flashback sections on other cultures at the moment Europeans first come into contact with them. Needless to say, that is still Eurocentric. Another way is to grant Western Civ merely an equal status, and to study each culture in turn: a month on China, a month on India, a month on Europe, and so forth. But that artificially disconnects civilizations from each other, ignoring perhaps the most powerful theme in McNeill's works, which is the cross-cultural borrowing, challenge, and response mechanism that is so often the engine of historical change.

What is more, the teacher who goes into some depth about other cultures on their own terms, clearly a good thing on the face of it, runs the risk of offending someone's self-esteem and landing in the principal's or dean's office on charges of insensitivity or even racism! But if we are going to teach about other cultures on their own terms, and not just as targets for Western imperialism, then we must stress the bad and ugly as well as the good: the oppression, slavery, and reciprocal racism and brutality among Asian and African peoples themselves. We must teach about the binding of girls' feet in China, the forced suicide of widows in India, the Islamic texts that place women somewhere above goats but below cattle, the genital mutilation of women in Africa. Now, we can try to deflect criticism by drumming into children's heads that they must not make value judgments, especially ones based, after all, on Western traditions: the Bible and the Enlightenment. But to try to be value-free about, for instance, Aztec human sacrifice, slavery in the Islamic world, or the barbaric tortures practiced by the Comanches and Apaches, is to do exactly what we all say must *not* be done with regard to the darker chapters of Western history. Thus, even as we try to explain to students why the Spanish Inquisition was set up, or how the Nazis could come to power in

Germany, we quickly add that whereas we must try to understand the past on its own terms, to understand is not to forgive: *zu verstehen ist nicht zu vergeben*. So we cannot just give all other cultures a "pass" when it comes to their inhumane practices. But to condemn the "bad" in other cultures is by definition to impose a Western standard of good and bad.

Above all, to treat other cultures in isolation, to censor aspects of their history that might damage some student's self-esteem, or to refrain from making any moral judgments at all, is to cheat students of the one thing they need to learn most, and which only multicultural history can teach them: and that is the many ways in which all human beings, all cultures and civilizations, are alike. For no real toleration among peoples can exist unless they are given a reason to imagine themselves and others as "we," and not just as "we" and "they." In what ways are all people alike? They are all *Homo sapiens*, they are all conceived and born the same way, and they all face the certainty of death. They all live on the same planet and need food and shelter. They all wonder about the meaning of life, love, tragedy, and what if anything happens after they die. They have different answers to the eternal questions, and they invent different political and social forms to order their brief and toilsome time on this earth. But at bottom they are all alike. Thus, Chinese are not angels, but neither are they aliens.

I have no solution to the curricular issues, except to insist that all high school students take at least three full years of history—one being world history. Alas, in many states the trend is to cut back, not expand, history requirements. But I did hit upon a technique this semester for handling the "self-esteem" issue, which seemed to work. (At least, I have not as yet been summoned to the office of the Penn ombudsperson.) In my last lecture in the modern history survey, I asked students to recall a question that I had posed in the first lecture: not why people and societies so often do bad things, but rather why on occasion they do good things, why on occasion people have taken risks and made sacrifices in order to improve the lot of others. Evil is banal and universal. What is shocking and in need of explanation in history is the good.

Thus, I granted that European and American civilization has been imperialistic and exploitative. But so has every other civilization in history. What is unique about the West is that it invented *anti*-imperialism. I granted that the West practiced slavery. But so has every other civilization in history. What is unique about the West is that it gave rise to an anti-slavery movement. I granted that the West has waged war on a ferocious scale. But so has every other civilization at one time or another. What is unique about the West is that it tried over and over to devise international systems that might prevent war. I granted that women were in a subordinate status throughout Western history. But so were they in every other civilization. What is unique about the West is that it spawned a movement for female equality. And I granted that the West has known tyranny and indeed totalitarianism of the most brutal sort. But forms of tyranny and even genocide have appeared in all other civilizations. What is unique about the West is that it alone has declared certain human rights to be universal and tried to devise governments that expand, not crush, liberty.

What is needed to ensure that multicultural education can be a glue and not a solvent of American community is dedicated, knowledgeable, and above all honest teaching. All civilizations are worthy of celebration by dint of their being civilizations, that is, extraordinary examples of collective human invention. But all have also been horribly flawed by dint of their being human creations. If Western civilization appears to have done more nasty things in recent centuries, it is not because it is worse than others, but only because it has lately been the most powerful. What is more, the three ways in which people from all the world, while cherishing their diversity, can nevertheless identify themselves as part of a single human community are themselves gifts of Western civilization. Those unifying forces are science and technology, the Enlightenment doctrine of natural law and natural rights, and the astounding Judeo-Christian theology to the effect that all human beings are children of one and the same loving God.

Unfortunately, the radical multiculturalists denounce science and technology as an evil, masculine "discourse" that oppresses the weak, pollutes the environment, and privileges "linear thinking." They attack the "Enlightenment Project" as an ideological cover for Western cultural imperialism. And they hate the Bible for promoting patriarchy and heterosexism. In so doing, they are attempting to destroy the very principles under which toleration of diverse cultures has in fact the best chance of flowering! In so doing, the multiculturalists help to perpetuate the tragedy that Alexander Solzhenitsyn called "A World Split Apart." Asked to deliver the Harvard commencement address in 1978, Solzhenitsyn, a survivor of the Soviet gulag, shocked his audience by proclaiming that the line that divides the world does not run between communism and capitalism, or along the boundaries between nations, races, social classes, or genders. The line that splits the world apart runs straight through the middle of each human heart.

Walter A. McDougall, who won a Pulitzer Prize for The Heavens and the Earth: A Political History of the Space Age, *is Alloy-Ansin Professor of International Relations and History at the University of Pennsylvania, co-director of the Foreign Policy Research Institute's (FPRI) History Academy, and the editor of* Orbis: A Journal of World Affairs.

This article was originally published in the Fall 1999 issue of Orbis and is based on Professor McDougall's address to the FPRI History Institute for secondary school and junior college teachers on the theme, "Multiculturalism in World History," held in Bryn Mawr, Pa., on May 1–2, 1999. For information about future History Institutes for teachers, e-mail: FPRI@FPRI.org

Finding
Real Love

Human beings crave intimacy, to love and be loved.
Why then do people feel isolated in their intimate relationships?
Four researchers and clinicians, Ayala Malach Pines, Shirley Glass,
Lisa Firestone and Joyce Catlett, discuss the alienation that affects
so many people and how to overcome it.

By Cary Barbor

We need to be close to other people as surely as we need food and water. But while it's relatively easy to get ourselves a good meal, it is difficult for many of us to create and maintain intimacy with others, particularly with a romantic partner. There are many variables that affect the quality of our relationships with others; it's difficult to pin it on one thing or another. But in this article, based on a symposium recently held at the annual American Psychological Association convention in Washington, D.C., four mental health professionals discuss their ideas about how we sabotage our intimate relationships—and what we can do to fix them.

---

*The first decision
we make about a
relationship is
the partner we choose.*

Choose to Lose?

Many factors influence the level of intimacy we enjoy in our relationships. The various decisions we make, and our behavior toward one another, are what foster closeness or drive us apart. These decisions are all under our control, although we are influenced by old patterns that we must work to change.

The first decision we make about a relationship is the partner we choose. Whom we fall in love with determines the level of intimacy in our relationships, according to Ayala Malach Pines, Ph.D., who heads the behavioral sciences in management program at Ben-Gurion University in Israel. We often choose partners who remind us of significant people from our childhood—often our parents—and we set out to recreate the patterns of our childhood. Let's look at an example:

Tara met Abe at a party. She was instantly attracted to the tall, lean man with a faraway look in his eyes. Abe, who had been standing alone, was delighted when Tara approached him with her open smile and outstretched hand. She was not only beautiful, but she struck him as warm and nurturing as well. The conversation between them flowed instantly. It felt comfortable and easy. Eventually, they fell in love, and after a year, they were married.

At first things were wonderful. They had the kind of closeness Tara had always dreamed about with her father. Though she was sure he loved her, she never felt she had her father completely to herself. Even when he held her on his lap, he had a faraway look. But with Abe things were different. He was there with her completely.

The intimacy between them also felt terrific to Abe. It was not the kind of suffocating closeness he always dreaded—the kind of intrusive closeness he experienced as a child with his mother, who used to enter his room uninvited and arrange his personal belongings with no regard to his privacy. But Tara was different. She did not intrude.

The View

People have conflicting views and beliefs about relationships. Here are a few common ones:

1. Relationships are important and central in affecting a person's life.

2. Relationships are generally unstable. Young people marrying for the first time face a 40% to 50% chance of divorce.

3. There is a good deal of dishonesty in relationships. People are duplicitous in many ways: sexually, emotionally, etc.

4. Relationships are often based on emotional hunger and desperation. People mistake longing and desperation for love.

5. Few long-term relationships are based on high-level choices. Often people "take what they can get."

6. Choices can be made for negative as well as positive reasons. For example, people have a tendency to select mates who are similar to a parent, which can be good or bad.

7. People confuse sex with love. During the early phase of a relationship, attraction and pleasure in sex are often mistaken for love.

8. People feel they are failures unless they succeed in finding mates.

(Source: *Fear of Intimacy*, 1999)

Many factors influence the level of intimacy we enjoy in our relationships. The various decisions we make, and our behavior toward one another, are what foster closeness or drive us apart.

But occasionally, Abe would come home from work tired and annoyed. All he wanted was a drink and to sit with the paper until he could calm down and relax. Seeing him that way, Tara would become concerned. "What is going on?" she would ask anxiously. "Nothing," he would answer. Sure that there was something very wrong, and assuming that it must be something about her or their marriage, Tara would insist that he tell her. She reminded him of his mother, and he responded the way he did with his mother: by withdrawing. To Tara, this felt similar to the way her father behaved. She responded in the same way she did when her father withdrew: by clinging. The struggle between them continued and became more and more intense over time, with Tara demanding more intimacy and Abe demanding more space.

Recreating the Family

Like Abe and Tara, people choose partners who help them recreate their childhood struggles. Tara fell in love with a man with "a faraway look in his eyes," and subsequently had to struggle for greater intimacy. Abe fell in love with a woman who was "warm and nurturing," then spent a lot of energy struggling for more space.

Tara's unresolved intimacy issues complement Abe's. For example, one partner (often the woman) will fight to break down defenses and create more intimacy while the other (often the man) will withdraw and create distance. So the "dance of intimacy" follows: If the woman gets too close, the man pulls back. If he moves too far away, she pursues, and so on.

To achieve greater intimacy, the partners must overcome the anxiety that compels them to take their respective parts in that dance. In the example, Tara needs to control her abandonment anxiety and not pursue Abe when he withdraws, and Abe needs to control his engulfment anxiety when Tara pursues him and not withdraw. Working to overcome these anxieties is an opportunity to resolve childhood issues and can be a major healing experience for both partners.

Infidelity: The Road Back

If a couple can't overcome their anxieties and achieve a balance, however, fear and an inability to achieve intimacy will linger. This can create a vulnerability to affairs, says Shirley P. Glass, Ph.D., a clinical psychologist in private practice in Baltimore. Either partner may feel burned out from trying to get his or her emotional intimacy needs met in the relationship. A pursuing woman, who wonders if her needs will ever be met, may withdraw out of hopelessness. Yet her partner may think that the relationship has improved because the complaining has stopped. Meanwhile, she could be supplementing her unmet intimacy needs through an extramarital relationship that could ultimately lead to separation or divorce.

Once an affair has occurred, it only serves to erode intimacy further. Intimacy requires honesty, openness and self-disclosure. The deception that accompanies an affair makes this impossible. In addition, if the affair partner becomes the confidante for problems in the marriage, it can be threatening to the marriage because it creates a bond of friendship between the affair partners that goes beyond sexuality.

For trust to be rebuilt and intimacy reestablished, the walls of deception created by the affair need to be broken down. The spouse needs to be back on the "inside" of the partnership and the extramarital partner on the "outside." The involved spouse must stop all personal exchanges with the affair partner and disclose to the marital partner any unavoidable encounters with the affair partner, without prompting. Unfaithful partners can only regain credibility by being completely honest. People report that they recover from their partner having a sexual relationship with another person before they recover from being deceived.

But if both partners can be totally honest, and if communication in the partnership improves, there is a good chance that the marriage can survive the infidelity and the relationship can become strong again.

Overcoming Fear of Intimacy

It is our fear of intimacy that inspires these ingenious ways of avoiding it. This raises the question: How can we overcome our fear of intimacy? We can start by breaking down our defenses.

We all bring defenses to relationships, and, unfortunately, it is often these defenses that spell trouble. We develop our defenses and negative beliefs in childhood. They are what we utilized to protect ourselves against emotional pain and, later, against anxiety about death.

A core defense that often leads to the downfall of a partnership is "the fantasy bond," according to Lisa Firestone, Ph.D., adjunct faculty at the University of California Santa Barbara Graduate School of

Education, and Joyce Catlett, M.A., co-author of *Fear of Intimacy*, published recently by the American Psychological Association. The fantasy bond is an illusion of a connection to another person. It develops first with the mother or primary parent figure, and people often try to recreate it in their adult relationships.

People use various techniques to reestablish this primary relationship. They may first select a partner who fits their model, someone they can relate to in the way they related to their parent or other family member. They can distort their partner and perceive them as being more like this significant person than they are. Third, if all else fails, they tend to provoke their partner into the behavior they seek. All of these mechanisms curtail their ability to relate and make it less likely that people will be successful in achieving true intimacy in their relationships.

A secondary defense that helps preserve the fantasy bond is, according to Firestone and Catlett, "the voice." All people tend to carry on some form of internal dialogue within themselves as though another person were talking to them: reprimanding them, denouncing them, divulging negative information about others, and so on.

In intimate relationships, both individuals may be listening to the dictates of their respective voices. Unfortunately, these only create more defensiveness. Both partners may use rationalizations promoted by "the voice" to ward off loving responses from the other and justify their distancing behavior.

Speak Up, Therapeutically

A technique developed by Robert Firestone, Ph.D., and used to reverse this process and allow greater intimacy is voice therapy. Voice therapy brings these internalized negative thoughts to consciousness. The goal of voice therapy with couples is to help each individual identify the "voice attacks" that are creating conflict and distance in the relationship. In identifying specific self-criticisms as well as judgmental, hostile thoughts about the other, each partner is able to relate more openly.

Here is an example of someone using voice therapy. Sheryl is in a four-year relationship and was starting to have problems. She and her partner Mark came to therapy for help, and they progressed through these four steps of voice therapy over the course of treatment. Following is a glimpse into Sheryl's process.

Formulate the problem each individual perceives is limiting his or her satisfaction within the relationship.

Sheryl: The feeling I have is that I've always liked Mark, but lately I feel like I can't stand it when he's nice to me. I feel like I have a mean streak.

Therapist: In response to his liking you.

Sheryl: Yes.

Verbalize self-critical thoughts and negative perceptions of the other in the form of the voice, and let go of the feelings associated with them.

Therapist: What are you telling yourself about the relationship?

Sheryl: It's like, 'Don't show him anything, don't show him you like him.' I tell myself, 'Just don't show it, you're such a sucker if you show it.' When he's vulnerable I just want to squash him. And it's for no reason except for he's being sweet.

Develop insight into the origins of the voice and make connections between past experience and present conflicts.

Sheryl: I've seen myself be like my mother millions of times. In previous relationships I've acted so much like her, I didn't even know it. I saw her as being a really critical person, she was very critical of my father. And she would be mean to him. Sometimes I act like that myself.

Alter behaviors and communications in a direction that counteracts the dictates of the voice.

Therapist: So the hope is for you to hang in there and to tolerate the anxiety of giving up these defenses and the fantasized connection you have with your mother. If you do sweat it out then you'll be able to have more in your life. It takes a lot of courage to go through that process but it's really worth it.

Sheryl: I feel like it would make me sad, too, because I would feel a lot. When I have that other point of view, I feel big and mean. And when I just let things be, and don't act in ways to push Mark away, I feel like a soft, sweet person.

After trying voice therapy, Sheryl reported that she felt closer to Mark. She noticed a shift in her feelings, both in accepting his caring about her and genuinely caring about him.

In therapy sessions, both partners reveal negative thoughts and attitudes toward himself or herself and each other. In this way, they share each other's individual psychotherapy. In tracing back the source of their self-attacks and cynical views to early family interactions, they gain perspective on each other's problems and feel more compassion for their mates as well as

The Ideal and Not So Ideal

Interactions in an ideal and healthy relationship:

1. Nondefensiveness and openness
2. Honesty and integrity
3. Respect for the other's boundaries, priorities and goals, separate from self
4. Physical affection and responsive sexuality
5. Understanding—lack of distortion of the other
6. Noncontrolling, nonmanipulative and nonthreatening behavior

(Source: *Fear of Intimacy*, 1999)

Interactions in an unhealthy relationship:

1. Angry and negative reactions to feedback; being closed to new experiences
2. Deception and duplicity
3. Overstepping boundaries Other seen only in relation to self
4. Lack of affection, inadequate or impersonal, routine sexuality
5. Misunderstanding—distortion of the other
6. Manipulations of dominance and submission

(Source: *Fear of Intimacy*, 1999: The Glendon Association)

themselves. Changing old patterns often brings up anxiety, so part of the treatment is to learn to tolerate the anxiety and work through it, so the partners can maintain the behavioral changes and ultimately increase intimacy.

Homework

For couples who are not in therapy, there are many ways to change destructive patterns that prevent intimacy. Partners could become aware of the times when they attack themselves or think negatively about their partner. They could record their self-critical thoughts and hostile attitudes in a journal; they could reveal the contents of their destructive thoughts to a trusted friend or to their mate. They could assess how close to reality these thoughts are (usually not very). Each could set goals for what he or she wants out of the relationship and then keep track of how closely his or her actions match these goals.

Another good idea for couples is to make an active effort to move away from isolated couple interaction and toward an extended circle of family and friends. This often affords a better perspective and provides a potential background for understanding and breaking destructive, habitual patterns of relating. Partners need to admit to themselves and their partner if they have become distant, and that their actions are no longer loving or respectful. By reawakening their feeling for one another, they can achieve a higher level of intimacy.

We always have choices to make about intimacy—from the partners we choose to the way we interact with them each day. Recognizing our patterns, tolerating our anxieties, and working together on our relationships will help us overcome our fear of intimacy. Learning how best to communicate with each other and treat one another will help us enjoy loving, lasting relationships.

READ MORE ABOUT IT

Fear of Intimacy, Robert Firestone and Joyce Catlett (American Psychological Association Books, 1999)

The Trauma of Infidelity: Research and Treatment, Shirley Glass (Norton Professional Books, 2001)

Falling in Love: Why We Choose the Lovers We Choose, Ayala Malach Pines (Routledge, 1999)

Combating Destructive Thought Processes: Voice Therapy and Separation Theory, Robert Firestone (Sage Publications, 1997)

Romantic Jealousy: Causes, Symptoms and Cures, Ayala Malach Pines (Routlege, 1998)

Cary Barbor is a freelance writer based in New York. Her work has appeared on CBS Healthwatch *and in* Walking *and* Women's Sports and Fitness, *among other publications.*

UNIT 10
Psychological Disorders

Unit Selections

Key Points to Consider

- Do you believe everyone has the potential for developing a mental disorder? Just how widespread is mental disorder in the United States? What circumstances lead an individual to mental illness? In general, what can be done to reduce the number of cases of mental disorder or to promote better mental health in the United States?

- Do you think that mental disorders are biologically or psychologically induced? If we discover that most mental disorders are caused by something physiological, do you think mental disorders will remain the purview of psychology? Why?

- If mental disorders are biological, do you think they might be "contagious" (caused by disease and passed from person to person)? Do you think that mental disorders are brain disorders, or do you think this is a hoax perpetrated by so-called experts on those diagnosed with mental illness? How do you think treatments might differ depending on the origin of a mental disturbance?

- What is depression? How widespread are depressive episodes? What causes depression? How are ordinary episodes of depression different from clinical depression? Why are the elderly of interest to specialists in the field of depression? What biological causes are implicated in depression? Are there psychological causes for depression? What are some promising treatments for this disorder?

- What is a phobia? What are some common phobias? Why are some individuals phobic and others not? Are there any treatments for phobias?

 **Links: www.dushkin.com/online/**
These sites are annotated in the World Wide Web pages.

Anxiety Disorders
http://www.adaa.org/aboutanxietydisorders/
Ask NOAH About: Mental Health
http://www.noah-health.org/english//illness/mentalhealth/mental.html
Mental Health Net Disorders and Treatments
http://www.mentalhelp.net/dxtx.htm
Mental Health Net: Eating Disorder Resources
http://www.mentalhelp.net/guide/eating.htm
National Women's Health Resource Center (NWHRC)
http://www.healthywomen.org
SAVE: Suicide Awareness/Voices of Education
http://www.save.org

Jay and Harry were two brothers who owned a service station. They were the middle children of four. The other two children were sisters, the oldest of whom had married and moved out of the family home. The service station was once owned by their father who had retired and turned it over to them.

Harry and Jay had a good working relationship. Harry was the "up-front" man. Taking customer orders, accepting payments, and working with parts distributors, Harry was the individual who dealt most directly with the customers and others. Jay worked behind the scenes. While Harry made the mechanical diagnoses, Jay was the one who did the corrective work. Some of his friends thought Jay was a mechanical genius.

Preferring to spend time by himself, Jay had always been a little odd and a bit of a loner. His emotions had been more inappropriate and intense than other people's emotional states. Harry was the stalwart in the family. He was the acknowledged leader and decision-maker when it came to family finances.

One day Jay did not show up for work on time. When he did, he was dressed in the most garish outfit and was laughing hysterically and talking to himself. Harry at first suspected that his brother had taken some illegal drugs. However, Jay's condition persisted. Out of concern, his family took him to their physician, who immediately sent Jay and his family to a psychiatrist. The diagnosis? Schizophrenia. Jay's uncle had also been schizophrenic. The family grimly left the psychiatrist's office. After several other appointments with the psychiatrist, they would travel to the local pharmacy to fill a prescription for antipsychotic medications that Jay would probably take for the rest of his life.

What caused Jay's drastic and rather sudden change in mental health? Was Jay destined to be schizophrenic because of his family genes? Did competitiveness with his brother and the feeling that he was a less revered family member than Harry cause Jay's descent into mental disorder? How can psychiatrists and clinical psychologists make accurate diagnoses? Once a diagnosis of mental disorder is made, can the individual ever completely recover?

These and other questions are the emphasis in this unit. Mental disorder has fascinated and, on the other hand, terrified us for centuries. At various times in our history, those who suffered from these disorders were persecuted as witches, tortured to drive out possessing spirits, punished as sinners, jailed as a danger to society, confined to insane asylums, or at best hospitalized for simply being too ill to care for themselves.

Today, psychologists propose that the view of mental disorders as "illnesses" has outlived its usefulness. We should think of mental disorders as either biochemical disturbances or disorders of learning in which the person develops a maladaptive pattern of behavior that is then maintained by an inappropriate environment. At the same time, we need to recognize that these reactions to stressors in the environment or to the inappropriate learning situations may be genetically preordained; some people may more easily develop the disorders than others. Serious disorders are serious problems and not just for the individual who is the patient or client. The impact of mental disorders on the family (just as for Jay's family) and friends deserves our full attention, too. Diagnosis, treatment, and the implications of the disorders are covered in some of the articles in this section. The

next unit will explore further the concept of treatment of mental disorders.

The first two articles in this unit offer a general introduction to the concept of mental disorder. In the first, "Mental Health Gets Noticed," David Satcher reveals his agenda for better mental health care in the United States. Mental disorder, he concludes, is more widespread than previously thought. Only an active policy of assisting those who need help can change the status of those with mental disorders in this country.

In the next article, a renowned critic of the mental health field, Thomas Szasz, proposes that mental disorders are not merely brain disorders or diseases. He says that to advance this notion dilutes attempts to argue that the mental health care system does a disservice to its clients. Only when we fully understand mental disorders can we assist those who have them. Mental disorders, in fact, may well be a myth created by the health care system.

We turn next to some specific problems of mental health. Depression is one of the common forms of mental disorder. Depression in its severe form can sometimes lead to suicide. Psychologists recently have been interested in the biochemical mechanisms underlying severe depression. In "Up From Depression," the author looks at the causes, symptoms, and treatments for depression. Special attention is paid to the depressed elderly, a group not well studied in psychology.

The final article in this series, "Fear Not!" reviews information about a peculiar disorder that plagues some Americans. In phobic disorders, individuals are overwhelmed by fear of ordinary objects or places. The article describes the disorder as well as biological and psychological treatments for it.

MENTAL HEALTH GETS NOTICED

The First-Ever Surgeon General's Report on Mental Health

BY DAVID SATCHER, M.D., PH.D., UNITED STATES SURGEON GENERAL

I am pleased to issue the first-ever Surgeon General's Report on Mental Health. In doing so, I am alerting the American people that mental illness is a critical public health problem that must be addressed immediately. As a society, we assign a high priority to disease prevention and health promotion; so, too, must we ensure that mental health and the prevention of mental disorders share that priority.

Mental illness is the second leading cause of disability in major market economies such as the United States, with mental disorders collectively accounting for more than 15% of all disabilities. Mental disorders—depression, schizophrenia, eating disorders, depressive (bipolar) illness, anxiety disorders, attention deficit hyperactivity disorder and Alzheimer's disease, to name a few—are as disabling and serious as cancer and heart disease in terms of premature death and lost productivity.

Few Americans are untouched by mental illness, whether it occurs within one's family or among neighbors, co-workers or members of the community. In fact, in any one year, one in five Americans—including children, adolescents, adults and the elderly—experience a mental disorder. Unfortunately, over half of those with severe mental illness do not seek treatment. This is mostly due to some very real barriers to access, foremost among them the stigma that people attach to mental illness and the lack of parity between insurance coverage for mental health services and other health care services.

Over the past 25 years, there has been a scientific revolution in the fields of mental health and mental illness that has helped remove the stigma. The brain has emerged as the central focus for studies of mental health and mental illness, with emphasis on the activities that underlie our abilities to feel, learn, remember and, when brain activity goes awry, experience mental health problems or a mental illness. We now know that not only do the workings of the brain affect behavior, emotions and memory, but that experience, emotion and behavior also affect the workings of the brain

As information about the brain accumulates, the challenge then becomes to apply this new knowledge to clinical practice.

Today, mental disorders can be correctly diagnosed and, for the most part, treated with medications or short-term

GREG GIANNINI

I'd describe myself as a regular person.... Most of the time I like taking walks around my house. Before I was living in a group home out in the country and there weren't that many stores or streets to walk on. I like walking to 7-Eleven and Mr. D's fast food.

ROSE CLARK

Sometimes I wake up so sick, but then I go to work and feel better. Being with animals makes me feel 100% better. Does that sound funny?

I love my boss. He's crazy. When he does surgery he dances, does the jitterbug. Sometimes I go into surgery with him to make sure all the animals are lying down straight and not awake. Mostly my responsibilities are taking care of the cages and general cleaning.

I've been with this program for four years. Since then I've gone back to school and gotten a job. I live in my own apartment, got two cats, and have a checking and savings account.

psychotherapy, or with a combination of approaches. The single most explicit recommendation I make in my report is to seek help if you have a mental health problem or think you have symptoms of a mental disorder. It is my firm conviction that mental health is indispensable to personal well-being and balanced living. Overall quality of life is tremendously improved when a mental disorder is diagnosed early and treated appropriately.

My report presents an in-depth look at mental health services in the U.S. and at the scientific research that supports treatment interventions for people with mental disorders. Summarized briefly below, it attempts to describe trends in the mental health field; explore mental health across the human life span; examine the organization and financing of mental health services; and recommend courses of action to further improve the quality and availability of mental health services for all Americans. The report's conclusions are based on a review of more than 3,000 research articles and other materials, including first person accounts from people who have experienced mental disorders.

A Vision for the Future

I cannot emphasize enough the principal recommendation of my report: Seek help if you think you have a mental health problem or symptoms of a mental disorder. But because stigma and substantial gaps in the accessibility to state-of-the-art mental health services keep many from seeking help, I offer the nation the following additional recommendations, which are intended to overcome some of these barriers:

- **Continue to Build the Science Base:** As scientific progress propels us into the next century, there should be a special effort to address pronounced gaps in current knowledge, including the urgent need for research relating to mental health promotion and illness prevention.
- **Overcome Stigma:** An emerging consumer and family movement has, through vigorous advocacy, sought to overcome stigma and prevent discrimination against people with mental illness. Powerful and pervasive, stigma prevents people from acknowledging their mental health problems and disclosing them to others. To improve access

to care, stigma must no longer be tolerated. Research and more effective treatments will help move this country toward care and support of the ill—and away from blame and stigma.

- **Improve Public Awareness of Effective Treatments:** Mental health treatments have improved by leaps and bounds over the past 25 years, but those treatments do no good unless people are aware they exist and seek them out. There are effective treatments for virtually every mental disorder. For more information on how to take advantage of them, call (877) 9MHEALTH.
- **Ensure the Supply of Mental Health Services and Providers:** Currently, there is a shortage of mental health professionals serving children and adolescents, elderly people with serious mental disorders and those who suffer from mental illness-related substance abuse. There is also a shortage of specialists with expertise in cognitive behavioral therapy and interpersonal therapy—two forms of psychotherapy that have proven effective for many types of mental health problems.
- **Ensure Delivery of State-of-the-Art Treatments:** A wide variety of effective, community-based services—carefully refined through years of research—exist for even the most severe mental illnesses, but they are not yet widely available in community settings. We need to ensure that mental health services are as universally accessible as other health services in the continuously changing health care delivery system. We must speed the transfer of new information from the research setting into the service delivery setting.
- **Tailor Treatment to Individuals, Acknowledging Age, Gender, Race and Culture:** To be optimally effective, diagnosis and treatment of mental illness must be attentive to these factors. Patients often prefer to be treated by mental health professionals who are of the same racial and ethnic background, a fact that underscores the need to train more minorities in the mental health professions.
- **Facilitate Entry into Treatment:** Access to mental health services

can be improved immediately if we enhance the abilities of primary care providers, public schools, the child welfare system and others to help people with mental health problems seek treatment. In addition, ensuring ready access to appropriate services for people with severe mental disorders promises to significantly reduce the need for involuntary care, which is sometimes required in order to prevent behavior that could be harmful to oneself or others.

- **Reduce Financial Barriers to Treatment:** Equality or parity between mental health coverage and other health coverage is an affordable and effective way to decrease the number of ill people who are not receiving proper treatment.

TONY RIVERA

When I first came to the Pastimes Cafe & Antiques I told them that it reminds me of the coffee shops in Baltimore and Maryland. They laughed and we've been friends for two years. They know my name when I walk in. I used to know all their names but I only come every few weeks now and I can't remember. They make me feel comfortable, like I'm not bothering anybody.

KATHY MOLYNEAUX

I didn't know I was depressed until after college. I just thought everyone felt the same way I did. I had problems sleeping, feeling down, overwhelmed, worried and not happy. My graduation from DePaul University in 1983 was a good day. After college, I worked successfully as a nurse for 13 years. I felt like I could relate to the patients because I had been there myself.

The U.S. system is extremely complex; it is a hybrid system that serves many people well, but often seems fragmented and inaccessible to those with the most extensive problems and fewest financial resources. Critical gaps exist between those who need services and those who receive them; only about 40% of those with severe disorders use any services at all.

Although research shows little direct evidence of problems with quality in mental health service programs, there are signs that programs could be better implemented, especially ones that serve children and people with serious impairment. While an array of quality monitoring and improvement methods have been developed, incentives to improve conditions lag behind incentives to reduce costs.

These inequities in insurance coverage for mental and physical health care have prompted 27 states to adopt legislation requiring parity, and compelled President Clinton to order the Federal Employees Health Benefits Program to provide parity for federal employees by the year 2001. Some localized attempts at creating parity so far have resulted in better mental health service access at negligible cost increases for managed care organizations.

Issues relating to mental health and mental illness have been overlooked or ignored in this country too often and for too long. While we cannot change the past, I am convinced that we can shape a better future.

SHERYL CAUDLE

My family at first didn't understand why I was so depressed. My dad kept asking me why couldn't I be happy?... I never thought I'd be able to work again because of my illness. I've had to quit other jobs in the past, but I don't want to quit cleaning the Roxy [a local movie theater]; I want to have an apartment someday and a job in the community. Both of these things would be special to me because it would mean I've come a long way.

PATTI REID

I used to live in a house with my family, but I have a rare disorder that makes me think about the past. In 1992, I got this disorder and I couldn't drive my car anymore. I miss driving the most. My two big battles are smiling and taking my medications. Both of these are very hard.

David Satcher, M.D., Ph.D., is the 16th surgeon general of the United States. He is also Assistant Secretary for Health, advising the Secretary on public health matters and directing the Office of Public Health and Science.

PSYCHOLOGY

Mental Disorders Are Not Diseases

Psychiatrists and their allies have succeeded in persuading the scientific community, courts, media, and general public that mental illnesses are phenomena independent of human motivation or will.

BY THOMAS SZASZ, M.D.

THE CORE CONCEPT of mental illness—to which the vast majority of psychiatrists and the public adhere—is that diseases of the mind are diseases of the brain. The equation of the mind with the brain and of mental disease with brain disease, supported by the authority of a large body of neuroscience literature, is used to render rational the drug treatment of mental illness and justify the demand for parity in insurance coverage for medical and mental disorders.

Reflecting the influence of these ideas, on Sept. 26, 1997, Pres. Clinton signed the Mental Health Parity Act of 1996, which took effect on Jan. 1, 1998. "This landmark law," according to the National Alliance for the Mentally Ill, "begins the process of ending the long-held practice of providing less insurance coverage for mental illnesses, or brain disorders, than is provided for equally serious physical disorders." Contrary to these views, I maintain that the mind is not the brain, that mental functions are not reducible to brain functions, and that mental diseases are not brain diseases—indeed, that mental diseases are not diseases at all.

When I assert the latter, I do not imply that distressing personal experiences and deviant behaviors do not exist. Anxiety, depression, and conflict do exist—in fact, are intrinsic to the human condition—but they are not diseases in the pathological sense.

According to the *Oxford English Dictionary*, disease is "a condition of the body, or of some part or organ of the body, in which its functions are disturbed or deranged; a morbid physical condition." Diagnosis, in turn, is "the determination of the nature of a diseased condition... also, the opinion (formally stated) resulting from such investigation."

The core medical concept of disease is a bodily abnormality. Literally, the term "disease" denotes a demonstrable lesion of cells, tissues, or organs. Metaphorically, it may be used to denote any kind of malfunctioning of individuals, groups, economies, etc. (substance abuse, violence, unemployment, *et al.*).

The psychiatric concept of disease rests on a radical alteration of the medical definition. The mind is not a material object; hence, it can be diseased only in a metaphorical sense. In his classic, *Lectures on Clinical Psychiatry*, Emil Kraepelin—the founder of modern psychiatry—wrote: "The subject of the following course of lectures will be the Science of Psychiatry, which, as its name implies, is that of the treatment of mental disease. It is true that, in the strictest terms, we cannot speak of the mind as becoming diseased."

If we accept the idea that the diagnoses of mental illnesses refer to real diseases, we are compelled to accept them as diagnoses on a par with those of bodily diseases, albeit the criterion for what counts as a mental disease is completely different from what counts as a bodily disease. For instance, in *Psychiatric Diagnosis*, Donald Goodwin and Samuel B. Guze, two of the most respected psychiatrists in the U.S., state: "When the term 'disease' is used, this is what is meant: A disease is a cluster of symptoms and/or signs with a more or less predictable course. Symptoms are what patients tell you; signs are what you see. The cluster may be associated with physical abnormality or may not. The essential point is that it results in consultation with a physician." According to these authorities, disease is not an observable phenomenon, but a social relationship.

In contrast to Goodwin and Guze's assertion that mental illness need not be associated with physical abnormality, Allen Frances, the chief architect of the American Psychiatric Association's *Diagnostic and Statistical Manual, DSM-IV*, states: "The special features of *DSM-IV* are...

elimination of the term 'organic mental disorder' because it incorrectly implied that other psychiatric disorders did not have a biological contribution."

Linguistic considerations help to illuminate the differences between bodily and mental disease, as well as between disease and diagnosis. We do not attribute motives to a person for having leukemia, do not say that a person has reasons for having glaucoma, and would be uttering nonsense if we asserted that diabetes has caused a person to shoot the President. However, we can and do say all of these things about a person with a mental illness. One of the most important philosophical-political features of the concept of mental illness is that, at one fell swoop, it removes motivation from action, adds it to illness, and thus destroys the very possibility of separating disease from non-disease and disease from diagnosis.

Diseases are physico-chemical phenomena or processes—for example, the abnormal metabolism of glucose (diabetes). Mental diseases are patterns of personal conduct, unwanted by the self or others. Psychopathology is diagnosed by finding behavioral, not physical, abnormalities in bodies. Disease qua psychopathology cannot be asymptomatic. Changing the official classification of mental diseases can transform non-disease into psychopathology and psychopathology into non-disease (*i.e.*, smoking from a behavioral habit into "nicotine dependence"). In short, medical diseases are *discovered* and then given a name, such as acquired immune deficiency syndrome (AIDS). Mental diseases are *invented* and then given a name, such as attention deficit disorder.

Nowadays, names routinely are given not only to somatic pathology (real or bodily diseases), but to behavioral pathology (psychopathology or mental diseases). Indeed, if we propose to treat misbehavior as a disease instead of a matter of law or social policy, we name it accordingly (for instance, "substance abuse"). Not surprisingly, we diagnose mental illnesses by finding abnormalities (unwanted behaviors) in persons, not abnormalities (lesions) in bodies. That is why forensic psychiatrists "interview" criminals called "patients" (who often do not regard themselves as patients), whereas forensic pathologists examine body fluids. In the case of bodily illness, the clinical diagnosis is a hypothesis, typically confirmed or disconfirmed through an autopsy. It is not possible to die of a mental illness or to find evidence of it in organs, tissues, cells, or body fluids during an autopsy.

To summarize, anthrax is a disease that is biologically constructed and can, and does, kill its host. Attention deficit disorder, on the other hand, is socially constructed and cannot kill the patient.

If we fail or refuse to distinguish between literal and metaphorical diseases, we confuse and deceive ourselves and others not only about the differences between treatments influencing the body and those influencing the person, but about the differences between medical treatments (such as performing an appendectomy for acute appendicitis) and medical interventions (performing an abortion terminating a healthy, but unwanted pregnancy). To be sure, there is something to be gained by not distinguishing between diseases and diagnoses, complaints and lesions, and/or treatments and interventions. It permits creation of a therapeutic utopia—a medical fairyland with "miracle cures" not only for diseases, but for non-diseases as well.

Mental diseases are behaviors

No one believes that love sickness is a disease, but nearly everyone believes that mental sickness is, and virtually no one realizes that, if this were true, it would prove the nonexistence of mental illness. If mental illnesses are brain diseases (like Parkinsonism), then they are diseases of the body, not the mind. A screwdriver may be a drink or a tool, but it would be foolish to do research in the hope of discovering that some cases of orange juice and vodka are hitherto unrecognized instances of carpenters' implements.

The contemporary American mind-set is so thoroughly psychiatrized that it is quite useless to demonstrate the logical-linguistic misconceptions inherent in the claim that "mental illness is like any other illness." Unless people are prepared to defy the combined forces of the state, science, medicine, law, and popular opinion, they must believe—or at least pretend to believe—that mental illnesses are brain diseases; scientists have identified the somatic lesions that cause such illnesses; and psychiatrists possess effective treatments for them. Conventional wisdom as well as political correctness preclude entertaining the possibility that mental illness, like spring fever, is a metaphor.

In short, psychiatrists and their allies have succeeded in persuading the scientific community, courts, media, and general public that the conditions they call mental disorders are diseases—that is, phenomena independent of human motivation or will. Because there is no empirical evidence to back this claim (indeed, there can be none), the psychiatric profession relies on supporting it with periodically revised versions of its pseudo-scientific bible, the *American Psychiatric Association's Diagnostic and Statistical Manual of Mental Disorders*.

The official view is that these manuals list the various "mental disorders" that afflict "patients." My view is that they are rosters of officially accredited psychiatric diagnoses, constructed by task forces appointed by officers of the American Psychiatric Association. Psychiatrists thus have constructed diagnoses, pretended that the terms they coined were morally neutral descriptions of brain diseases, and few in political power have challenged their pretensions.

My argument may be put another way: The existence of John Smith's bodily disease—say, astrocytoma, a nerve tissue tumor—is discovered and empirically verified. Radiologists identify the tumor; neurosurgeons verify its presence by observing the lesion with their naked eyes; and pathologists confirm the diagnosis by examination of the tissues. In contrast, the existence of John Smith's mental disease—say, schizophrenia—is declared and socially verified. His alleged illness is identified by psychiatrists, who diagnose his behavior as schizophrenia; other psychiatrists verify its presence by committing him to a mental hospital, where he acquires the right to refuse treatment, which he exercises; and a judge confirms the diagnosis by declaring him mentally incompetent to refuse treatment.

Because the idea of mental illness combines a mistaken conceptualization (of non-disease as disease) with an immoral justification (of coercion as cure), the effect is two-pronged—it corrupts language and curtails freedom and responsibility. Because psychiatrists have power over persons denominated as patients, their descriptive statements typically function as covert prescriptions. For instance, psychiatrists may describe a man who asserts that he hears God's voice telling him to kill his wife as schizophrenic. This "diagnosis" functions as a prescription—for example, to hospitalize the patient involuntarily (lest he kill his wife) or, after he has killed her, to acquit him as not guilty by reason of insanity and again hospitalize him against his will. This coercive-tactical feature of psychiatric diagnosis is best appreciated by contrasting medical with psychiatric diagnosis. Diagnosis of bodily illness is the operative word that justifies a physician to admit to a hospital a patient who wants to be so admitted. Diagnosis of mental illness is the operative word that justifies a judge to incarcerate in a mental hospital a sex criminal who has completed his prison sentence.

So long as there are no objective, physico-chemical observations shown to be causally related to depression and schizophrenia, the claim that they are brain diseases is unsubstantiated. In the absence of such evidence, psychiatrists rest their claim that these major mental diseases are brain diseases largely on the contention that drugs keep the disease processes "under control." The absurdity of this claim lies in its own consequences.

Diabetes is kept under control by insulin. When patients stop taking their medication, the disease process flares up and kills them. Lupus is kept under control by steroids. When patients stop taking their medication, the disease process flares up and kills them.

This is not what happens when patients with serious mental diseases stop taking their medication. Depression is kept under control by antidepressants. When patients stop taking their medication, the disease process flares up, but the disease does not kill them. They kill themselves, an act psychiatrists attribute to their so-called mental illness. Schizophrenia is kept under control by anti-psychotic drugs. When patients stop taking their medication, the disease process flares up, but the disease does not kill them. They kill someone else, an act psychiatrists attribute to their supposed illness.

If we restrict the concept of treatment to a voluntary relationship between a medical practitioner and a competent client, then a coerced medical intervention imposed on persons not legally incompetent is, by definition, assault and battery, not treatment.

Psychiatry is thus a systematic violation of this legal-political principle, one that is especially odious because most persons treated against their will by psychiatrists are defined as legally competent—they can vote, marry and divorce, etc. It is important to keep in mind that, in a free society, the physician's "right" to treat a person rests not on the diagnosis, but on the subject's consent to treatment.

Regardless of psychiatric diagnosis, the typical mental patient is entitled to liberty, unless convicted of a crime punishable by imprisonment. If that patient breaks the law and is convicted, then he or she ought to be punished for it as prescribed by the criminal law. In a free society, a person ought not to profit from psychiatric excuses or suffer from psychiatric coercions.

Thomas Szasz *is professor of psychiatry emeritus, State University of New York Health Science Center, Syracuse.*

Up from depression

Wiser diagnosis, better treatment offer new hope

BY PEGGY EASTMAN

In recent visits with your mother, you notice she has lost her customary spark, her sense of humor. She has stopped going out, rarely sees her longtime pals and instead stays at home, staring dully at the TV. Even the grandkids can't cheer her up.

She's just slowing down, you tell yourself. Possibly, but there may be another reason: She may be among the growing number of Americans with serious depression, a draining condition that can ruin the quality of life and often goes unrecognized—especially in older people—by doctors or family members.

Some 19 million Americans experience persistent, or clinical, depression. Of these, 6 million are over age 65, a number that is rising sharply as the older population expands. Experts say the problem, if not brought under control, will only worsen as baby boomers age and confront life changes and losses that can cause depression.

"We're talking about an epidemic," says William E. Reichman, M.D., a psychiatrist at the University of Medicine and Dentistry of New Jersey and president of the American Association for Geriatric Psychiatry (AAGP). "There's a demographic imperative that compels us to pay attention to depression in late life."

On the bright side: In most cases, depression is highly treatable. A deeper understanding of what leads to the disorder is producing better ways to fight it, with everything from self-help measures like exercise and diet to new, more effective drugs.

Overcoming depression "can add years of productivity and happiness to someone who had given up on those aspects of life," says Nathan Billig, M.D., a geriatric psychiatrist in Washington and author of "Growing Older & Wiser" (Lexington Books, 1995).

But fighting depression takes more than the efforts of professionals. "The challenge for baby boomers who may care for an older adult is to gain an understanding of the issue, identify disorders early and help her or him get ap-propriate treatment," says Soo Borson, M.D., director of geriatric psychiatry services at the University of Washington Medical Center in Seattle.

Your Health

Ten warning signs of depression

AS A RULE of thumb, the time has come to seek help when five or more of the following symptoms occur for at least two weeks:

- feeling guilty, worthless, "empty," unloved, hopeless
- no longer enjoying things
- feeling very tired and lethargic
- feeling nervous, restless or irritable
- unable to concentrate
- crying frequently
- sleeping more or less than usual
- eating more or less than usual
- having persistent headaches, stomachaches or pain
- having thoughts of death, especially suicide

NOT JUST THE BLUES

It's normal to be sad after major life events like illness, divorce, losing a job, moving far from home and the death of a spouse or close friend. Most people begin to bounce back after a few days or weeks.

But clinical depression is more than the blues or a reaction to grief. Untreated, the feelings of sorrow, hopelessness and anxiety can last for months or years, leading to impaired functioning, isolation, physical ailments and even suicide.

"[Depression] is a medical disorder, like hypertension or diabetes," says Billig. "It can and must be treated when it interferes with otherwise healthy functioning."

The condition, he stresses, is not a part of normal aging.

Looking for help?...

A FEW OF THE NUMEROUS organizations offering information on depression:

- American Association for Geriatric Psychiatry, 7910 Woodmont Ave., Suite 1050, Bethesda, MD 20814-3004, **www.aagpgpa.org**.
- National Alliance for the Mentally Ill, (800) 950-6264, **www.nami.org**.
- National Alliance for Research on Schizophrenia and Depression, (800) 829-8289, **www.narsad.org**.
- National Institute of Mental Health, (800) 421-4211, **www.nimh.nih.gov**.
- National Mental Health Association, (800) 969-6642, **www.nmha.org**.
- National Depressive and Manic-Depressive Association, (800) 826-3632, **www.ndmda.org**.

But some 90 percent of depressed older adults don't get relief, says the National Mental Health Association, because they are reluctant to seek help or because their doctors don't recognize their illness.

While younger people may be comfortable discussing their troubles, their elders may be more reticent, notes Billig. Depressed older people may hide their true feelings by focusing instead on physical ills or using alcohol.

Thus, experts say, adult children need to know the signs of depression. Asking the older person certain questions—How are you sleeping? Are you seeing your friends?—can yield some clues, too. [See "Ten warning signs."]

If depression is suspected, it's important to help the person recognize the symptoms and seek help from a doctor or psychotherapist (or if the individual is in a nursing home, to ask for a consultation with a mental health professional).

What if the person resists such overtures? One answer is to enlist the persuasive powers of a trusted friend or member of the clergy to encourage him or her to get assistance.

Allan Anderson, M. D. medical director for geriatric psychiatry at Shore Behavioral Health Services in Cambridge, Md., says he tells reluctant patients: "Look, I'm wearing eyeglasses. It's a pain, but I choose to wear them so I can see and not suffer. Depression is an illness. You can get treatment, or you can suffer. I don't want you to suffer."

'MISSING' THE DIAGNOSIS

Primary care doctors generally are not trained in psychiatry and sometimes "miss" depression in their older patients. One study of suicides showed that 20 percent of older adults had seen their doctor about other health conditions on the same day they took their lives, 40 percent had seen their doctor within a week, and 70 percent within one month.

At the least, says Ira R. Katz, M.D., director of geriatric psychiatry at the University of Pennsylvania Medical Center, "the doctor has to ask, 'What have you enjoyed doing lately?' If the answer is 'nothing,' that's very important. The trick is to ask."

... paying for treatment

WHILE DEPRESSION and other mental health problems are gradually being accorded more importance as a public health problem, insurance coverage for treatment is, at best, mixed. Many health plans cover all or some care, but prescription drug coverage varies widely.

Traditional Medicare pays 50 percent of most outpatient mental health care but does not pay for prescription drugs. Coverage in Medicare HMOs varies from plan to plan.

DEPRESSION TRIGGERS

Clinical depression often has no obvious cause but emerges gradually, imperceptibly.

"When I look back on my life and I'm honest with myself, I think I've had this problem all my life," says Pittsburgh resident Marian Schwartz, 85, who recently waged a successful battle against depression.

She went through some hard times that may have set the stage for her condition. She had cared for her invalid husband for about 10 years, and she had had heart surgery. Her son died at age 38, and her daughter struggled with depression.

Over time, Schwartz began having sleep problems and wide appetite swings; she stopped driving and no longer devoured newspapers and books as she once had. She felt lethargic, sad.

Sorrow over misfortune is normal. But it can be compounded in late life, a time when people may become more isolated as they lose spouses and old friends. Without social and emotional support, AAGP's Reichman says, depression can take hold.

Other risk factors:
- family history of the disorder;
- imbalance of brain chemicals that govern mood;
- chronic pain and illnesses like cancer, heart disease and Parkinson's disease;

- dementia (more than half of people with Alzheimer's disease are depressed);
- certain medications, such as beta blockers for heart problems;
- seasonal changes;
- hormonal changes (such as occur at menstruation and menopause); and
- stress.

More than twice as many women experience depression than men. Just why is unclear, but the National Mental Health Association speculates that hormonal changes and the stress of family responsibilities may explain the high rate among women.

Marian Schwartz knows about that kind of pressure. "I was the 'Let Marian do it' person," says Schwartz, a middle child in a family of six children. "All my life I have been the family caregiver."

With counseling, she came to a more realistic understanding of her own needs and the limits of what she can do for others.

DIGGING OUT

Minor depression usually lifts on its own. But it's likely to need active measures to banish a lingering case. As a first step, experts say, get adequate sleep, eat a nourishing diet and spend more time with friends and family.

Exercise is a powerful antidote. A recent Duke University study of 156 people age 50 or older showed that exercise was about as effective as medicine in relieving depression.

In more persistent cases, psychological counseling, or "talk therapy," can reveal underlying causes of depression and help the patient reverse negative attitudes and find better ways of handling problems.

Antidepressant drugs can help, too. Many are available and more are in the pipeline. Selective serotonin reuptake inhibitors (SSRIs), a class that includes Prozac and Zoloft, boost serotonin, a mood-enhancing chemical in the brain.

SSRIs tend to have fewer side effects than the older antidepressants—tricyclics and monoamine oxidase (MAO) inhibitors—and are better tolerated, says Bruce G. Pollack, M.D., director of the Geriatric Psychopharmacology Program at the University of Pittsburgh School of Medicine.

Another new drug is venlafaxine (Effexor), which acts on at least two mood-regulating brain chemicals.

Just as adult children can be key in spotting depression, says the University of Pennsylvania's Katz, they can help determine if a given drug is working for their elder relative or causing side effects like insomnia, loss of balance or sleepiness.

"If Mom is on an antidepressant and she's still depressed, that's a time to speak up," he says, and perhaps change drugs or dosages.

Whatever the drug, relief is not immediate. "It takes a number of weeks for medication to work in treating depression," stresses Anderson of Shore Behavioral Health Services.

The most effective treatment for severe clinical depression may be a one-two punch using drugs and psychotherapy.

Researchers at Brown University said in the New England Journal of Medicine that combined treatment produced an 85 percent positive response rate among the 681 participants in their study. The drug alone elicited a 55 percent positive response rate and talk therapy 52 percent.

Electroconvulsive—or shock—therapy is generally reserved for severely depressed people who don't respond to other treatments. The controversial procedure, in which the brain is electrically stimulated to break the course of depression, is deemed highly effective by some doctors. One possible side effect: temporary memory loss.

Researchers are exploring another treatment in which the vagus nerve in the neck is stimulated with electrical impulses, sending signals to brain areas that control mood.

Says one lifelong sufferer of depression who participated in the University of Texas Southwestern Medical Center's study of the treatment, "For the first time in years, I can feel joy, real joy."

Marian Schwartz is experiencing some joy, too. She has reclaimed her life, beating her depression via therapy and an antidepressant drug. Her message to others who feel depressed: "Please get help. I have benefited greatly. I have more confidence in myself [and] see things in a different perspective now."

AARP would like to learn more about how being denied medical care for depression might affect people. If you or someone close to you has ever been harmed by the inability to get treatment for depression, please write to AARP Foundation Litigation, P. O. Box 50228-D, Washington, DC 20091-0228. All correspondence will be kept confidential.

Peggy Eastman is a Washington-based free-lance writer.

PHOBIAS

FEAR NOT!

For millions of sufferers of phobias, science is offering new treatments— and new hope

By JEFFREY KLUGER

IT'S NOT EASY MOVING THROUGH THE world when you're terrified of electricity. "Donna," 45, a writer, knows that better than most. Get her in the vicinity of an appliance or a light switch or—all but unthinkable—a thunderstorm, and she is overcome by a terror so blinding she can think of nothing but fleeing. That, of course, is not always possible, so over time, Donna has come up with other answers. When she opens the refrigerator door, rubber-soled shoes are a must. If a light bulb blows, she will tolerate the dark until someone else changes it for her. Clothes shopping is done only when necessary, lest static on garments send her running from the store. And swimming at night is absolutely out of the question, lest underwater lights electrocute her. When there's a possibility that lightning may strike, she simply shuts off everything in her house and sits alone in a darkened room until the danger passes.

There is a word—a decidedly straightforward one—for Donna's very extreme condition: *electrophobia*, or a morbid fear of electricity. You will find it listed right below *eisoptrophobia* (fear of mirrors) and not far above *enetophobia*, *eosophobia* and *ereuthrophobia* (fear of pins, daylight and blushing, respectively). And those are just some of the Es.

For every phobia the infinitely inventive—and infinitely fearful—human mind can create, there is a word that has been coined to describe it. There's *nephophobia*, or fear of clouds, and *coulrophobia*, the fear of clowns. There's *kathisophobia*,

fear of sitting, and *kyphophobia*, fear of stooping. There are *xanthophobia*, *leukophobia* and *chromophobia*, fear of yellow, white and colors in general. There are *alektorophobia* and *apiphobia*, fear of chickens and bees. And deep in the list, lost in the Ls, there's *lutraphobia*, or fear of otters— a fear that's useful, it would seem, only if you happen to be a mollusk.

The list of identified phobias is expanding every day and is now, of course, collected online (*phobialist.com*), where more than 500 increasingly quirky human fears are labeled, sometimes tongue-in-cheek, and cataloged alphabetically. Some have more to do with neology than psychology. (It's one thing to invent a word like *arachibutyrophobia*, another thing to find someone who's really afraid of peanut butter sticking to the roof of the mouth.) Other phobias, however—like *acrophobia* (fear of heights), *claustrophobia* (fear of enclosed spaces) and *agoraphobia* (a crushing, paralyzing terror of anything outside the safety of the home)—can be deadly serious business.

If the names of phobias can be found online, the people who actually suffer from at least one of them at some point in their life—about 50 million in the U.S. by some estimates—are everywhere. They may be like "Beth," a pseudonym, a middle school student in Boston whose hemophobia, or fear of blood, was so severe that even a figure of speech like "cut it out" could make her faint. Or they may be like "Jean," 38, an executive assistant in New Jersey who is so terrified of balloons that just walking

into a birthday party can make her break out in a sweat.

For most people, the treatment of phobias has been a cope-as-you-go business: preflight cocktails for the fearful flyer, stairways instead of elevators for the claustrophobe. But such home-brew tactics are usually only stopgaps at best. Happily, safe and lasting phobia treatments are now at hand. In an era in which more and more emotional disorders are falling before the scythe of science, phobias are among the disorders falling fastest.

Researchers are making enormous progress in determining what phobias are, what kinds of neurochemical storms they trigger in the brain and for what evolutionary purpose the potential for such psychic squalls was encoded into us in the first place. With this understanding has come a magic bag of treatments: exposure therapy that can stomp out a lifetime phobia in a single six-hour session; virtual-reality programs that can safely simulate the thing the phobic most fears, slowly stripping it of its power to terrorize; new medications that can snuff the brain's phobic spark before it can catch. In the past year, the U.S. Food and Drug Administration approved the first drug—an existing antidepressant called Paxil—specifically for the treatment of social phobias. And just last week the Anxiety Disorders Association of America held a four-day seminar in Atlanta on a wide range of topics, including how to recognize and overcome social phobias, how to spot phobia and anxiety disorders in

FIGHTING FEAR OF FLYING

All Aboard Exposure Airlines

Were you able to fix it? someone asks. My head snaps to the right. A man in a fur hat and red ski parka pauses before answering. That's it, I think. There's some mechanical problem with the plane. My mind races ahead, spinning out of control. I hate 737s. They have bad rudders, right? Maybe there's another flight home. Or even better, I could take the train…

Fur hat finally answers, "Yup. Just the wheel," as he point to his carry-on suitcase.

Classic. My mind had leaped in the space of a nanosecond from a waiting room in Logan Airport to a death spiral over the Atlantic. Dr. Curtis Hsia of Boston University's Center for Anxiety and Related Disorders calls this automatic thinking. It was even worse a few hours earlier when, as part of my treatment for a debilitating case of aviophobia (fear of flying), Dr. Hsia had booked me on Exposure Airlines. It's the newest thing in phobic therapy: a virtual airplane of hardware, software and fancy head-mounted display screens that feels like the real thing.

I hate window seats, I remember thinking just before my virtual flight took off. You can see how far you'd fall if… Oops. Don't go there. I want to speak to the crew for reassurance, but there is no one. Instead I'm squeezed into a row of four seats, alone.

I take a hurried glance out the window to check the weather. Just a few stratus clouds. That's O.K. The sound of jet engines drowns me as my virtual airplane heads down the runway. My legs are stiff, and I arch my back in anticipation. No g-force in this simulation. A small break for me. We level off. Sky is still good. I begin to relax. Look around. Not so bad.

A humongous noise sparks my body upward. Another glance out the window. Not good. We're in the middle of a thunderstorm. The seats ahead of me are shaking. I can feel the thunder in my bones. I know this isn't real, but I can't seem to control

my fear. Through the din, I hear Dr. Hsia ask me how I'm feeling on an anxiety scale of 1 to 10: total relaxation to panic. I'm pushing 9. The storm thunders on. I am hating this.

"Why isn't the pilot saying anything?" I ask Dr. Hsia. I crave reassurance. The pilot must be fighting to stay aloft, I think. Maybe he's drunk.

"What about the co-pilot?" Dr. Hsia asks.

He's probably drunk, too. Otherwise someone would be saying something to reassure me.

"What's the likelihood that both pilots would be out of it?" he asks.

Probably nil, I answer reluctantly. All right. They got bad weather information. I start looking around the cabin, searching the seams of the fuselage for any signs of strain. Don't know what I'm expecting. A loosened panel. Dripping water. A broken bolt. Still no word from the crew. I'm getting ticked. They should be talking to me. My head is pounding. I'm fingering my necklace. My legs ache.

It's over. The sky is clear again. I get my breath back. My back is just sinking into the seat when—Gotcha! We're in another storm. Just as bad. Panic level back up to 9. Still no pilot. Damn him! Does this plane have a lightning rod? My head is bursting now.

"What do you think would happen if lightning did hit the plane?" Dr. Hsia asks. I don't know. It would break apart. "Has that happened before?" Not that I know of. "If the pilots are flying through this, it's because they know the plane can take it," he says calmly.

Maybe the plane can, but I can't.

Another calm. I think it's over. Wrong. A third storm. Still nothing from the pilot. Seams are holding. I lean in to the window as far as I can. Nothing but black, punctuated by flashes and that dreadful crash of thunder. I'm wearing out my necklace. I

want out of this. I close my eyes. Maybe that'll help me cope. Eyes pop back open. Need to see what's going on! Have to get through this. The pilot apparently is. Plane isn't breaking apart.

I look out the window again. Blue sky, buildings rising to meet us. We're coming down. I collapse against my seat. It's over.

Not quite. Ten minutes later, I'm back in the air. Another storm. This one lasts the whole flight. I run through my bleak assumptions. This time, I answer them for myself. Pilot. Lousy communicator. Plane. Holding together. Made for this. Look out the window. The pulsing clouds remind me of Van Gogh. My hands stay on my lap. I play with my rings. I'll be coming down soon enough. I register between a 3 and a 4. I can do this.

Back at Logan Airport, they're boarding Continental Flight No. 367 to Newark. As I head down the aisle toward seat 8E—a window—I hear a passenger say, "Did I tell you what a bad flight I had coming up here?" I shut him out. Don't need this. Squeeze into my seat. Look out the window. Beautiful. Clear. Almost no wind. The right engine is just below me. Could keep this plane up by itself, if the other engine quits. It roars to life, and my stomach tightens.

This is real. What do I think can happen? None of my worst-case scenarios seem very likely. And if we do run into trouble, there are tons of airports below for an emergency landing. We'll be O.K. Perfect takeoff to the south over Boston Harbor, and then bank slightly right toward home. Level off at 16,000 ft. I hear the crackle of the intercom. The pilot says it'll be a smooth flight. Safety-belt sign is turned off. I love his voice. I push back my seat and stare out the window.

No miracle cure here, but I do feel a bit calmer, more in control. I'm going to take it one flight at a time.

—By Joëlle Attinger/Boston

children and how to help patients maintain gains achieved in treatment.

"There's been nothing like this in the field of mental health," says psychologist David H. Barlow, director of the Center for Anxiety and Related Disorders at Boston University. "In the past few years, we've

had a complete turnaround in the treatment of phobic disorders."

For something that can cause as much suffering as a phobia, it's remarkable how many people lay claim to having one—and how many of them are wrong. Self-described computer phobics are probably

nothing of the kind. They may not care for the infernal machines and may occasionally want to throw one out the window, but that's not the same as a full-fledged phobia. Self-described claustrophobics often misdiagnose as well. The middle seat on a transatlantic flight may be something you

ARE YOU PHOBIC?

Phobias can be slippery things. It's not always clear when an aversion to cockroaches becomes something more serious. The signs are not just physical reactions but also emotional ones: Do you fret about the object of your phobia? Do you alter your life to avoid it? A few yes or no questions can help you take the measure of your fear:

Yes or No? Do you...

...Have a persistent and excessive fear of an object or situation, such as flying, heights, animals, blood or being in a public place from which there is no escape?
❑YES   ❑NO

...Experience symptoms including pounding heart, trembling, shortness of breath, lightheadedness, weak knees, dry mouth, feeling of unreality, feelings that you may go crazy or die, when you think of or encounter the object or situation you fear?
❑YES   ❑NO

...Have an excessive and ongoing fear of social situations, such as going to the mall, the movies or a restaurant?
❑YES   ❑NO

...Fear that you will be judged or will humiliate yourself socially?
❑YES   ❑NO

...Fear of traveling without a companion?
❑YES   ❑NO

...Fear that people will notice that you are blushing, sweating, trembling or showing other signs of anxiety?
❑YES   ❑NO

...Take elaborate excessive steps to avoid the object or situation you fear?
❑YES   ❑NO

...Find that your fears or your reactions to them have interfered with your ability to function at home, professionally or socially?
❑YES   ❑NO

If you answered yes to these questions, contact your health-care provider. A phobia is hard to bear but is treatable. Adapted from *Diagnostic and Statistical Manual of Mental Disorders*, American Psychiatric Association.

approach with dismay, but unless you also experience a racing heart and ragged breath, you are probably not phobic. Drawing the distinction between distaste and the singular terror of a phobia is not always easy—and it's made all the harder by the fact that fear in some circumstances is perfectly appropriate. If flying into a storm or easing into weaving traffic isn't the right time to go a little white knuckled, what is?

Experts, however, say a true phobic reaction is a whole different category of terror, a central nervous system wildfire that's impossible to mistake. In the face of the thing that triggers fear, phobics experience sweating, racing heart, difficulty breathing and even a fear of imminent death—all accompanied by an overwhelming need to flee. In addition, much of the time that they are away from the feared object or situation is spent dreading the next encounter and developing elaborate strategies intended to avoid it. "Jeanette," 44, a teacher's assistant, is so terrified of cats that she sends her daughter, 21, into an unfamiliar store to scout around and sound a feline all clear before she enters. The daughter has been walking point this way since age five. "Nora," 50, a social worker, will circumnavigate a block with a series of right turns rather than make a single left, so afraid is she of facing the stream of traffic that a left turn requires.

Most psychologists now assign phobias to one of three broad categories: social phobias, in which the sufferer feels paralyzing fear at the prospect of social or professional encounters; panic disorders, in which the person is periodically blindsided by overwhelming fear for no apparent reason; and specific phobias—fear of snakes and enclosed spaces and heights and the like. Of the three, the specific phobias are the easiest to treat, partly because they are the easiest to understand.

The human brain may be a sophisticated thing, but there is an awful lot of ancient programming still etched into it. For "Martin," 21, a dental student in London, Ontario, his fear of snakes is so overwhelming that he stapled together pages in a textbook to avoid flipping to a photo of a snake. He often wakes with nightmares that he is sitting in a bar or a stadium and suddenly sees a snake slithering toward him. "It's odd," he says, "because I'm not in situations where I would ever see snakes."

His brain, however—or at least the oldest parts of it—may have been. One of the things that helped early humans survive was a robust fear-and-flight response: an innate sense of the places and things that represent danger and a reflexive impulse to hightail it when one of them is encountered. When the species became top predator a few million years later, those early lessons were not easy to unlearn.

Contemporary researchers believe it's no coincidence that specific phobias usually fall into one of four subcategories, all of which would have had meaning for our ancient ancestors: fear of insects or animals; fear of natural environments, like heights and the dark; fear of blood or injury; and fear of dangerous situations, like being trapped in a tight space. "Phobias are not random," says Michelle Craske, psychologist at UCLA's Anxiety and Behavioral Disorders Program. "We tend to fear anything that threatens our survival as a species." When times change, new fears develop, but the vast majority still fit into one of the four groups.

It turns out that we process the fear of these modern menaces in the same area of the brain our ancient ancestors did—the paralimbic region, which mediates a whole range of primal responses, including anger and sexual arousal. "It seems that contemporary people learned from their ancient ancestors what to be afraid of and how to handle it," Barlow says.

Not all of us, however, parlay that ancient history into a modern-day phobia. It may be our distant ancestors who predispose us to phobias, but it's our immediate ancestors—specifically our parents—who seal the deal. As many as 40% of all people suffering from a specific phobia have at least one phobic parent, seemingly a clue that phobias could be genetically influenced. In recent years, a number of scientists have claimed to have found the phobia gene, but none of those claims have held up to scrutiny. If phobias are genetically based at all, they almost certainly require a whole tangle of genes to get the process going.

But genetics doesn't even have to be involved as long as learning is. A childhood trauma—a house fire, say, or a dog bite—may be more than enough to seize the brain's attention and serve as a repository for incipient fears. "Temperament also seems to be critical," says Craske. "Two people can go through the exact same traumatic event, but the high-strung, emotionally sensitive person is more vulnerable to the fear." Even secondhand fears—watching Mom or Dad react with exaggerated terror to a cockroach or a drop of blood, for example—may play a role. The journal *Nature* last week reported a study in which researchers performed scans on the fear centers of volunteers' brains and found that when the subjects were merely told to expect an electric shock, the neurological reaction to the anticipated jolt was as powerful as fears based on actual experience. "There is a lot of legitimacy to the idea that phobias can be learned," says Edna B. Foa, professor of psychology and psychiatry at the University of Pennsylvania. "We respond to what we see or experience."

IN MANY CASES, THE BRAIN MAY THINK it's doing the child's psyche a favor by developing a phobia. The world is a scary place, and young kids are inherently fearful until they start to figure it out. If you are living with a generalized sense of danger, it can be profoundly therapeutic to find a single object on which to deposit all that unformed fear—a snake, a spider, a rat. A specific phobia becomes a sort of backfire for fear, a controlled blaze that prevents other blazes from catching. "The thinking mind seeks out a rationale for the primitive mind's unexplained experiences," says psychologist Steven Phillipson, clinical director of the Center for Cognitive-Behavioral Psychotherapy in New York City.

But a condition that is so easy to pick up is becoming almost as easy to shake, usually without resort to drugs. What turns up the wattage of a phobia the most is the strategy the phobics rely on to ease their discomfort: avoidance. The harder phobics work to avoid the things they fear, the more the brain grows convinced that the threat is real. "The things you do to reduce anxiety just make it worse," says Barlow. "We have to strip those things away."

And that's what doctors do. A patient visiting Barlow's Boston clinic is first assessed for the presence of a specific phobia and then guided through an intensive day or two of graduated exposure. People who are afraid of syringes and blood, for example, may first be shown a magazine photo with a trace of blood depicted in it. Innocuous photos give way to graphic ones, and graphic ones to a display of a real, empty syringe. Over time, the syringe is brought

closer, and the patient learns to hold it and even tolerate having blood drawn.

None of this is remotely easy for the phobic person, and the body's anxiety Klaxons may go off the instant the therapy begins. Gradually, however, as each exposure level is reached, the alarms start to quiet; they sound again only when the intensity of the exposure is turned up. "Just as people become habituated to the noise of traffic or background chatter, so too can phobics become nonresponsive to the thing that once frightened them," says Phillipson.

With that habituation comes profound recovery. In studies recently conducted by Lars Goran Ost, a psychology professor at Stockholm University and one of the pioneers of one-day phobia treatments, a staggering 80% to 95% of patients get their phobias under control after just one session. And when symptoms disappear, they usually stay gone. Patients, he says, rarely experience a significant phobic relapse, and almost never replace the thing they no longer fear with a fresher phobia object.

Given the apparent simplicity of exposure therapy, phobics may be tempted to try it themselves. That can be a mistake. It is important that exposure take place under the care of a professional, since it takes a trained person to know when patients are being pushed too far and when it's safe to go further. For some situations impossible to re-create in a doctor's office—like heights and flying in airplanes—virtual-reality programs are available to provide simulated exposure under professional supervision. Software for other fears is being written all the time. "Not all people respond to virtual reality," says Barlow, "but on average, it's just as effective for treating certain phobias." If specific phobias were the only type of phobias around, things would be decidedly easier for doctors and patients. But the two other members of the phobia troika—social phobias and panic disorders—can be a little trickier.

Of the 50 million Americans who have experienced or will someday suffer from a phobia (and many will have more than one), 35 million will suffer from social phobia, and the battle they fight is a harrowing one. Richard Heimberg at Temple University's Adult Anxiety Clinic often thinks of the 50-year-old patient who talked frequently about getting married and having a family—a reasonable dream, except that his terror of rejection had kept him from ever going out on a date. After much encouragement and counseling, he finally screwed up his courage enough to ask

a woman out. The next day, when Heimberg asked him if he'd had a good time, he said yes. But when asked if he were going to invite her out again, the patient slumped and said no. "She's only going to give to charity once," he explained.

For this patient, the problem wasn't mere low self-esteem but outright terror. To a social phobic, the mere prospect of a social encounter is frightening enough to cause sweating, trembling, light-headedness and nausea, accompanied by an overwhelming feeling of inadequacy. For some sufferers, the disorder is comparatively circumscribed—occurring only at large parties, say—making avoidance strategies seem easy. But social phobias can encroach into more and more areas of life, closing more and more doors. As sufferers grow increasingly isolated, they grow increasingly hopeless and risk developing such conditions as depression and alcoholism.

But things don't have to be so bleak. While social phobias do not respond to a single intensive exposure session as specific phobias do, therapy can still be relatively straightforward. A successful treatment regimen may involve no more than a dozen sessions of cognitive-behavioral therapy, in which patients slowly expose themselves to the places and circumstances that frighten them and reframe the catastrophic thinking that torments them. They are taught to tone down their "attentional bias," a tendency to stress their supposed social stumbles, and their "interpretation bias," a habit of picking up neutral cues from other people and interpreting them as evidence of failing socially. Often group therapy works better than one-on-one therapy. It provides more than a supportive circle of fellow sufferers: the very act of gathering with other people can serve as a first, critical rebellion against the disorder.

If such therapy doesn't help social phobics, drugs can. Ever since the popularization of Prozac in the early 1990s, the family of modern psychopharmacological drugs has grown steadily. Most of these medications are selective serotonin reuptake inhibitors—or SSRIs—which, as the name implies, selectively block the brain's reabsorption of the neurotransmitter serotonin, helping produce feelings of satisfaction and kick-start recovery. Last year the drug manufacturer SmithKline Beecham asked the Food and Drug Administration to take a second look at the popular SSRI Paxil and consider approving it specifically for the treatment of social-anxiety disorder. The FDA agreed, making Paxil the first drug ever to be formally endorsed for such use. While the flood of marketing tends to overstate the case, the fact is, Paxil works—not by eliminating anxiety entirely but by controlling it enough for traditional therapy to take hold. And with the pharmacological door now open, makers of similar drugs like Luvox, Prozac and Celexa will probably seek the same certification. "Paxil is not unique among these drugs," says Barlow. "It was just first in line."

Progress in treating social-anxiety disorder is also providing hope for the last—and most disabling—of the family of phobias: panic disorder. Panic disorder is to anxiety conditions what a tornado is to weather conditions: a devastating sneak attack that appears from nowhere, wreaks havoc and then simply vanishes. Unlike the specific phobic and the social phobic who know what will trigger their fear, the victim of panic attacks never knows where or when one will hit. Someone who experiences an attack in, say, a supermarket will often not return there, associating the once neutral place with the traumatic event. But the perceived circle of safety can quickly shrink, until sufferers may be confined entirely to their homes. When this begins to happen, panic disorder mutates into full-blown agoraphobia. "For some people, even the house becomes too big,"

says Fordham University psychology professor Dean McKay. "They may limit their world to just a few rooms."

The treatment for agoraphobia is much the same as it is for social phobia: cognitive-behavioral therapy and drugs. In many cases, recovery takes longer than it does for social phobias because agoraphobic behavior can become so entrenched. Nonetheless, once therapy and drug treatments get under way, they sometimes move surprisingly quickly. "The best way to treat agoraphobia," says Ost, "is by individual therapy, once a week for 10 or 12 weeks."

If science has so many phobias on the run, does that mean that the problem as a whole can soon be considered solved? Hardly. Like all other emotional disorders, phobias cause a double dip of psychic pain: from the condition and from the shame of having the problem in the first place. Over the years, researchers have made much of the fact that the large majority of phobia sufferers are women—from 55% for social phobias and up to 90% for specific phobias and extreme cases of agoraphobia. Hormones, genes and culture have all been explored as explanations. But the simplest answer may be that women own up to the condition more readily than men do. If you don't come forward with your problem, you can't be included in the epidemiologists' count. Worse, you can never avail yourself of the therapists' cure.

Making things even tougher, phobias are often hard to distinguish from other anxiety disorders. A person who feels compelled to wash or shower dozens of times a day may have a phobic's terror of germs, but a clinician would easily peg the problem as obsessive-compulsive disorder, not a specific phobia. The survivor of an airline crash may exhibit a phobic's panic at even a picture of a plane, but likely as not, the fear is one component of a larger case of post-traumatic stress disorder. Different conditions require different treatments, and without the right care, the problem is unlikely to clear up.

The fact that phobias, of all the anxiety disorders, can be overcome so readily is one of psychology's brightest bits of clinical news in a long time. Phobias can beat the stuffing out of sufferers because the feelings they generate seem so real and the dangers they warn of so great. Most of the time, however, the dangers are mere neurochemical lies—and the lies have to be exposed. "Your instincts tell you to escape or avoid," says Phillipson. "But what you really need to do is face down the fear." When you spend your life in a cautionary crouch, the greatest relief of all may come from simply standing up.

—With reporting by Dan Cray/Los Angeles, Brad Liston/ New Orleans, Ulla Plon/Copenhagen and other bureaus.

PHOBIAS

The online phobia list is an A, B, C of terror. Below are just half of the named fears

A—B—C

Ablutophobia… Fear of washing or bathing.
Acarophobia… Fear of itching or of the insects that cause itching.
Acerophobia… Fear of sourness.
Achluophobia… Fear of darkness.
Acousticophobia… Fear of noise.
Acrophobia… Fear of heights.
Aerophobia… Fear of drafts, air swallowing, or airborne noxious substances.
Aeroacrophobia… Fear of open high places.
Aeronausiphobia… Fear of vomiting secondary to airsickness.
Agateophobia… Fear of insanity.
Agliophobia… Fear of pain.
Agoraphobia… Fear of open spaces or of being in crowded, public places like markets. Fear of leaving a safe place.

Agraphobia… Fear of sexual abuse.
Agrizoophobia… Fear of wild animals.
Agyrophobia… Fear of streets or crossing the street.
Aichmophobia… Fear of needles or pointed objects.
Ailurophobia… Fear of cats.
Albuminurophobia… Fear of kidney disease.
Alektorophobia… Fear of chickens.
Algophobia… Fear of pain.
Alliumphobia… Fear of garlic.
Allodoxaphobia… Fear of opinions.
Altophobia… Fear of heights.
Amathophobia… Fear of dust.
Amaxophobia… Fear of riding in a car.
Ambulophobia… Fear of walking.
Amnesiphobia… Fear of amnesia.
Amychophobia… Fear of scratches or being scratched.

Anablephobia… Fear of looking up.
Ancraophobia or Anemophobia… Fear of wind.
Androphobia… Fear of men.
Anemophobia… Fear of air drafts or wind.
Anginophobia… Fear of angina, choking or narrowness.
Anglophobia… Fear of England, English culture, etc.
Angrophobia… Fear of anger or of becoming angry.
Ankylophobia… Fear of immobility of a joint.
Anthrophobia or Anthophobia… Fear of flowers.
Anthropophobia… Fear of people or society.
Antlophobia… Fear of floods.
Anuptaphobia… Fear of staying single.
Apeirophobia… Fear of infinity.

Aphenphosmphobia... Fear of being touched. (Haphephobia)

Apiphobia... Fear of bees.

Apotemnophobia... Fear of persons with amputations.

Arachibutyrophobia... Fear of peanut butter sticking to the roof of the mouth.

Arachnephobia or Arachnophobia... Fear of spiders.

Arithmophobia... Fear of numbers.

Arrhenphobia... Fear of men.

Arsonphobia... Fear of fire.

Asthenophobia... Fear of fainting or weakness.

Astraphobia or Astrapophobia... Fear of thunder and lightning.

Astrophobia... Fear of stars and celestial space.

Asymmetriphobia... Fear of asymmetrical things.

Ataxiophobia... Fear of ataxia (muscular incoordination).

Ataxophobia... Fear of disorder or untidiness.

Atelophobia... Fear of imperfection.

Atephobia... Fear of ruin or ruins.

Athazagoraphobia... Fear of being forgotton or ignored or forgetting.

Atomosophobia... Fear of atomic explosions.

Atychiphobia... Fear of failure.

Aulophobia... Fear of flutes.

Aurophobia... Fear of gold.

Auroraphobia... Fear of Northern lights.

Autodysomophobia... Fear of one that has a vile odor.

Automatonophobia... Fear of ventriloquist's dummies, animatronic creatures, wax statues...anything that falsely represents a sentient being.

Automysophobia... Fear of being dirty.

Autophobia... Fear of being alone or of oneself.

Aviophobia or Aviatophobia... Fear of flying.

Bacillophobia... Fear of microbes.

Bacteriophobia... Fear of bacteria.

Ballistophobia... Fear of missiles or bullets.

Bolshephobia... Fear of Bolsheviks.

Barophobia... Fear of gravity.

Basophobia or Basiphobia... Inability to stand. Fear of walking or falling.

Bathmophobia... Fear of stairs or steep slopes.

Bathophobia... Fear of depth.

Batophobia... Fear of heights or being close to high buildings.

Batrachophobia... Fear of amphibians, such as frogs, newts, salamanders, etc.

Belonephobia... Fear of pins and needles. (Aichmophobia)

Bibliophobia... Fear of books.

Blennophobia... Fear of slime.

Bogyphobia... Fear of bogies or the bogey-man.

Botanophobia... Fear of plants.

Bromidrosiphobia or Bromidrophobia... Fear of body smells.

Brontophobia... Fear of thunder and lightning.

Bufonophobia... Fear of toads.

Cacophobia... Fear of ugliness.

Cainophobia or Cainotophobia... Fear of newness, novelty.

Caligynephobia... Fear of beautiful women.

Cancerophobia... Fear of cancer.

Carcinophobia... Fear of cancer.

Cardiophobia... Fear of the heart.

Carnophobia... Fear of meat.

Catagelophobia... Fear of being ridiculed.

Catapedaphobia... Fear of jumping from high and low places.

Cathisophobia... Fear of sitting.

Catoptrophobia... Fear of mirrors.

Cenophobia or Centophobia... Fear of new things or ideas.

Ceraunophobia... Fear of thunder.

Chaetophobia... Fear of hair.

Cheimaphobia or Cheimatophobia... Fear of cold.

Chemophobia... Fear of chemicals or working with chemicals.

Cherophobia... Fear of gaiety.

Chionophobia... Fear of snow.

Chiraptophobia... Fear of being touched.

Chirophobia... Fear of hands.

Cholerophobia... Fear of anger or the fear of cholera.

Chorophobia... Fear of dancing.

Chrometophobia or Chrematophobia... Fear of money.

Chromophobia or Chromatophobia... Fear of colors.

Chronophobia... Fear of time.

Chronomentrophobia... Fear of clocks.

Cibophobia or Sitophobia or Sitiophobia... Fear of food.

Claustrophobia... Fear of confined spaces.

Cleithrophobia or Cleisiophobia... Fear of being locked in an enclosed place.

Cleptophobia... Fear of stealing.

Climacophobia... Fear of stairs, climbing or of falling down stairs.

Clinophobia... Fear of going to bed.

Clithrophobia or Cleithrophobia... Fear of being enclosed.

Cnidophobia... Fear of stings.

Cometophobia... Fear of comets.

Coimetrophobia... Fear of cemeteries.

Coitophobia... Fear of coitus.

Contreltophobia... Fear of sexual abuse.

Coprastasophobia... Fear of constipation.

Coprophobia... Fear of feces.

Coulrophobia... Fear of clowns.

Counterphobia... The preference by a phobic for fearful situations.

Cremnophobia... Fear of precipices.

Cryophobia... Fear of extreme cold, ice or frost.

Crystallophobia... Fear of crystals or glass.

Cyberphobia... Fear of computers or working on a computer.

Cyclophobia... Fear of bicycles.

Cymophobia... Fear of waves or wavelike motions.

Cynophobia... Fear of dogs or rabies.

Cypridophobia, Cypriphobia, Cyprianophobia, or Cyprinophobia... Fear of prostitutes or venereal disease.

D—E—F

Decidophobia... Fear of making decisions.

Defecaloesiophobia... Fear of painful bowel movements.

Deipnophobia... Fear of dining or dinner conversations.

Dementophobia... Fear of insanity.

Demonophobia or Daemonophobia... Fear of demons.

Demophobia... Fear of crowds. (Agoraphobia)

Dendrophobia... Fear of trees.

Dentophobia... Fear of dentists.

Dermatophobia... Fear of skin lesions.

Dermatosiophobia or Dermatophobia or Dermatopathophobia... Fear of skin disease.

Dextrophobia... Fear of objects at the right side of the body.

Diabetophobia... Fear of diabetes.

Didaskaleinophobia... Fear of going to school.

Dikephobia... Fear of justice.

Dinophobia... Fear of dizziness or whirlpools.

Diplophobia... Fear of double vision.

Dipsophobia... Fear of drinking.

Dishabiliophobia... Fear of undressing in front of someone.

Domatophobia or Oikophobia... Fear of houses or being in a house.

Doraphobia... Fear of fur or skins of animals.

Doxophobia... Fear of expressing opinions or of receiving praise.

Dromophobia... Fear of crossing streets.

Dutchphobia... Fear of the Dutch.

Dysmorphophobia... Fear of deformity.

Dystychiphobia... Fear of accidents.

Ecclesiophobia... Fear of church.

Ecophobia... Fear of home.

Eicophobia or Oikophobia... Fear of home surroundings.

Eisoptrophobia... Fear of mirrors or of seeing oneself in a mirror.

Electrophobia… Fear of electricity.
Eleutherophobia… Fear of freedom.
Elurophobia… Fear of cats. (Ailurophobia)
Emetophobia… Fear of vomiting.
Enetophobia… Fear of pins.
Enochlophobia… Fear of crowds.
Enosiophobia or Enissophobia… Fear of having committed an unpardonable sin or of criticism.
Entomophobia… Fear of insects.
Eosophobia… Fear of dawn or daylight.
Ephebiphobia… Fear of teenagers.
Epistaxiophobia… Fear of nosebleeds.
Epistemophobia… Fear of knowledge.
Equinophobia… Fear of horses.
Eremophobia… Fear of being oneself or of loneliness.
Ereuthrophobia… Fear of blushing.
Ergasiophobia… 1) Fear of work or functioning. 2) Surgeon's fear of operating.
Ergophobia… Fear of work.
Erotophobia… Fear of sexual love or sexual questions.
Euphobia… Fear of hearing good news.
Eurotophobia… Fear of female genitalia.
Erythrophobia, Erytophobia or Ereuthophobia… 1) Fear of red lights. 2) Blushing. 3) Red.
Febriphobia, Fibriphobia or Fibriophobia… Fear of fever.
Felinophobia… Fear of cats. (Ailurophobia, Elurophobia, Galeophobia, Gatophobia)
Francophobia… Fear of France, French culture. (Gallophobia, Galiophobia)
Frigophobia… Fear of cold, cold things.

G—H—I—J

Galeophobia or Gatophobia… Fear of cats.
Gallophobia or Galiophobia… Fear of France, French culture. (Francophobia)
Gamophobia… Fear of marriage.
Geliophobia… Fear of laughter.
Geniophobia… Fear of chins.
Genophobia… Fear of sex.
Genuphobia… Fear of knees.
Gephyrophobia, Gephydrophobia, or Gephysrophobia… Fear of crossing bridges.
Germanophobia… Fear of Germany, German culture, etc.
Gerascophobia… Fear of growing old.
Gerontophobia… Fear of old people or of growing old.
Geumaphobia or Geumophobia… Fear of taste.
Glossophobia… Fear of speaking in public or of trying to speak.
Gnosiophobia… Fear of knowledge.
Graphophobia… Fear of writing or handwriting.
Gymnophobia… Fear of nudity.

Gynephobia or Gynophobia… Fear of women.
Hadephobia… Fear of hell.
Hagiophobia… Fear of saints or holy things.
Hamartophobia… Fear of sinning.
Haphephobia or Haptephobia… Fear of being touched.
Harpaxophobia… Fear of being robbed.
Hedonophobia… Fear of feeling pleasure.
Heliophobia… Fear of the sun.
Hellenologophobia… Fear of Greek terms or complex scientific terminology.
Helminthophobia… Fear of being infested with worms.
Hemophobia or Hemaphobia or Hematophobia… Fear of blood.
Heresyphobia or Hereiophobia… Fear of challenges to official doctrine or of radical deviation.
Herpetophobia… Fear of reptiles or creepy, crawly things.
Heterophobia… Fear of the opposite sex. (Sexophobia)
Hierophobia… Fear of priests or sacred things.
Hippophobia… Fear of horses.
Hippopotomonstrosesquippedaliophobia… Fear of long words.
Hobophobia… Fear of bums or beggars.
Hodophobia… Fear of road travel.
Hormephobia… Fear of shock.
Homichlophobia… Fear of fog.
Homilophobia… Fear of sermons.
Hominophobia… Fear of men.
Homophobia… Fear of sameness, monotony or of homosexuality or of becoming homosexual.
Hoplophobia… Fear of firearms.
Hydrargyophobia… Fear of mercurial medicines.
Hydrophobia… Fear of water or of rabies.
Hydrophobophobia… Fear of rabies.
Hyelophobia or Hyalophobia… Fear of glass.
Hygrophobia… Fear of liquids, dampness, or moisture.
Hylephobia… Fear of materialism or the fear of epilepsy.
Hylophobia… Fear of forests.
Hypengyophobia or Hypegiaphobia… Fear of responsibility.
Hypnophobia… Fear of sleep or of being hypnotized.
Hypsiphobia… Fear of height.
Iatrophobia… Fear of going to the doctor or of doctors.
Ichthyophobia… Fear of fish.
Ideophobia… Fear of ideas.
Illyngophobia… Fear of vertigo or feeling dizzy when looking down.
Iophobia… Fear of poison.
Insectophobia…Fear of insects.

Isolophobia… Fear of solitude, being alone.
Isopterophobia… Fear of termites, insects that eat wood.
Ithyphallophobia… Fear of seeing, thinking about or having an erect penis.
Japanophobia… Fear of Japanese.
Judeophobia… Fear of Jews.

K—L—M

Kainolophobia… Fear of novelty.
Kainophobia… Fear of anything new, novelty.
Kakorrhaphiophobia… Fear of failure or defeat.
Katagelophobia… Fear of ridicule.
Kathisophobia… Fear of sitting down.
Kenophobia… Fear of voids or empty spaces.
Keraunophobia… Fear of thunder and lightning.
Kinetophobia or Kinesophobia… Fear of movement or motion.
Kleptophobia… Fear of stealing.
Koinoniphobia… Fear of rooms.
Kolpophobia… Fear of genitals, particularly female.
Kopophobia… Fear of fatigue.
Koniophobia… Fear of dust. (Amathophobia)
Kosmikophobia… Fear of cosmic phenomenon.
Kymophobia… Fear of waves.
Kynophobia… Fear of rabies.
Kyphophobia… Fear of stooping.
Lachanophobia… Fear of vegetables.
Laliophobia or Lalophobia… Fear of speaking.
Leprophobia or Lepraphobia… Fear of leprosy.
Leukophobia… Fear of the color white.
Levophobia… Fear of things to the left side of the body.
Ligyrophobia… Fear of loud noises.
Lilapsophobia… Fear of tornadoes and hurricanes.
Limnophobia… Fear of lakes.
Linonophobia… Fear of string.
Liticaphobia… Fear of lawsuits.
Lockiophobia… Fear of childbirth.
Logizomechanophobia… Fear of computers.
Logophobia… Fear of words.
Luiphobia… Fear of lues, syphillis.
Lutraphobia… Fear of otters.
Lygophobia… Fear of darkness.
Lyssophobia… Fear of rabies or of becoming mad.
Macrophobia… Fear of long waits.
Mageirocophobia… Fear of cooking.
Maieusiophobia… Fear of childbirth.

Malaxophobia… Fear of love play. (Sarmassophobia)

Maniaphobia… Fear of insanity.

Mastigophobia… Fear of punishment.

Mechanophobia… Fear of machines.

Medomalacuphobia… Fear of losing an erection.

Medorthophobia… Fear of an erect penis.

Megalophobia… Fear of large things.

Melissophobia… Fear of bees.

Melanophobia… Fear of the color black.

Melophobia… Fear or hatred of music.

Meningitophobia… Fear of brain disease.

Menophobia… Fear of menstruation.

Merinthophobia… Fear of being bound or tied up.

Metallophobia… Fear of metal.

Metathesiophobia… Fear of changes.

Meteorophobia… Fear of meteors.

Methyphobia… Fear of alcohol.

Metrophobia… Fear or hatred of poetry.

Microbiophobia… Fear of microbes. (Bacillophobia)

Microphobia… Fear of small things.

Misophobia… Fear of being contaminated with dirt or germs.

Mnemophobia… Fear of memories.

Molysmophobia or Molysomophobia… Fear of dirt or contamination.

Monophobia… Fear of solitude or being alone.

Monopathophobia… Fear of definite disease.

Motorphobia… Fear of automobiles.

Mottephobia… Fear of moths.

Musophobia or Murophobia… Fear of mice.

Mycophobia… Fear or aversion to mushrooms.

Mycrophobia… Fear of small things.

Myctophobia… Fear of darkness.

Myrmecophobia… Fear of ants.

Mysophobia… Fear of germs or contamination or dirt.

Mythophobia… Fear of myths or stories or false statements.

Myxophobia… Fear of slime. (Blennophobia)

N—O—P—Q

Nebulaphobia… Fear of fog. (Homichlophobia)

Necrophobia… Fear of death or dead things.

Nelophobia… Fear of glass.

Neopharmaphobia… Fear of new drugs.

Neophobia… Fear of anything new.

Nephophobia… Fear of clouds.

Noctiphobia… Fear of the night.

Nomatophobia… Fear of names.

Nosocomephobia… Fear of hospitals.

Nosophobia or Nosemaphobia… Fear of becoming ill.

Nostophobia… Fear of returning home.

Novercaphobia… Fear of your step-mother.

Nucleomituphobia… Fear of nuclear weapons.

Nudophobia… Fear of nudity.

Numerophobia… Fear of numbers.

Nyctohylophobia… Fear of dark wooded areas, of forests at night.

Nyctophobia… Fear of the dark or of night.

Obesophobia… Fear of gaining weight. (Pocrescophobia)

Ochlophobia… Fear of crowds or mobs.

Ochophobia… Fear of vehicles.

Octophobia…Fear of the figure 8.

Odontophobia… Fear of teeth or dental surgery.

Odynophobia or Odynephobia… Fear of pain. (Algophobia)

Oenophobia… Fear of wines.

Oikophobia… Fear of home surroundings, house.

Olfactophobia… Fear of smells.

Ombrophobia… Fear of rain or of being rained on.

Ommetaphobia or Ommatophobia… Fear of eyes.

Oneirophobia… Fear of dreams.

Oneirogmophobia… Fear of wet dreams.

Onomatophobia… Fear of hearing a certain word or of names.

Ophidiophobia… Fear of snakes. (Snakephobia)

Ophthalmophobia… Fear of being stared at.

Opiophobia… Fear medical doctors experience of prescribing needed pain medications for patients.

Optophobia… Fear of opening one's eyes.

Ornithophobia… Fear of birds.

Orthophobia… Fear of property.

Osmophobia or Osphresiophobia… Fear of smells or odors.

Ostraconophobia… Fear of shellfish.

Ouranophobia… Fear of heaven.

Pagophobia… Fear of ice or frost.

Panthophobia… Fear of suffering and disease.

Panophobia or Pantophobia… Fear of everything.

Papaphobia… Fear of the Pope.

Papyrophobia… Fear of paper.

Paralipophobia… Fear of neglecting duty or responsibility.

Paraphobia… Fear of sexual perversion.

Parasitophobia… Fear of parasites.

Paraskavedekatriaphobia… Fear of Friday the 13th.

Parthenophobia… Fear of virgins or young girls.

Pathophobia… Fear of disease.

Patroiophobia… Fear of heredity.

Parturiphobia… Fear of childbirth.

Peccatophobia… Fear of sinning. (imaginary crime)

Pediculophobia… Fear of lice.

Pediophobia… Fear of dolls.

Pedophobia… Fear of children.

Peladophobia… Fear of bald people.

Pellagrophobia… Fear of pellagra.

Peniaphobia… Fear of poverty.

Pentheraphobia… Fear of mother-in-law. (Novercaphobia)

Phagophobia… Fear of swallowing or of eating or of being eaten.

Phalacrophobia… Fear of becoming bald.

Phallophobia… Fear of a penis, esp erect.

Pharmacophobia… Fear of taking medicine.

Phasmophobia… Fear of ghosts.

Phengophobia… Fear of daylight or sunshine.

Philemaphobia or Philematophobia… Fear of kissing.

Philophobia… Fear of falling in love or being in love.

Philosophobia… Fear of philosophy.

Phobophobia… Fear of phobias.

Photoaugliaphobia… Fear of glaring lights.

Photophobia… Fear of light.

Phonophobia… Fear of noises or voices or one's own voice; of telephones.

Phronemophobia… Fear of thinking.

Phthiriophobia… Fear of lice. (Pediculophobia)

Phthisiophobia… Fear of tuberculosis.

Placophobia… Fear of tombstones.

Plutophobia… Fear of wealth.

Pluviophobia… Fear of rain or of being rained on.

Pneumatiphobia… Fear of spirits.

Pnigophobia or Pnigerophobia… Fear of choking or being smothered.

Pocrescophobia… Fear of gaining weight. (Obesophobia)

Pogonophobia… Fear of beards.

Poliosophobia… Fear of contracting poliomyelitis.

Politicophobia… Fear or abnormal dislike of politicians.

Polyphobia… Fear of many things.

Poinephobia… Fear of punishment.

Ponophobia… Fear of overworking or of pain.

Porphyrophobia… Fear of the color purple.

Potamophobia… Fear of rivers or running water.

Potophobia… Fear of alcohol.

Pharmacophobia… Fear of drugs.

Proctophobia… Fear of rectum.

Prosophobia… Fear of progress.

Psellismophobia… Fear of stuttering.

Psychophobia… Fear of mind.

Psychrophobia... Fear of cold.
Pteromerhanophobia... Fear of flying.
Pteronophobia... Fear of being tickled by feathers.
Pupaphobia... Fear of puppets.
Pyrexiophobia... Fear of fever.
Pyrophobia... Fear of fire.

R—S—T—U

Radiophobia... Fear of radiation, x-rays.
Ranidaphobia... Fear of frogs.
Rectophobia... Fear of rectum or rectal diseases.
Rhabdophobia... Fear of being severely punished or beaten by a rod, or of being severely criticized. Also fear of magic. (wand)
Rhypophobia... Fear of defecation.
Rhytiphobia... Fear of getting wrinkles.
Rupophobia... Fear of dirt.
Russophobia... Fear of Russians.
Samhainophobia... Fear of Halloween.
Sarmassophobia... Fear of love play. (Malaxophobia)
Satanophobia... Fear of Satan.
Scabiophobia... Fear of scabies.
Scatophobia... Fear of fecal matter.
Scelerophobia... Fear of bad men, burglars.
Sciophobia or Sciaphobia... Fear of shadows.
Scoleciphobia... Fear of worms.
Scolionophobia... Fear of school.
Scopophobia or Scoptophobia... Fear of being seen or stared at.
Scotomaphobia... Fear of blindness in visual field.
Scotophobia... Fear of darkness. (Achluophobia)
Scriptophobia... Fear of writing in public.
Selachophobia... Fear of sharks.
Selaphobia... Fear of light flashes.
Selenophobia... Fear of the moon.
Seplophobia... Fear of decaying matter.
Sesquipedalophobia... Fear of long words.
Sexophobia... Fear of the opposite sex. (Heterophobia)
Siderodromophobia... Fear of trains, railroads or train travel.
Siderophobia... Fear of stars.
Sinistrophobia... Fear of things to the left, left-handed.
Sinophobia... Fear of Chinese, Chinese culture.
Sitophobia or Sitiophobia... Fear of food or eating. (Cibophobia)

Snakephobia... Fear of snakes. (Ophidiophobia)
Soceraphobia... Fear of parents-in-law.
Social Phobia... Fear of being evaluated negatively in social situations.
Sociophobia... Fear of society or people in general.
Somniphobia... Fear of sleep.
Sophophobia... Fear of learning.
Soteriophobia... Fear of dependence on others.
Spacephobia... Fear of outer space.
Spectrophobia... Fear of specters or ghosts.
Spermatophobia or Spermophobia... Fear of germs.
Spheksophobia... Fear of wasps.
Stasibasiphobia or Stasiphobia... Fear of standing or walking. (Ambulophobia)
Staurophobia... Fear of crosses or the crucifix.
Stenophobia... Fear of narrow things or places.
Stygiophobia or Stigiophobia... Fear of hell.
Suriphobia... Fear of mice.
Symbolophobia... Fear of symbolism.
Symmetrophobia... Fear of symmetry.
Syngenesophobia... Fear of relatives.
Syphilophobia... Fear of syphilis.
Tachophobia... Fear of speed.
Taeniophobia or Teniophobia... Fear of tapeworms.
Taphephobia Taphophobia... Fear of being buried alive or of cemeteries.
Tapinophobia... Fear of being contagious.
Taurophobia... Fear of bulls.
Technophobia... Fear of technology.
Teleophobia... 1) Fear of definite plans. 2) Religious ceremony.
Telephonophobia... Fear of telephones.
Teratophobia... Fear of bearing a deformed child or fear of monsters or deformed people.
Testophobia... Fear of taking tests.
Tetanophobia... Fear of lockjaw, tetanus.
Teutophobia... Fear of Germany or German things.
Textophobia... Fear of certain fabrics.
Thaasophobia... Fear of sitting.
Thalassophobia... Fear of the sea.
Thanatophobia or Thantophobia... Fear of death or dying.
Theatrophobia... Fear of theaters.
Theologicophobia... Fear of theology.
Theophobia... Fear of gods or religion.
Thermophobia... Fear of heat.

Tocophobia... Fear of pregnancy or childbirth.
Tomophobia... Fear of surgical operations.
Tonitrophobia... Fear of thunder.
Topophobia... Fear of certain places or situations, such as stage fright.
Toxiphobia or Toxophobia or Toxicophobia... Fear of poison or of being accidently poisoned.
Traumatophobia... Fear of injury.
Tremophobia... Fear of trembling.
Trichinophobia... Fear of trichinosis.
Trichopathophobia or Trichophobia or Hypertrichophobia... Fear of hair. (Chaetophobia)
Triskaidekaphobia... Fear of the number 13.
Tropophobia... Fear of moving or making changes.
Trypanophobia... Fear of injections.
Tuberculophobia... Fear of tuberculosis.
Tyrannophobia... Fear of tyrants.
Uranophobia... Fear of heaven.
Urophobia... Fear of urine or urinating.

V—W—X—Y—Z

Vaccinophobia... Fear of vaccination.
Venustraphobia... Fear of beautiful women.
Verbophobia... Fear of words.
Verminophobia... Fear of germs.
Vestiphobia... Fear of clothing.
Virginitiphobia... Fear of rape.
Vitricophobia... Fear of step-father.
Walloonphobia... Fear of the Walloons.
Wiccaphobia... Fear of witches and witchcraft.
Xanthophobia... Fear of the color yellow or the word yellow.
Xenoglossophobia... Fear of foreign languages.
Xenophobia... Fear of strangers or foreigners.
Xerophobia... Fear of dryness.
Xylophobia... 1) Fear of wooden objects. 2) Forests.
Xyrophobia... Fear of razors.
Zelophobia... Fear of jealousy.
Zeusophobia... Fear of God or gods.
Zemmiphobia... Fear of the great mole rat.
Zoophobia... Fear of animals.
Source: www.phobialist.com
Compiled by Fredd Culbertson

UNIT 11
Psychological Treatments

Unit Selections

Key Points to Consider

- Are Americans nuts? Why do you agree or disagree? Do you know what varieties of psychotherapy are available? Does psychotherapy work? Do you think laypersons can be effective therapists? Is professional assistance for psychological problems always necessary? According to Mary McNamara, how and why is psychotherapy replacing spirituality?

- Can people successfully change themselves? Why do people turn to self-help books rather than to friends or professionals? What is some of the advice commonly provided by today's self-help books? Is the advice true? How can we be sure whether we are given good advice by self-help gurus and their books?

- Do you know what types of medications are now available for use by people with psychological disorders? What would you prefer, psychotherapy or medication? How does clinical depression differ from the everyday blues we sometimes experience? What are some of the treatments for severe depression? What is Prozac? How does Prozac work? What are some of its side effects and disadvantages? If you were a psychiatrist, would your first line of treatment for depression be Prozac? Why?

- What is schizophrenia? Why is schizophrenia hard to treat? Do you think schizophrenia is a brain disorder as some claim? What are some treatments for schizophrenia? What do you think would be the best treatment for this perplexing disorder?

 **Links: www.dushkin.com/online/**
These sites are annotated in the World Wide Web pages.

Knowledge Exchange Network (KEN)
   http://www.mentalhealth.org
Links to the World of Carl Jung
   http://www.cisnet.com/teacher-ed/jung.html
Sigmund Freud and the Freud Archives
   http://plaza.interport.net/nypsan/freudarc.html

Have you ever had the nightmare that you are trapped in a dark, dismal place? No one will let you out. Your pleas for freedom go unanswered and, in fact, are suppressed or ignored by domineering authority figures around you. You keep begging for mercy but to no avail. What a nightmare! You are fortunate to awake to your normal bedroom and to the realities of your daily life. For the mentally ill, the nightmare of institutionalization, where individuals can be held against their will in what are sometimes terribly dreary, restrictive surroundings, is a reality. Have you ever wondered what would happen if we took perfectly normal individuals and institutionalized them? In one well-known and remarkable study, that is exactly what happened.

In 1973, eight people, including a pediatrician, a psychiatrist and some psychologists, presented themselves to psychiatric hospitals. Each claimed that he or she was hearing voices. The voices, they reported, seemed unclear but appeared to be saying "empty" or "thud." Each of these individuals was admitted to a mental hospital, and most were diagnosed as being schizophrenic. Upon admission, the "pseudopatients" or fake patients gave truthful information and thereafter acted like their usual, normal selves.

Their hospital stays lasted anywhere from 7 to 52 days. The nurses, doctors, psychologists, and other staff members treated them as if they really were schizophrenic and never saw through their trickery. Some of the real patients in the hospital did recognize, however, that the pseudopatients were perfectly normal. Upon discharge almost all of the pseudopatients received the diagnosis of "schizophrenic in remission," meaning that they were still clearly construed as schizophrenic; they just weren't exhibiting any of the symptoms at the time.

What does this study demonstrate about mental illness? Is true mental illness readily detectable? If we can't always detect mental disorders, the more professionally accepted term for mental illness, how can we treat them? What treatments are available and which work better for various diagnoses? The treatment of mental disorders is a challenge. The array of available treatments is ever increasing and can be downright bewildering—and not just to the patient or client! In order to demystify

and simplify your understanding of various treatments, we will look at them in this unit.

We commence with two general articles on treatment. In the first, Mary McNamara asks, "Are We Nuts?" If one examines how popular psychotherapy is today, then one might indeed conclude that, yes, Americans appear to be crazy. Why we are in love with psychotherapy and whether therapy is truly helpful are investigated in her article.

In a companion article, Annie Murphie Paul questions whether self-help books really are helpful. She believes they are not. By juxtaposing scientific studies against advice given in these books, Paul shatters some of the myths and bad guidance that the books provide.

In the third article, the common cold of mental health—depression—is again explored with a special eye on its treatment. Depression afflicts many of us. Some individuals suffer from chronic and intense depression, known as clinical depression. This article, "The Quest for a Cure," not only details the symptoms of depression, it also provides a good discussion of the possible treatments for severe depression, in particular, the revolutionary drug Prozac.

The final article of this unit and of the book investigates treatments for schizophrenia. Schizophrenia is a psychosis that causes more profound disturbance than the disorders discussed previously. In this final article, Bruce Bower asserts that the best treatment for this baffling illness is a combination of medication and psychotherapy.

ARE WE Nuts?

By Mary McNamara Los Angeles Times

Americans have long been in love with the idea of psychotherapy. When Sigmund Freud made his first and only visit to the United States in 1909, American intelligentsia flocked to his lectures. Since then, psychotherapy has spread like kudzu, morphing from the medical treatment of specific, diagnosable mental illnesses into a sort of societal support system offered by psychiatrists, psychologists, counselors, therapists, self-help gurus and TV talk-show hosts.

"Seek professional help" is our standard answer to everything from episodes of psychotic rage to dating problems, and "self-help" has become its own industry. We use terms like "manic depressive," "obsessive compulsive" and "neurotic" to describe the most benign, everyday sort of behaviors.

And should true tragedy occur, the psychologists and counselors are there on the front lines, elbowing out the friends and clergy if not the paramedics. No other area of science or medicine so informs our national discussions or perceptions of who we are and who we should be.

But is it working? Are we getting any better? Is our mental health improving? And is our increased self-awareness benefiting society?

"It's difficult to gauge, compared to other parts of medicine," says Rochester, N.Y., psychiatrist John McIntyre. "There's no question that treatment of specific mental disorders is very effective—the efficacy rate is often higher than in other medical procedures. But when you broaden it to other issues, it gets fuzzy. It's had the overall beneficial effect of increasing knowledge of human nature, but are people better? How do you measure that?"

'Hysterical misery'

There is no arguing the fact that psychotherapy and psychiatry have improved the lives of millions suffering from often devastating chemical and mental imbalances. And, certainly, Freud had no personal illusions about transforming the human condition. He was content, he once said, to turn people's "hysterical misery into ordinary human unhappiness."

But here in America, we want to teach the world to sing, in perfect harmony. And so we look to psychology to provide us with answers and solutions to everything from a president's mendacity (there was that abusive stepfather) to relations between the sexes (which planet am I from?) to a baseball player's overt racism and homophobia (don't fire him, send him to a therapist).

According to Surgeon General David Satcher, the next decades will put the effectiveness of psychotherapy and psychiatry to the test. One out of five baby boomers can expect to suffer a mental disorder, from substance abuse to late-onset schizophrenia, while almost 21 percent of children ages 9 to 17 suffer from diagnosable mental disorders.

But measuring a nation's mental health is a difficult thing to undertake. One traditional method is to look at a society's tendency toward "social deviance"—its rates of crime, divorce, suicide, drug use and out-of-wedlock births. Most of these have decreased in recent years, although the divorce rate is significantly higher than it was even half a century ago.

But how valid are these numbers as indicators of mental health?

"Crime is not a good measure because there are a lot of social and economic reasons for crime," says Wendy Kaminer, pop psychology critic and author of "I'm Dysfunctional, You're Dysfunctional" and more recently "Sleeping With Extraterrestrials." "And to use divorce, well, if you have a sick norm [of troubled marriages], what is mentally healthy? To conform or rebel?"

Even using drug use as an indicator of mental instability is dangerous, she says, because there are many possible reasons for drug abuse; many in the scientific community believe the propensity for abuse is genetic.

Political movements have a complex relationship with the psychoanalytical movement. At one level, political movements by definition reject the psychological paradigm, their premise being that discontent stems not from our selves but from the System. On the other hand, Freud's identification of the id and the unconscious had a profound effect, particularly on the youth movements of the '60s and '70s.

Age of the id

"The id really came out in the '60s," says Peter Wolson, a Beverly Hills, Calif., psychoanalyst. "Suddenly, the thing is to be happy, not to lead a good life. Have fun, have orgasms, and this leads into the '70s and '80s, which is about getting ahead, still about 'me,' and then you have a backlash, mainly from fundamentalists. But even the backlash is very self-centered, very much of the id."

The United States has a long, complicated relationship with the culture of self—with self-government, self-actualization, self-discovery, self-aggrandizement. We celebrate nonconformity in a way that absolutely defines conformity and claim to treasure individualism while mass-producing more products than any other country in the world. "I gotta be me," we say, and if that "me" doesn't work out, well, we'll just try on a new one.

Psychology seems to provide both the means and the motive for the culture of self, and therein lies its greatest strength and its greatest failings.

"In a way, psychology has replaced religion," says David Blankenhorn of the Institute for American Values, based in New York. "It is who we are, the air we breathe. And it can truly help people who suffer and can yield important insights. But the assumptions of the paradigm are so relentlessly centered on self, all other structures of meaning and authority evaporate. 'What do I want?' becomes the governing question."

Much of Blankenhorn's work centers on marriage and fatherhood, two areas greatly affected by the mass marketing of psychological theories in very different ways.

"For men, there are clearly advantages," he says. "They are more able to express emotions. Most fathers today hug their children and say, 'I love you.' For our fathers and grandfathers, such emotional intimacy was not there, and there is a whole generation of men walking around wounded from that."

But while fatherhood has benefited, he says, marriage has not.

"If talking about marriage and relationships was the basis of good marriage and relationships, we'd have the best in the history of the world," he says. "But they are now more fragile than they have ever been. Men and women seem unhappier with each other than ever."

Self-invention

Freud argued that it is pointless to try to make people happy because that's not what they want. Yet happiness seems to be the carrot at the end of psychology's stick—if you know yourself, you can change yourself and you can be happy. All the time. The creation of such expectations may be one of the psych-culture's greatest drawbacks.

"It's a mixed blessing," says University of Washington sociologist Pepper Schwartz. "We've hugely increased our sensitivity to each other. We understand, for example, how much damage words can do. More people take responsibility for their actions, and if they don't, someone makes them. But we've also created whole new categories of what people should worry about, hundreds of new ways in which we can fail or people can fail us."

Our expectations from relationships have become much higher.

"Just look at the area of sex therapy," she says. "We have a hundred new ways to create inadequacies."

On the other hand, we have become more informed consumers, of theories as well as products.

"It used to be if Dr. So-and-So said something in the newspaper, readers would assume it was true," Schwartz says. "Not anymore. An easy example is how we have examined and rejected corporal punishment."

Like Blankenhorn, Schwartz believes the successes of the psychological movement are most evident in our attitudes toward parenting.

"If nothing else, I know we've made better fathers, although the numbers of fathers who leave is an area where we have possibly slid. But the ones who stay are much more participatory. No one's shocked to see a man in the grocery store alone with his kids. When I was a young woman, you would have assumed the mother was dead."

But again, are such changes the result of psychologically increased self-awareness, or the women's movement?

"The only real answer to 'Are we better yet?' " says Kaminer, "is, 'We don't know yet.' "

Self-Help:

Shattering the Myths

BOOKSTORES AND THE INTERNET ARE SPILLING OVER WITH ADVICE FROM THE LATEST SELF-HELP GURUS. PT FINDS OUT WHETHER ANY OF IT MAKES SENSE.

IT'S NO SURPRISE THAT AMERICA—LAND OF SECOND CHANCES, FABLED site of self-invention—also harbors an endless appetite for self-help. From Poor Richard to Dale Carnegie to Tony Robbins, we love the idea that we can fix what's broken by ourselves, without the expensive ministrations of doctor or shrink. The limits of HMOs, and the limitlessness of the Internet, have lately made self-help even more appealing: Americans spent $563 million on self-help books last year, and surfed more than 12,000 Web sites devoted to mental health. An estimated 40% of all health-related Internet inquiries are on mental health topics, and depression is the number-one most researched illness on the Web.

By Annie Murphy Paul

In the spirit of pioneers, we're concocting our own remedies and salving our own wounds. But is it good medicine? Once the preserve of charlatans and psychobabblers, self-help has undergone its own reinvention, emerging as a source of useful information presented by acknowledged authorities. That's not to say snake oil isn't still for sale. Often, the messages of self-help books tend to be vast oversimplifications, misrepresenting a part of the truth for the whole, as the following list of popular misconceptions and distortions demonstrates.

The antidote—the "good" kind of self-help, grounded in research—is also available to those who help themselves. Just keep in mind that even the best self-help may be too simplistic to manage complex prob-

lems, and that research, with its emphasis on straight science, may not always offer a clear course of action.

Does venting anger make you more angry?

DISTORTION 1
VENT YOUR ANGER, AND IT'LL GO AWAY.

SELF-HELP BOOKS SAY: "Punch a pillow or punching bag. And while you do it, yell and curse and moan and holler," advises *Facing the Fire: Expressing and Experiencing Anger Appropriately* (Bantam Doubleday Dell, 1995). "Punch with all the frenzy you can. If you are an-

gry at a particular person, imagine his or her face on the pillow or punching bag, and vent your rage physically and verbally."

RESEARCHERS SAY: Pillow punching, like other forms of vigorous exercise, might be helpful for stress management, but recent studies suggest that venting anger may be counterproductive. "Venting anger just keeps it alive," says Brad Bushman, Ph.D., a psychologist at Iowa State University. "People think it's going to work, and when it doesn't, they become even more angry and frustrated."

In addition, several studies show that the outward expression of anger leads to dangerously elevated cardiovascular activity, which may contribute to the development of cardiovascular disease.

THE BEST SELF-HELP BOOKS

GENERAL RESOURCES
The Authoritative Guide to Self-Help Resources in Mental Health By John C. Norcross, Linda Frye Campbell and Thomas P. Smith (Guilford, 2000)

THE BEST SELF-HELP AND SELF-AWARENESS BOOKS
A Topic-by-Topic Guide to Quality Information By Stephen B. Fried and G. Ann Schultis (American Library Association, 1995)

Caring for the Mind: The Comprehensive Guide to Mental Health By Dianne and Robert Hales (Bantam, 1995)

RESOURCES ON ANXIETY
An End to Panic: Breakthrough Techniques for Overcoming Panic Disorder By Elke Zuercher-White (New Harbinger Publications, 1998)

Anxiety & Depression: The Best Resources to Help You Cope Edited By Rich Wemhoff (Resource Pathways, 1998)

RESOURCES ON DEPRESSION
Feeling Good: The New Mood Therapy By David D. Burns (Avon, 1992)

Understanding Depression: A Complete Guide to Its Diagnosis and Treatment By Donald F. Klein, M.D., and Paul H. Wender, M.D. (Oxford University Press, 1993)

SELF-HELP RESOURCES ON OBSESSIVE-COMPULSIVE DISORDER
Getting Control: Overcoming Your Obsessions and Compulsions By Lee Baier (Plume, 1992)

The OCD Workbook: Your Guide to Breaking Free from Obsessive-Compulsive Disorder By Bruce M. Hyman and Cherry Pedrick (New Harbinger Publications, 1999)

RESOURCES FOR TRAUMA AND PTSD
Coping with Post-Traumatic Stress Disorder By Carolyn Simpson and Dwain Simpson (Rosen Publishing Group, 1997)

Coping with Trauma: A Guide to Self-Understanding By Jon G. Allen (American Psychiatric Press, 1995)

THE BEST SELF-HELP WEB SITES

GOVERNMENT-SPONSORED WEB SITES:
Knowledge Exchange Network (operated by the U.S. Dept. of Health and Human Services, Substance Abuse and Mental Health Services Administration, and the Center for Mental Health Services) www.mentalhealth.org
- National Center for PTSD (operated by the U.S. Department of Veterans Affairs) www. dartmouth.edu/dms/ptsd
- National Institute of Mental Health www.nimh.nih.gov

NON-PROFIT SITES

- American Psychiatric Association www.psych.org
- Anxiety Disorders Association of America www.adaa.org
- The Help Center of the American Psychological Association www.helping.apa.org
- The International Society for Mental Health Online www. ismho.org
- National Alliance for the Mentally Ill www.nami.org
- National Depressive and Manic-Depressive Association www.ndmda.org

COMMERCIAL WEB SITES

- Online Psych www.onlinepsych.com
- Basic Information www.realpsychology.com
- Self-Help and Psychology Magazine www.shpm.com

Bushman recently put the so-called "catharsis hypothesis" to the test, deliberately inducing anger in a group of college students by marking nasty comments on essays they had written. Those who slammed a punching bag afterward were more, not less, aggressive to people they subsequently encountered.

"It may be better to do things incompatible with anger like watching a funny movie or listening to music"

WHAT TO DO INSTEAD: A better tack, says Bushman, is to do "anything that's incompatible with anger and aggression." That includes watching a funny movie, reading an absorbing novel, sharing a laugh with a friend, or listening to music. Given time, your anger will dissipate, and then you'll be able to deal with the situation in a more constructive way.

Though Bushman has found that exercise can actually heighten physical arousal and keep anger alive, other studies have concluded that sustained strenuous activity might indeed release anger and improve mood. And nontraditional exercise programs like tai chi, yoga and stretching may not only dissipate negative feelings such as anger but make people more conscious of their mood states, paving the way for them to do something constructive about them.

DISTORTION 2
WHEN YOU'RE DOWN IN THE DUMPS, THINK YOURSELF HAPPY BY FOCUSING ON THE POSITIVE.

SELF-HELP BOOKS SAY: "Close your mental doors behind you on unpleasant circumstances or failures you have experienced," commands Napoleon Hill's *Keys to Positive Thinking* (Plume, 1998). "Use your brain for controlled, optimistic thinking. Take possession of your mind and direct it to images of your choosing. Do not let circumstances or people dictate negative visual images."

RESEARCHERS SAY: Research shows that when we're anxious or stressed—in other words, exactly when we need a mood boost—our minds become unable to provide one.

That's because we're so preoccupied with our troubles that we don't have enough brainpower left over to suppress negative thoughts. And when we try to distract ourselves, pessimistic notions are the only ones that come to mind. "If you're really under stress, putting yourself in a good mood by thinking positive thoughts becomes not only difficult—in fact it backfires, and you get the opposite of what you want," says Daniel Wegner, Ph.D., a psychologist at the University of Virginia.

Feeling down? Go to the mall and lift your spirits

In an experiment, Wegner asked a group of people to put themselves in a good mood—which they did, fairly easily. But when they were also told to keep a nine-digit number in mind, they actually felt worse. The energy they had available to control their mood was reduced by the effort of remembering the number.

If you're upset or anxious, make a list of positive things

WHAT TO DO INSTEAD: "You have to enlist the help of other people," Wegner says. "Talk to friends or relatives or clergy or a therapist, or anyone else who might be able to help you think about other things." Or go to a place where people are enjoying themselves, like a party or the park or the mall, and you'll soon feel your spirits lift. Finally, if you know in advance that you're going to be upset or anxious about something, make a list of positive things that you can refer to when you need it most: your five favorite memories, say, or three occasions to look forward to.

DISTORTION 3
VISUALIZE YOUR GOAL, AND YOU'LL HELP MAKE IT COME TRUE.

SELF-HELP BOOKS SAY: "Hold the image of yourself succeeding, visualize it so vividly, that when the desired success comes, it seems to be merely echoing a reality that has already existed in your mind," suggests *Positive Imaging: The Powerful Way to Change Your Life* (Fawcett Book Group, 1996).

RESEARCHERS SAY: Sports psychologists have shown the power that visualization has on improving performance, but simply imagining that you've achieved your goal won't bring it any closer—and might even put it further out of reach.

Shelley Taylor, Ph.D., a psychologist at UCLA, has reservations about visualizing your goals. "First of all, it separates the goal from what you need to do to get it. And second, it enables you to enjoy the feeling of being successful without actually having achieved anything. That takes away the power of the goal"—and can even make you complacent, unwilling to work hard or take risks to get what you already have in your daydreams.

WHAT TO DO INSTEAD: In addition to picturing your goal as a fait accompli, "you should figure out what the steps to get there are, and then mentally rehearse them," says Taylor.

In an experiment, Taylor asked some students preparing for an exam to imagine their happiness at having received an 'A' on the test, and others to picture themselves sitting in the library, studying their textbooks and going over lecture notes. Those in the second group performed better on the test, and experienced less stress and worry.

For short-term goals, Taylor recommends running through the steps you've laid out once a day; for bigger dreams, you can revisit your plan every time you make some progress, and see if it needs adjusting.

DISTORTION 4
SELF-AFFIRMATIONS WILL HELP YOU RAISE LOW SELF-ESTEEM.

SELF-HELP BOOKS SAY: "Write affirmations on paper and put them in places you will see them—on the bathroom mirror, next to your bed, on the car dashboard," recommends *Life 101: Everything We Wish We Had Learned About Life In School—But Didn't* (Prelude Press, 1991). "You can also record them on endless-loop cassette tapes and play them in the background all day (and night)."

RESEARCHERS SAY: Psychologists say this technique may not be very helpful. Changing how we feel about ourselves is a lot more complicated, explains William Swann, Ph.D., of the University of Texas-Austin. "Self-esteem is based on two components: first, our sense of how likable and lovable we are, and second, our sense of how competent we are" at our jobs and at other activities that demand talent and skill. On those scores, we've been hearing from other people—parents, teachers, bosses, siblings, friends, romantic partners—all our lives, and their opinions of us continue to reinforce our notions of ourselves, good or bad. Self-affirmations, even when endlessly repeated, don't make much of a dent—and when they fail to work, they may leave us even more demoralized.

"The more specific the problem-solving strategies, the more useful. All the strategies presented should be based squarely on science or professional science."

What's more, people with low self-esteem may be especially unpersuaded by self-affirmations. Preliminary research by Swann's colleague at UT, Robert Josephs, Ph.D., indicates that those with poor self-images

SIFTING SCIENCE FROM SNAKE OIL:
How to Find Top Psychology in Pop Psychology

By Stephen B. Fried, Ph.D

AMERICANS TURN RELENTLESSLY TO BOOKS, MAGA-zines, radio, TV and the Internet in the hopes of finding their way to a better, less problem-filled life. But there's a catch. Some of this popular psychology is based on solid psychological science and practice, and some is not. How to distinguish which is which?

• Consider the source of the information. Does it come from a mental health professional? Beware of materials written by fellow sufferers who are laypersons. Experiencing a problem doesn't automatically confer the ability to help others. And what works for one may not work for all.

• The problem that's addressed has to be one that is amenable to change. Psychological states that are genetic, like manic-depressive disorder, are extraordinarily difficult to change. So are those that are at the core of what we think or do, such as sexual orientation. Depression is more responsive to deliberate efforts at change, and panic disorder and issues of sexual performance more susceptible still.

• The material must provide both facts about and specific strategies for dealing with the psychological concern. It's important that the information review the symptoms of any condition, and ideally a self-diagnosis questionnaire should be provided.

• Quality information also takes into account individual differences among readers. Most helpful is an array of techniques for tackling the problem. The more specific the problem-solving strategies, the more useful. And all of the strategies presented should be based squarely on science or professional practice.

• The material should refer the reader to authoritative sources, such as professional organizations. Does it contain a bibliography? A resource guide? These are important for possible follow-ups.

Along with G. Ann Schultis, I have analyzed self-help books and offer these additional guidelines in choosing good ones. The book's title should reflect its contents. The purpose of the book should be stated in the preface or the first chapter.

• Some radio and TV stations air entire programs devoted to psychological matters, often hosted by a "mental health professional." Highly dependent on the skills and knowledge of the host, these programs may play on the voyeuristic interests of listeners who may be titillated tuning into the intimate details of an anonymous caller's life. On the other hand, such programs may reach millions and motivate some to seek professional help because of what they heard.

• TV talk shows may feature "victims" of a particular problem—but they often encourage the very behaviors they are purporting to fix. For instance, a couple with poor interpersonal skills is goaded into fighting before the studio audience. Then a guest therapist (typically the author of a topical self-help book) suggests a quick fix to the problem. In this way, the program reinforces both the antisocial behavior and the idea of overly simple solutions to far more complex matters.

• Psychologically related sites have virtually exploded on the web. Look for those hosted by a reputable organization and that present in-depth coverage of issues. The best Web sites offer bibliographies of relevant articles and books; they also offer a listing of professional organizations.

No matter where you turn for information, you can't abandon your critical thinking skills.

Until he succumbed to a long-term illness last May, Dr. Fried was professor and chairman of psychology at Park University in Missouri.

---

simply don't believe the statements, because they don't value their own opinions very highly. In Josephs' experiment, high self-esteem people were able to pat themselves on the back for solving a set of problems, while "lows" had to hear praise from someone else before they would credit it.

WHAT TO DO INSTEAD: The only way to change the final product—your self-esteem—is to change what goes into making it—feedback from other people. "If you find yourself in bad relationships where your negative self-view is getting reinforced, then either change the way

those people treat you by being more assertive, or change who you interact with," says Swann. "If you're in a job where you're getting denigrated, insist that you be treated more appropriately, or change jobs. Try to do your job better than you've done it before."

IN OTHER WORDS: Stand up for yourself. Surround yourself with people who think you're great, and tell you so. Do your best to live up to their high opinions. And be patient. Self-esteem is the sum of your interactions with others over a lifetime, and it's not going to change overnight.

DISTORTION 5
"ACTIVE LISTENING" CAN HELP YOU COMMUNICATE BETTER WITH YOUR PARTNER.

SELF-HELP BOOKS SAY: "The technique of 'active listening' ensures that you not only hear, but really understand what your partner is trying to tell you," reads *Going the Distance: Finding and Keeping Lifelong Love* (Plume, 1993). You do it by "paraphrasing your partner's words, then repeating in your own words what you believe your partner is trying to communicate to you."

RESEARCHERS SAY: There's only one problem with active listening: hardly anyone does it. Although the technique has been promoted by therapists for over three decades, research shows that actual couples—including the long-lasting, lovey-dovey ones—completely ignore it when they argue. "It just doesn't happen," says Sybil Carrere, Ph.D., a psychologist at the University of Washington who's been leading a six-year study of how newlyweds interact. "Intuitively it does make sense, but the fact is that when you look at happy couples, they're not doing it. They're being affectionate, they're using humor to break up tension, they're indicating interest in what their partner has to say—they're doing a lot of positive things. But they're not doing active listening." In fact, one of the few studies that has been conducted on the effects of active listening shows that it does nothing to help couples in distress.

WHAT TO DO INSTEAD: According to Carrere, couples should focus their efforts on three other areas. First, women should try to present their complaints in a calm way: Research shows that men are more likely to listen if their partners tone down hostility and avoid contemptuousness. Second, men need to really listen to their partners, taking their feelings and opinions into account. And third, both sides should do what they can to keep the male half cool and collected. "Men have a tendency when they get into conflict to get physiologically aroused, and then they tend to withdraw from the conflict in order to soothe themselves, which only makes the woman more angry," says Carrere. If the two of you can work together to head his anger off at the pass—by throwing in a joke, maybe, or offering a hug—you'll both be better off.

The five distortions presented here are only a few of the misconceptions you may encounter. To protect yourself against others, be sure to take self-help prescriptions with a measure of skepticism and a healthy dose of common sense.

Reprinted with permission from *Psychology Today*, March/April 2001, pp. 60-68. © 2001 by Sussex Publishers, Inc.

THE QUEST FOR A CURE

BY MARK NICHOLS

Every few weeks, several teenage girls arrive at Halifax's Queen Elizabeth II Health Sciences Centre to take part in a study that may someday ease the crippling misery of depression. For two nights, the girls, a different group each time, bunk down in a sleep laboratory with tiny electrodes attached to their heads. Through the night, electronic equipment monitors their brain activity as they pass through the various stages of sleep, including the periods of rapid eye movement (REM) when dreaming occurs. Half of the roughly 80 girls who will take part in the study have no family history of depression. The others do—their mothers have had major depression and researchers know that these girls have a 30 percent chance of being victims, too. Dr. Stan Kutcher, a Dalhousie University psychiatrist who is involved in the study, wants to see whether a feature of sleep in depressed adults—they reach the REM stage faster than others—shows up in the kids. If it does, doctors for the first time would have a way of predicting depression and starting treatment early. Kutcher has been working with troubled youngsters most of his life. "It's a tremendous feeling to be able to help kids get better," he says. "It's a privilege to be let into their lives."

A pioneer in studying and treating adolescent depression, Kutcher is part of an army of medical researchers whose efforts are bringing new drugs, new therapies and new ways of thinking to bear in the war on the debilitating disorder. One of the biggest breakthroughs came in capsule form when Indianapolis's Eli Lilly and Co. introduced a product called Prozac almost 10 years ago. The first of a new class of drugs that can alleviate depression without the same nasty side effects of many older antidepressants, it profoundly improved the quality of life for millions of people. Thanks to Prozac and drugs like it, says Dr. Sid Kennedy, head of the mood disorders program at Toronto's Clarke Institute of Psychiatry, "depressed people are able to live normal, productive lives in a way that wouldn't have been possible 10 years ago."

Now, drugs that are potentially even better are undergoing tests, while researchers study the intricate universe of the brain in search of clues that could someday banish depression entirely. "Things are really moving quickly," says Dr. Trevor Young, a neuroscientist at McMaster University in Hamilton. "They're really getting close to understanding the biochemical changes that occur in depressed brains."

And doctors are coming closer to the time when they may be able to start treatment, in some cases, even before depression takes hold. After the Dalhousie researchers finish their current series of tests early next year, they will keep track of their young subjects for five years to see whether their REM sleep patterns pinpoint which of them will become depressed. If they do, then doctors in the future may be able to test children from families with a history of depression, and identify potential victims. One possibility, says Kutcher, would be to begin treating those children with antidepressants even before the first bout of depression occurred—in the hope that it never will.

New drugs and therapies join the battle against depression

Underpinning the new wave of research is a quiet revolution that has transformed thinking about depression over the past two decades. As recently as in the 1960s, when Sigmund Freud's psychoanalytic philosophy was still pervasive, depression and most other forms of mental illness were regarded as the consequences of emotional turmoil in childhood. Now, scientists have clear evidence that inherited flaws in the brain's biochemistry are to blame for many mental problems, including manic-depressive illness—with its violent swings between depressive lows and manic highs—and, according to some experts, recurring severe depression. Beyond that, many experts think that damaging events in childhood—sexual or physical abuse, poisoned parental relationships and other blows to the child's psyche—may cause depression later by disrupting development of crucial chemical pathways in the brain. "Losses early in life," says Dr. Jane Garland, director of the mood and anxiety clinic at the British Columbia Children's Hospital in Vancouver, "can raise the brain's level of stress hormones that are associated with depression."

When the dark curtain of depression descends, today's victims have access to quick and effective treatment. Short-term "talk therapies" now in use can help haul a patient out of depression in as little as four months—as opposed to years on a psychoanalyst's couch. The purpose of such therapy, says Dr. Marie Corral, a psychiatrist at the British Columbia Women's Hospital in Vancouver, is "to deal with the skewed thinking that develops when a person has been depressed for a long time." The most widely used methods: interpersonal therapy, which focuses on specific people-related problems, and cognitive therapy, which tries to counter the feelings of worthlessness and hopelessness that plague depressed people. "We try to show the patient that much of this thinking may be unfounded," says Zindel Segal, a Toronto psychologist.

But along with the new approaches to dealing with depression, a treatment introduced nearly 60 years ago that has earned a grim public image—electroconvulsive therapy (ECT)—is still a mainstay. Popularly known as shock treatment, it remains "one of our most potent forms of therapy" for severely depressed patients who do not respond to other treatment, says Dr. David Goldbloom, chief of staff at Toronto's Clarke Institute. ECT is routinely used every year on thousands of depressed Canadians, including older patients who cannot tolerate some of the side-effects of drug therapies.

ECT's bad reputation owes much to the 1975 movie *One Flew over the Cuckoo's Nest*, in which staff members of a mental institution punish a rebellious patient, played by Jack Nicholson, with repeated ECT sessions. Patients *did* endure painful ordeals in the early days of ECT when larger electrical shocks were used to induce a limb-shaking seizure in unanesthetized patients. Electroconvulsive treatment is gentler now. Doctors administer a muscle relaxant and a general anesthetic before subjecting the patient's brain to the amount of current needed to light a 60-watt bulb for one second.

ECT's aftereffects can include painful headaches lasting half an hour or so, and some memory loss. ECT does its job, they add, by altering the brain's electrical and chemical activity. The therapy has some bitter opponents, who claim that it can cause lasting memory loss and impair other brain functions, such as concentration. "ECT damages people's brains—that's really the whole point of it," says Wendy Funk, a 41-year-old Cranbrook, B.C., housewife. Funk says that after receiving electroconvulsive therapy for depression in 1989 and 1990, she lost virtually all memory—she could not recall even her own name or that she was married and had two children.

Meanwhile, for the approximately 70 per cent of patients who respond to them, Prozac and the family of drugs it spawned—Paxil, Zoloft, Luvox and Serzone—are making life far more bearable. Collectively, the drugs are known as SSRIs (for selective serotonin reuptake inhibitors) because they increase the brain's supply of the chemical messenger serotonin. The SSRIs have foes: the Internet bristles with accusations that the drugs can cause panic attacks, aggressive behavior and suicidal tendencies. But most doctors have nothing but praise for the drugs. It's not that they are better than their predecessors at relieving depression—most physicians say they are not.

But SSRIs are easier to live with than some older antidepressants, which often caused dry mouth, daytime sleepiness, constipation, vision problems and other unpleasant side effects. "The SSRIs are better tolerated," says Dr. Russell Joffe, dean of health sciences at McMaster University, "and it is much harder to overdose on them than the older drugs"—a vital consideration in treating people who may be at risk from suicide. The SSRIs can have side effects of their own, including insomnia and a diminished interest in sex that sometimes persuade patients to stop taking them. "You just don't get sexually aroused," says Giselle, a 41-year-old Manitoba resident who requested anonymity. "There's just nothing there."

Another problem with the SSRIs is that patients usually have to take them for three weeks or more before they start to work. The reason: when an SSRI increases the flow of serotonin in the brain, the thermostat-like mechanism that normally controls the flow of the chemical shuts down—and then takes three to six weeks to adapt and allow serotonin to flow again. "If you have a severely depressed patient who may be thinking about suicide," says Dr. Pierre Blier, a professor of psychiatry at Montreal's McGill University, "telling him he may have to wait that long for relief isn't good enough."

Most doctors praise the Prozac-like drugs

After studying the problem exhaustively, Blier and another McGill psychiatrist, Dr. Claude deMontigny, proposed in 1993 that the SSRIs would probably take effect more rapidly if used in conjunction with another drug that could block the brain mechanism causing the delay. Such a drug, a hypertension medication called Pindolol, existed. And the following year, a Spanish physician tried the combination—and found that it worked. Since then, studies have shown that the Pindolol-SSRI combination can cut the waiting time for SSRIs to take effect to about 10 days. Working with that knowledge, several major drug companies now are trying to develop a new generation of fast-acting SSRIs.

Meanwhile, efforts to lay bare the roots of depression are being pursued by a number of Canadian research teams:

• While most antidepressants concentrate on two of the brain's chemical messengers—serotonin and noradrenaline—a research team at the University of Alberta in Edmonton headed by neurochemist Glen Baker is studying a substance called GABA. Another of the brain's neurotransmitters, GABA appears to play a role in quelling the panic attacks that often accompany depression. GABA (for gamma-aminobutyric acid) seems to work in the brain by preventing selected nerve cells from sending signals down the line. To find out more, Baker's team is studying the action of two older antidepressants that are used to treat panic, imipramine and phenelzine. They want to find out whether the drugs work by increasing GABA activity in the brain. A possible payoff: a new class of drugs that could some day stem panic by boosting the flow of GABA in the brain.

• At McMaster, Young's team is focusing on manic-depressive illness in an effort to discover which brain chemicals are involved. One approach to the puzzle involves dosing rats—which have many of the same genes as humans—with antidepressants or mood stabilizers and examining tissue samples to see which genes are activated. Eventually, Young hopes to learn more about the signalling process inside the brain that can go awry and lead to depression or mania. He also wants to identify which defective chemical pathways make that happen. "Once we know more about these things," says Young, "we may be able to correct the problems with drugs."

• In Toronto, a Clarke Institute team co-headed by psychiatrists Sid Kennedy and Franco Vaccarino is using high-tech imaging equipment to look at brain functioning before and after treatment with antidepressants. Images produced by a PET scan machine show that, in depressed people, some parts of the brain's pre-frontal region—an area associated with emotion—are less active than normal. Surprisingly, when antidepressant drugs start acting on the brain, those areas be come even *less* active. Kennedy thinks that may be because in depression, the brain deliberately dampens down pre-frontal activity to cope with high levels of stress, and antidepressants may help the process by reducing activity even further. Kennedy hopes next to study brains in people who had remained well on antidepressants for at least a year, and thinks "we may find that by then activity in the pre-frontal areas has returned to something normal"—meaning that the brain's overstressed condition has been corrected.

The best antidepressants can banish depression—but they do not necessarily protect patients from relapses. Susan Boning, who organizes volunteer services for the Society for Depression and Manic Depression of Manitoba at its Winnipeg headquarters, had been taking Prozac for two years when she felt her mood "dipping" last March. Her condition worsened to the point where she made what she calls "a suicidal gesture" by drinking half a bottle of rum and passing out on her living-room floor. Boning, 37, has stopped taking Prozac and has turned to three other drugs, including Serzone. Boning's experience, like countless others, shows that while medical science is making rapid progress in treating depression, for many in the remorseless grip of the disease it is still not fast enough.

From *Maclean's*, December 1, 1997, pp. 60-62. © 1997 by Maclean Hunter Publishing Ltd. Reprinted by permission.

Back from the brink

Psychological treatments for schizophrenia attract renewed interest

By BRUCE BOWER

Leslie Greenblat learned she had schizophrenia long after she had begun to hear, in her words, "thought-voices." She heard them all the time, whether she was driving, reading, shopping, or talking with friends. The disembodied remarks seemed to come from someone whose intimidating and demoralizing pronouncements couldn't be ignored.

Greenblat's condition first landed her in a psychiatric hospital in 1990. Over the next 3 years, the young woman was briefly hospitalized another dozen times. After each discharge, she took antipsychotic medications for a few months until the thought-voices receded. Invariably, however, they returned.

Then Greenblat began psychotherapy with psychiatrist Ann Alaoglu at Chestnut Lodge, a private psychiatric hospital in Rockville, Md. Although trained as a psychoanalyst, Alaoglu didn't have Greenblat lie on a couch and dissect her childhood. Instead, Alaoglu provided a relaxed environment and gentle, straightforward questioning to convince Greenblat that she finally had found a partner in healing. In that atmosphere, the cacophony of thought-voices started to ease.

"Before I met her, I didn't trust doctors," Greenblat wrote in an article last year for SCHIZOPHRENIA BULLETIN (Vol. 26, No. 1). "Doctors doped me up, locked me in, and were generally distant. Dr. Alaoglu... was willing to put herself on the line, sharing with me her sense of my progress and lapses."

Alaoglu's methods hardly represent the norm for schizophrenia treatment. But her success with Greenblat and other patients helps explain why the search for effective treatments has expanded beyond medication in the past decade. Researchers are increasingly exploring ways to combine psychological and social approaches with antipsychotic drugs, especially in the early stages of the disorder. Techniques in the spotlight include family-education sessions, job training, social rehabilitation, and several forms of one-on-one psychotherapy.

Consider Alaoglu's approach. She regards hallucinated voices as having meaning for the person who hears them. Unlike Greenblat's previous doctors, Alaoglu offered Greenblat ways to make sense of the voices.

Before a flight home, for instance, Greenblat once told Alaoglu that the trees were warning her not to go. "You seem a bit nervous about your trip," the therapist responded.

Such observations "gave me a sense of how I was communicating," Greenblat says. She was often conveying her feelings indirectly, through personally significant symbols that seemed bizarre to others. Such realizations, Greenblat says, also helped her develop intimate and safe contact with Alaoglu, easing schizophrenia's terrifying isolation and stigma.

"Psychotherapy doesn't fix schizophrenia," Alaoglu says. "But it can help to improve a person's functioning."

As Greenblat's condition improved over the next few years, she collaborated with her psychiatrist in adjusting her doses of antipsychotic medication. She also participated in a vocational rehabilitation program.

Greenblat, now in her 30s, is studying for a master's in health science. The rigors of school sometimes cajole her thought-voices out of hiding, but she pulls through these rough times with the help of family members, friends, and Alaoglu.

Greenblat's ongoing struggle illustrates a bitter truth: There are no quick fixes for schizophrenia. It's a severe mental disorder that draws most of its public attention in rare cases when a sufferer commits an act of violence.

Over the past century, schizophrenia treatments have included isolation in pastoral settings or hospital wards, intensive psychotherapy, brain surgery, dialysis, and a growing number of medications. The fiercest theoretical battle has pitted psychoanalysts—some of whom have regarded schizophrenia as a product of emotionally callous parents—against biological psychiatrists—who view schizophrenia as a brain disease.

Psychoanalysts and other psychotherapists now emphasize the need to build healing relationships in treating schizophrenia. More biologically oriented psychiatrists stress the use of antipsychotic drugs.

Combining these approaches may take treatment to another level. "People aren't blaming families for schizophrenia anymore," says psychiatrist Courtenay Harding of Boston University. "But they're also starting to realize that a pill doesn't reclaim a life."

Merely defining the disease has evoked a century of controversy. Increasingly, however, psychiatrists are agreeing on three general categories of symptoms known, respectively, as positive, disorganized, and negative. Still, many researchers suspect that there are different types of schizophrenia with different causes.

Positive, or psychotic, symptoms include delusions, such as believing that secret agents are monitoring one's thoughts, and hallucinations, in which a person experiences imaginary but disturbing sights and sounds.

Disorganized symptoms include confused thinking and bizarre speech and behavior, as well as inappropriate emotions, incoherent sentences, and wild gestures. Some schizophrenia sufferers also have difficulty interpreting everyday sights, sounds, and feelings.

Negative symptoms include apathy, a lack of verbal and emotional expression, and an inability to hold down a job or interact with others.

Most cases of schizophrenia—which afflicts 1 in 100 people—are diagnosed in young adults.

The causes of schizophrenia remain unknown. In the past decade,

researchers have sought to identify problems in brain structure and chemistry, as well as genetic mutations that underlie this mental disorder.

The scientific emphasis on brains and genes has accompanied a growing clinical reliance on antipsychotic medications to treat schizophrenia. The first of these drugs, chlorpromazine, appeared in 1954. One major consequence of this in the 1960s was the mass release of schizophrenia patients from state mental hospitals, antipsychotic prescriptions in hand. However, few community-based mental-health centers materialized to offer treatment to supplement the drugs.

A new wave of antipsychotic drugs has since raised expectations for improved schizophrenia treatment. Even for the roughly one-half of schizophrenia sufferers who clearly benefit from antipsychotic drugs, most face a long-term struggle with disabling symptoms and poor social skills, according to psychiatrist Juan R. Bustillo of the University of New Mexico School of Medicine in Albuquerque. These same people stand a good chance of sinking back into a full-blown psychotic state at some point, even if they dutifully take their medication, Bustillo adds.

When drugs alone are not an answer, combination therapies of drugs and other treatments show promise, argue Bustillo and his colleagues in a review of recent schizophrenia-treatment research in the February AMERICAN JOURNAL OF PSYCHIATRY.

Family therapy and so-called assertive community treatment show particular promise in preventing the return of psychotic symptoms and the need for hospitalization, Bustillo's group holds.

In family therapy, teams of clinicians meet regularly with patients and their families. The primary goal here is to provide information about schizophrenia and ways to cope with it. Another critical goal is to re-

duce the tendency of family members to react to their schizophrenic relatives with expressions of exasperation and discouragement. These negative responses don't cause schizophrenia, but research has linked the social stress that comes with them to renewed bouts of psychosis.

Assertive community treatment consists of caregivers meeting with patients and family members in their homes and providing practical advice on living independently with schizophrenia. These programs also give advice to schizophrenia patients on finding and keeping a job.

A combination of these approaches substantially improves the quality of life for schizophrenia sufferers and their families, according to the research of psychiatrist William R. McFarlane of the Maine Medical Center in Portland.

Efforts to reclaim psychoanalysis as part of schizophrenia treatment often get the cold shoulder in the United States

---

His approach employs teams of mental-health workers, each of which conducts educational sessions with groups of six to nine patients and their relatives. Families learn to help each other and get a big morale boost from expanded social contacts, McFarlane says. The addition of multifamily sessions to assertive community treatment improves the capability of schizophrenia sufferers to avoid sinking back into psychosis and to stay employed, at least over the 1-to-2-year periods studied so far.

Individual psychotherapy represents the most controversial form of schizophrenia treatment at least in the United States. Fifty years ago, psychoanalysts were the primary purveyors of psychotherapy for all sorts of mental problems. Their attempts to cure schizophrenia by untangling family conflicts met with little success, however. To make matters worse, psychoanalysts left many parents feeling unjustly blamed as the cause of their children's schizophrenia.

A set of treatment recommendations in 1998 from the Schizophrenia Patient Outcome Research Team (PORT), which was sponsored by the National Institute of Mental Health in Bethesda, Md., advised against using a "psychodynamic model" in psychotherapy with schizophrenia sufferers. In other words, it recommended to health-care professionals that they offer support without probing for ostensibly unconscious, family-related discord.

A revision of the PORT guidelines will make major changes, says psychiatrist Anthony F. Lehman of the University of Maryland School of Medicine in Baltimore, who directs the project.

Despite its marred reputation, psychoanalysis deserves consideration by the PORT revisers, asserts Brian Martindale, a psychiatrist in London, who conducts psychotherapy with schizophrenia sufferers. He says a psychoanalytic approach to individual and group psychotherapy helps in establishing a working relationship with these patients. Efforts to reclaim psychoanalysis as part of schizophrenia treatment often get the cold shoulder in the United States.

Europeans currently conduct most of the research in this area. Updates on several treatment projects that include a psychoanalytic perspective appear in *Psychosis: Psychological Approaches and Their Effectiveness* (2000, B. Martindale et al., eds., Gaskell), a compendium published last year.

The British government plans to finance 50 early intervention teams that will treat people soon after their first psychotic episodes, Martindale says. These teams will include clinicians trained in a psychoanalytic approach much like that employed by Alaoglu.

"The most essential requirements in psychosis therapy are persistence, honesty, and an ability to convey to the patient hope for a better future, even if it's a distant one," says psychiatrist Yrjö O. Alanen of the University of Turku, Finland. He has done psychotherapy with schizophrenia sufferers for 40 years.

Alanen and his coworkers have organized schizophrenia-treatment teams in communities throughout Finland. These teams offer a variety of services based on a person's particular symptoms and circumstances. Treatments include individual and family therapy, vocational training, and antipsychotic medication.

Among patients tracked for up to 8 years after entering treatment, about two-thirds remain free of psychotic symptoms and a majority hold down jobs.

Young adults who first became psychotic as part of an identity crisis and had warm family ties at the time of their psychotic episode, have benefited mainly from psychoanalysis, Alanen says. These individuals did best without antipsychotic medication, he adds.

Young people who became psychotic in the context of stormy family relationships and an unstable personality profited from drugs as well as family and individual therapy. Particularly severe cases of schizophrenia, in which people had become isolated and unable to maintain social contacts or to express emotions, required both medication and basic forms of rehabilitation.

Bustillo's group sees potential in two other forms of individual psychotherapy for schizophrenia.

One technique, called personal therapy, attempts to reduce patients' anguish by helping them recognize their own psychotic symptoms. In combination with medication, this technique has fostered social adjustment and reduced psychotic relapses among schizophrenia sufferers (SN: 11/8/97, p. 293). U.S. therapists have now expanded personal therapy to include computer and group exercises in abstract thinking and social communication.

The second method that Bustillo deems potentially valuable is based on a treatment for depression called cognitive-behavior therapy. Given help in problem-solving and social-coping skills, patients with schizophrenia are encouraged to challenge their own psychotic beliefs and experiences and to consider more reasonable explanations for them.

It's clear that a mix of psychological treatments and antipsychotic drugs constitutes the best medicine for schizophrenia, Lehman says. However, most schizophrenia sufferers can neither find nor afford community-based services and experienced psychotherapists.

Nor will this situation change soon, Lehman says. To begin with, he notes, antipsychotic drugs generate huge profits for pharmaceutical companies. Aggressive marketing campaigns for these medications bombard psychiatrists, most of whom now get little medical school training in psychotherapy. What's more, drug prescriptions and brief office visits are easier on managed medical care's bottom line than are more complicated and expensive psychological treatments. "Our system of care for people with schizophrenia is inadequate," says Harding. Over the long haul, integrated treatment provided by clinicians who maintain close ties to patients will save money and change lives for the better, she says.

From *Science News*, April 28, 2001, pp. 68-69 by Bruce Bower. © 2001 by Sci Service Inc. Reproduced with permission.

Glossary

This glossary of psychology terms is included to provide you with a convenient and ready reference as you encounter general terms in your study of psychology and personal growth and behavior that are unfamiliar or require a review. It is not intended to be comprehensive, but taken together with the many definitions included in the articles themselves, it should prove to be quite useful.

abnormal behavior Behavior that contributes to maladaptiveness, is considered deviant by the culture, or that leads to personal psychological distress.

absolute threshold The minimum amount of physical energy required to produce a sensation.

accommodation Process in cognitive development; involves altering or reorganizing the mental picture to make room for a new experience or idea.

acculturation The process of becoming part of a new cultural environment.

acetylcholine A neurotransmitter involved in memory.

achievement drive The need to attain self-esteem, success, or status. Society's expectations strongly influence the achievement motive.

achievement style The way people behave in achievement situations; achievement styles include the direct, instrumental, and relational styles.

acquired immune deficiency syndrome (AIDS) A fatal disease of the immune system.

acquisition In conditioning, forming associations in first learning a task.

actor-observer bias Tendency to attribute the behavior of other people to internal causes and our own behavior to external causes.

acupuncture Oriental practice involving the insertion of needles into the body to control pain.

adaptation The process of responding to changes in the environment by altering responses to keep a person's behavior appropriate to environmental demands.

adjustment How we react to stress; some change that we make in response to the demands placed upon us.

adrenal glands Endocrine glands involved in stress and energy regulation.

adrenaline A hormone produced by the adrenal glands that is involved in physiological arousal; adrenaline is also called epinephrine.

aggression Behavior intended to harm a member of the same or another species.

agoraphobia Anxiety disorder in which an individual is excessively afraid of places or situations from which it would be difficult or embarrassing to escape.

alarm reaction The first stage of Hans Selye's general adaptation syndrome. The alarm reaction is the immediate response to stress; adrenaline is released and digestion slows. The alarm reaction prepares the body for an emergency.

all-or-none law The principle that states that a neuron only fires when a stimulus is above a certain minimum strength (threshold), and when it fires, it does so at full strength.

alogia Individuals with schizophrenia that show a reduction in speech.

alpha Brain-wave activity that indicates that a person is relaxed and resting quietly; 8–12 Hz.

altered state of consciousness (ASC) A state of consciousness in which there is a redirection of attention, a change in the aspects of the world that occupy a person's thoughts, and a change in the stimuli to which a person responds.

ambivalent attachment Type of infant-parent attachment in which the infant seeks contact but resists once the contact is made.

amphetamine A strong stimulant; increases arousal of the central nervous system.

amygdala A part of the limbic system involved in fear, aggression, and other social behaviors.

anal stage Psychosexual stage during which, according to Sigmund Freud, the child experiences the first restrictions on his or her impulses.

anorexia nervosa Eating disorder in which an individual becomes severely underweight because of self-imposed restrictions on eating.

antidepressants Drugs used to elevate the mood of depressed individuals, presumably by increasing the availability of the neurotransmitters norepinephrine and/or serotonin.

antisocial personality disorder Personality disorder in which individuals who engage in antisocial behavior experience no guilt or anxiety about their actions; sometimes called sociopathy or psychopathy.

anxiety disorder Fairly long-lasting disruption of a person's ability to deal with stress; often accompanied by feelings of fear and apprehension.

applied psychology The area of psychology that is most immediately concerned with helping to solve practical problems; includes clinical and counseling psychology as well as industrial, environmental, and legal psychology.

aptitude test Any test designed to predict what a person with the proper training can accomplish in the future.

archetypes In Carl Jung's personality theory, unconscious universal ideas shared by all humans.

arousal theory Theory that focuses on the energy (arousal) aspect of motivation; it states that we are motivated to initiate behaviors that help to regulate overall arousal level.

asocial phase Phase in attachment development in which the neonate does not distinguish people from objects.

assertiveness training Training that helps individuals stand up for their rights while not denying rights of other people.

assimilation Process in cognitive development; occurs when something new is taken into the child's mental picture.

attachment Process in which the individual shows behaviors that promote proximity with a specific object or person.

attention Process of focusing on particular stimuli in the environment.

attention deficit disorder Hyperactivity; inability to concentrate.

attitude Learned disposition that actively guides us toward specific behaviors; attitudes consist of feelings, beliefs, and behavioral tendencies.

attribution The cognitive process of determining the motives of someone's behavior, and whether they are internal or external.

autism A personality disorder in which a child does not respond socially to people.

autonomic nervous system The part of the peripheral nervous system that carries messages from the central nervous system to the endocrine glands, the smooth muscles controlling the heart, and the primarily involuntary muscles controlling internal processes; includes the sympathetic and parasympathetic nervous systems.

aversion therapy A counterconditioning therapy in which unwanted responses are paired with unpleasant consequences.

avoidance conditioning Learning situation in which a subject avoids a stimulus by learning to respond appropriately before the stimulus begins.

avolition Individuals with schizophrenia who lack motivation to follow through on an activity.

Glossary

backward conditioning A procedure in classical conditioning in which the US is presented and terminated before the termination of the CS; very ineffective procedure.

basal ganglia An area of the forebrain that is important to smooth muscle movement and actions. This area works in conjunction with the midbrain to help us avoid moving in choppy, fragmented ways.

behavior Anything you do or think, including various bodily reactions. Behavior includes physical and mental responses.

behavior genetics How genes influence behavior.

behavior modification Another term for behavior therapy; the modification of behavior through psychological techniques; often the application of conditioning principles to alter behavior.

behaviorism The school of thought founded by John Watson; it studied only observable behavior.

belongingness and love needs Third level of motives in Maslow's hierarchy; includes love and affection, friends, and social contact.

biological motives Motives that have a definite physiological basis and are biologically necessary for individual or species survival.

biological response system Systems of the body that are important in behavioral responding; includes the senses, muscles, endocrine system, and the nervous system.

biological therapy Treatment of behavior problems through biological techniques; major biological therapies include drug therapy, psychosurgery, and electroconvulsive therapy.

bipolar disorder Mood disorder characterized by extreme mood swings from sad depression to joyful mania; sometimes called manic depression.

blinding technique In an experiment, a control for bias in which the assignment of a subject to the experimental or control group is unknown to the subject or experimenter or both (a double-blind experiment).

body dysmorphic disorder Somatoform disorder characterized by a preoccupation with an imaginary defect in the physical appearance of a physically healthy person.

body language Communication through position and movement of the body.

bottom-up processing The psychoanalytic process of understanding communication by listening to words, then interpreting phrases, and finally understanding ideas.

brief psychodynamic therapy A therapy developed for individuals with strong egos to resolve a core conflict.

bulimia nervosa Eating disorder in which an individual eats large amounts of calorie-rich food in a short time and then purges the food by vomiting or using laxatives.

California Psychological Inventory (CPI) An objective personality test used to study normal populations.

Cannon-Bard theory of emotion Theory of emotion that states that the emotional feeling and the physiological arousal occur at the same time.

cardinal traits In Gordon Allport's personality theory, the traits of an individual that are so dominant that they are expressed in everything the person does; few people possess cardinal traits.

catatonic schizophrenia A type of schizophrenia that is characterized by periods of complete immobility and the apparent absence of will to move or speak.

causal attribution Process of determining whether a person's behavior is due to internal or external motives.

central nervous system The part of the human nervous system that interprets and stores messages from the sense organs, decides what behavior to exhibit, and sends appropriate messages to the muscles and glands; includes the brain and spinal cord.

central tendency In statistics, measures of central tendency give a number that represents the entire group or sample.

central traits In Gordon Allport's personality theory, the traits of an individual that form the core of the personality; they are developed through experience.

cerebellum The part of the hindbrain that is involved in balance and muscle coordination.

cerebral cortex The outermost layer of the cerebrum of the brain where higher mental functions occur. The cerebral cortex is divided into sections, or lobes, which control various activities.

cerebrum (cerebral hemisphere) Largest part of the forebrain involved in cognitive functions; the cerebrum consists of two hemispheres connected by the corpus callosum.

chromosome Bodies in the cell nucleus that contain the genes.

chunking Process of combining stimuli in order to increase memory capacity.

classical conditioning The form of learning in which a stimulus is associated with another stimulus that causes a particular response. Sometimes called Pavlovian conditioning or respondent conditioning.

clinical psychology Subfield in which psychologists assess psychological problems and treat people with behavior problems using psychological techniques (called psychotherapy).

cognition Mental processes, such as perception, attention, memory, language, thinking, and problem solving; cognition involves the acquisition, storage, retrieval, and utilization of knowledge.

cognitive behavior therapy A form of behavior therapy that identifies self-defeating attitudes and thoughts in a subject, and then helps the subject to replace these with positive, supportive thoughts.

cognitive development Changes over time in mental processes such as thinking, memory, language, and problem solving.

cognitive dissonance Leon Festinger's theory of attitude change that states that, when people hold two psychologically inconsistent ideas, they experience tension that forces them to reconcile the conflicting ideas.

cognitive expectancy The condition in which an individual learns that certain behaviors lead to particular goals; cognitive expectancy motivates the individual to exhibit goal-directed behaviors.

cognitive learning Type of learning that theorizes that the learner utilizes cognitive structures in memory to make decisions about behaviors.

cognitive psychology The area of psychology that includes the study of mental activities involved in perception, memory, language, thought, and problem solving.

cognitive restructuring The modification of the client's thoughts and perceptions that are contributing to his or her maladjustments.

cognitive therapy Therapy developed by Aaron Beck in which an individual's negative, self-defeating thoughts are restructured in a positive way.

cognitive-motivational-relational theory of emotion A theory of emotion proposed by Richard Lazarus that includes cognitive appraisal, motivational goals, and relationships between an individual and the environment.

collective unconscious Carl Jung's representation of the thoughts shared by all humans.

collectivistic cultures Cultures in which the greatest emphasis is on the loyalty of each individual to the group.

comparative psychology Subfield in which experimental psychologists study and compare the behavior of different species of animals.

compulsions Rituals performed excessively such as checking doors or washing hands to reduce anxiety.

concept formation (concept learning) The development of the ability to respond to common features of categories of objects or events.

concrete operations period Stage in cognitive development, from 7 to 11 years, in which the child's ability to solve problems with reasoning greatly increases.

conditioned response (CR) The response or behavior that occurs when the conditioned stimulus is presented (after the CS has been associated with the US).

conditioned stimulus (CS) An originally neutral stimulus that is associated with an unconditioned stimulus and takes on the latter's capability of eliciting a particular reaction.

conditioned taste aversion (CTA) An aversion to particular tastes associated with stomach distress; usually considered a unique form of classical conditioning because of the extremely long interstimulus intervals involved.

conditioning A term applied to two types of learning (classical and operant). Conditioning refers to the scientific aspect of the type of learning.

conflict Situation that occurs when we experience incompatible demands or desires; the outcome when one individual or group perceives that another individual or group has caused or will cause harm.

conformity Type of social influence in which an individual changes his or her behavior to fit social norms or expectations.

connectionism Recent approach to problem solving; the development of neural connections allows us to think and solve problems.

conscientiousness The dimension in the five-factor personality theory that includes traits such as practical, cautious, serious, reliable, careful, and ambitious; also called dependability.

conscious Being aware of experiencing sensations, thoughts, and feelings at any given point in time.

conscious mind In Sigmund Freud's psychoanalytic theory of personality, the part of personality that we are aware of in everyday life.

consciousness The processing of information at various levels of awareness; state in which a person is aware of sensations, thoughts, and feelings.

consensus In causal attribution, the extent to which other people react as the subject does in a particular situation.

conservation The ability to recognize that something stays the same even if it takes on a different form; Piaget tested conservation of mass, number, length, and volume.

consistency In causal attribution, the extent to which the subject always behaves in the same way in a situation.

consolidation The biological neural process of making memories permanent; possibly short-term memory is electrically coded and long-term memory is chemically coded.

contingency model A theory that specific types of situations need particular types of leaders.

continuum of preparedness Martin Seligman's proposal that animals are biologically prepared to learn certain responses more readily than they are prepared to learn others.

control group Subjects in an experiment who do not receive the independent variable; the control group determines the effectiveness of the independent variable.

conventional morality Level II in Lawrence Kohlberg's theory, in which moral reasoning is based on conformity and social standards.

conversion disorder Somatoform disorder in which a person displays obvious disturbance in the nervous system without a physical basis for the problem.

correlation Statistical technique to determine the degree of relationship that exists between two variables.

counterconditioning A behavior therapy in which an unwanted response is replaced by conditioning a new response that is incompatible with it.

creativity A process of coming up with new or unusual responses to familiar circumstances.

critical period hypothesis Period of time during development in which particular learning or experiences normally occur; if learning does not occur, the individual has a difficult time learning it later.

culture-bound The idea that a test's usefulness is limited to the culture in which it was written and utilized.

cumulative response curve Graphed curve that results when responses for a subject are added to one another over time; if subjects respond once every 5 minutes, they will have a cumulative response curve value of 12 after an hour.

curiosity motive Motive that causes the individual to seek out a certain amount of novelty.

cyclothymia disorder A moderately severe problem with numerous periods of hypomanic episodes and depressive symptoms.

death instinct (also called Thanatos) Freud's term for an instinct that is destructive to the individual or species; aggression is a major expression of death instinct.

decay Theory of forgetting in which sensory impressions leave memory traces that fade away with time.

defense mechanisms Psychological techniques to help protect ourselves from stress and anxiety, to resolve conflicts, and to preserve our self-esteem.

delayed conditioning A procedure in classical conditioning in which the presentation of the CS precedes the onset of the US and the termination of the CS is delayed until the US is presented; most effective procedure.

delusion The holding of obviously false beliefs; for example, imagining someone is trying to kill you.

dendrites The branch-like structures of neurons that extend from the cell body (soma). The dendrites are the receivers of neural impulses (electrical and chemical signals) from the axons of other neurons. Although there are some areas of the body that contain dendrites that can act like axon terminals, releasing neurotransmitters in response to impulses and local voltage changes, most dendrites are the receiving branches of the neuron.

dependent variable In psychology, the behavior or response that is measured; it is dependent on the independent variable.

depersonalization disorder Dissociative disorder in which the individual escapes from his or her own personality by believing that he or she does not exist or that his or her environment is not real.

depolarization Any change in which the internal electrical charge becomes more positive.

depression A temporary emotional state that normal individuals experience or a persistent state that may be considered a psychological disorder. Characterized by sadness and low self-esteem.

descriptive statistics Techniques that help summarize large amounts of data information.

developmental psychology Study of physical and mental growth and behavioral changes in individuals from conception to death.

Diagnostic and Statistical Manual of Mental Disorders (DSM) Published by the American Psychiatric Association in 1952, and revised in 1968, 1980, 1987, and 1994, this manual was provided to develop a set of diagnoses of abnormal behavior patterns.

diffusion of responsibility Finding that groups tend to inhibit helping behavior; responsibility is shared equally by members of the group so that no one individual feels a strong commitment.

disorganized schizophrenia A type of schizophrenia that is characterized by a severe personality disintegration; the individual often displays bizarre behavior.

displacement Defense mechanism by which the individual directs his or her aggression or hostility toward a person or object other than the one it should be directed toward; in Freud's dream theory, the process of reassigning emotional feelings from one object to another one.

dissociative disorder Psychological disorder that involves a disturbance in the memory, consciousness, or identity of an individual; types include multiple personality disorder, depersonalization disorder, psychogenic amnesia, and psychogenic fugue.

dissociative fugue Individuals who have lost their memory, relocated to a new geographical area, and started a new life as someone else.

dissociative identity disorder (multiple personality disorder) Dissociative disorder in which several personalities are present in the same individual.

distinctiveness In causal attribution, the extent to which the subject reacts the same way in other situations.

Down syndrome Form of mental retardation caused by having three number 21 chromosomes (trisomy 21).

Glossary

dream analysis Psychoanalytic technique in which a patient's dreams are reviewed and analyzed to discover true feelings.

drive Motivational concept used to describe the internal forces that push an organism toward a goal; sometimes identified as psychological arousal arising from a physiological need.

dyssomnia Sleep disorder in which the chief symptom is a disturbance in the amount and quality of sleep; they include insomnia and hypersomnia.

dysthymic disorder Mood disorder in which the person suffers moderate depression much of the time for at least two years.

ego Sigmund Freud's term for an individual's sense of reality.

egocentric Seeing the world only from your perspective.

eidetic imagery Photographic memory; ability to recall great detail accurately after briefly viewing something.

Electra complex The Freudian idea that the young girl feels inferior to boys because she lacks a penis.

electroconvulsive therapy (ECT) A type of biological therapy in which electricity is applied to the brain in order to relieve severe depression.

emotion A response to a stimulus that involves physiological arousal, subjective feeling, cognitive interpretation, and overt behavior.

empiricism The view that behavior is learned through experience.

encoding The process of putting information into the memory system.

encounter group As in a sensitivity training group, a therapy where people become aware of themselves in meeting others.

endorphins Several neuropeptides that function as neurotransmitters. The opiate-like endorphins are involved in pain, reinforcement, and memory.

engram The physical memory trace or neural circuit that holds memory; also called memory trace.

episodic memory Highest memory system; includes information about personal experiences.

Eros Sigmund Freud's term for an instinct that helps the individual or species survive; also called life instinct.

esteem needs Fourth level of motives in Abraham Maslow's hierarchy; includes high evaluation of oneself, self-respect, self-esteem, and respect of others.

eustress Stress that results from pleasant and satisfying experiences; earning a high grade or achieving success produces eustress.

excitement phase First phase in the human sexual response cycle; the beginning of sexual arousal.

experimental group Subjects in an experiment who receive the independent variable.

experimental psychology Subfield in which psychologists research the fundamental causes of behavior. Many experimental psychologists conduct experiments in basic research.

experimenter bias Source of potential error in an experiment from the action or expectancy of the experimenter; might influence the experimental results in ways that mask the true outcome.

external locus of control In Julian Rotter's personality theory, the perception that reinforcement is independent of a person's behavior.

extraversion The dimension in the five-factor personality theory that includes traits such as sociability, talkativeness, boldness, fun-lovingness, adventurousness, and assertiveness; also called surgency. The personality concept of Carl Jung in which the personal energy of the individual is directed externally.

factor analysis A statistical procedure used to determine the relationship among variables.

false memories Memories believed to be real, but the events never occurred.

fast mapping A process by which children can utilize a word after a single exposure.

fetal alcohol syndrome (FAS) Condition in which defects in the newborn child are caused by the mother's excessive alcohol intake.

five-factor model of personality tracts A trait theory of personality that includes the factors of extraversion, agreeableness, conscientiousness, emotional stability, and openness.

fixed action pattern (FAP) Unlearned, inherited, stereotyped behaviors that are shown by all members of a species; term used in ethology.

fixed interval (FI) schedule Schedule of reinforcement where the subject receives reinforcement for a correct response given after a specified time interval.

fixed ratio (FR) schedule Schedule of reinforcement in which the subject is reinforced after a certain number of responses.

flashbulb memory Memory of an event that is so important that significant details are vividly remembered for life.

forgetting In memory, not being able to retrieve the original learning. The part of the original learning that cannot be retrieved is said to be forgotten.

formal operations period Period in cognitive development; at 11 years, the adolescent begins abstract thinking and reasoning. This period continues throughout the rest of life.

free association Psychoanalytic technique in which the patient says everything that comes to mind.

free recall A verbal learning procedure in which the order of presentation of the stimuli is varied and the subject can learn the items in any order.

frequency theory of hearing Theory of hearing that states that the frequency of vibrations at the basilar membrane determines the frequency of firing of neurons carrying impulses to the brain.

frustration A cause of stress that results from the blocking of a person's goal-oriented behavior.

frustration-drive theory of aggression Theory of aggression that states that it is caused by frustration.

functionalism School of thought that studied the functional value of consciousness and behavior.

fundamental attribution error Attribution bias in which people overestimate the role of internal disposition and underestimate the role of external situation.

gate-control theory of pain Theory of pain that proposes that there is a gate that allows pain impulses to travel from the spinal cord to the brain.

gender-identity disorder (GID) Incongruence between assigned sex and gender identity.

gender-identity/role Term that incorporates gender identity (the private perception of one's sex) and gender role (the public expression of one's gender identity).

gene The basic unit of heredity; the gene is composed of deoxyribonucleic acid (DNA).

general adaptation syndrome (GAS) Hans Selye's theory of how the body responds to stress over time. GAS includes alarm reaction, resistance, and exhaustion.

generalized anxiety disorder Anxiety disorder in which the individual lives in a state of constant severe tension, continuous fear, and apprehension.

genetics The study of heredity; genetics is the science of discovering how traits are passed along generations.

genotype The complete set of genes inherited by an individual from his or her parents.

Gestalt therapy Insight therapy designed to help people become more aware of themselves in the here and now and to take responsibility for their own actions.

grandiose delusion Distortion of reality; one's belief that he or she is extremely important or powerful.

group therapy Treatment of several patients at the same time.

groupthink When group members are so committed to, and optimistic about, the group that they feel it is invulnerable; they become so concerned with maintaining consensus that criticism is muted.

GSR (galvanic skin response) A measure of autonomic nervous system activity; a slight electric current is passed over the skin, and the more nervous a subject is, the easier the current will flow.

hallucinations A sensory impression reported when no external stimulus exists to justify the report; often hallucinations are a symptom of mental illness.

hallucinogens Psychedelic drugs that result in hallucinations at high doses, and other effects on behavior and perception in mild doses.

halo effect The finding that once we form a general impression of someone, we tend to interpret additional information about the person in a consistent manner.

Hawthorne effect The finding that behavior can be influenced just by participation in a research study.

health psychology Field of psychology that studies psychological influences on people's health, including how they stay healthy, why they become ill, and how their behavior relates to their state of health.

heuristic Problem-solving strategy; a person tests solutions most likely to be correct.

hierarchy of needs Abraham Maslow's list of motives in humans, arranged from the biological to the uniquely human.

hippocampus Brain structure in the limbic system that is important in learning and memory.

homeostasis The state of equilibrium that maintains a balance in the internal body environment.

hormones Chemicals produced by the endocrine glands that regulate activity of certain bodily processes.

humanistic psychology Psychological school of thought that believes that people are unique beings who cannot be broken down into parts.

hyperphagia Disorder in which the individual continues to eat until he or she is obese; can be caused by damage to ventromedial hypothalamus.

hypersomnia Sleep disorder in which an individual falls asleep at inappropriate times; narcolepsy is a form of hypersomnia.

hypnosis Altered state of consciousness characterized by heightened suggestibility.

hypochondriasis Somatoform disorder in which the individual is obsessed with fears of having a serious medical disease.

hypothalamus Part of the brain's limbic system; involved in motivational behaviors, including eating, drinking, and sex.

hypothesis In the scientific method, an educated guess or prediction about future observable events.

iconic memory Visual information that is encoded into the sensory memory store.

id Sigmund Freud's representation of the basic instinctual drives; the id always seeks pleasure.

identification The process in which children adopt the attitudes, values, and behaviors of their parents.

identity diffusion In Marcia's adolescent identity theory, the status of individuals who have failed to make a commitment to values and roles.

illusion An incorrect perception that occurs when sensation is distorted.

imitation The copying of another's behavior; learned through the process of observation.

impression formation Developing an evaluation of another person from your perceptions; first, or initial, impressions are often very important.

imprinting A form of early learning in which birds follow a moving stimulus (often the mother); may be similar to attachment in mammals.

independent variable The condition in an experiment that is controlled and manipulated by the experimenter; it is a stimulus that will cause a response.

indiscriminate attachment phase Stage of attachment in which babies prefer humans to nonhumans, but do not discriminate among individual people.

individuation Carl Jung's concept of the process leading to the unification of all parts of the personality.

inferential statistics Techniques that help researchers make generalizations about a finding based on a limited number of subjects.

inferiority complex Adler's personality concept that states that because children are dependent on adults and cannot meet the standards set for themselves they feel inferior.

inhibition Restraint of an impulse, desire, activity, or drive.

insight A sudden grasping of the means necessary to achieve a goal; important in the Gestalt approach to problem solving.

insight therapy Therapy based on the assumption that behavior is abnormal because people do not adequately understand the motivation causing their behavior.

instinct Highly stereotyped behavior common to all members of a species that often appears in virtually complete form in the absence of any obvious opportunities to learn it.

instrumental conditioning Operant conditioning.

intelligence Capacity to learn and behave adaptively.

intelligence quotient (IQ) An index of a person's performance on an intelligence test relative to others in the culture; ratio of a person's mental age to chronological age.

interference Theory of forgetting in which information that was learned before (proactive interference) or after (retroactive interference) causes the learner to be unable to remember the material of interest.

internal locus of control In Rotter's personality theory, the perception that reinforcement is contingent upon behavior.

interstimulus interval Time interval between two stimuli; in classical conditioning, it is the elapsed time between the CS and the US.

intrinsic motivation Motivation inside the individual; we do something because we receive satisfaction from it.

introspection Method in which a subject gives a self report of his or her immediate experience.

introversion The personality concept of Carl Jung in which the personal energy of the individual is directed inward; characterized by introspection, seriousness, inhibition, and restraint.

James-Lange theory of emotion Theory of emotion that states that the physiological arousal and behavior come before the subjective experience of an emotion.

kinesthesis The sense of bodily movement.

labeling of arousal Experiments suggest that an individual experiencing physical arousal that cannot be explained will interpret those feelings in terms of the situation she or he is in and will use environmental and contextual cues.

language acquisition device (LAD) Hypothesized biological structure that accounts for the relative ease of acquiring language, according to Noam Chomsky.

latent dream content In Sigmund Freud's dream theory, the true thoughts in the unconsciousness; the true meaning of the dream.

latent learning Learning that occurs when an individual acquires knowledge of something but does not show it until motivated to do so.

law of effect Edward Thorndike's law that if a response produces satisfaction it will be repeated; reinforcement.

learned helplessness Condition in which a person learns that his or her behavior has no effect on his or her environment; when an individual gives up and stops trying.

learned social motives Social motives that are learned; include achievement and affiliation.

learning The relatively permanent change in behavior or behavioral ability of an individual that occurs as a result of experience.

Glossary

learning styles The preferences students have for learning; theories of learning styles include personality differences, styles of information processing, and instructional preferences.

life instinct (also called Eros) Sigmund Freud's term for an instinct that helps the individual or species survive; sex is the major expression of life instinct.

life structure In Daniel Levinson's theory of adult personality development, the underlying pattern of an individual's life at any particular time; seasonal cycles include preadulthood, early adulthood, middle adulthood, and late adulthood.

linguistic relativity hypothesis Proposal that the perception of reality differs according to the language of the observer.

locus of control Julian Rotter's theory in which a person's beliefs about reinforcement are classified as internal or external.

long-term memory The permanent memory where rehearsed information is stored.

love An emotion characterized by knowing, liking, and becoming intimate with someone.

low-ball procedure The compliance technique of presenting an attractive proposal to someone and then switching it to a more unattractive proposal.

magic number 7 The finding that most people can remember about seven items of information for a short time (in short-term memory).

magnetic resonance imaging (MRI) A method of studying brain activity using magnetic field imaging.

major depressive disorder Severe mood disorder in which a person experiences one or more major depressive episodes; sometimes referred to simply as depression.

maladjustment Condition that occurs when a person utilizes inappropriate abilities to respond to demands placed upon him or her.

manic depressive reaction A form of mental illness marked by alternations of extreme phases of elation (manic phase) and depression.

manifest dream content In Sigmund Freud's dream theory, what is remembered about a dream upon waking; a disguised representation of the unconscious wishes.

maturation The genetically controlled process of growth that results in orderly changes in behavior.

mean The arithmetic average, in which the sum of scores is divided by the number of scores.

median The middle score in a group of scores that are arranged from lowest to highest.

meditation The practice of some form of relaxed concentration while ignoring other sensory stimuli.

memory The process of storing information so that it can be retrieved and used later.

memory attributes The critical features of an event that are used when the experience is encoded or retrieved.

mental age The age level on which a person is capable of performing; used in determining intelligence.

mental set Condition in which a person's thinking becomes so standardized that he or she approaches new problems in fixed ways.

microexpressions Facial expressions that last a fraction of a second. Since microexpressions do not last long, they go undetected in our everyday lives. Microexpressions are a type of nonverbal communication.

Minnesota Multiphasic Personality Inventory (MMPI-2) An objective personality test that was originally devised to identify personality disorders.

mnemonic technique Method of improving memory by combining and relating chunks of information.

modeling A process of learning by imitation in a therapeutic situation.

mood disorder Psychological disorder in which a person experiences a severe disruption in mood or emotional balance.

moral development Development of individuals as they adopt their society's standards of right and wrong; development of awareness of ethical behavior.

motivated forgetting (repression) Theory that suggests that people want to forget unpleasant events.

motivation The forces that initiate and direct behavior, and the variables that determine the intensity and persistence of the behavior.

motivator needs In Federick Herzberg's theory, the factors that lead to job satisfaction; they include responsibility, the nature of the work, advancement, and recognition.

motive Anything that arouses the individual and directs his or her behavior toward some goal. Three categories of motives include biological, stimulus, and learned social.

Müller-Lyer illusion A well-known illusion, in which two horizontal lines have end lines either going in or out; the line with the end lines going in appears longer.

multiple approach-avoidance conflict Conflict that occurs when an individual has two or more goals, both of which have positive and negative aspects.

multiple attachment phase Later attachment stage in which the baby begins to form attachments to people other than the primary caretaker.

multiple intelligences Howard Gardner's theory that there exists several different kinds of intelligence.

Myers-Briggs Type Indicator (MBTI) Objective personality test based on Carl Jung's type theory.

narcotic analgesics Drugs that have an effect on the body similar to morphine; these relieve pain and suppress coughing.

naturalistic observation Research method in which behavior of people or animals in their normal environment is accurately recorded.

Necker cube A visual illusion. The Necker cube is a drawing of a cube designed so that it is difficult to determine which side is toward you.

negative reinforcement Removing something unpleasant to increase the probability that the preceding behavior will be repeated.

NEO Personality Inventory (NEO-PI) An objective personality test developed by Paul Costa Jr. and Robert McCrae to measure the five major factors in personality; consists of 181 questions.

neodissociation theory Idea that consciousness can be split into several streams of thought that are partially independent of each other.

neuron A specialized cell that functions to conduct messages throughout the body.

neurosis A Freudian term that was used to describe abnormal behavior caused by anxiety; it has been eliminated from *DSM-IV*.

neutral stimulus A stimulus that does not cause the response of interest; the individual may show some response to the stimulus but not the associated behavior.

norm A sample of scores representative of a population.

normal curve When scores of a large number of random cases are plotted on a graph, they often fall into a bell-shaped curve; as many cases on the curve are above the mean as below it.

observational learning In social learning theory, learning by observing someone else behave; people observe and imitate in learning socialization.

obsessions Fears that involve the inability to control impulses.

obsessive compulsive disorder Anxiety disorder in which the individual has repetitive thoughts (obsessions) that lead to constant urges (compulsions) to engage in meaningless rituals.

object permanence The ability to realize that objects continue to exist even if we can no longer see them.

Oedipus complex The Freudian idea that the young boy has sexual feelings for his mother and is jealous of his father and must identify with his father to resolve the conflict.

olfaction The smell sense.

openness The dimension in the five-factor personality theory that includes traits such as imagination, creativity, perception, knowledge, artistic ability, curiosity, and analytical ability; also called intellect.

operant conditioning Form of learning in which behavior followed by reinforcement (satisfaction) increases in frequency.

opponent-process theory Theory that when one emotion is experienced, the other is suppressed.

optimum level of arousal Motivation theory that states that the individual will seek a level of arousal that is comfortable.

organic mental disorders Psychological disorders that involve physical damage to the nervous system; can be caused by disease or by an accident.

organizational psychology Area of industrial psychology that focuses on worker attitudes and motivation; derived primarily from personality and social psychology.

orgasm The climax of intense sexual excitement; release from building sexual tension, usually accompanied by ejaculation in men.

paired-associate learning A verbal learning procedure in which the subject is presented with a series of pairs of items to be remembered.

panic disorder Anxiety disorder characterized by the occurrence of specific periods of intense fear.

paranoid schizophrenia A type of schizophrenia in which the individual often has delusions of grandeur and persecution, thinking that someone is out to get him or her.

partial reinforcement Any schedule of reinforcement in which reinforcement follows only some of the correct responses.

partial reinforcement effect The finding that partial reinforcement produces a response that takes longer to extinguish than continuous reinforcement.

pattern recognition Memory process in which information attended to is compared with information already permanently stored in memory.

Pavlovian conditioning A bond or association between a neutral stimulus and a response; this type of learning is called classical conditioning.

perception The active process in which the sensory information that is carried through the nervous system to the brain is organized and interpreted; the interpretation of sensation.

persecutory delusion A delusion in which the individual has a distortion of reality; the belief that other people are out to get him or her.

person perception The process of using the information we gather in forming impressions of people to make evaluations of others.

personal unconscious Carl Jung's representation of the individual's repressed thoughts and memories.

personality disorder Psychological disorder in which there are problems in the basic personality structure of the individual.

phantom-limb pain Phenomenon in which people who have lost an arm or leg feel pain in the missing limb.

phobias Acute excessive fears of specific situations or objects that have no convincing basis in reality.

physiological needs First level of motives in Abraham Maslow's hierarchy; includes the biological needs of hunger, thirst, sex, exercise, and rest.

placebo An inert or inactive substance given to control subjects to test for bias effects.

plateau phase Second phase in the human sexual response cycle, during which the physiological arousal becomes more intense.

pleasure principle In Freudian theory, the idea that the instinctual drives of the id unconsciously and impulsively seek immediate pleasure.

positive reinforcement Presenting a subject something pleasant to increase the probability that the preceding behavior will be repeated.

Positron Emission Tomography (PET) Similar to the MRI, this method enables psychologists and doctors to study the brain (or any other living tissue) without surgery. PET uses radioactive glucose (instead of a strong magnetic field) to help study activity and locate structures in the body.

postconventional morality Level III in Lawrence Kohlberg's theory, in which moral reasoning is based on personal standards and beliefs; highest level of moral thinking.

posttraumatic stress disorder (PTSD) Condition that can occur when a person experiences a severely distressing event; characterized by constant memories of the event, avoidance of anything associated with it, and general arousal.

Prägnanz (law of) Gestalt psychology law that states that people have a tendency to group stimuli according to rules, and that people do this whenever possible.

preconscious mind In Sigmund Freud's psychoanalytic theory of personality, the part of personality that contains information that we have learned but that we are not thinking about at the present time.

preconventional morality Level I of Lawrence Kohlberg's theory, in which moral reasoning is largely due to the expectation of rewards and punishments.

prejudice An unjustified fixed, usually negative, way of thinking about a person or object.

Premack principle Principle that states that, of any two responses, the one that is more likely to occur can be used to reinforce the response that is less likely to occur.

preoperational thought period Period in cognitive development; from two to seven years, the period during which the child learns to represent the environment with objects and symbols.

primary appraisal Activity of determining whether a new stimulus event is positive, neutral, or negative; first step in appraisal of stress.

primary narcissism A Freudian term that refers to the oral phase before the ego has developed; the individual constantly seeks pleasure.

primary reinforcement Reinforcement that is effective without having been associated with other reinforcers; sometimes called unconditioned reinforcement.

probability (p) In inferential statistics, the likelihood that the difference between the experimental and control groups is due to the independent variable.

procedural memory The most basic type of long-term memory; involves the formation of associations between stimuli and responses.

projection Defense mechanism in which a person attributes his or her unacceptable characteristics or motives to others rather than himself or herself.

projective personality test A personality test that presents ambiguous stimuli to which subjects are expected to respond with projections of their own personality.

proximity Closeness in time and space. In perception, it is the Gestalt perceptual principle in which stimuli next to one another are included together.

psyche According to Carl Jung, the thoughts and feelings (conscious and unconscious) of an individual.

psychoactive drug A drug that produces changes in behavior and cognition through modification of conscious awareness.

psychoanalysis The school of thought founded by Sigmund Freud that stressed unconscious motivation. In therapy, a patient's unconscious motivation is intensively explored in order to bring repressed conflicts up to consciousness; psychoanalysis usually takes a long time to accomplish.

psychobiology (also called biological psychology or physiological psychology) The subfield of experimental psychology concerned with the influence of heredity and the biological response systems on behavior.

psychogenic amnesia A dissociative disorder in which an individual loses his or her sense of identity.

psychogenic fugue A dissociative disorder in which an individual loses his or her sense of identity and goes to a new geographic location, forgetting all of the unpleasant emotions connected with the old life.

Glossary

psychographics A technique used in consumer psychology to identify the attitudes of buyers and their preferences for particular products.

psycholinguistics The psychological study of how people convert the sounds of a language into meaningful symbols that can be used to communicate with others.

psychological dependence Situation in which a person craves a drug even though it is not biologically needed by the body.

psychological disorder A diagnosis of abnormal behavior; syndrome of abnormal adjustment, classified in *DSM*.

psychological types Carl Jung's term for different personality profiles; Jung combined two attitudes and four functions to produce eight psychological types.

psychopharmacology Study of effects of psychoactive drugs on behavior.

psychophysics An area of psychology in which researchers compare the physical energy of a stimulus with the sensation reported.

psychosexual stages Sigmund Freud's theoretical stages in personality development.

psychosomatic disorders A variety of body reactions that are closely related to psychological events.

psychotherapy Treatment of behavioral disorders through psychological techniques; major psychotherapies include insight therapy, behavior therapy, and group therapy.

psychotic disorders The more severe categories of abnormal behavior.

puberty Sexual maturation; the time at which the individual is able to perform sexually and to reproduce.

quantitative trait loci (QTLs) Genes that collectively contribute to a trait for high intelligence.

rational-emotive therapy A cognitive behavior modification technique in which a person is taught to identify irrational, self-defeating beliefs and then to overcome them.

reaction formation Defense mechanism in which a person masks an unconsciously distressing or unacceptable trait by assuming an opposite attitude or behavior pattern.

reality principle In Freudian theory, the idea that the drives of the ego try to find socially acceptable ways to gratify the id.

reciprocal determinism The concept proposed by Albert Bandura that the behavior, the individual, and the situation interact and influence each other.

reciprocal inhibition Concept of Joseph Wolpe that states that it is possible to break the bond between anxiety provoking stimuli and responses manifesting anxiety by facing those stimuli in a state antagonistic to anxiety.

reflex An automatic movement that occurs in direct response to a stimulus.

regression Defense mechanism in which a person retreats to an earlier, more immature form of behavior.

reinforcement Any event that increases the probability that the behavior that precedes it will be repeated; also called a reinforcer; similar to a reward.

reinforcement therapy A behavior therapy in which reinforcement is used to modify behavior. Techniques in reinforcement therapy include shaping, extinction, and token economy.

REM Sleep There are two main categories of sleep, Non-Rapid Eye Movement Sleep (NREM; which contains stages 1–4; basically everything except REM), and Rapid Eye Movement Sleep (REM). REM sleep is a sleep period during which your brain is very active, and your eyes move in a sharp, back-and-forth motion as opposed to a slower, more rolling fashion that occurs in other stages of sleep. People often believe mistakenly that humans only dream during REM sleep, although humans also dream during slow wave sleep (stages 3 and 4). However it is true that the majority of our dreaming occurs during REM sleep.

repression Defense mechanism in which painful memories and unacceptable thoughts and motives are conveniently forgotten so that they will not have to be dealt with.

residual schizophrenia Type of schizophrenia in which the individual currently does not have symptoms but has had a schizophrenic episode in the past.

resistance Psychoanalytic term used when a patient avoids a painful area of conflict.

resolution phase The last phase in the human sexual response cycle; the time after orgasm when the body gradually returns to the unaroused state.

Restricted Environmental Stimulation Technique (REST) Research technique in which environmental stimuli available to an individual are reduced drastically; formerly called sensory deprivation.

retrograde amnesia Forgetting information recently learned because of a disruptive stimulus such as an electric shock.

reversible figure In perception, a situation in which the figure and ground seem to reverse themselves; an illusion in which objects alternate as the main figure.

Rorschach Inkblot Test A projective personality test in which subjects are asked to discuss what they see in cards containing blots of ink.

safety needs Second level of motives in Abraham Maslow's hierarchy; includes security, stability, dependency, protection, freedom from fear and anxiety, and the need for structure and order.

Schachter-Singer theory of emotion Theory of emotion that states that we interpret our arousal according to our environment and label our emotions accordingly.

scheme A unit of knowledge that the person possesses; used in Jean Piaget's cognitive development theory.

schizophrenia Severe psychotic disorder that is characterized by disruptions in thinking, perception, and emotion.

scientific method An attitude and procedure that scientists use to conduct research. The steps include stating the problem, forming the hypothesis, collecting the information, evaluating the information, and drawing conclusions.

secondary appraisal In appraisal of stress, this is the evaluation that an individual's abilities and resources are sufficient to meet the demands of a stressful event.

secondary reinforcement Reinforcement that is effective only after it has been associated with a primary reinforcer; also called conditioned reinforcement.

secondary traits In Gordon Allport's personality theory, the less important situation-specific traits that help round out personality; they include attitudes, skills, and behavior patterns.

secure attachment Type of infant-parent attachment in which the infant actively seeks contact with the parent.

self-actualization A humanistic term describing the state in which all of an individual's capacities are developed fully. Fifth and highest level of motives in Abraham Maslow's hierarchy, this level, the realization of one's potential, is rarely reached.

self-efficacy An individual's sense of self-worth and success in adjusting to the world.

self-esteem A measurement of how people view themselves. People who view themselves favorably have good self-esteem whereas people who view themselves negatively have poor self-esteem. Self-esteem affects a person's behavior dramatically.

self-evaluation maintenance model (SEM) Tesser's theory of how we maintain a positive self-image despite the success of others close to us.

self-handicapping strategy A strategy that people use to prepare for failure; people behave in ways that produce obstacles to success so that when they do fail they can place the blame on the obstacle.

self-serving bias An attribution bias in which an individual attributes success to his or her own behavior and failure to external environmental causes.

semantic memory Type of long-term memory that can use cognitive activities, such as everyday knowledge.

sensation The passive process in which stimuli are received by sense receptors and transformed into neural impulses that can be carried through the nervous system; first stage in becoming aware of environment.

sensitivity training group (T-group) Therapy group that has the goal of making participants more aware of themselves and their ideas.

sensorimotor period Period in cognitive development; the first two years, during which the infant learns to coordinate sensory experiences with motor activities.

sensory adaptation Tendency of the sense organs to adjust to continuous stimulation by reducing their functioning; a stimulus that once caused sensation and no longer does.

sensory deprivation Situation in which normal environmental sensory stimuli available to an individual are reduced drastically; also called REST (Restricted Environmental Stimulation Technique).

serial learning A verbal learning procedure in which the stimuli are always presented in the same order, and the subject has to learn them in the order in which they are presented.

sex roles The set of behaviors and attitudes that are determined to be appropriate for one sex or the other in a society.

shaping In operant conditioning, the gradual process of reinforcing behaviors that get closer to some final desired behavior. Shaping is also called successive approximation.

short-term memory Part of the memory system in which information is only stored for roughly 30 seconds. Information can be maintained longer with the use of such techniques as rehearsal. To retain the information for extended periods of time, it must be consolidated into long-term memory where it can then be retrieved. The capacity of short-term memory is also limited. Most people can only store roughly 7 chunks of information plus or minus 2. This is why phone numbers only have seven digits.

signal detection theory Research approach in which the subject's behavior in detecting a threshold is treated as a form of decision making.

similarity Gestalt principle in which similar stimuli are perceived as a unit.

simple phobia Excessive irrational fear that does not fall into other specific categories, such as fear of dogs, insects, snakes, or closed-in places.

simultaneous conditioning A procedure in classical conditioning in which the CS and US are presented at exactly the same time.

Sixteen Personality Factor Questionnaire (16PF) Raymond Cattell's personality test to measure source traits.

Skinner box B. F. Skinner's animal cage with a lever that triggers reinforcement for a subject.

sleep terror disorder (pavor nocturnus) Nonrapid eye-movement (NREM) sleep disorder in which the person (usually a child) wakes up screaming and terrified, but cannot recall why.

sleepwalking (somnambulism) NREM sleep disorder in which the person walks in his or her sleep.

social cognition The process of understanding other people and ourselves by forming and utilizing information about the social world.

social cognitive theory Albert Bandura's approach to personality that proposes that individuals use observation, imitation, and cognition to develop personality.

social comparison Theory proposed by Leon Festinger that we tend to compare our behavior to others to ensure that we are conforming.

social exchange theory Theory of interpersonal relationships that states that people evaluate the costs and rewards of their relationships and act accordingly.

social facilitation Phenomenon in which the presence of others increases dominant behavior patterns in an individual; Richard Zajonc's theory states that the presence of others enhances the emission of the dominant response of the individual.

social influence Influence designed to change the attitudes or behavior of other people; includes conformity, compliance, and obedience.

social learning theory An approach to social psychology that emphasizes observation and modeling; it states that reinforcement is involved in motivation rather than in learning, and proposes that aggression is a form of learned behavior.

social phobia Excessive irrational fear and embarrassment when interacting with other people. Social phobias may include fear of assertive behavior, fear of making mistakes, or fear of public speaking.

social psychology The study of how an individual's behavior, thoughts, and feelings are influenced by other people.

sociobiology Study of the genetic basis of social behavior.

sociocultural Emphasizes the importance of culture, gender, and ethnicity in how we think, feel, and act.

somatic nervous system The part of the peripheral nervous system that carries messages from the sense organs and relays information that directs the voluntary movements of the skeletal muscles.

somatization disorder Somatoform disorder in which a person has medical complaints without physical cause.

somatoform disorders Psychological disorders characterized by physical symptoms for which there are no obvious physical causes.

specific attachment phase Stage at about six months of age, in which the baby becomes attached to a specific person.

split-brain research Popular name for Roger Sperry's research on the syndrome of hemisphere deconnection; research on individuals with the corpus callosum severed. Normal functioning breaks down in split-brain subjects when different information is presented to each hemisphere.

SQ5R A technique to improve learning and memory. Components include survey, question, read, record, recite, review, and reflect.

stage of exhaustion Third stage in Hans Selye's general adaptation syndrome. As the body continues to resist stress, it depletes its energy resources and the person becomes exhausted.

stage of resistance Second stage in Hans Selye's general adaptation syndrome. When stress is prolonged, the body builds some resistance to the effects of stress.

standardization The process of obtaining a representative sample of scores in the population so that a particular score can be interpreted correctly.

Stanford-Binet Intelligence Scale An intelligence test first revised by Lewis Terman at Stanford University in 1916; still a popular test used today.

state-dependent learning Situation in which what is learned in one state can only be remembered when the person is in that state of mind.

statistically significant In inferential statistics, a finding that the independent variable did influence greatly the outcome of the experimental and control group.

stereotype An exaggerated and rigid mental image of a particular class of persons or objects.

stimulus A unit of the environment that causes a response in an individual; a physical or chemical agent acting on an appropriate sense receptor.

stimulus discrimination Responding to relevant stimuli.

stimulus generalization Responding to stimuli similar to the stimulus that had caused the response.

stimulus motives Motivating factors that are internal and unlearned, but do not appear to have a physiological basis; stimulus motives cause an individual to seek out sensory stimulation through interaction with the environment.

stimulus trace The perceptual persistence of a stimulus after it is no longer present.

strange-situation procedure A measure of attachment developed by Mary Ainsworth that consists of eight phases during which the infant is increasingly stressed.

Glossary

stress Anything that produces demands on us to adjust and threatens our well-being.

Strong Interest Inventory An objective personality test that compares people's personalities to groups that achieve success in certain occupations.

structuralism First school of thought in psychology; it studied conscious experience to discover the structure of the mind.

subject bias Source of potential error in an experiment from the action or expectancy of a subject; a subject might influence the experimental results in ways that mask the true outcome.

subjective organization Long-term memory procedures in which the individual provides a personal method of organizing information to be memorized.

sublimation Defense mechanism; a person redirects his or her socially undesirable urges into socially acceptable behavior.

successive approximation Shaping; in operant conditioning, the gradual process of reinforcing behaviors that get closer to some final desired behavior.

superego Sigmund Freud's representation of conscience.

surface traits In Raymond Cattell's personality theory, the observable characteristics of a person's behavior and personality.

symbolization In Sigmund Freud's dream theory, the process of converting the latent content of a dream into manifest symbols.

systematic desensitization Application of counterconditioning, in which the individual overcomes anxiety by learning to relax in the presence of stimuli that had once made him or her unbearably nervous.

task-oriented coping Adjustment responses in which the person evaluates a stressful situation objectively and then formulates a plan with which to solve the problem.

test of significance An inferential statistical technique used to determine whether the difference in scores between the experimental and control groups is really due to the effects of the independent variable or to random chance. If the probability of an outcome is extremely low, we say that outcome is significant.

Thanatos Sigmund Freud's term for a destructive instinct such as aggression; also called death instinct.

Thematic Apperception Test (TAT) Projective personality test in which subjects are shown pictures of people in everyday settings; subjects must make up a story about the people portrayed.

theory of social impact Latané's theory of social behavior; it states that each member of a group shares the responsibility equally.

Theory X Douglas McGregor's theory that states that the worker dislikes work and must be forced to do it.

Theory Y Douglas McGregor's theory that states that work is natural and can be a source of satisfaction, and, when it is, the worker can be highly committed and motivated.

therapy In psychology, the treatment of behavior problems; two major types of therapy include psychotherapy and biological therapy.

time and motion studies In engineering psychology, studies that analyze the time it takes to perform an action and the movements that go into the action.

tip-of-the-tongue phenomenon A phenomenon in which the closer a person comes to recalling something, the more accurately he or she can remember details, such as the number of syllables or letters.

token economy A behavior therapy in which desired behaviors are reinforced immediately with tokens that can be exchanged at a later time for desired rewards, such as food or recreational privileges.

trace conditioning A procedure in classical conditioning in which the CS is a discrete event that is presented and terminated before the US is presented.

trait A distinctive and stable attribute in people.

trait anxiety Anxiety that is long-lasting; a relatively stable personality characteristic.

transference Psychoanalytic term used when a patient projects his feelings onto the therapist.

transsexualism A condition in which a person feels trapped in the body of the wrong sex.

trial and error learning Trying various behaviors in a situation until the solution is found.

triangular theory of love Robert Sternberg's theory that states that love consists of intimacy, passion, and decision/commitment.

triarchic theory of intelligence Robert Sternberg's theory of intelligence that states that it consists of three parts: componential, experiential, and contextual subtheories.

Type-A behavior A personality pattern of behavior that can lead to stress and heart disease.

unconditional positive regard Part of Carl Rogers's personality theory; occurs when we accept someone regardless of what he or she does or says.

unconditioned response (UR) An automatic reaction elicited by a stimulus.

unconditioned stimulus (US) Any stimulus that elicits an automatic or reflexive reaction in an individual; it does not have to be learned in the present situation.

unconscious mind In Sigmund Freud's psychoanalytic theory of personality, the part of personality that is unavailable to us; Freud suggests that instincts and unpleasant memories are stored in the unconscious mind.

undifferentiated schizophrenia Type of schizophrenia that does not fit into any particular category, or fits into more than one category.

variable interval (VI) schedule Schedule of reinforcement in which the subject is reinforced for the first response given after a certain time interval, with the interval being different for each trial.

variable ratio (VR) schedule Schedule of reinforcement in which the subject is given reinforcement after a varying number of responses; the number of responses required for reinforcement is different for every trial.

vestibular sense Sense that helps us keep our balance.

vulnerability-stress model Theory of schizophrenia that states that some people have a biological tendency to develop schizophrenia if they are stressed enough by their environment.

Weber's Law Ernst Weber's law that states that the difference threshold depends on the ratio of the intensity of one stimulus to another rather than on an absolute difference.

Wechsler Adult Intelligence Scale (WAIS) An intelligence test for adults, first published by David Wechsler in 1955; it contains verbal and performance subscales.

Wechsler Intelligence Scale for Children (WISC-III) Similar to the Wechsler Adult Intelligence Scale, except that it is designed for children ages 6 through 16, and helps diagnose certain childhood disorders such as dyslexia and other learning disabilities.

Wechsler Preschool and Primary Scale of Intelligence (WPPSI-R) Designed for children between the ages of 4 and 7; helps diagnose childhood disorders, such as dyslexia and other learning disabilities.

withdrawal Unpleasant physical reactions that a drug dependent user experiences when he or she stops taking the drug.

within-subject experiment An experimental design in which each subject is given all treatments, including the control condition; subjects serve in both experimental and control groups.

working memory The memory store, with a capacity of about 7 items and enduring for up to 30 seconds, that handles current information.

Yerkes-Dodson Law Popular idea that performance is best when arousal is at a medium level.

Sources for the Glossary: The majority of terms in this glossary are from Psychology: A ConnecText, *4th Edition, Terry F. Pettijohn. ©1999 Dushkin/ McGraw-Hill, Guilford, CT 06437. The remaining terms were developed by the* Annual Editions *staff, 2001.*

Index

Index

Test Your Knowledge Form

We encourage you to photocopy and use this page as a tool to assess how the articles in *Annual Editions* expand on the information in your textbook. By reflecting on the articles you will gain enhanced text information. You can also access this useful form on a product's book support Web site at *http://www.dushkin.com/online/*.

NAME:

DATE:

TITLE AND NUMBER OF ARTICLE:

BRIEFLY STATE THE MAIN IDEA OF THIS ARTICLE:

LIST THREE IMPORTANT FACTS THAT THE AUTHOR USES TO SUPPORT THE MAIN IDEA:

WHAT INFORMATION OR IDEAS DISCUSSED IN THIS ARTICLE ARE ALSO DISCUSSED IN YOUR TEXTBOOK OR OTHER READINGS THAT YOU HAVE DONE? LIST THE TEXTBOOK CHAPTERS AND PAGE NUMBERS:

LIST ANY EXAMPLES OF BIAS OR FAULTY REASONING THAT YOU FOUND IN THE ARTICLE:

LIST ANY NEW TERMS/CONCEPTS THAT WERE DISCUSSED IN THE ARTICLE, AND WRITE A SHORT DEFINITION:

We Want Your Advice

ANNUAL EDITIONS revisions depend on two major opinion sources: one is our Advisory Board, listed in the front of this volume, which works with us in scanning the thousands of articles published in the public press each year; the other is you—the person actually using the book. Please help us and the users of the next edition by completing the prepaid article rating form on this page and returning it to us. Thank you for your help!

ANNUAL EDITIONS: Psychology 02/03

ARTICLE RATING FORM

Here is an opportunity for you to have direct input into the next revision of this volume.
We would like you to rate each of the articles listed below, using the following scale:

1. **Excellent: should definitely be retained**
2. **Above average: should probably be retained**
3. **Below average: should probably be deleted**
4. **Poor: should definitely be deleted**

Your ratings will play a vital part in the next revision.
Please mail this prepaid form to us as soon as possible.
Thanks for your help!

RATING	ARTICLE	RATING	ARTICLE
	1. A Dance to the Music of the Century: Changing Fashions in 20th-Century Psychiatry		34. Disarming the Rage
	2. Science and Pseudoscience		35. Rational and Irrational Fears Combine in Terrorism's Wake
	3. Good and Evil and Psychological Science		36. Nobody Left to Hate
	4. Psychology's Tangled Web: Deceptive Methods May Backfire on Behavioral Researchers		37. Merits and Perils of Teaching About Other Cultures
	5. The Tangled Skeins of Nature and Nurture in Human Evolution		38. Finding Real Love
	6. Decoding the Human Body		39. Mental Health Gets Noticed
	7. The Future of the Brain		40. Mental Disorders Are Not Diseases
	8. The Senses		41. Up From Depression
	9. Vision: A Window on Consciousness		42. Fear Not!
	10. Noise Busters		43. Are We Nuts?
	11. For Some, Pain Is Orange		44. Self-Help: Shattering the Myths
	12. Dreamspeak		45. The Quest for a Cure
	13. Memory and Learning		46. Back From the Brink
	14. Different Strokes for Different Folks?		
	15. Regarding Rewards: Should You Be a Gold-Sticker Sticker?		
	16. Repression Tries for Experimental Comeback		
	17. The Seven Sins of Memory: How the Mind Forgets and Remembers		
	18. Cognitive Development in Social and Cultural Context		
	19. Who Owns Intelligence?		
	20. Can Animals Think?		
	21. His Goal: Making Intelligence Tests Smarter		
	22. Into the Zone		
	23. The Weighting Game		
	24. What's in a Face?		
	25. Emotional Intelligence: What the Research Says		
	26. Fetal Psychology		
	27. Parenting: The Lost Art		
	28. A World of Their Own		
	29. Live to 100? No Thanks		
	30. Start the Conversation		
	31. Making Sense of Self-Esteem		
	32. Nurturing Empathy		
	33. Secrets of Happiness		

(Continued on next page)

NO POSTAGE
NECESSARY
IF MAILED
IN THE
UNITED STATES

BUSINESS REPLY MAIL
FIRST-CLASS MAIL PERMIT NO. 84 GUILFORD CT
POSTAGE WILL BE PAID BY ADDRESSEE

McGraw-Hill/Dushkin
530 Old Whitfield Street
Guilford, Ct 06437-9989

III....II...I..I..II.I..II.I..I.I..I.I..I.I..I.I.I

- -

ABOUT YOU

Name   Date
_____   _____

Are you a teacher? ☐   A student? ☐
Your school's name
_____

Department
_____

Address   City   State   Zip
_____

School telephone #
_____

YOUR COMMENTS ARE IMPORTANT TO US!

Please fill in the following information:
For which course did you use this book?
_____

Did you use a text with this ANNUAL EDITION?   ☐ yes ☐ no
What was the title of the text?
_____

What are your general reactions to the *Annual Editions* concept?
_____

Have you read any pertinent articles recently that you think should be included in the next edition? Explain.
_____

Are there any articles that you feel should be replaced in the next edition? Why?
_____

Are there any World Wide Web sites that you feel should be included in the next edition? Please annotate.
_____

May we contact you for editorial input?   ☐ yes ☐ no
May we quote your comments? ☐ yes ☐ no